# V. I. LENIN

# ALLIANCE
## OF THE
# WORKING CLASS
## AND THE
# PEASANTRY

FOREIGN LANGUAGES PUBLISHING HOUSE

Moscow 1959

## PUBLISHER'S NOTE

The present volume contains Lenin's articles and speeches dealing with the policy of the Communist Party toward the peasantry and showing how the task of building a lasting alliance with the peasantry was solved at various stages of the revolutionary struggle waged by the working class in Russia. They cover a period of nearly a quarter of a century and reflect the momentous events in which this span of history abounded.

In the first articles in this volume, written in the early years of the century, Lenin demonstrates the necessity of an alliance of the workers and peasants, with the working class playing the leading role, to bring about the overthrow of tsarism and the emancipation of the people from feudal exploitation. Articles written during the revolutionary years of 1905-07 set forth the fundamental political slogans relating to the peasantry in the conditions of the bourgeois-democratic revolution. Lenin elaborates the concept of the revolutionary-democratic dictatorship of the proletariat and the peasantry and shows that, like everything else in the world, this type of dictatorship has its past and its future. Its past was autocracy, feudalism, monarchy, class privilege; its future, the fight for socialism.

The articles and speeches in which Lenin charts the transition to socialist revolution and, basing himself on an analysis of the concrete historical situation, formulates slogans in regard to the various sections of the peasantry at a new and higher stage of the revolution relate to the period between February 1917, when the masses in Russia overthrew tsarism, and October 1917.

Considerable space is given to Lenin's writings after the victory of the socialist revolution in Russia. In the report on work in the countryside delivered at the Eighth Congress of the Party (March 1919) and in other speeches and articles Lenin brilliantly substantiates the policy of co-operation and firm alliance with the middle peasantry, the unswerving implementation of which enabled the working class of the Soviet country to forge ahead to socialism together with the broad masses of the peasantry. The volume closes with Lenin's last articles, written in 1923—"On Co-operation" and "Better Fewer, but Better." These articles outline the plan for directing agriculture on to socialist lines which underlies all the Soviet people's efforts in the socialist reorganization of the countryside.

The contents of the present volume is in strictly chronological order. Most of the articles and speeches are given in full. There are, however, a few exceptions, when only separate chapters or excerpts have been included.

The translation follows the Fourth Edition of the *Collected Works* of Lenin, published in Moscow by the Institute of Marxism-Leninism of the C.C. C.P.S.U. In each case the source is given on the right-hand side under the corresponding speech or article.

# CONTENTS

# THE WORKERS' PARTY AND THE PEASANTRY

Forty years have passed since the peasants were emancipated. It is quite natural that the public should celebrate with particular enthusiasm February 19[1]—the anniversary of the fall of old feudal Russia and the beginning of an epoch which promised the people liberty and prosperity. But we must not forget that besides genuine loathing of serfdom and all its manifestations, there is also much hypocrisy in the laudatory orations delivered on the occasion. The now fashionable estimation of the "great" reform as "the emancipation of the peasantry with a grant of land *with the aid* of state compensation" is utterly hypocritical and false. Actually, the peasants were emancipated *from* the land, for the plots they had tilled for centuries were ruthlessly cut down,[2] and hundreds of thousands of peasants were deprived of all their land and settled on a wretched fourth of an allotment.[3] In fact, the peasants were doubly robbed: not only were their allotments cut down, but they had to pay "compensation" for the portion which was left to them and which had always been in their possession, and, moreover, the price was set far above the actual value. Ten years after the emancipation of the peasantry the landlords themselves admitted to government officials investigating the state of agriculture that the peasants were made to pay not only for their land, but also for their personal liberty. And although the peasants paid for their liberation, they did not become free men; for twenty years they remained "temporarily bound";[4] they were left and have remained to this day the lower estate, who can be flogged, who pay special taxes, who have no right freely to leave the semi-feudal community, freely to dispose of their own land, or to settle freely in any part of the country. Our peasant reform is not a tribute to the magnanimity of the government; on the contrary, it serves as a great historical example of how the autocratic government befouls everything it touches. Military defeat, appalling financial difficulties, and menacing discontent among the peasantry *compelled* the government to take the step. The tsar himself admitted that the peasants had to be emancipated from above, lest they emancipate themselves from below. But in embarking on emancipation, the government did all it possibly could to satisfy the greed of the "injured" serf owners. The government did not even stop at the base device of reshuffling the men who were to carry out the reform, although these men had been selected from among the nobility themselves. The first body of *miroviye posredniki*[5] was dissolved and replaced by men who could not but help the serf owners cheat the peasantry in the very process of parcelling out the land. Nor could the great reform be carried out without resort to military punitive action and the shooting down of peasants who refused to accept the charters.[6] It is not surprising, therefore, that the best men of the time, muzzled by the censors, met this great reform with the silence of condemnation.

The peasant, "emancipated" from serf labour, emerged from the hands of the reformers crushed, plundered, degraded, tied to his plot of land, so much so that nothing was left for him to do but "voluntarily" accept serf labour. And he began to cultivate the land of his former master, "renting" from him the very land that had been cut off from his own allotment, hiring himself out in the winter for summer work in return for the corn he had to borrow from the landlord to feed his hungry family. The "free labour," for which the manifesto drawn up by a Jesuit priest called upon the peasantry to ask the "blessing of God," turned out to be nothing more nor less than serf labour and bondage.

To oppression by the landlords, which was preserved thanks to the magnanimity of the officials who introduced and carried out the reform, was added oppression by capital. The power of money, which crushed even the French peasant who was emancipated from the power of the feudal landlords not by miserable, half-hearted reforms but by a mighty popular revolution—this power of money bore down with all its weight upon our semi-serf muzhik. The peasant had to obtain money at all costs—in order to pay the taxes which had increased as a result of the beneficent reform, in order to rent land, to buy the few miserable articles of factory-made goods which began to squeeze out the home manufactures of the peasant, to buy corn, etc. The power of money not only crushed the peasantry, but split it up. An enormous number of peasants were steadily ruined and turned into proletarians. From the minority arose a small group of grasping kulaks and thrifty muzhiks who laid hands upon the peasant economy and the peasants' lands, and who represented the kernel of the rising rural bourgeoisie. The forty years since the reform have been marked by this constant process of "de-peasantizing" the peasants, a process of slow and painful extinction of the peasantry. The peasant was reduced to beggary. He lived together with his cattle, was clothed in rags, and fed on weeds; he fled from his allotment if he had anywhere to go, and even *paid* to be relieved of it, if he could induce anyone to take over a plot of land the payments on which exceeded the income it yielded. The peasants were in a state of chronic starvation, and died by the tens of thousands from famine and epidemics in bad harvest years, which recurred with increasing frequency.

This is the state of our countryside even at the present time. One might ask: what is the way out, and how can the lot of the peasantry be improved? The small peasantry can free itself from the yoke of capital only by joining the labour movement, by helping the workers in their fight for the socialist system, to make the land as well as other means of production (factories, works, machines, etc.) public property. To try to save the peasantry by protecting small-scale farming and small holdings from the onslaught of capitalism would be a useless attempt to retard social development; it would mean deceiving the peasantry with illusions about the possibility of prosperity even under capitalism, disuniting the toiling classes and creating a privileged position for the minority at the expense of the majority. That is why Social-Democrats shall always fight against senseless and vicious institutions such as that prohibiting the peasant from disposing of his land, such as collective responsibility,[7] the system of prohibiting the peasants from freely leaving the community and freely accepting into it persons belonging to any estate. But, as we have seen, our peasants are suffering not only and not so much from oppression by capital as from oppression by the landlords and the survivals of serfdom. Ruthless struggle against these shackles, which immeasurably worsen the condition of the peasantry and tie it hand and foot, is not only possible but even necessary in the interest of the country's social development in general; for the hopeless poverty, ignorance, tyranny, and degradation, from which the peasants suffer, lay an Asiatic imprint upon the entire life of our country. Social-Democrats would not be doing their duty if they did not render every assistance to this struggle. This assistance should take the form, to put it briefly, of *carrying the class war to the countryside.*

We have seen that in the modern Russian countryside two kinds of class antagonism exist side by side: first, antagonism between the rural workers and the rural employers, and second, between the peasantry as a whole and the landlord class as a whole. The first antagonism is developing and becoming more acute; the second is gradually diminishing. The first is still wholly in the future; the second to a considerable degree already belongs to the past. And yet in spite of this, it is the second antagonism that has the most vital and most practical significance for Russian Social-Democrats at the present time. It goes without saying that we must utilize all the opportunities that present themselves to us to develop the class-consciousness of the agricultural wage-workers, that we must pay attention to the urban workers who go to the countryside (for example, mechanics employed on steam threshing-machines, etc.) and to the markets where agricultural labourers are hired. This is an axiom for every Social-Democrat.

But our rural labourers are still too closely connected with the peasantry, they are still too heavily burdened with the misfortunes of the peasantry generally to enable the

movement of the rural workers to assume national significance, either now or in the immediate future. On the other
hand, the question of sweeping away the survivals of serfdom, of driving the spirit of class inequality and degradation of tens of millions of the "common people" out of the
whole of the Russian state system is already a matter of
national significance, and the party which claims to be the
vanguard in the fight for freedom cannot ignore it.

The deplorable state of the peasantry has now become (in
a more or less general form) almost universally recognized. The phrase about "the defects" of the Reform of 1861,
and about the need for state aid, has become a current tru-
ism. It is our duty to point out that peasant distress arises
precisely from the class oppression of the peasantry; that
the government is the loyal champion of the oppressing
classes, and that those who sincerely and seriously desire
a radical improvement in the condition of the peasantry
must seek not aid from the government, but freedom from
its oppression, and win political liberty. There is talk about
the compensation payments[8] being too high, and about benevolent measures on the part of the government to reduce
them and postpone the dates of payment. Our reply to this
is: all payment of compensation is nothing more nor less
than robbery of the peasantry by the landlords and the government, screened by legal forms and official phrases; it
is nothing more nor less than tribute paid to the serf owners for emancipating their slaves. We shall put forward
the demand for the immediate and complete abolition of
compensation payments and quitrents, and the demand for
the return to the people of the hundreds of millions which
the tsarist government has extorted from them in the
course of the years to satisfy the greed of the slave-owners.
There is talk about the peasants not having sufficient land,
about the need for state aid in providing them with more
land. Our reply to this is: it is precisely *because* of state
aid (aid to the landlords, of course) that the peasants in
such an enormous number of cases were deprived of land
they vitally needed. We shall put forward the demand for
the restoration to the peasantry of the land of which they
were deprived and the lack of which still keeps them in a

state of bondage and forced labour, i.e., actually in a state
of serfdom. We shall put forward the demand for the establishment of peasant committees to remove the crying in-
justices committed against the emancipated slaves by the
committees of the nobles set up by the tsarist government.
We shall demand the establishment of courts empowered
to reduce the excessively high payment for land extorted
from the peasants by the landlords by taking advantage of
their hopeless position, courts in which the peasants could
prosecute for usury all those who take advantage of
their extreme need to impose extortionate terms upon them.
We shall take advantage of every opportunity to explain to
the peasantry that the people who talk to them about the
tutelage or the aid of the present state are either fools or
charlatans, and their worst enemies; that what the peasants stand in need of most is relief from the tyranny and
oppression of the officials, recognition of their complete and
absolute equality in all respects with all other classes, complete freedom to migrate and move freely from place to
place, freedom to dispose of their lands as they please and
freedom to manage their own communal affairs and dispose of the communal revenues. The most common facts in
the life of any Russian village provide a thousand themes
for agitation on behalf of the above demands. This agitation must be based upon the local, concrete, and most pressing needs of the peasantry; yet it must not be confined to
these needs, but must be steadily directed towards widen-
ing the outlook of the peasantry, towards developing their
political consciousness. The peasants must be made to understand the special place occupied in the state by the
landlords and the peasants respectively, and they must be
taught that the only way to free the countryside from the
tyranny and oppression that reigns in it is to convene an
assembly of representatives of the people and to overthrow
the arbitrary rule of the officials. It is absurd and stupid to
assert that the demand for political liberty would not be
understood by the workers: not only the workers who have
engaged the factory-owners and the police in direct battle
for years and who constantly see their best fighters sub-
jected to arbitrary arrests and persecution—not only these

workers who are already infected with socialism, but every
intelligent peasant who thinks at all about the things he
sees going on around him will understand what the workers are fighting for and what the significance is of the
national assembly which will emancipate the whole country from the tyranny of the hated officials. Agitation on the
basis of the direct and most urgent needs of the peasants
will fulfil its purpose, i.e., carry the class war to the countryside, only when it succeeds in combining every exposure
of some "economic" evil with definite political demands.

But the question arises whether the Social-Democratic
Labour Party can include in its programme demands like
those referred to above. Can it undertake to carry on agitation among the peasantry? Will it not lead to the scattering and diversion of our revolutionary forces, which are
not very numerous as it is, from the principal and only reliable channel of the movement?

Such objections are based on a misunderstanding. We
must unfailingly include in our programme demands for the
emancipation of our countryside from all the survivals of
slavery, demands capable of rousing among the best section
of the peasantry, if not independent political action, then at
all events a readiness consciously to support the working
class struggle for emancipation. We would be committing
a mistake if we advocated measures which may retard social development, or artificially shield the small peasantry
against growing capitalism, against the development   of
large-scale production; but it would be a much more fatal
mistake if we failed to utilize the labour movement for the
purpose of spreading among the peasantry the democratic
demands which the Reform of February 19, 1861, failed to
carry out because it was distorted by the landlords and the
officials. Our Party must include such demands in its programme if it wants to take the lead of the whole people in
the struggle against the autocracy.* But to include these

---

* We have already drafted a Social-Democratic programme
which includes the above-mentioned demands. We hope—after this
draft has been discussed and amended with the participation of the
Emancipation of Labour group[9]—to publish it as the draft programme of our Party in one of our forthcoming issues.

points does not imply urging any transfer of active revolutionary forces from the towns to the villages. Such a thing
is out of the question. There can be no doubt that all the
militant elements of the Party must strive to go to the towns
and industrial centres; that only the industrial proletariat
is capable of conducting a steadfast and mass struggle
against the autocracy, that only the industrial proletariat is
capable of employing such methods of struggle as organizing public demonstrations, or of issuing regularly and widely circulating a *popular* political newspaper. We must
include peasant demands in our programme not in order to
transfer convinced Social-Democrats from the towns to the
countryside, not in order to chain them to the village, but
to guide the activities of those forces which *cannot* find an
outlet anywhere except in the rural localities and to utilize
for the cause of democracy, for the political struggle for
freedom, the ties which, owing to the force of circumstances,
a good many faithful Social-Democratic intellectuals
and workers have with the countryside—ties that are growing and necessarily will continue to grow with the growth
of the movement. We have long since outgrown the stage
when we were a small detachment of volunteers, when the
reserves of Social-Democratic forces were limited to circles
of young people who all "went to the workers." Our movement now has a whole army at its command, an army
of workers, inspired by the struggle for socialism and freedom—an army of intellectuals who have been taking part
in the movement and who can already be found over the
whole length and breadth of Russia—an army of sympa-
thizers whose eyes are turned with faith and hope upon the
labour movement and who are prepared to render it a thousand services. We are confronted with the great task of
organizing all these armies in such a manner as will enable us not only to organize transient outbreaks, not only
to strike casual and sporadic (and therefore not dangerous)
blows at the enemy, but also to pursue the enemy steadily
and persistently, in a determined struggle all along the
line, to harass the autocratic government wherever it sows
oppression and gathers a harvest of hatred. Can this aim
be achieved without sowing the seeds of the class struggle

and political consciousness among the many millions of the peasantry? Do not say it is impossible to sow these seeds! It is not only possible, it is already being done in a thousand ways which escape our attention and influence. This will proceed much more widely and rapidly when we issue slogans that will bring our influence to bear and unfurl the banner of the emancipation of the Russian peasantry from all the survivals of shameful serfdom. Country people coming to the towns already regard with curiosity and interest the workers' struggle, and although they do not understand it, they carry the news of this struggle to the most remote parts of the country. We can and must bring about a situation when this curiosity of spectators is replaced, if not by full understanding, then at least by a vague consciousness that the workers are fighting for the interests of the whole people, by growing sympathy for their struggle. And when that is done, the day of the victory of the revolutionary workers' party over the police government will come more quickly than we ourselves ever expected or even guessed.

Written in February 1901
Published in April 1901, in the
newspaper *Iskra*, No. 3

Vol. IV, pp. 394-401

# TO THE RURAL POOR

## An Explanation to Peasants:
## What the Social-Democrats Want

### 1. THE STRUGGLE OF THE URBAN WORKERS

Many peasants have probably already heard about the labour unrest in the towns. Some of them have themselves been in the capitals and in the factories and have seen the riots, as the police call them. Others know workers who were involved in the unrest and were deported back to their villages by the authorities. Others again must have seen the leaflets issued by the workers, or pamphlets about the workers' struggle. Still others have only heard stories about what is going on in the towns from people who have been there.

Formerly, only students rebelled, but now thousands and tens of thousands of workers have risen in all the big towns. In most cases they fight against their employers, against the factory-owners, against the capitalists. The workers declare strikes, all the workers at a factory stop work at the same time and demand higher wages, and that they should be made to work not eleven or ten hours a day, but only eight hours. The workers also demand other things that would make the working-man's life easier. They want the workshops to be in better condition and the machines to be protected by special appliances so as to prevent them from maiming the workers; they want their children to be able to go to school and the sick to be given proper aid in the hospitals; they want the homes of the workers to be like human dwellings instead of being like dogs' kennels.

The police intervene in the workers' struggle. The police seize the workers, throw them into prison, deport them without trial back to their villages or even to Siberia. The government has outlawed strikes and workers' meetings. But the workers wage their fight against the police and against the government. The workers say: we, millions of working people, have bent our backs long enough! We have worked for the rich and remained paupers long enough! We have allowed them to rob us long enough! We want to unite in unions, to unite all the workers in one big workers' union (a workers' *party*) and jointly to strive for a better life. We want to achieve a new and better order of society: in this new and better society there must be neither rich nor poor; all will have to work. Not a handful of rich people, but all the working people must enjoy the fruits of common labour. Machines and other improvements must serve to ease the work of all and not to enable a few to grow rich at the expense of millions and tens of millions of people. This new and better society is called *socialist society*. The teachings about this society are called *socialism*. The workers' unions which fight for this better society are called *Social-Democratic* parties. Such parties exist openly in nearly all countries (except Russia and Turkey), and our workers, together with Socialists from among the educated people, have also formed such a party: the *Russian Social-Democratic Labour Party*.

The government persecutes that Party, but it exists in secret, in spite of all prohibitions; it publishes newspapers and pamphlets and organizes secret unions. The workers not only meet in secret, they come out into the streets in crowds and unfurl their banners bearing the inscriptions: "Long live the eight-hour day! Long live freedom! Long live socialism!" The government savagely persecutes the workers for this. It even sends troops to shoot the workers. Russian soldiers have killed Russian workers in Yaroslavl, in St. Petersburg, in Riga, in Rostov-on-Don and in Zlatoust.

But the workers do not surrender. They continue the fight. They say: neither persecution, nor prison, nor deportations, nor penal servitude, nor death can frighten us.

Our cause is a just cause. We are fighting for freedom and
happiness for all who work. We are fighting to free tens
and hundreds of millions of people from violence, oppression and poverty. The workers are becoming more and
more class-conscious. The number of Social-Democrats is
growing fast in all countries. We shall win in spite of all
persecution.

The rural poor must clearly understand who these Social-Democrats are, what they want, and what must be
done in the countryside to help the Social-Democrats to
win happiness for the people.

## 2. WHAT DO THE SOCIAL-DEMOCRATS WANT?

The Russian Social-Democrats are first and foremost
striving to win *political freedom*. They need freedom in order to unite all the Russian workers widely and openly in
the struggle for the new and better socialist order of society.

What is political freedom?

To understand this, the peasant must first compare his
present state of freedom with serfdom. Under serfdom the
peasant could not marry without the landlord's permission.
Today the peasant is free to marry without anyone's permission. Under serfdom the peasant had to work for his
landlord on the days fixed by the latter's bailiff. Today
the peasant is free to decide which employer to work for,
on which days, and for what pay. Under serfdom the peasant could not leave his village without the landlord's permission. Today the peasant is free to go wherever he
pleases—if the *mir* (the village community) allows him to
go, if he is not in arrears with his taxes, if he can get a
passport, and if the governor or the police do not forbid his
changing residence. Thus, even today the peasant is not
quite free to go where he pleases, he does not enjoy complete freedom of movement, the peasant is still a semi-serf.
Later on we shall explain in detail why the Russian peasant is still a semi-serf and what he must do to change his
condition.

Under serfdom the peasant had no right to acquire property without the landlord's permission, he could not buy land. Today the peasant is free to acquire all kinds of property (but even today he is not quite free to leave the *mir*, he is not quite free to dispose of his land as he pleases). Under serfdom the peasant could be flogged by order of the landlord. Today the peasant cannot be punished by his landlord, although he is still liable to corporal punishment.

This freedom is called *civil* freedom—freedom in family matters, in private matters, in matters concerning property. The peasant and the worker are free (although not quite) to arrange their family life and their private affairs, to dispose of their labour (choose their employer) and of their property.

But neither the Russian workers nor the Russian people as a whole are yet free to arrange their *public* affairs. The people as a whole are the serfs of the government officials, just as the peasants were the serfs of the landlords. The Russian people have no right to choose their officials, nor the right to elect representatives to legislate for the whole country. The Russian people have not even the right to arrange meetings for the discussion of *state* affairs. We cannot even print newspapers or books, we cannot even speak to all and for all on matters concerning the whole state without the permission of the officials who have been put in authority over us without our consent, just as the landlord used to appoint his bailiff without the consent of the peasants!

Just as the peasants were the slaves of the landlords, so the Russian people are still the slaves of the officials. Just as the peasants under serfdom lacked civil freedom, so the Russian people still lack *political* freedom. Political freedom means the freedom of the people to arrange their public, their state affairs. Political freedom means the right of the people to elect their representatives (deputies) to a State Duma (parliament). All laws should be discussed and passed, all taxes and imposts should be fixed only by such a State Duma (parliament) elected by the people. Political freedom means the right of the people themselves to choose all their officials, to arrange all kinds of meetings for the discussion of all state affairs, to publish whatever papers and books they please without having to ask for permission.

All the other European peoples won political freedom for themselves long ago. Only in Turkey and in Russia are the people still politically enslaved to the Sultan's government and to the tsarist autocratic government. Tsarist autocracy means the unlimited power of the tsar. The people play no part in the development of the state or in the administration of the state. All the laws are made and all the officials are appointed by the tsar alone, by his personal, unlimited, autocratic authority. But, of course, the tsar *cannot even know* all the Russian laws and all the Russian officials. The tsar cannot even know all that goes on in the country. The tsar simply endorses the will of a few score of the most high-ranking and most high-born officials. However much he may want to, one man cannot govern a vast country like Russia. It is not the tsar who governs Russia—one can only talk about autocratic, one-man rule; Russia is governed by a handful of the richest and most high-born officials. The tsar learns only what this handful is pleased to tell him. The tsar is quite powerless to go against the will of this handful of high-rank nobles: the tsar himself is a landlord and one of the nobility; from his earliest childhood he has lived only among these high-born people; it was they who brought him up and educated him; he knows about the Russian people as a whole only what is known by these noble gentry, these rich landlords, and the few very rich merchants who are received at the tsar's court.

In every volost administration office you will find the same picture hanging on the wall; it depicts the tsar (Alexander III, the father of the present tsar) speaking to the volost headmen who have come to his coronation. The tsar is saying to them: *"Obey your marshals of the nobility!"* And the present tsar, Nicholas II, has repeated those words. Thus, the tsars themselves admit that they can govern the country only with the aid of the nobility and through the nobility. We must firmly remember those words of the tsars about the peasants having to obey the nobility.

We must clearly understand what a lie is being told  the people by those who try to make out that tsarist government is the best form of government. In other countries—those people say—the government is elected; but it is the rich who are elected, and they govern unjustly and oppress the poor. In Russia the government is not elected; an autocratic tsar governs the whole country. The tsar stands above everyone, rich and poor. The tsar, they tell us, is just to everyone, to the poor and to the rich alike.

Such talk is sheer hypocrisy. Every Russian knows the kind of justice that is dispensed by our government. Everybody knows whether a plain working-man or a farm-labourer in our country can become a member of the State Council. In all other European countries, however, factory workers and farm-hands too have been elected to the State Duma (parliament); and they have freely spoken to all the people about the miserable condition of the workers, and called upon the workers to unite and fight for better conditions. And no one has dared to stop these speeches of the people's representatives, no policeman has dared to lay a finger on them.

In Russia there is no elective government, and she is governed not merely by the rich and the high-born, but by the worst of these. She is governed by the most skilful intriguers at the tsar's court, by the most artful backbiters, by those who carry lies and slanders to the tsar, who flatter and toady to him. They govern in secret; the people do not and cannot know what new laws are being drafted, what wars are being hatched, what new taxes are being introduced, which officials are being rewarded and for what services, and which are being dismissed. In no country is there such a multitude of officials as in Russia. These officials tower above the voiceless people like a dark forest—a mere working-man can never make his way through this forest, can never obtain justice. Not a single complaint against the bribery, the robbery or the violence of the officials is ever brought to light; every complaint is smothered in official red tape. The voice of an isolated individual never reaches the people, it is lost in this dark jungle, it is stifled in the police torture-chamber. An army of officials, who were

never elected by the people and who are not responsible to
the people, has woven a thick web, and people are struggling in this web like flies.

Tsarist autocracy is an autocracy of officials. Tsarist autocracy means the feudal dependence of the people upon
the officials and especially upon the police. Tsarist autocracy is police autocracy.

That is why the workers come out into the streets with
banners bearing the inscriptions: "Down with the autocracy!" "Long live political freedom!" That is why the tens
of millions of the village poor must also support and take
up this battle-cry of the urban workers. Like them, undaunt-
ed by persecution, fearless of the enemy's threats and violence, and undeterred by the first reverses, the agricultural
labourers and the poor peasants must come forward for a
decisive struggle for the freedom of the whole of the Russian people and demand first of all the *convocation of the
representatives of the people*. Let the people themselves all
over Russia elect their deputies. Let those deputies form a
supreme assembly, which will introduce elective government in Russia, free the people from feudal dependence
upon the officials and the police, secure for the people the
right to meet freely, to speak freely, and to have a free
press!

That is what the Social-Democrats want first and foremost. That is the meaning of their first demand: the *demand for political freedom*.

We know that political freedom, free elections to the State
Duma (parliament), freedom of meetings, freedom of the
press, will not at once deliver the working people from poverty and oppression. There is no means of immediately delivering the poor of town and country from the burden of
working for the rich. The working people have no one to
place their hopes in and no one to rely upon *but themselves*.
Nobody will free the working-man from poverty *if he does
not free himself*. And to free themselves the workers of the
whole country, of the whole of Russia, must unite in one
union, in one party. But millions of workers cannot unite
if the autocratic police government forbids all meetings,
all workers' newspapers, the election of workers' deputies.

To unite they must have the right to form unions of every kind, they must have freedom to unite, they must have political freedom.

Political freedom will not at once deliver the working people from poverty, *but it will give the workers a weapon with which to fight poverty*. There is no other means and there can be no other means of fighting poverty except the *unity of the workers themselves*. But millions of people cannot unite unless there is *political freedom*.

In all European countries where the people have won political freedom the workers began to unite long ago. Throughout the whole of Europe, workers who own no land and no workshops, who work for other people for wages all their lives, are called *proletarians*. Over fifty years ago the call was sounded for the working people to unite. "Proletarians of all countries, unite!"—during the past fifty years these words have sounded and resounded all over the world, they are repeated at tens and hundreds of thousands of workers' meetings, they can be read in millions of Social-Democratic pamphlets and newspapers in every language.

Of course, to unite millions of workers in one union, in one party, is a very difficult task; it requires time, persistence, perseverance, and courage. The workers are crushed by poverty, numbed by back-breaking toil for the capitalists and landlords; often they have not even the time to think of why they remain eternal paupers, or how to be delivered from this. Everything is done to prevent the workers from uniting: either by means of direct and brutal violence, as in countries like Russia where there is no political freedom, or by refusing to employ workers who preach the doctrines of socialism, or, lastly, by means of deceit and corruption. But no violence, no persecution will stop the proletarian workers who are fighting for the great cause of the emancipation of all the working people from poverty and oppression. The number of Social-Democratic workers is constantly growing. Take our neighbour country, Germany; there they have elective government. Formerly, in Germany, too, there was an unlimited, autocratic monarchist government. But long ago, more than fifty years ago, the German people destroyed the autocracy and won polit-

ical freedom by force. In Germany laws are not made by a
handful of officials, as in Russia, but by an *assembly of
people's representatives*, by a parliament, by the *Reichstag*,
as the Germans call it. All adult males take part in electing
deputies to this assembly. This makes it possible to count
how many votes were cast for the Social-Democrats. In
1887, *one-tenth* of all the votes were cast for the Social-
Democrats. In 1898, (when the last elections to the Reichstag
took place) the Social-Democratic vote *increased    nearly
threefold*. This time *more than one-fourth* of all the votes
were cast for the Social-Democrats. *Over two million* adult
males voted for *Social-Democratic parliamentary candi-
dates*. Among the farm-labourers of Germany socialism is
not yet widespread, but it is now making very rapid progress
among them. And when the masses of farm-hands,    day-
labourers and poor, pauperized peasants unite with their
brothers in the towns, the German workers will win and
establish conditions under which the toilers will suffer neither poverty nor oppression.

By what means do the Social-Democratic workers want
to deliver the people from poverty?

To know this, one must clearly understand the cause of
the poverty of the vast masses of the people under the present social order. Rich cities are growing, magnificent shops
and houses are being built, railways are being construct-
ed, all kinds of machines and improvements are being introduced in industry and in agriculture,   but millions   of
people remain in poverty, continue to work all their lives
to provide a bare subsistence for their families. And that is
not all: more and more people are becoming unemployed.
Both in town and country there are more and more people
who can find no work at all. In the villages they starve, in
the towns they swell the ranks of the "tramps" and "down
and outs," they find refuge like beasts in dug-outs on the
outskirts of towns, or in dreadful slums and cellars,   such
as those in the Khitrov Market in Moscow.

Why is this? Wealth and luxury are increasing, and yet
the millions and millions who by their labour   create   all
this wealth remain in poverty and want! The peasants are
dying of starvation, the workers wander about workless, and

yet merchants export millions of poods of grain from Russia to foreign countries, factories and mills are closed down because the goods cannot be sold, there is no market for them!

The cause of all this is, first of all, that most of the land, and also the factories, workshops, machines, buildings, ships, etc., belong to a small number of rich people. Tens of millions of people work on this land and in these factories and workshops, but they are all owned by a few thousand or tens of thousands of rich people, landlords, merchants and factory-owners. The people work for those rich men for hire, for wages, for a crust of bread. All that is produced over and above what is required to provide a bare subsistence for the workers goes to the rich owners; it is their profit, their "income." All the benefits arising from the use of machines and from improvements in methods of production go to the landlords and capitalists: they accumulate countless wealth, while the working people get only miserable crumbs. The working people are brought together for work; on large estates and in big factories several hundred and sometimes even several thousand workers are employed. When labour is united in this way, and when the most diverse kinds of machines are employed, work becomes more productive: one worker produces much more than scores of workers did working separately and without the aid of machines. But the benefits of this more productive labour go not to all the toilers, but to an insignificant number of big landowners, merchants, and factory-owners.

One often hears it said that the landlords and merchants "*provide* work" for the people, that they "provide" earnings for the poor. It is said, for instance, that a neighbouring factory or a neighbouring landlord "*maintains*" the local peasants. Actually, however, the workers by their labour maintain themselves and also all those who do not work. *But for permission* to work on the landlord's land, in a factory, or on a railway, the worker *gives* the owner *for nothing* all he produces, while the worker himself gets only enough for a bare subsistence. Actually, therefore, it is not the landlords and the merchants who maintain the workers, but the workers who by their labour maintain everybody, surrendering the greater part of the results of their labour for nothing.

Further. In all modern countries the poverty of the people is due to the fact that the workers produce all sorts of articles for sale, for the market. The factory-owner and the artisan, the landlord and the well-to-do peasant produce goods, raise cattle, sow and harvest grain *for sale*, in order to obtain *money*. Money has everywhere become the principal power. All the goods produced by human labour are exchanged for money. With money you can buy anything. With money you can even buy men, that is to say, force a man who owns nothing to work for another who has money. Formerly, land used to be the principal power—that was the case under serfdom: whoever possessed land possessed power and authority. Today, however, money, capital, has become the principal power. With money you can buy as much land as you like. Without money you will not be able to do much even if you have land: you must have money to buy a plough or other implements, to buy livestock, to buy clothes and other town-made goods, not to speak of paying taxes. For the sake of money nearly all the landlords have mortgaged their land to the banks. To get money the government borrows from rich people and bankers all over the world, and pays hundreds of millions of rubles yearly in interest on these loans.

For the sake of money everyone today is waging a fierce war against everyone else. Each tries to buy cheap and to sell dear, each tries to outcompete the other, to sell a larger quantity of goods, to undercut the other, to conceal from him a profitable market or a profitable contract. In this general scramble for money the small man, the small artisan, or the small peasant, fares worse than all: he is always outcompeted by the big merchant or the rich peasant. The small man never has any reserves; he lives from hand to mouth; the first difficulty, the first accident compels him to pawn his last belongings or to sell his draught animals at a trifling price. Once he has fallen into the clutches of a kulak or of a usurer he very rarely succeeds in freeing himself from the shackles and in most cases he is utterly ruined. Every year tens and hundreds of thousands of

small peasants and artisans lock up their cottages, surrender their plot of land to the community free of charge and
become wage-labourers, farm-hands, unskilled workers,
proletarians. But the rich grow richer and richer in this
struggle for money. They pile up millions and hundreds of
millions of rubles in the banks and make profit not only
with their own money, but also with the money deposited in
the banks by others. The small man who deposits a few
score or a few hundred rubles in a bank or a savings bank
receives interest at the rate of three or four kopeks on the
ruble; but the rich make millions out of these scores and
use those millions to enlarge their turnover and make ten
and twenty kopeks on the ruble.

That is why the Social-Democratic workers say that the
only way to put an end to the poverty of the people is to
change the existing order from top to bottom, throughout
the country, and to establish a *socialist order:* in other
words, to take the land from the big landowners, the factories from the factory-owners, the money capital from the
bankers, to abolish their *private property* and turn it over
to the whole working people throughout the country. When
that is done the labour of the workers will be made use of
not by the rich who live on the labour of others, but by the
workers themselves and by those elected by them. The
fruits of common labour and the benefits that arise from all
improvements and machines will then go to all the toilers,
to all the workers. Wealth will then grow at a still faster
rate because, working for themselves, the workers will work
better than they worked for the capitalists, the working-
day will be shorter, the workers' standard of living will
be higher, all their conditions of life will be completely
changed.

But it is not an easy matter to change the existing order
throughout the country. That requires a great deal of effort,
a long and stubborn struggle. All the rich, all the property-
owners, all the bourgeoisie* will defend their riches with

----

* Bourgeois means a property-owner. The bourgeoisie are all the
property-owners taken together. A big bourgeois is the owner of
big property. A petty bourgeois is the owner of small property. The
words bourgeoisie and proletariat mean property-owners and work-

all their might. The officials and the army will rise to defend the *rich class*, because the government itself is in the
hands of the rich class. The workers must rally as one man
for the fight against all those who live on the labour of
others; the workers themselves must unite and help to unite
all the propertyless in a single *working class*, in a single
*proletarian class*. The struggle will not be easy for the
working class, but it will certainly end in the victory of the
workers, because the bourgeoisie, the people who live on the
labour of others, are an insignificant minority of the population, while the working class is the vast majority. Workers
against property-owners means millions against thousands.

The workers in Russia are already beginning to unite for
this great struggle in a single workers' Social-Democratic
Party. Difficult as it is to unite in secret, hiding from the
police, nevertheless the organization is growing and gaining strength. When the Russian people have won political
freedom, the work of uniting the working class, the cause
of socialism, will advance much more rapidly, more rapidly
than it is advancing among the German workers.

### 3. RICHES AND POVERTY, PROPERTY-OWNERS AND WORKERS IN THE COUNTRYSIDE

We know now what the Social-Democrats want. They
want to fight the whole of the rich class to free the people
from poverty. In our countryside there is no less and, perhaps, even more poverty than there is in the towns. We
shall not speak here about how great the poverty in the
countryside is. Every worker who has been in the country
and every peasant are well acquainted with want, hunger,
cold and ruin in the countryside.

But the peasant does not know the *cause* of his distress,
hunger, and ruin, or *how* to rid himself of want. To know
this we must first find out what causes all want and poverty in both town and country. We have already dealt  with

---

ers, the rich and the poor, or those who live on the labour of others
and those who work for others for wages.

this briefly, and we have seen that the poor peasants and rural workers must unite with the urban workers. But that is not enough. We must find out what sort of people in the countryside will follow the rich, the property-owners, and what sort of people will follow the workers, the Social-Democrats. We must find out whether there are many peasants who no less than the landlords are able to acquire capital and live on the labour of others. Unless we get to the bottom of this matter, no amount of talking about poverty will be of any use, and the rural poor will not know *who* in the countryside must unite among themselves and with the urban workers, or *what* must be done to make it a *real* union and to prevent the peasant from being hoodwinked by his own kind, the rich peasant, as well as by the landlord.

To get to the bottom of this let us now see how strong the landlords are and how strong the rich peasants are in the countryside.

Let us begin with the landlords. We can judge of their strength first of all by the amount of land they own. The total amount of land in European Russia, including peasant allotment land and privately owned land, was calculated at about 240,000,000 dessiatins* (exclusive of the state land, of which we shall speak separately). Out of this total of 240,000,000 dessiatins, 131,000,000 dessiatins of allotment land are held by the peasants, that is to say, by *over ten million households*; whereas 109,000,000 dessiatins are held by private owners, i.e., by *less than half a million families*. Thus, even if we take the average, every peasant family holds 13 dessiatins, while every family of private owners owns 218 dessiatins! But the inequality in the distribution of the land is far greater than this, as we shall presently see.

---

* These and all subsequent figures concerning the amount of land are very much out of date. They refer to the years 1877-78. But we have no more up-to-date figures. The Russian government can only survive by living in the dark, and that is why complete and truthful information about the life of the people throughout our country is so rarely collected.

Of the 109,000,000 dessiatins owned by private   owners
*seven* million are *appanage lands*, in other words, the private property of the members of the imperial family. The
tsar, with his family, is the first landlord, the biggest landlord, in Russia. *One* family possesses *more* land than *half
a million* peasant families! Further, the churches and monasteries own about *six* million  dessiatins  of  land.  Our
priests preach frugality and abstinence to the peasants, but
they themselves have, by fair means and foul, accumulated
an enormous amount of land.

Further, about two million dessiatins are owned by the
cities and towns, and an equal amount by various commercial and industrial companies and corporations. Ninety-
two million dessiatins (the exact figure is 91,605,845, but
to simplify matters we will quote round figures) belong to
*less than half a million* (481,358) families of private owners. Half these families are quite small owners, owning
less than ten dessiatins of land each, and all of them together own less than one million dessiatins. On the other
hand, *sixteen thousand* families own *over   one   thousand*
dessiatins each; and the total land owned by them amounts
to *sixty-five million dessiatins*. What vast areas of land are
concentrated in the hands of the big landowners is seen
from the fact that *just under one thousand families* (924)
*own more than ten thousand dessiatins* each,  and all together they own *twenty-seven million dessiatins*! One thousand families own as much land as is owned by two million peasant families.

Obviously, millions and tens of millions of people  are
*bound* to live in distress and starvation and *will go on* living in distress and starvation as long as such vast areas
of land are owned by a few thousand rich families. Obviously, the state authorities, the government (even the tsar's
government) will always dance to the tune of these big
landowners. Obviously, the rural poor can expect no help
from anyone, or from any quarter, as long as they do not
unite, combine in a single class to wage a fierce and stubborn struggle against the landlord class.

At this point we must observe that very many people in
this country (including many educated people) have a to-

tally wrong idea about the strength of the landlord class; they say that the "state" owns much more land. These bad counsellors of the peasant say: "A large portion of the territory (i.e., of all the land) of Russia already belongs to the state." (These words are taken from the newspaper *Revolyutsionnaya Rossiya*, No. 8, p. 8.) The mistake these people make arises from the following. They have heard that the *state* owns 150,000,000 dessiatins of land in European Russia. That is true. But they forget that these 150,000,000 dessiatins consist almost entirely of *uncultivable land and forests in the Far North*, in the Arkhangelsk, Vologda, Olonets, Vyatka, and Perm gubernias. Thus, the state has retained only that land which up to the present has been quite unfit for cultivation. The cultivable land owned by the state amounts to *less than four million dessiatins*. And these cultivable state lands, (for example, in the Samara Gubernia, where they are particularly extensive), are let for very low rents, for next to nothing, to the rich. The rich rent thousands and tens of thousands of dessiatins of these lands and sublet them to the peasants at exorbitant rents.

The people who say that the state owns a great deal of land are truly very bad counsellors of the peasant. The actual case is that the big private landowners (including the tsar personally) own a lot of good land, and the state itself is in the hands of these big owners. Until the rural poor unite and by uniting become a formidable force, the "state" will always remain the obedient servant of the landlord class. There is another thing that must not be forgotten: formerly, nearly all the landlords were nobles. The nobility still owns a vast amount of land (in 1877-78, 115,000 nobles owned 73,000,000 dessiatins). But today money, capital, has become the principal power. Merchants and well-to-do peasants have bought very large amounts of land. It is estimated that in the course of thirty years (from 1863 to 1892) the nobility lost (i.e., sold more than they bought) land to the value of over 600,000,000 rubles. And merchants and honorary citizens bought land to the value of 250,000,000 rubles. Peasants, Cossacks, and "other rural inhabitants" (as our government calls the common folk, to distinguish them from the "gentry," the "clean public")

3*

bought land to the value of 300,000,000 rubles. Thus, on
the average, every year the peasants in the whole of Russia
acquire land as private property to the value of 10,000,000
rubles.

And so, there are different sorts of peasants: some live in
distress and starvation; others grow rich. Consequently, the
number of rich peasants who lean towards the landlords
and who will take the side of the rich against the workers
is increasing. The rural poor who want to unite with the
urban workers must carefully ponder over this and find out
whether there are many rich peasants of this kind, how
strong they are, and what kind of a union we need to fight
this force. We have just mentioned the bad counsellors of
the peasant. Those bad counsellors are fond of saying that
the peasants already have such a union. That union is the
*mir*, the village community. The *mir*, they say, is a great
force. The *mir* unites the peasants very closely; the organization (i.e., the association, unity) of the peasants in the
*mir* is colossal (i.e., enormous, boundless).

That is not true. It is a fairy-tale. A fairy-tale invented
by kind-hearted people, but a fairy-tale nevertheless. If we
listen to fairy-tales we shall only wreck our cause, the
cause of uniting the rural poor with the urban workers. Let
every rural inhabitant look round carefully: is the unity of
the *mir*, is the peasant community, at all like a union of
the poor to fight *all* the rich, *all* those who live on the labour of others? No, it is not, and it cannot be. In every village, in every community, there are many labourers, many
impoverished peasants, and there are rich peasants who
employ labourers and buy land "in perpetuity." These rich
peasants are also members of the community, and it is they
who boss the community because they are a power. But do
we need a union to which the rich belong, and which is
bossed by the rich? Of course not. We need a union to fight
the rich. And so, the unity of the *mir* is no good to us at
all.

What we need is a voluntary union, a union only of people who have realized that they must unite with the urban workers. The village community is not a voluntary
union; it is enforced by the state. The village community

does not consist of people who work for the rich and who want to unite to fight the rich. The village community consists of all sorts of people, not because they want to be in it, but because their parents lived on the same land and worked for the same landlord, because the authorities registered them as members of that community. The poor peasants are not free to leave the community; they are not free to receive into the community a man whom the police have registered in another volost, but whom we, our union, may need for this particular village. No, we need a very different kind of union, a voluntary union consisting only of labourers and poor peasants to fight all those who live on the labour of others.

The times when the *mir* was a force have long passed, never to return. The *mir* was a force when hardly any of the peasants were landless labourers, or workers wandering over the length and breadth of Russia in search of a job, when there were hardly any rich peasants, when all were equally crushed by the feudal landlords. But now money has become the principal power. Even members of the same community will now fight one another for money like wild beasts. The moneyed peasants sometimes oppress and fleece their fellow-peasants worse than the landlords. What we need today is not the unity of the *mir*, but a union against the *power of money*, against the rule of capital, a union of all the rural labourers and of all the poor peasants of different communities, a union of all the rural poor with the urban workers to fight both the landlords and the rich peasants.

We have seen how strong the landlords are. We must now see whether there are many rich peasants and how strong they are.

We measured the strength of the landlords by the size of their estates, by the amount of land they own. The landlords are able freely to dispose of their land, they are free to buy land and to sell it. That is why it is possible to judge their strength very accurately by the amount of land they own. The peasants, however, still lack the right freely to dispose of their land, they are still semi-serfs, tied to their village community. Hence, the strength of the rich peasants cannot be judged by the amount of allotment land they hold. The rich peasants do not grow rich on their allotments; they *buy* a considerable amount of land, they buy "in perpetuity" (i.e., as their private property) and "for a number of years" (i.e., on lease); they buy from the landlords and from their fellow-peasants, from those peasants who abandon the land, who are compelled by want to let their holdings. It will therefore be more correct to divide the rich, the middle, and the poor peasants according to the number of horses they own. A peasant who owns many horses will nearly always be a rich peasant; if he keeps many draught animals it shows that he cultivates much land, owns land besides his communal allotment, and has money saved up. Moreover, we can find out the number of peasants owning many horses in the whole of Russia (European Russia, not including Siberia or the Caucasus). Of course, it must not be forgotten that we can speak of the whole of Russia only in averages: the different uyezds and gubernias vary to a considerable degree. For instance, in the neighbourhood of cities we often find rich peasant farmers who keep very few horses. Some of them engage in market gardening—a very profitable business; others keep few horses but many cows and sell milk. In all parts of Russia there are also peasants who do not make money out of the land, but engage in trade, run creameries, hulling-mills, and other enterprises. Whoever lives in the country very well knows rich peasants in his own village or district. But we want to know how many there are in the whole of Russia and how strong they are, so that the poor peasant shall not have to guess and go about blindfolded, as it were, but know exactly his friends and his foes.

Well then, let us see whether there are many peasants who are rich or poor in the possession of horses. We have already said that the total number of peasant households in Russia is estimated at about *ten million*. Between them they now own, probably, about *fifteen million* horses (about fourteen years ago the number was seventeen million, but it is smaller now). Thus, on the average, every *ten* households have *fifteen* horses. But the whole point is that some

of them—a few—own many horses, while others—very
many—own no horses, or very few. There are *at least three
million* horseless peasants, and about three and a half million own *only one horse each.* All these are either utterly
ruined or very poor peasants. We call these the rural poor.
They number *six and a half* million out of a total of ten
million, that is to say, *almost two-thirds!* Next come the
middle peasants who own a pair of horses each. These
peasants number *about two* million households, with
*about four* million horses between them. Then come the
rich peasants, each of whom owns more than one pair of
horses. Such comprise *one and a half million* households,
but between them they own *seven and a half* million
horses.* Thus, about one-sixth of the total households own
half the total number of horses.

Now that we know this we are in a position to judge
fairly accurately the strength of the rich peasants. In number they are very few: in the different communities and volosts they will muster from ten to twenty households in
every hundred. But these few households are the richest.
Taking Russia as a whole, they own almost as many horses
as all the other peasants put together. That means that
their crop area must also amount to nearly half the total
peasant crop area. Such peasants harvest much more grain
than they require for the needs of their families. They sell
large quantities of grain. They grow grain not merely to
feed themselves, they grow it chiefly to sell, to make

* We must repeat that the figures quoted are average, approx-
imate figures. The number of rich peasants may not be exactly a
million and a half, but a million and a quarter, or a million and
three-quarters, or even two million. That is not a big difference. The
important thing here is not to count them up to the last thousand
or last hundred, but clearly to realize the strength and the
position of the rich peasants so that we may be able to recognize
our enemies and our friends, that we shall not allow ourselves to
be deceived by fairy-tales and empty talk, but to find out the exact
position of the poor and the position of the rich.

Let every rural worker carefully study his own volost and the
neighbouring volosts. He will see that we have counted correctly,
and that, on the average, this will be the position everywhere: out
of every hundred households there will be ten, at most twenty, rich
families, some twenty middle peasants, and all the rest—poor.

money. Peasants like these can save money. They deposit it
in savings banks and banks. They buy land outright. We
have already said how much land the peasants all over
Russia buy every year; nearly all this land goes to these
few rich peasants. The rural poor cannot think of buying
land; it is as much as they can do to provide themselves
with food. Often they have not enough money to buy grain,
let alone land. Therefore, the banks in general, and the
Peasants' Bank in particular, do not help all the peasants
to buy land (as is sometimes asserted by people who try
to deceive the peasant or by people who are very simple-
minded), but only an insignificant number of peasants,
only the rich peasants. Therefore, the bad counsellors of
the peasant we mentioned tell an untruth about the peasants buying land when they claim that the land is passing from capital to labour. The land can never pass to labour, that is, to the poor working-man, because land has
to be paid for with money. But the poor never have any
spare money. The land can only pass to the rich, moneyed
peasants, to capital, to those people against whom the rural poor must *fight* in alliance with the urban workers.

The rich peasants not only buy land in perpetuity; most
often they take land for a number of years, on lease. They
prevent the poor from getting land by renting large plots.
For example, in one uyezd in the Poltava Gubernia (Kon-
stantinograd) the amount of land rented by the rich peasants has been calculated. And what do we find? The number who rented thirty dessiatins or more per household is
very small, only two out of every fifteen households. But
those rich peasants laid hold of *one-half* of all the rented
land, and each of them has on the average *seventy-five
dessiatins* of the rented land! Or take the Taurida Gubernia, where a calculation was made of how much of the land
rented by the peasants from the state through the *mir*,
through the village community, was grabbed by the rich.
It was found out that the rich, who account for only *one-
fifth* of the total number of households, grabbed *three-
fourths* of the rented land. Everywhere land goes to those
who have money, and only the few rich have money.

Further, much land is now let by the peasants themselves. The peasants abandon their holdings, because they have no livestock, no seeds, nothing with which to run their farms. Today even land is of no use unless you have money. For instance, in the Novouzensk Uyezd in the Samara Gubernia, one, sometimes even two, out of every three rich peasant households *rent allotment land* in their own or in another community. The allotments are let by those who have no horses, or only one horse. In the Taurida Gubernia as much as *one-third* of the peasant households let allotments. *One-fourth* of the peasant allotments, a quarter of a million dessiatins is let. Of this quarter of a million dessiatins, one hundred and fifty thousand dessiatins (three-fifths) is rented by rich peasants! This, too, shows whether the unity of the *mir*, of the community, is of any use for the poor. In the village community, he who has money has power. What we need is the unity of the poor of all communities.

As is the case with talk about buying land, the peasants are deceived by talk about buying cheap ploughs, reapers and all sorts of improved implements. Zemstvo stores and co-operatives are set up and it is said: improved implements will improve the conditions of the peasantry. This is mere deception. All these improved implements go to the rich; the poor get next to nothing. They cannot think of buying ploughs and reapers; they have enough to do to keep body and soul together! All this sort of "helping the peasants" is nothing but helping the rich. As for the mass of the poor who have neither land, nor livestock, nor reserves, they will not benefit by the fact that the improved implements will be cheaper. Here is an example. In one of the uyezds of the Samara Gubernia all the improved implements belonging to the poor and to the rich peasants were counted. It was found that *one-fifth* of all the households, i.e., the most well-to-do, owned almost *three-fourths* of the improved implements, while the poor—*half* the households—had only *one-thirtieth*. Out of a total of 28,000 households, 10,000 were horseless and one-horse households; these 10,000 had only *seven* improved implements out of total of 5,724 improved implements owned by all the peasant households in that uyezd. Seven out of 5,724—that is the share of the rural poor in all these farm improvements, in all this increase in the number of ploughs and reapers which are supposed to help "all the peasantry"! That is what the rural poor must expect from the people who talk about "improving peasant farming"!

Finally, one of the main features of the rich peasants is that they *hire farm-hands and day-labourers*. Like the landlords, the rich peasants also live on the labour of others. Like the landlords, they grow rich because the mass of the peasants are ruined and pauperized. Like the landlords, they try to squeeze as much work as they can out of their farm-hands and to pay them as little as possible. If millions of peasants were not utterly ruined and compelled to go to work for others, to become hired labourers, to sell their labour power, the rich peasants could not exist, could not carry on their farms. There would be no "abandoned" allotments for them to pick up and no labourers for them to hire. The million and a half rich peasants throughout Russia certainly hire no less than a *million* farm-hands and day-labourers. Obviously, in the great struggle between the propertied class and the propertyless, between masters and workers, between the bourgeoisie and the proletariat, the rich peasants will take the side of the property-owners against the working class.

Now we know the position and the strength of the rich peasantry. Let us examine the conditions of the rural poor.

We have already said that the rural poor comprise the vast majority, almost two-thirds of the peasant households throughout Russia. To begin with, the number of horseless households cannot be less than *three million*—probably more than that today, perhaps three and a half million. Every famine, every crop failure, ruins tens of thousands of farms. The population grows, the people become more congested, but all the best land has been grabbed by the landlords and rich peasants. And so, every year more and more people are ruined, they go to the towns and to the factories, they take work as farm-hands, or become unskilled labourers. A horseless peasant is a peasant who has become quite propertyless. He is a proletarian. He gains his living (if you can call it living; it would be truer to say that he just contrives to keep body and soul together) not from the land, not from his farm, but *by working for wages.* He is the brother of the town worker. Even land is of no use to the horseless peasant: half the horseless peasants *let their allotments,* some even surrender them to the community for nothing (and sometimes even pay the difference between the taxes and the expected income from the land!) because they are not in a position to till their land. A horseless peasant sows one dessiatin, or two at the very most. He always has to buy additional grain (if he has the money to buy it with)—his own crop is never sufficient. The one-horse peasants, of whom there are about three and a half million households throughout Russia, are not very much better off. Of course, there are exceptions, and we have already said that, here and there, there are one-horse peasants who are doing middling well, or are even rich. But we are not speaking of exceptions, of individual localities, but of Russia as a whole. If we take the entire mass of one-horse peasants, there can be no doubt that they are a mass of paupers. Even in the agricultural gubernias the one-horse peasant sows only three or four dessiatins, rarely five; his crop, too, does not suffice. Even in a good year his food is no better than that of the horseless peasant—which means that he is always underfed, always starves. His farm is in decay, his livestock is poor and short of fodder, he is not in a position to till his land properly. On the whole of his farm the one-horse peasant—in the Voronezh Gubernia, for instance—can afford to spend (not counting expenditure on fodder) not more than *twenty rubles a year!* (A rich peasant spends *ten times as much.*) Twenty rubles a year for rent, for buying livestock, for repairing his wooden plough and other implements, for paying the shepherd, and for everything else! Do you call that farming? It is sheer misery, hard labour, eternal drudgery. It is natural that some of the one-horse peasants, and not a few, should also *let their allotments.* Even land is of little use to a pauper. He has no money and his land does not even provide him with enough to eat, let alone with money. But money is needed for everything: for food, for clothing, for the farm, and to pay taxes. In the Voronezh Gubernia, a one-horse peasant usually has to pay *about eighteen rubles* a year in taxes alone, and to meet *all* his expenses he cannot make more than seventy-five rubles a year. Under these circumstances it is sheer mockery to talk about buying land, about improved implements, about agricultural banks: those things were not invented for the poor.

Where is the peasant to get the money from? He has to look for "earnings" on the side. A one-horse peasant, like a horseless one, ekes out a living only with the help of "earnings." But what does "earnings" mean? It means working for others, working for hire. It means that the one-horse peasant has half ceased to be an independent farmer and has become a hireling, a proletarian. That is why such peasants are called *semi-proletarians*. They, too, are the brothers of the town workers because they, too, are fleeced in every way by all sorts of employers. They, too, have no way out, no salvation, except by uniting with the Social-Democrats to fight all the rich, all the property-owners. Who works on the building of railways? Who is fleeced by the contractors? Who goes out lumbering and timber-floating? Who works as a farm-hand? Or as a day-labourer? Who does the unskilled work in the towns and ports? It is always the rural poor, the horseless and one-horse peasants. It is always the rural proletarians and semi-proletarians. And what vast numbers of these there are in Russia! It has been calculated that throughout Russia (not including the Caucasus and Siberia) eight and sometimes even nine *million* passports are taken out yearly. Those are all for migratory workers. They are peasants only in name; actually, they are hirelings, wage-labourers. They must all unite with the town workers—and every ray of light and knowledge that reaches the countryside will strengthen and consolidate this unity.

There is one more point about "earnings" that must not be forgotten. Officials, and all sorts of people who think like officials, are fond of saying that the peasant, the muzhik, "needs" two things: land (but not too much of it—besides, he cannot get much, because the rich have grabbed it all!) and "earnings." Therefore, they say, in order to help the people, it is necessary to introduce more trades in the rural districts, to "provide" more "earnings." Such talk is sheer hypocrisy. For the poor, "earnings" mean wage-labour. To "provide earnings" for the peasant means transforming him into a wage-labourer. Fine sort of assistance this! For the rich peasants there are other kinds of "earnings," which require capital—for instance, the building of a flour-mill or some other plant, the purchase of threshing-machines, commerce, and so on. To confuse the earnings of the moneyed people with the *wage-labour* of the poor means deceiving the poor. Of course, this deception is to the advantage of the rich; it is to their advantage to make it appear that all kinds of "earnings" are open to and within the reach of *all* the peasants. But he who really cares for the welfare of the poor will tell *the whole truth and nothing but the truth.*

It remains for us to consider the middle peasants. We have already seen that, on the average, taking Russia as a whole, we must regard as a middle peasant one who has a pair of horses, and that out of a total of ten million households there are about two million middle-peasant households in the country. The middle peasant stands between the rich peasant and the proletarian, and that is why he is called a middle peasant. His standard of living, too, is middling: in a good year he makes ends meet on his farm, but poverty is always knocking at the door. He has either very little savings or none at all. That is why his farm is in a rather precarious position. He finds it hard to get money: only very seldom can he make as much money out of his farm as he needs, and if he does, it is just barely enough. To go out for earnings would mean neglecting the farm and everything would go to rack and ruin. Nevertheless, many of the middle peasants cannot possibly dispense with earnings: they, too, have to hire themselves, want compels them to go into bondage to the landlord, to fall into debt. And once in debt the middle peasant is hardly ever able to get out of it, for unlike the rich peasant he has no steady income. Therefore, once he falls into debt it is as if he had put his neck in a halter. He remains a debtor until he is utterly ruined. It is chiefly the middle peasant who falls into bondage to the landlord because for piece-

work the landlord must have a peasant who is not quite
ruined, a peasant who has a pair of horses and all that is
needed for farming. It is not so easy for the middle peasant
to go away to look for earnings, so he goes into bondage
to the landlord in return for grain, in return for permission
to use pastureland, for the lease of the cut-off lands, for
advances of money in winter. Besides the landlord and the
kulak, the middle peasant is hard pressed by his rich neighbour, who always snatches land from under his nose and
never misses an opportunity to squeeze him in some way
or other. Such is the life of the middle peasant; he is neither fish nor fowl. He can be neither a real master nor a
worker. All the middle peasants strive towards the masters;
they want to be property-owners,  but very few succeed.
There are a few, a very few who hire farm-hands or day-labourers, try to become rich on the labour of others, to rise
to wealth on the backs of others. But the majority of the
middle peasants have no money with which to hire labourers
—in fact, they have to hire themselves out.

Wherever a struggle begins between the rich and the
poor, between the property-owners and the workers, the
middle peasant remains in between, not knowing which
side to take. The rich call him to their side: you, too, are
a master, a man of property, they say to him, you have
nothing to do with the penniless workers. But the workers
say: the rich will cheat and fleece you, and there is no
salvation for you except by helping us in our fight against
all the rich. This fight for the middle peasant is going on
everywhere, in all countries, wherever the Social-Democratic workers are fighting to emancipate the working people. In Russia the fight is just beginning. That is why we
must carefully study the matter and understand clearly the
deceits the rich resort to in order to win over the middle
peasant, we must learn how to expose those deceits, and
help the middle peasant to find his real friends. If the Russian Social-Democratic workers at once take the right road,
we shall establish a firm alliance between the rural working people and the urban workers more quickly than our
comrades the German workers, and we shall speedily
achieve victory over all the enemies of the toilers.

## 4. WHERE SHOULD THE MIDDLE PEASANT GO?
### SHOULD HE TAKE THE SIDE OF THE PROPERTY-OWNERS AND OF THE RICH, OR THE SIDE OF THE WORKERS AND OF THE POOR?

All the property-owners, the entire bourgeoisie, try to draw the middle peasant to their side by promising him all sorts of measures for improving his farm (cheap ploughs, agricultural banks, the introduction of grass sowing, cheap livestock and fertilizers, and so on) and also by inducing the peasant to join all sorts of agricultural societies (co-operatives, as they are called in books) which unite all kinds of farmers with the object of improving the methods of farming. In this way the bourgeoisie tries to keep the middle and even the small peasant, even the semi-proletarian, from uniting with the workers, and tries to induce them to side with the rich, with the bourgeoisie, in its fight against the workers, against the proletariat.

To this the Social-Democratic workers reply: improved farming is an excellent thing. There is nothing wrong in buying cheaper ploughs; nowadays even a merchant, if he is not a fool, tries to sell cheap to attract customers. But when a poor or a middle peasant is told that improved farming and cheaper ploughs will help all of them to rid themselves of poverty and to get on to their feet, and that this can be done without touching the rich, *it is deception*. All these improvements, lower prices and co-operatives (societies for the sale and purchase of goods) *benefit the rich far more than anybody*. The rich grow stronger and oppress the poor and middle peasants more and more. As long as the rich remain rich, as long as they own most of the land, livestock, implements, and money—as long as all this lasts, the poor, or even the middle peasants, will *never* be able to escape from want. One or two middle peasants may be able to grow rich with the aid of all these improvements and co-operatives, but the people as a whole, and all the middle peasants, will sink deeper and deeper into poverty. In order that *all* the middle peasants may become rich, the rich must be turned out, and they can be

turned out only if the urban workers and the rural poor
are united.

The bourgeoisie says to the middle (and even to the small)
peasant: we will sell you land at a low price, and ploughs
at a low price, but in return you sell us your soul, give up
fighting the rich.

The Social-Democratic worker says: if you are really offered goods at a low price, why not buy them, if you have
the money; that is sound business. But never sell your soul.
To give up the fight in alliance with the urban workers
against the entire bourgeoisie would mean remaining in
poverty and want for ever. If goods become cheaper, the
rich will gain still more and become richer. But those who
have no money will gain nothing from the cheapening of
goods until they take that money from the bourgeoisie.

Let us take an example. Those who support the bourgeoisie make much ado about all sorts of co-operatives (societies for buying cheap and selling profitably). There are
even people who call themselves "Socialist-Revolutionaries," who, echoing the bourgeoisie, also talk loudly about
the peasant needing nothing so much as co-operatives. All
sorts of co-operatives are beginning to spring up in Russia,
too, although there are still very few of them here, and there
will not be many until we have political freedom. But take
Germany: there the peasants have many co-operatives of all
kinds. But see who gains most from these co-operatives. In
the whole of Germany, 140,000 farmers belong to societies
for the sale of milk and dairy produce, and these  140,000
farmers (we take round figures for the sake of simplicity)
own 1,100,000 cows. It is calculated that there are *four million* poor peasants in Germany. Of these, only 40,000 belong
to co-operatives: thus, *only one* out of every hundred  poor
peasants enjoys the benefits of these  co-operatives.  These
40,000 poor peasants own only 100,000 cows. Further,  the
middle farmers, the middle peasants, number *one million*; of
these, 50,000 belong to co-operatives (that is to say, five out
of every hundred) and they own 200,000 cows. Finally, the
rich farmers (i. e., both landlords and rich peasants) number *one-third of a million*; of these, 50,000 belong to co-oper-

atives (that is to say, *seventeen* out of every hundred!) and they own 800,000 cows!

That is whom the co-operatives help first and foremost. That is how the peasant is led by the nose by those people who talk loudly about saving the middle peasant by means of such societies for buying cheap and selling profitably. It is, indeed, at a very low price that the bourgeoisie wants to "buy off" the middle peasant from the Social-Democrats who call upon both the poor and the middle peasant to join them.

In our country, too, co-operative creameries and joint dairies are beginning to be formed. In our country, too, there are plenty of people who shout: artels, the unity of the *mir* and co-operatives—that is what the peasant needs. But see who gains by these artels, co-operatives, and communal renting. Out of every hundred households in our country, at least twenty have no cows at all; thirty have only one cow each: these sell milk from dire need, their own children have to go without milk, starve, and die like flies. The rich peasants, however, have three, four and more cows each, and these rich peasants own half the total number of cows owned by peasants. Who, then, gains from co-operative creameries? Obviously, the landlords and the peasant bourgeoisie gain first of all. Obviously, it is *to their advantage* that the middle peasants and the poor should strive after them and that they should believe that the means of escaping from want is not the struggle of all the workers against the entire bourgeoisie, but the striving of individual small farmers to climb out of their present position into the ranks of the rich.

This striving is fostered and encouraged in every way by all the champions of the bourgeoisie who pretend to be the champions and friends of the small peasant. And many simple-minded people fail to see the wolf in sheep's clothing, and repeat this bourgeois deception in the belief that they are helping the poor and middle peasants. For instance, they argue in books and in speeches that small-scale farming is the most profitable, most remunerative form of farming, that small-scale farming is flourishing, and that is why, they say, there are so many small producers in agriculture everywhere, and why they cling so tightly to their

4—1928

land (and not because all the best lands are owned by the bourgeoisie, and all the money, too, while the poor have to live all their lives penned up on tiny patches of land!). The small peasant does not need much money, say these smooth-tongued people; the small and the middle peasants are more thrifty and more industrious than the big farmers, and know how to live a simple life; instead of buying hay for their cattle, they are content to feed them on straw. Instead of buying an expensive machine, they get up earlier and toil longer and do as much as a machine does; instead of paying money to strangers for doing repairs, the peasant himself takes his hatchet on a Sunday and works a bit as a carpenter—and that is much cheaper than the way a big farmer goes about it; instead of feeding an expensive horse or an ox, he uses his cow for ploughing. In Germany all the poor peasants plough with cows, and in our country, too, the people have become so impoverished that they are beginning to plough not only with cows, but with men and women! How profitable, how cheap all this is! How praiseworthy of the middle and small peasants to be so industrious, so diligent, to live such simple lives, not to waste their time on nonsense, not to think of socialism, but only of their farms, not to strive towards the workers who organize strikes against the bourgeoisie, but towards the rich and respectable! If only all were so industrious and so diligent, and lived frugally, and did not drink, and saved more money, and spent less on calico, and had fewer children—all would be happy and there would be no poverty and no want!

Such are the sweet songs the bourgeoisie sings to the middle peasant, and there are simpletons who believe these songs and repeat them!* Actually all these honeyed words

---

* In Russia these simpletons who wish the peasant well, but who every now and then start this sort of honeyed talk, are called "Narodniks" or the "advocates of small-scale farming." The "Socialist-Revolutionaries," for lack of understanding, follow in their footsteps. In Germany also there are many smooth-tongued people. One of them, Eduard David, has just written a big book, in which he says that small farms are infinitely more profitable than large ones, because the small peasant does not spend money needlessly, keeps no horses for ploughing, and is content to use his milch cow for ploughing.

are nothing but deceit and mockery of the peasant. What these smooth-tongued people call cheap and profitable farming is the want, the dire need, which forces the middle and small peasant to work from morning till night, to begrudge himself a bit of bread, to grudge every penny he spends. Of course, what can be "cheaper" and "more profitable" than to wear the same pants for three years, to go about barefooted in the summer, to repair one's wooden plough with a bit of string and to feed one's cow on rotten straw from the roof! Put a bourgeois or a rich peasant on such a "cheap" and "profitable" farm, and he will soon forget all this honeyed talk!

The people who extol small farming sometimes want to help the peasant, but actually they only do him harm. With their honeyed words they deceive the peasant in the same way as people are deceived by a *lottery*. I shall tell you what a lottery is. Let us suppose I have a cow, worth 50 rubles. I want to sell the cow by means of a lottery, so I offer everyone tickets at a ruble each. Everyone has a chance of getting the cow for one ruble! People are tempted, rubles pour in. When I have collected a hundred rubles I proceed to draw the lottery: the one whose ticket is drawn gets the cow for a ruble, the others get nothing. Was the cow "cheap" for the people? No, it was very dear, because the total money they paid was double the value of the cow, because two persons (the one who ran the lottery and the one who won the cow) gained without doing any work, and gained at the expense of the ninety-nine who lost their money. Thus, those who say that lotteries are advantageous for the people are simply deceiving the people. Those who promise to deliver the peasants from poverty and misery by means of co-operatives (societies for buying cheap and selling profitably), improved farming, banks, and all that sort of thing, are deceiving them in exactly the same way. Just as in a lottery where there is one winner and all the rest are losers, so it is with these things: one middle peasant may be clever enough to get rich, but ninety-nine of his fellow-peasants bend their backs all their lives, never rid themselves of want, and even sink more deeply into poverty. Let every villager examine his community and the whole district a little more

closely: are there many middle peasants who become rich
and forget want? And how many are there who can never
rid themselves of want? How many are ruined and leave
their village? As we have seen, it is calculated that in the
whole of Russia there are not more than two million middle
peasant households. Suppose there were ten times as many
societies of all kinds for buying cheap and selling profitably as there are now. What would the result be? It would
be a lot if a hundred thousand middle peasants succeeded
in raising themselves to the level of the rich. What would
that mean? It would mean that out of every hundred middle
peasants, five would have become rich. But what about the
other ninety-five? They would be in the same straits as ever,
and many of them would be in even greater difficulties! And
the poor would only be ruined all the more!

Of course, the bourgeoisie wants nothing more than that
the largest possible number of poor and middle  peasants
should strive after the rich, should *believe* in the possibility
of abolishing poverty without fighting the bourgeoisie,
should place their *hopes* in diligence and frugality  and in
becoming rich, and not in uniting with the rural and urban
workers. The bourgeoisie does all it can to foster this decep-
tive faith and hope in the peasant and tries to lull him with
honeyed words.

To expose the deception practised by these smooth-
tongued people it is sufficient to ask them three questions.

First question: can the working people rid themselves of
want and poverty when, in Russia, a hundred million dessiatins out of two hundred and forty million dessiatins of
cultivable land are owned by private  landowners?  When
sixteen thousand very big landowners own sixty-five million
dessiatins?

Second question: can the working people rid themselves
of want and poverty when one and a half million rich peasant households (out of a total of ten million) have concentrated in their hands half of the total peasant  crop   area,
half of the total number of horses and livestock owned by
peasants, and much more than half of the  total  peasant
stocks and savings? When the peasant bourgeoisie is grow-

TO THE RURAL POOR

ing richer and richer, oppressing the poor and middle peasants, making money out of the labour of others, of the farm-
hands and day-labourers? When six and a half million peasant households are ruined, poor, always starving, and reduced to winning a miserable crust of bread by all kinds of
wage-labour?

Third question: can the working people rid themselves of
want and poverty when money has become the principal
power, when everything can be bought for money—factories
and land, and even men and women can be bought to serve
as wage-labourers, as wage-slaves? When no one can live
or run a farm without money? When a small farmer, a poor
peasant, has to wage a struggle against the big farmer to
get money? When a few thousand landlords, merchants, factory-owners and bankers have concentrated in their hands
hundreds of millions of rubles, and, moreover, control all
the banks, where thousands of millions of rubles are deposited?

No honeyed words about the advantages of small-scale
farming or of co-operatives will allow you to evade these
questions. To these questions there can be only one answer:
the real "co-operation" that can save the working people is
the *union* of the rural poor with the Social-Democratic workers in the towns to fight the entire bourgeoisie. The faster
*this* union grows and becomes strong, the sooner will the
middle peasant realize that the promises of the bourgeoisie
are all lies, and the sooner will the middle peasant come
over to our side.

The bourgeoisie knows this, and that is why, in addition
to honeyed words, they spread all sorts of lies about the Social-Democrats. They say that the Social-Democrats want to
deprive the middle and poor peasants of their property. *That
is a lie.* The Social-Democrats want to deprive of their property only big proprietors, *only those who live on the labour
of others.* The Social-Democrats *will never take away the
property of the small and middle farmers who do not hire labourers.* The Social-Democrats defend and champion the interests of all the working people, not only the interests of the
urban workers, who are more class-conscious and more united than the others, but also of the agricultural workers, and

of those small artisans and peasants who do not hire workers, do not strive towards the rich, and do not go over to the
side of the bourgeoisie. *The Social-Democrats are fighting
for all improvements in the conditions of the workers and
peasants* which can be introduced immediately, even before we have destroyed the rule of the bourgeoisie, and which
will help them in the fight against the bourgeoisie. But the
Social-Democrats do not deceive the peasant, they tell him
*the whole truth*, they plainly tell him in advance that no improvements will rid the people of want and poverty as long
as the bourgeoisie is in power. To enable *all the people* to
know what the Social-Democrats are and what they want,
the Social-Democrats have drawn up a *programme*. A programme is a brief, plain and precise statement of *all the
things a party is striving and fighting for*. The Social-Democratic Party is the only party that advances a plain and
precise programme in order that all the people may know and
see it, and in order that the party may consist only of people
who really want to fight for the emancipation of all the working people from the yoke of the bourgeoisie, and who understand who must unite for this fight and how the fight must
be conducted. Furthermore, the Social-Democrats believe
that they must *explain* in their programme, in a plain, open,
and precise way, *the causes of the poverty and distress of the
working people*, and why the unity of the workers is becoming wider and stronger. It is not enough to say that life is
hard and to call for revolt; every tub-thumper can do that,
but that is of little use. The working people must crearly
understand *why* they are living in such distress and *with
whom they must unite* in order to fight to liberate themselves from want.

We have already stated what the Social-Democrats want;
we have explained the causes of the want and poverty of
the working people; we have indicated whom the rural
poor must fight and with whom they must unite for this
fight.

We shall now explain *what improvements* we can win *at
once* by fighting for them, improvements in the lives of the
workers and in the lives of the peasants.

## 5. WHAT IMPROVEMENTS ARE THE SOCIAL-DEMOCRATS STRIVING TO OBTAIN FOR THE WHOLE PEOPLE AND FOR THE WORKERS?

The Social-Democrats are fighting for the liberation of all the working people from all robbery, oppression, and injustice. To become free the working class must first of all become united. And to become united it must have freedom to unite, it must have the right to unite, it must have *political freedom*. We have already said that autocratic government means the feudal subordination of the people to the officials and the police. Political freedom is therefore needed by the whole people, except a handful of courtiers and a few money-bags and high dignitaries who are received at court. But most of all, political freedom is needed by the workers and the peasants. The rich can buy for themselves freedom from the tyranny and caprices of the officials and of the police. The rich can make their complaints heard in the highest places. That is why the police and the officials take less liberties with the rich than with the poor. The workers and the peasants have no money with which to bribe the police or the officials, they have no one to complain to, they are not in a position to sue them in court. The workers and the peasants will never rid themselves of the extortions, the tyranny, or the insults of the police and the officials as long as there is no *elective government*, as long as there is no *national assembly of deputies*. Only such a national assembly of deputies can free the people from feudal dependence upon the officials. Every intelligent peasant must stand for the Social-Democrats, who first and foremost demand of the tsarist government *the convocation of a national assembly of deputies*. The deputies must be elected by all, irrespective of social estate, irrespective of wealth or poverty. The elections must be free, without any interference on the part of the officials; they must be carried out under the supervision of the people's delegates and not of police officers or of Zemstvo chiefs.[10] Under such conditions, the deputies representing the entire people will be able to discuss all the needs of the people, and introduce a better state of affairs in Russia.

The Social-Democrats demand that the police should not have the power to imprison anyone without trial. Officials must be severely punished for making arbitrary arrests. To stop them from taking the law into their own hands, the officials must be chosen by the people, and everyone must have the right to lodge a complaint against any official directly in a court. What is the use of complaining about the police to the Zemstvo chief, or about the Zemstvo chief to the governor? The Zemstvo chief will, of course, always protect the police, and the governor will always protect the Zemstvo chief, and the plaintiff runs a fair chance of being punished himself, of being put into prison or deported to Siberia. The officials will be curbed only when everyone in Russia (as in all other countries) has the right to complain to the national assembly, to the elected courts, and to speak freely of his needs, to write about them in the newspapers.

The Russian people are still in feudal dependence upon the officials. Without the permission of the officials the people cannot call meetings, they cannot print books or newspapers! Is that not feudal dependence? If meetings cannot be freely called, or pamphlets freely printed, how can one obtain redress against the officials, or against the rich? Of course, the officials suppress every pamphlet and every utterance that tell the truth about the people's poverty. The present pamphlet, too, has to be printed by the Social-Democratic Party secretly and circulated secretly: anyone who is found in possession of this pamphlet will see no end of courts and prisons. But the Social-Democratic workers are not afraid of this: they print more and more, and give the people more and more truthful pamphlets to read. And no prisons, no persecution can stop the fight for the people's freedom!

The Social-Democrats demand that social estates be abolished, and that all the citizens of the state have exactly the same rights. Today we have poll-tax-paying and non-poll-tax-paying estates, privileged and non-privileged estates, blue blood and common blood; even the birch has

been retained for the common people. In no other country are the workers and peasants in such a position of
inferiority. In no country except Russia are there different
laws for different social estates. It is time the Russian
people, too, demanded that every peasant should possess
*all the rights* that are possessed by the nobility. Is it not
a disgrace that the birch should still be used and that
a *poll-tax-paying* estate be in existence more than forty
years after the abolition of serfdom?

The Social-Democrats demand that the people shall
have complete freedom of movement and the right to
engage in any occupation. What does *freedom of movement* mean? It means that the peasant should be free to
go wherever he pleases, to move to whatever place he
wants to, to live in any village or town he chooses without having to ask for permission from anyone. It means
that passports must be abolished in Russia too (in other
countries passports were abolished long ago), that no police officer, no Zemstvo chief shall be allowed to stop any
peasant from settling or working in any place he pleases.
The Russian peasant is still so much the serf of the officials that he is not free to move to a town, or to settle in
a new district. The Minister issues orders that the governors should not allow *unauthorized* settlement! A governor
knows better than the peasant what place is good for the
peasant! The peasant is a little child and must not dare
move without permission of the authorities! Is that not
feudal dependence? Is it not an insult to the people when
every profligate nobleman is allowed to lord it over grown-
up farmers?

There is a book called *Crop Failure and the Distress of
the People* (famine) written by the present "Minister
of Agriculture," Mr. Yermolov. This book says in so many
words: the peasant must not change residence as long
as their worships the local landlords need hands. The
Minister says this quite openly, without the least hesitation: he thinks the peasant will not hear what he is saying,
will not understand. Why allow the people to go away
when the landlords need cheap labour? The more crowded the people are on the land the better for the landlords;

the poorer the peasants are the more cheaply can they be hired and the more meekly will they submit to oppression of every kind. Formerly, the bailiffs looked after the landlord's interests, now the Zemstvo chiefs and governors do that. Formerly, the bailiffs ordered the flogging of peasants in the stables, now the Zemstvo chief in the volost office orders the flogging.

The Social-Democrats demand that the standing army be abolished and that a militia be established in its stead, that all the people be armed. A standing army is an army that is divorced from the people and trained to shoot the people. If the soldier were not locked up for years in barracks and inhumanly drilled there, would he ever agree to shoot his brothers, the workers, and the peasants? Would he go against the starving peasants? A standing army is not needed in the least to protect the country from attack by an enemy; a people's militia is sufficient. If every citizen is armed, Russia need fear no enemy. And the people would be relieved of the burden of militarism: militarism costs *hundreds of millions of rubles a year*, and all this money is collected from the people; that is why the taxes are so heavy and why it becomes increasingly difficult to live. Militarism still further increases the power of the officials and of the police over the people. Militarism is needed to plunder foreign peoples, for instance, to take the land from the Chinese. This does not ease but, on the contrary, increases the people's burden because of the increased taxes. The substitution of the armed nation for the standing army would enormously ease the burden of all the workers and all the peasants.

Similarly, *the abolition of indirect taxation*, which the Social-Democrats demand, would be an enormous relief for them. Indirect taxes are those taxes which are not imposed on land or on a house, but are paid by the people *indirectly*, in the form of higher prices for what they buy. The Treasury imposes taxes on sugar, vodka, kerosene, matches, and all sorts of articles of consumption; the taxes are paid to the Treasury by the merchant or by the manufacturer, but, of course, he does not pay it out of his own pocket, but out of the money his customers pay

him. The price of vodka, sugar, kerosene, and matches is
raised and every purchaser of a bottle of vodka or of a
pound of sugar has to pay the tax in addition to the
price of the goods. For instance, if, say, you pay fourteen
kopeks for a pound of sugar, four kopeks (approximately)
constitute the tax: the sugar-manufacturer has already
paid the tax to the Treasury and is now exacting the sum
he has paid from every customer. Thus, indirect taxes
are taxes on articles of consumption, taxes which are
paid by the consumer in the form of higher prices for
the articles he buys. It is sometimes said that indirect taxation is the fairest form of taxation: you pay according
to the amount you buy. But this is not true. Indirect taxation is the most unfair form of taxation, because it
is harder for the poor to pay indirect taxes than it is for
the rich. The rich man's income is ten times or, perhaps,
a hundred times as large as that of the peasant or the
worker. But does the rich man need a hundred times as
much sugar? Or ten times as much vodka, or matches,
or kerosene? Of course not! A rich family will buy twice,
at most three times as much kerosene, vodka, or sugar
as a poor family. But that means that the rich man will
pay a *smaller part* of his income in taxes than the poor
man. Let us suppose that the poor peasant's income is
two hundred rubles a year; let us suppose he buys sixty
rubles' worth of such goods as are taxed and which are
consequently dearer (the tax on sugar, matches, kerosene,
is an *excise duty*, i.e., the manufacturer pays the duty before placing the goods on the market; in the case of vodka, a state monopoly, the Treasury has simply raised the
price; cotton goods, iron and other goods have risen in
price because cheap foreign goods are not admitted into
Russia unless a heavy duty is paid on them). Of these
sixty rubles *twenty rubles* constitute the tax. Thus, out of
every ruble of his income the poor peasant has to pay
*ten kopeks* in indirect taxes, (not counting direct taxes,
land compensation payments, quitrent, land tax, Zemstvo,
volost and village rates). The rich peasant has an income of one thousand rubles; he will buy one hundred
and fifty rubles' worth of taxed goods and pay *fifty rubles*

in taxes (included in these one hundred and fifty rubles).
Thus, out of every ruble of his income the rich peasant
pays only *five kopeks* in indirect taxes. The richer the man
the *smaller* is the share of his income that he pays in indirect taxes. That is why indirect taxation is *the most unfair* form of taxation. Indirect taxes are taxes on the poor.
The peasants and the workers together form nine-tenths
of the population and pay nine- or eight-tenths of the
indirect taxes. And, in all probability, the income of the
peasants and workers amounts to no more than four-tenths
of the whole national income! And so, the Social-Democrats demand the abolition of indirect taxation and the
introduction of a *graduated* tax on incomes and inherit-
ances. That means, the higher the income the higher the
tax. Those who have an income of a thousand rubles must
pay one kopek in the ruble; if the income is two thousand,
two kopeks in the ruble must be paid, and so on. The
smallest incomes (let us say incomes of under four hundred rubles) do not pay anything at all. The richest pay
the highest taxes. Such a tax, an *income* tax, or more
exactly, a *graduated income* tax, would be much fairer
than indirect taxes. And that is why the Social-Democrats
are striving to secure the abolition of indirect taxation
and the introduction of a graduated income tax. Of
course, all the property-owners, all the bourgeoisie, object
to this measure and resist it. Only by a firm alliance between the rural poor and the urban workers can this
improvement be *won* from the bourgeoisie.

Finally, a very important improvement for the whole
of the people, and for the rural poor in particular, would
be the *free education* of children, which the Social-Democrats demand. Today there are far fewer schools in the
countryside than in the towns, and, moreover, everywhere it is only the rich classes, only the bourgeoisie,
who are in a position to give their children a good education. Only the free and compulsory education of *all
children* can free the people at least to some extent from
their present state of ignorance. The rural poor suffer most
from this ignorance and stand in particular need of edu-

cation. But, of course, we need real, free education, and not the sort the officials and the priests prefer.

The Social-Democrats further demand that everybody shall have unrestricted right to profess any religion he pleases. Of the European countries Russia and Turkey are the only ones which have retained shameful laws against persons belonging to any other religion than the Orthodox religion, laws against Dissenters, Non-conformists, and Jews. These laws either totally ban a certain religion, or prohibit the spreading of it, or deprive those who belong to it of certain rights. All these laws are as unjust, as arbitrary, and as disgraceful as can be. Everybody must be perfectly free not only to profess whatever religion he pleases, *but also to spread it, or to change his religion.* No official should have the right even to ask anyone about his religion: that is a matter for each person's conscience and no one has any right to interfere. There must be no *"dominant"* religion or church. All religions, all churches must be equal before the law. The clergy of the various religions must be maintained by those who belong to their religions, but the state must not use state money to support any religion whatever, must not grant money to maintain any clergy, Orthodox, Dissenting, Non-conformist, or any other. That is what the Social-Democrats are fighting for, and until these measures are carried out without any reservation and without any subterfuge, the people will not be freed from the disgraceful police persecution of religion, or from the no less disgraceful police doles to any one of those religions.

* * *

We have seen what improvements the Social-Democrats demand for all the people, and especially for the poor peasants. Now let us see what improvements they demand for the workers, not only for the factory and urban workers, but also for the agricultural labourers. The factory workers live in more crowded, congested conditions; they work in large workshops; it is easier for them to avail themselves of the assistance of educated Social-Democrats. For all these reasons the urban workers started the

struggle against the employers much earlier than the
others and have obtained more considerable improvements; they have also obtained the passing of factory
laws. But the Social-Democrats are fighting for the extension of these improvements to *all* the workers: to the
handicraftsmen both in town and country who work for
employers at home, to the wage-workers employed by
small proprietors and artisans, to the workers in the building trades (carpenters, bricklayers, etc.), to the lumber-
jacks, and the unskilled labourers, *and in equal measure
to the agricultural labourers*. All over Russia, all these
workers are now beginning to unite, following the example and with the aid of the factory workers, to unite for
the struggle for better conditions of life, for a shorter
working-day, *for higher wages*. And the Social-Democratic Party has set itself the task of supporting *all* workers
in their struggle for a better life, of helping them to organize (to unite) the most resolute and the most reliable
workers in strong unions, of helping them by circulating
pamphlets and leaflets, by sending experienced workers
to those new to the movement and helping them in every
possible way. When we have obtained political freedom,
we shall have our people in the national assembly of deputies, worker deputies, Social-Democrats, and like their
comrades in other countries, they will demand laws for
the benefit of the workers.

We shall not enumerate here *all* the improvements the
Social-Democratic Party is striving to obtain for the workers: they have been set forth in our programme and explained in detail in the pamphlet *The Workers' Cause in
Russia*. Here it will be sufficient to mention the most
important of those improvements. The working-day must
not be longer than eight hours. One day a week must
always be a rest day. Overtime must be absolutely forbidden, and so must night work. Children up to the age
of sixteen must be given free education and, consequently, must not be allowed to work for hire until that age.
Women must not work in trades dangerous to their health.
The employer must compensate the workers for all injury
caused during work, for example, for injury caused when

working on threshing-machines, winnowing-machines, and so forth. All wage-workers must be paid *weekly*, and not once in two months or once in a quarter as is often the case with agricultural labourers. It is very important for the workers to be paid regularly every week and to be paid in cash, and not in goods. Employers are very fond of making the workers accept all sorts of worthless goods at exorbitant prices in payment of wages; to put an end to this disgraceful practice the payment of wages in goods must be absolutely prohibited by law. Further, aged workers must receive pensions from the state. The workers by their labour maintain all the rich classes and the whole state, and that gives them as much right to receive a pension as the government officials. To prevent employers from taking advantage of their position to disregard the rules introduced to protect the workers, inspectors must be appointed to supervise not only the factories, but also the big landlord farms and, in general, all enterprises where wage-labour is employed. But those inspectors must not be government officials, they must not be appointed by ministers or governors, they must not be in the service of the police. The inspectors must *be elected by the workers*; the state must pay salaries to persons who enjoy the confidence of the workers and whom they have freely elected. These elected deputies of the workers must see to it that the workers' dwellings are kept in proper condition, that the employers do not dare compel the workers to live in some sort of dogs' kennels or in dug-outs (as is often the case with agricultural labourers), that the rules concerning the workers' rest are observed, and so on. It must not be forgotten, however, that no elected workers' deputies will be of any use as long as there is no political freedom, as long as the police are all-powerful, and are not responsible to the people. Everyone knows that the police now arrest without trial not only workers' deputies, but every worker who dares speak in the name of all his fellow-workers, who dares to expose breaches of the law, or to call on the workers to unite. But when we have political freedom, the workers' deputies will be of great use.

All employers (factory-owners, landlords, contractors, rich peasants) must *be absolutely forbidden* to make any arbitrary deductions from the wages of their workers, for example, deductions for defective goods, deductions in the form of fines, etc. It is lawlessness and tyranny for employers *arbitrarily* to make deductions from the wages of the workers. The employer must not reduce a worker's wage by means of fines and deductions, or in any way whatsoever. The employer cannot act as judge and executioner (a fine sort of judge who pockets the deductions from the worker's wages!), he must go to a *proper court*, and this court must consist of deputies elected by the workers and the employers in equal numbers. Only such a court will be able to judge fairly all the grievances of the employers against the workers and of the workers against the employers.

Such are the improvements the Social-Democrats are striving to obtain for the whole of the working class. The workers on every estate, on every farm, in the employ of every contractor, must meet and discuss with trustworthy persons what improvements they must strive to obtain and what demands they should advance (for the demands of the workers will, of course, be different in different factories, in different farms and with different contractors).

*Social-Democratic committees* all over Russia are helping the workers to formulate their demands in a clear and precise way, and are helping them to issue printed leaflets where all these demands are set out, so that they may be known to all the workers, and to the employers and the authorities. When the workers unite as one man in support of their demands, the employers always have to give way and agree to them. In the towns the workers have already obtained many improvements in this way, and now the handicraftsmen, the artisans and the agricultural labourers are also beginning to unite (to organize) and to fight for their demands. As long as we have no political freedom we carry on the fight in secret, hiding from the police who prohibit the publication of leaflets and all association of workers. But when we have won political freedom, we shall carry on the fight on a wider scale and openly, so that the working people all over Russia may unite and defend themselves more vigorously from oppression. The larger the number of workers who unite *in the workers' Social-Democratic Party* the stronger will they be, the sooner will they be able to achieve the complete emancipation of the working class from all oppression, from all wage-labour, from all toil for the benefit of the bourgeoisie.

* * *

We have already said that the Social-Democratic Labour Party is striving to obtain improvements not only for the workers, but also for *all the peasants*. Now let us see what improvements it is striving to obtain for all the peasants.

## 6. WHAT IMPROVEMENTS ARE THE SOCIAL-DEMOCRATS STRIVING TO OBTAIN FOR ALL THE PEASANTS?

To secure the complete emancipation of all the toilers, the rural poor must, in alliance with the urban workers, fight against the whole of the bourgeoisie, including the rich peasants. The rich peasants will strive to pay their farm-hands as little as possible and make them work as long and as hard as possible; but the workers in town and country will try to secure better wages, better conditions, and regular periods of rest also for the farm-hands who work for the rich peasants. That means that the rural poor must form their own unions separately from the rich peasants. We have already said this, and we shall always repeat it.

But in Russia, all the peasants, rich and poor, are still serfs in many respects; they all are an *inferior, "black," poll-tax-paying estate*; they are all the serfs of the police officers and of the Zemstvo chiefs; very often they have to work for the landlord in payment for the use of the cut-off lands, watering-places, pastures, or meadows, just as they worked for the feudal lord under serfdom. *All* the peasants want to be free from this new serfdom, *all* of them want to have full rights, *all* of them hate the landlords who still compel them *to perform serf labour*, to pay "labour rent" for the use of the gentry's land and pastures, watering-places, and meadows, to work also "for trespassing," and to send their womenfolk to reap the landlord's field merely "as a token of respect." All this work for the landlord is a heavier burden for the poor peasants than for the rich peasants. The rich peasant is sometimes able to pay the landlord money in lieu of this work, but even the rich peasant is in most cases badly squeezed by the landlord. Hence, the rural poor must fight side by side with the rich peasants against their lack of rights, against every kind of serf labour, against every kind of labour rent. We shall be able to abolish *all* bondage, *all* poverty only when we defeat the bourgeoisie *as a whole* (including the rich peasants). But there is a form of bondage of which we will get rid of *before that time*, because even the rich peasant suffers badly from it. There are still many localities and many districts in Russia where very often all the peasants are quite like serfs. That is why the Russian workers and all the rural poor must *fight with both hands and on two sides*: with one hand—*fight against all the bourgeois*, in alliance with all the workers; and with the other hand— *fight against the rural officials, against the feudal landlords*, in alliance with all the peasants. If the rural poor do not form their own union separately from the rich peasants they will be taken in and deceived by the rich peasants, who will become landlords themselves, while the poor will not only remain poor, but will not even be granted freedom to unite. If the rural poor do not fight side by side with the rich peasants against feudal bondage, they will remain fettered and tied to one spot, and they will not gain full freedom to unite with the urban workers.

The rural poor must first strike at the landlords and throw off at least the most vicious and most pernicious, feudal bondage; in this fight many of the rich peasants and adherents of the bourgeoisie will take the side of the poor, because everybody is fed up with the arrogance of the landlords. But as soon as we have curtailed the power of the landlords, the rich peasant will at once reveal his true character and stretch out his paws to grab everything; they are rapacious paws and they have already grabbed a great deal. Hence, we must be on our guard and form a strong, indestructible alliance with the urban workers. The urban workers will help to knock the old aristocratic habits out of the landlords and to tame the rich peasants a bit (as they have already tamed their bosses, the factory-owners, somewhat). Without an alliance with the urban workers the rural poor will *never* rid themselves of bondage, of poverty, and distress; except for the urban workers, there is *no one* to help the village poor, and they can count on no one but themselves. But there are improvements which we can obtain earlier, which we can obtain at the very outset of this great struggle. There is much bondage in Russia of a kind which has long ceased to exist in other countries, and it is from this bondage to the officials, to the landlords, this feudal bondage that *the Russian peasantry as a whole* can free itself *immediately*.

Let us now see what improvements the workers' Social-Democratic Party is striving first of all to obtain so as to free the Russian peasantry as a whole from at least the most vicious, feudal bondage and to untie the hands of the rural poor for struggle against the Russian bourgeoisie as a whole.

The first demand of the workers' Social-Democratic Party is the immediate abolition of all land compensation payments, all quitrent and all the dues imposed upon the "tax-paying" peasantry. When the committees of nobles, and the Russian tsar's government which consisted of nobles, "emancipated" the peasants from serfdom, the peasants were compelled to *buy out their own* land, to buy out the land which they had tilled for generations! That was *robbery*. The committees of nobles, assisted by the tsarist government, simply *robbed* the peasants. The tsarist government sent troops to many places to impose the charters upon the peasants *by force*, to take military punitive measures against the peasants

who refused to accept the curtailed "pauper" holdings.
Without the help of the troops, without torture and shooting, the committees of nobles would never have been
able to rob the peasants in the brazen way they did at
the time of the emancipation from serf dependence. The
peasants must always remember how they were robbed
and defrauded by those committees of nobles and landlords, because even today the tsarist government still
appoints committees of nobles and officials whenever it
is a question of passing new laws concerning the peasants. Recently, the tsar issued a manifesto (February 26,
1903) in which he promises to revise and improve the
laws concerning the peasants. Who will revise? Who
will improve? Again the nobility, again the officials!
The peasants will always be defrauded until they secure
the setting up of *peasant committees* for the purpose of
improving their conditions of life. The landlords, Zemstvo chiefs, and all kinds of officials have lorded it over
the peasants long enough! It is time to put a stop to
this serf dependence of the peasant upon every police
officer, upon every drink-sodden scion of the nobility who
is called a Zemstvo chief, a police captain, or a governor!
The peasants must demand freedom to manage their
affairs *themselves*, freedom to think out, pass and carry
out new laws *themselves*. The peasants must demand the
setting up of free, elected *peasant committees*, and until
they obtain this they will always be defrauded and robbed
by the nobility and the officials. No one will free the peasants
from the official leeches if they do not free themselves, if
they do not unite and take their fate into *their own* hands.

The Social-Democrats not only demand the complete
and immediate abolition of land compensation payments,
quitrent and imposts of all kinds; they also demand that
the land compensation payments already taken from the
people *be refunded to the people*. The peasants all over
Russia have paid hundreds of millions of rubles since they
were emancipated from serfdom by the committees of nobles. The peasants must demand that this money be returned to them. Let the government impose a special tax
on the big landed nobility, let the land be taken from

the monasteries and from the Department of Appanages (i.e., from the tsar's family), let the national assembly of deputies use this money for the benefit of the peasants. Nowhere in the world is the peasant so downtrodden or so impoverished as in Russia and nowhere do millions of peasants die of starvation as they do in Russia. The peasants in Russia have been reduced to starvation because they were robbed long ago by the committees of nobles, and are being robbed to this day by being forced to pay tribute to the heirs of the feudal landlords every year in the form of compensation payments and quitrent. The robbers must be made to answer for their crimes! Let money be taken from the big landed nobility in order to provide real relief for the famine-stricken. The starving peasant does not need charity, he does not need doles; he must demand the return of the money he has paid for years and years to the landlords and to the state. The national assembly of deputies and the peasant committees will then be able to give real, effective assistance to the starving.

Further. The Social-Democratic Labour Party demands the immediate abolition of collective responsibility and of *all laws which restrict the peasant in the free disposal of his land*. The tsar's manifesto of February 26, 1903 promises the abolition of collective responsibility. A law to this effect has already been passed. But this is not enough. *All the laws* that prevent the peasant from freely disposing of his land must be abolished immediately; otherwise, even without collective responsibility the peasant will not be free and will remain a semi-serf. The peasant must have *complete freedom* to dispose of his land: to let or sell it to whomever he pleases without having to ask for permission. That is what the tsar's ukase does not permit: the nobility, the merchants, and the burghers are free to dispose of their land, but the peasant is not. The peasant is treated like an infant, he must have a Zemstvo chief to look after him, like a nurse. The peasant must not be allowed to sell his allotment, for he will squander the money! That is how the feudal die-hards argue, and there are simpletons who believe them and, wishing the peasant well, they say that he must not be allowed to sell his land. Even the Narodniks (of whom we have already spoken) and the people who call themselves "Socialist-Revolutionaries" yield to this argument and agree that it is better that the peasant should remain a bit of a serf rather than be allowed to sell his land.

The Social-Democrats say: that is sheer hypocrisy, aristocratic talk, merely honeyed words! When we have attained socialism, when the working class has defeated the bourgeoisie, the land will be owned in common and *nobody* will have the right to sell land. But what in the meantime? Are the nobleman and the merchant to be allowed to sell their land and the peasant not? Are the nobleman and the merchant to be free, while the peasant remains a semi-serf? Is the peasant to continue to have to beg permission from the authorities?

All this is mere deceit, covered up by honeyed words, but deceit for all that.

As long as the nobleman and the merchant are allowed to sell land, the peasant must also have *full right* to sell his land and to dispose of it with *complete freedom*, in exactly the same way as the nobleman and the merchant. When the working class has defeated the entire bourgeoisie, it will take the land away from the big proprietors and introduce *co-operative farming* on the big estates, so that the workers will farm the land together, in common, and freely elect trustworthy men to manage the farms. They will have all kinds of labour-saving machines; they will work in shifts for not more than eight (or even six) hours a day. Then, the small peasant who prefers to carry on his farm in the old way on individual lines will not produce for the market, to sell to the first comer, but for the workers' co-operatives; the small peasant will supply the workers' co-operatives with grain, meat, vegetables, and the workers in return will, without money, provide him with machines, livestock, fertilizers, clothes, and whatever else he needs. There will be no struggle for money between the big and the small farmer, there will be no working for hire for others; all the workers will work for themselves, all improvements in methods of production and all machines will benefit the workers and help to make their work easier, to improve their standard of living.

But every sensible man will understand that socialism cannot be attained at once: to attain it a fierce struggle must be waged against the entire bourgeoisie and all governments; all the urban workers all over Russia must unite in a firm and unbreakable alliance with all the rural poor. That is a great cause, and to that cause it is worth devoting one's whole life. But until we have attained socialism, the big owner will always fight the small owner for money. Is the big landowner to be free to sell his land, and the small peasant not? We repeat: the peasants are not infants and they will not allow anyone to lord it over them; the peasants must receive without any restriction *all the rights* that are enjoyed by the nobility and the merchants.

It is also said: the peasant's land is not his own, it is communal land. Everyone cannot be allowed to sell communal land. This, too, is a deception. Have not the nobles and the merchants their communities? Do not the nobles and the merchants combine to form companies to buy land and factories, or any other thing in common? Why then are no restrictions invented for the associations of the nobility, while all the police scoundrels zealously invent restrictions and prohibitions for the peasantry? The peasants have never received anything good from the officials, they have secured only beatings, extortions, and bullying. The peasants will never receive anything good until they take their affairs into their own hands, until they obtain complete equality and complete freedom. If the peasants want their land to be communal, no one will dare to interfere with them; and they will voluntarily form a community which will include whomever they like, and on whatever terms they like; they will quite freely draw up a communal contract in whatever form they like. And let no official dare poke his nose into the communal affairs of the peasants. Let no one exercise his wits on the peasants to invent restrictions and prohibitions for them.

\* \* \*

Lastly, there is one more important improvement which the Social-Democrats are striving to obtain for the peasants. They want the immediate restriction of the peasants' bondage to the nobility, their feudal bondage. Of course bondage cannot be completely abolished as long as poverty exists, and poverty cannot be abolished as long as the land and the factories are in the hands of the bourgeoisie, as long as money is the principal power in the world, and until *socialist society* has been established. But in the rural districts of Russia there is still much bondage of a particularly vicious sort which no longer exists in other countries, although socialism has not yet been introduced there. There is still much *feudal bondage* in Russia which is profitable to all the landlords, which weighs heavily on all the peasants, and which can and must be abolished immediately, first of all.

Let us explain the sort of bondage we call feudal bondage.

Everyone who lives in the country knows cases like the following. The landlord's land adjoins the peasant's land. At the time of the emancipation the peasants were deprived of land that was indispensable to them: pastures, woods and watering-places for cattle were cut off. The peasants cannot do without this cut-off land, without pastures, without watering-places. Whether they like it or not the peasants are forced to go to the landlord to ask him to permit their cattle to go to the water, to graze on the pastures, and so forth. The landlord does not farm any land himself and, perhaps, has no money; he lives only by enthralling the peasants. In return for the use of the cut-off lands the peasants work for him for nothing; they plough his land with their horses, they harvest his grain and mow his hay, they thresh his grain, and in some places they even have to cart their manure to the landlord's fields, or bring him homespun cloth, and eggs and poultry. Just as under serfdom! Under serfdom the peasants had to work for nothing for the landlord on whose estate they lived, and today they very often have to work for nothing for the landlord in return for the very same land which the committees of nobles filched from them at the time of the emancipation. It is just the same as *barshchina*.* In some gubernias the peasants actually call it *barshchina* or *panshchina*. Well, that is what we call feudal bondage. At the time of the emancipation from serfdom the committees of landlords, of nobles, arranged matters so as to keep the peasants in bondage in the old way. They deliberately cut the peasants' allotments; they deliberately drove a wedge of landlord's land in between the peasants' holdings so as to make it impossible for peasants even to let a hen out without trespassing; they deliberately transferred the peasants to inferior land, blocked the way to the watering-place by a strip of landlord's land—in short, they arranged matters in such a way that the peasants found themselves in a trap, and could easily be taken captive. There are still countless numbers of villages where the peasants are in captivity to the local landlords, just as much as they were under serfdom. In villages like those, the rich peasant and the poor peasant are both bound hand and foot and at the mercy of the landlords. The poor peasant fares even worse than the rich peasant from this state of affairs. The rich peasant sometimes owns some land and sends his labourer to work for the landlord instead of going himself, but the poor peasant has no way out and the landlord does what he likes to him. Under this bondage the poor peasant often has not a moment's breathing space; he cannot even go to look for work elsewhere because of the work he has to do for his landlord; he has no time to think of freely uniting in one union, in one party with all the rural poor and the urban workers.

Now let us see whether it is possible to abolish this sort of bondage at once, forthwith, immediately. The Social-Democratic Labour Party proposes to the peasants *two* means to this end. But we must repeat that only socialism can deliver all the poor from bondage of every kind, for as long as the rich have power they will always oppress the poor in one way or another. It is impossible to abolish all bondage at once, but it is possible greatly to

---

* The Russian term for serf labour.—*Tr.*

restrict the most vicious, the most revolting form of bondage, feudal bondage, which weighs heavily on the poor,
on the middle and even on the rich peasants; it is possible
to obtain immediate relief for the peasants.

There are two means to this end.

First means: the establishment of freely elected courts
consisting of delegates of the farm-hands and poor
peasants, as well as of the rich peasants and the landlords.

Second means: freely elected *peasant committees*. These
peasant committees must have the right not only to discuss and adopt measures for abolishing serf labour, for
abolishing the survivals of serfdom, but they must also
have the right *to confiscate the cut-off lands and restore
them to the peasants*.

Let us consider these two means a little more closely.
The freely elected delegate courts will consider all cases
arising out of complaints of peasants against bondage.
Such courts will have the right to reduce rents if the landlords, taking advantage of the peasants' poverty, have
fixed them too high. Such courts will have the right to
free the peasants from excessive payments: for instance,
if a landlord engages a peasant in the winter for summer
work at an excessively low wage the court will judge
the case and fix a fair wage. Of course, such courts must
not consist of officials, but of freely elected delegates, and
the agricultural labourers and the rural poor must also
elect their delegates, whose number must not in any case
be less than those elected by the rich peasants and the
landlords. Such courts must also try disputes between
labourers and employers. They would make it easier for
the labourers and all the rural poor to defend their rights,
to unite, and to find out exactly who can be trusted to
stand up faithfully for the poor and for the labourers.

The other means is still more important: the establishment of free *peasant committees* consisting of elected delegates of the farm-hands and of the poor, middle, and rich
peasants in every uyezd (or, if the peasants think fit, they
may elect several committees in each uyezd; perhaps they
will even prefer to establish a peasant committee in every

volost and in every large village). No one knows better
than the peasants themselves what kind of bondage op-
presses them. No one will be able to expose the landlords
who to this day live on the backs of the enthralled peasants better than the peasants themselves. The peasant
committees will decide what cut-off lands, what meadows,
pastures, and so forth, were taken from the peasants unfairly; they will decide whether those lands shall be taken
back without compensation, or whether the people who
bought them should be paid compensation at the expense
of the high nobility. At all events, the peasant committees
will release the peasants from the traps into which they
were driven by very many committees of the landed nobility. The peasant committees will relieve the peasants of
the interference of the officials, they will show that the
peasants want to, and can, manage their own affairs, they
will help the peasants to come to a common understanding concerning their needs and to recognize those who
really stand for the rural poor and for an alliance with the
urban workers. The peasant committees will be the *first
step* towards enabling the peasants even in remote villages to get on to their feet and to take their fate into
their own hands.

That is why the Social-Democratic workers warn the
peasants:

*Place no faith in any committees of nobles, or in any
commissions consisting of officials.*

*Demand a national assembly of deputies.*

*Demand the establishment of peasant committees.*

*Demand complete freedom to publish pamphlets and
newspapers of every kind.*

When all have the right freely and fearlessly to express
their opinions and their wishes in the national assembly
of deputies, in the peasant committees and in the newspapers, it will very soon be seen who is on the side of the
working class and who is on the side of the bourgeoisie.
Today, the great majority of the people do not think about
these things at all, some conceal their real views, some
do not yet know their own minds, some lie deliberately.
But when everyone begins to think about it, there will

be no reason for concealing anything, and everything will soon become clear. We have already said that the bourgeoisie will draw the rich peasants to its side. The sooner and the more completely we succeed in abolishing serf bondage, and the more real freedom the peasants obtain for themselves, the sooner will the rural poor unite among themselves, and the sooner will the rich peasants unite with the rest of the bourgeoisie. Let them unite: we are not afraid of that, although we know perfectly well that this will strengthen the rich peasants. But we, too, will unite, and *our union*, the union between the rural poor and the urban workers, will embrace far more people, it will be a union of tens of millions against a union of hundreds of thousands. We also know that the bourgeoisie will try (it is already trying!) to attract the middle and even the small peasants; it will try to deceive them, to entice them, to sow dissension among them by promising to pull everyone of them into the ranks of the rich. We have already seen the tricks and deceits the bourgeoisie resorts to in order to win over the middle peasant. We must therefore open the eyes of the rural poor beforehand, and beforehand consolidate their separate union with the urban workers against the entire bourgeoisie.

Let every villager look around carefully. How often we hear the rich peasants talking against the nobility, against the landlords! How they complain of the oppression which the people suffer! Or of the landlords' land lying waste! How they love to talk (in private conversation) about what a good thing it would be if the peasants took possession of the land!

Can we believe what the rich say? No. They do not want the land for the people, they want it for themselves. They have already got hold of a great deal of land, bought outright and rented, and still they are not satisfied. *Hence, the rural poor will not long have to march side by side with the rich against the landlords*. Only the first step will have to be taken in their company, after that their ways will part.

*That is why we must draw a clear distinction between this first step and subsequent steps and our last and most*

*important step.* The first step in the countryside will be
the complete emancipation of the peasant, full rights for
the peasant and the establishment of peasant committees
for the purpose of restoring the cut-off lands. But our last
step will be the same in both town and country: *we shall
take all the land and all the factories from the landlords
and the bourgeoisie and set up a socialist society.* We
shall have to go through a big struggle in the period between our first step and the last *and whoever confuses the
first step with the last impedes that struggle and unwittingly helps to hoodwink the rural poor.*

The rural poor will take the first step together with all
the peasants: a few kulaks may fall out, perhaps one peasant in a hundred is willing to put up with any kind of
bondage. But the overwhelming mass of the peasants will,
as yet, advance as one whole: all the peasants want equal
rights. Bondage to the landlords ties everyone hand and
foot. But the last step will never be taken by all the peasants together: then, all the rich peasants will turn
against the labourers. Then, we shall already need a strong
union of the rural poor and the *urban Social-Democratic
workers.* Whoever tells the peasants that they can take
the first and the last step simultaneously is deceiving the
peasants. He forgets about the great struggle that is
going on among the peasants themselves, the great struggle between the rural poor and the rich peasants.

That is why the Social-Democrats do not promise the
peasants a land flowing with milk and honey *at once.* That
is why the Social-Democrats first of all demand complete
freedom for the struggle, for the great, wide, popular
struggle of the entire working class against the entire
bourgeoisie. That is why the Social-Democrats advise a
*small but sure first step.*

Some people think that our demand for the establishment of peasant committees for the purpose of restricting
bondage and of restoring the cut-off lands is a sort of
fence or barrier as if we meant to say: stop, you cannot
go any further. These people have not sufficiently thought
about what the Social-Democrats want. The demand for
the establishment of peasant committees for the purpose

of restricting bondage and of restoring the cut-off lands is not a barrier. It is a *door*. We must pass through this door *in order to go further*, to march along the wide and open road *to the very end*, to the complete emancipation of all the working people in Russia. Until the peasants pass through this door they will remain in ignorance and bondage, without full rights, without complete, real freedom; they will not even be able to decide among themselves who is the friend of the working-man and who his enemy. That is why the Social-Democrats point to this door and say that the entire people must all together first force this door and break it down completely. But there are people who call themselves Narodniks and Socialist-Revolutionaries, who also wish the peasant well, who shout and make a noise and wave their arms about and want to help him, but *they do not see that door*! Those people are so blind that they even say: there is no need to give the peasant the right freely to dispose of his land! They wish the peasant well, but they sometimes argue exactly like the feudal die-hards! Such friends can be of little assistance. What is the use of wishing the peasant all the best if you don't see the first door that must be forced? What is the use of wanting socialism if you don't see the way out to the road of free, people's struggle for socialism not only in the towns, but also in the country, not only against the landlords, but also *against the rich peasants in the village community, in the "mir"*?

That is why the Social-Democrats point so insistently to this first and nearest door. The difficult thing at this stage is not to express a lot of good wishes, but to point to the right road, to clearly understand *how the very first step should be taken*. All the friends of the peasant have been talking and writing for the past forty years about the Russian peasant being crushed by bondage and about his being a semi-serf. Long before there were any Social-Democrats in Russia the friends of the peasant wrote many books describing how shamefully the landlords robbed and enslaved the peasant by means of the various cut-off lands. All honest people now realize that the peasant must be given assistance at once, immediately, that he must get at least some relief from this bondage; even the officials of our police government are beginning to talk about this. The whole question is: *how to set about it, how to take the first step,* which door must be forced first?

To this question different people (among those who wish the peasant well) give two different answers. Every rural proletarian must try to understand these two answers as clearly as possible and form a definite and firm opinion about them. One answer is given by the Narodniks and the Socialist-Revolutionaries. The first thing to be done, they say, is to develop among the peasants all sorts of societies (co-operatives). The unity of the *mir* must be strengthened. The peasant must not be given the right to dispose of his land freely. Let the rights of the community, the *mir,* be extended, and let all the land in Russia gradually become communal land. The peasants must be granted every assistance to purchase land, so that the land may more easily pass from capital to labour.

The other answer is given by the Social-Democrats. The peasant must first of all obtain for himself all the rights possessed by the nobility and the merchants, all without exception. The peasant must have full right freely to dispose of his land. In order to abolish the most revolting forms of bondage, peasant committees must be set up for the purpose of restoring the cut-off lands. We need not the unity of the *mir*, but the unity of the rural poor in the different village communities all over Russia, the unity of the rural proletarians with the urban proletarians. All sorts of societies (co-operatives) and the communal purchase of land will always benefit the rich peasants most, and will always serve to hoodwink the middle peasants.

The Russian government realizes that some relief must be given to the peasants, but it wants to make shift with trifles, it wants everything to be done by the officials. The peasants must be on the alert, because commissions of officials will cheat them just as they were cheated by the committees of nobles. The peasants must demand the election of free peasant committees. The important thing is not to expect improvement from the officials, the peasants themselves must take their fate into their own hands. Let us at first take only one step, let us at first abolish only the worst forms of bondage—as long as the peasants become conscious of their strength, as long as they freely reach an understanding with one another and unite. No honest person can deny that the cut-off lands often serve as the instruments of the most outrageous feudal bondage. No honest person can deny that our demand is the very first and fairest of demands: let the peasants freely elect *their own* committees, without the officials, for the purpose of abolishing all feudal bondage.

In the free peasant committees (just as in the free all-Russian assembly of deputies) the Social-Democrats will at once do all in their power to consolidate the separate union of the rural proletarians with the urban proletarians. The Social-Democrats will demand all measures for the benefit of the rural proletarians and will help them to follow up the first step, as quickly as possible and as unanimously as possible, with the second and the third step, and so on to the very end, to the complete *victory of the proletariat.* But can we say today, at once, what demand will arise tomorrow as the second step? No, we cannot, because we do not know what stand will be taken tomorrow by the rich peasants, and by many of the educated people who are concerned about all sorts of co-operatives, and about the land passing from capital to labour.

Perhaps they will not join the landlords on the morrow; perhaps they will want to finish off landlord rule completely. Very good! The Social-Democrats would very much like this to happen, and they will advise the rural and the urban proletarians to demand that all the land be taken from the landlords and be transferred to the free people's state. The Social-Democrats will vigilantly see to it that the rural proletarians are not cheated in the course of this, and that they still further consolidate their forces for the final struggle for the complete emancipation of the proletariat.

But things may turn out quite differently. In fact, it is more likely that they will turn out differently. On the very day after the worst forms of bondage have been restricted and curtailed, the rich peasants, and many of the educated people, may unite with the landlords, and then the entire rural bourgeoisie will rise against the entire rural proletariat. In that event it would be ridiculous for us to fight only the landlords. We would then have to fight the entire bourgeoisie and demand first of all the greatest possible freedom and elbow-room for this fight, demand better conditions of life for the workers in order to make it easier for them to fight.

In any case, whichever way things turn out, our first, our principal and indispensable task is *to strengthen the alliance between the rural proletarians and semi-proletarians and the urban proletarians.* For this alliance we need at once, immediately, *complete political freedom for the people, complete equality of rights for the peasants and the abolition of feudal bondage.* And when that alliance is established and strengthened, we shall easily expose all the deceits to which the bourgeoisie resorts in order to attract the middle peasant, we shall easily and quickly take the second, the third, and the last step against the entire bourgeoisie, against all the government forces, and we shall march straight to victory and quickly achieve the *complete emancipation of all the working people.*

## 7. THE CLASS STRUGGLE IN THE COUNTRYSIDE

What is the *class struggle*? It is the struggle of one part of the people against the other; the struggle waged by the masses of the rightless, the oppressed, the toilers, against the privileged, the oppressors, the parasites; the struggle of the wage-labourers, or proletarians, against the property-owners, or bourgeoisie. This great struggle has always gone on and is now going on in the Russian countryside too, although not everyone sees it, and although not everyone understands its significance. In the period of serfdom the entire mass of the peasants fought against their oppressors, the landlord class, which was protected, defended, and supported by the tsarist government. The peasants then were unable to unite; they were utterly crushed by ignorance; they had no helpers and

6—1928

brothers among the urban workers; nevertheless they fought as best they could. They were not deterred by the brutal persecution of the government, they were not daunted by flogging and bullets, they did not believe the priests who tried with all their might to prove that serfdom was approved by Holy Scripture and sanctioned by God (that is what Metropolitan Philaret actually said!); the peasants rose in rebellion, now in one place and now in another, and at last the government gave in, fearing a general uprising of all the peasants.

Serfdom was abolished, but not altogether. The peasants remained without rights, they remained an inferior, poll-tax-paying, "black" estate, they remained in the clutches of feudal bondage. Unrest among the peasants continued, they continued to seek complete, real freedom. Meanwhile, after the abolition of serfdom, a new class struggle arose, the *struggle of the proletariat against the bourgeoisie*. Wealth increased, railways and large factories were built, the towns grew still more populous and more luxurious, but all this wealth was appropriated by a very few, while the people became poorer, more impoverished and starved, and they had to leave their homes to go and work for wages among strangers. The urban workers started a new, great struggle of all the poor against all the rich. The urban workers united in the *Social-Democratic Party* and are waging their struggle stubbornly, staunchly and solidly, advancing step by step, preparing for the great final struggle, demanding political freedom for all the people.

At last the peasants, too, lost patience. In the spring of last year, 1902, the peasants of the Poltava, Kharkov, and other gubernias rose and went against the landlords, broke open their barns, shared the contents among themselves, distributed among the starving the grain that had been sown and reaped by the peasants but appropriated by the landlords, and demanded a new division of the land. The peasants could no longer bear the endless oppression and began to seek a better lot. The peasants decided—and rightly decided—that it was better to die fighting the oppressors than to die from starvation without a fight. But they did not win a better lot for themselves. The tsarist government proclaimed them common rioters and robbers (for having taken from the robber landlords grain which the peasants themselves had sown and reaped!); the tsarist government sent troops against them as against an enemy, and the peasants were defeated; the peasants were shot down, many were killed; the peasants were brutally flogged, many were flogged to death; they were tortured worse than the Turks torture their enemies, the Christians. The tsar's envoys, the governors, were the worst torturers, real executioners. The soldiers raped the wives and daughters of the peasants. And after all this, the peasants were tried by a court of officials, they were compelled to pay the landlords 800,000 rubles, and at the trials, those infamous secret trials, trials in a torture-chamber, counsel for the defence were not even allowed to tell how the peasants had been ill-treated and tortured by the tsar's envoys, Governor Obolensky and the other servants of the tsar.

The peasants fought in a just cause. The Russian working class will always honour the memory of the martyrs who were shot down and flogged to death by the servants of the tsar. Those martyrs fought for the freedom and happiness of the working people. The peasants were defeated, but they will rise again and again, they will not lose heart because of this first defeat. The class-conscious workers will do all in their power to inform the largest possible number of working people in town and country about the peasants' struggle and to get them to prepare for another and more successful fight. The class-conscious workers will do all in their power to help the peasants *clearly to understand why the first peasant uprising* (1902) *was put down and what must be done so that the peasants and workers and not the servants of the tsar should win.*

The peasant uprising was put down because it was an uprising of an ignorant and unthinking mass, an uprising without clear and definite *political* demands, i.e., without the demand for a change in the *political* order. The peasant uprising was put down because *no preparations had been made* for it. The peasant uprising was put down because the rural proletarians had not yet allied themselves

with the urban proletarians. Such were the three causes
of the failure of the peasants' first fight. To be successful
an insurrection must have a conscious aim, preparations
must be made for it in advance, it must spread throughout
the whole of Russia and be in alliance with the urban
workers. And every step in the struggle of the urban workers, every Social-Democratic pamphlet or newspaper,
every speech made by a class-conscious worker to the rural proletarians will bring nearer the time when the insurrection will be repeated and end in victory.

The peasants rose without a conscious aim, simply because they could not bear their sufferings any longer, because they did not want to die like dumb brutes without a
fight. The peasants had suffered so much from robbery,
oppression, and torment that they could not but believe,
if only for a moment, the vague rumours about the tsar's
mercy, they could not but believe that every sensible man
would regard it as just that grain should be distributed
among starving people, among those who had worked all
their lives for others, who had sown and reaped, and were
now dying of starvation, while the "gentry's" barns were
full to overflowing. The peasants seemed to have forgotten that all the best land and the factories had been seized
by the rich, by the landlords and the bourgeoisie, precisely
for the purpose of compelling the starving people to go
to work for the property-owners. The peasants forgot that
not only do the priests preach sermons in defence of the
rich class, but the entire tsarist government with its host
of bureaucrats and soldiers rise in its defence. The tsarist
government reminded the peasants of that. The tsarist
government, with brutal cruelty, showed the peasants
what state power is, whose servant and whose protector
it is. We need only remind the peasants of this lesson more
often and they will easily understand why it is necessary
to *change the political order*, and why we need *political
freedom*. Peasant uprisings will have a conscious aim
when larger and larger numbers of people understand that,
when every peasant who can read and write and who
thinks for himself becomes familiar with the *three principal demands* which must be fought for first of all. First

demand—the convocation of a *national assembly of deputies for the purpose of establishing popular elective government in Russia in place of the present autocratic government.* Second demand—*freedom for all to publish any book or newspaper.* Third demand—*recognition by the law of the complete equality of the peasants with the other social estates and the institution of elected peasant committees, with the primary object of abolishing all forms of feudal bondage.* Such are the chief and fundamental demands of the Social-Democrats, and it will now be very easy for the peasants to understand them, to understand *what to begin with* in the struggle for the people's freedom. When the peasants understand these demands, they will also understand that long, persistent and persevering *preparations* must be made for the fight, not in isolation, but together with the workers in the towns—the Social-Democrats.

Let every class-conscious worker and peasant rally around himself the most intelligent, reliable, and fearless comrades. Let him strive to explain to them what the Social-Democrats want, so that every one of them may understand what struggle must be waged and what demands must be advanced. Let the class-conscious Social-Democrats begin gradually, circumspectly, but unswervingly, to teach the peasants the doctrines of Social-Democracy, give them Social-Democratic pamphlets to read and explain those pamphlets at small gatherings of trustworthy people.

But the doctrines of Social-Democracy must be taught not from books alone; every instance, every case of oppression and injustice we see around us must be used for this purpose. Social-Democracy is the doctrine of struggle against all oppression, against all robbery, against all injustice. Only he who knows the causes of oppression and who *all his life fights every case of oppression* is a real Social-Democrat. How can this be done? The class-conscious Social-Democrats, gathering in their town or village, must decide themselves how it can be done to the best advantage of the entire working class. To show how it can be done I shall quote one or two examples. Let us suppose that a Social-Democratic worker has come on a visit to his village, or that any Social-Democratic worker has come to any village. The entire village is in the clutches of the neighbouring landlord like a fly in a spider's web; it is in this state of bondage all its life and cannot escape from it. The worker must at once pick out the most sensible, intelligent and trustworthy peasants, those who are seeking justice and will not be frightened by the first sleuth who comes along, and explain to them the causes of this hopeless bondage, tell them how the landlords cheated the peasants and robbed them with the aid of the committees of nobles, tell them how strong the rich are and how they are supported by the tsarist government, and also tell them about the demands of the Social-Democratic workers. When the peasants understand all these simple things they must put their heads together and discuss whether it is possible to put up a united resistance to that landlord, whether it is possible to put forward the first and principal demands (in the same way as the urban workers present their demands to the factory-owners). If that landlord holds one big village or several villages in bondage, the best thing would be to obtain through trustworthy people a *leaflet* from the nearest Social-Democratic committee. In that leaflet the Social-Democratic committee will correctly describe, from the very beginning, the bondage the peasants suffer from and formulate their first demands (reduction of rent, proper rates and not half-rates of pay for winter hiring, or less severe persecution for trespass, or various other demands). From a leaflet like that all the peasants who can read and write will learn what the issue is, and then explain things to the illiterate. The peasants will then clearly see that the Social-Democrats are on their side, that the Social-Democrats condemn all robbery. The peasants will then begin to understand what relief, if only slight, but relief for all that, can be obtained immediately if all stand together, and what big improvements for the whole country must be fought for by waging a great battle together with the Social-Democratic workers in the towns. The peasants will then prepare more and more for that great struggle, they will learn how to find trustworthy people and how to stand unitedly for their demands. Perhaps they may succeed sometimes in organizing a strike, as the urban workers do. True, this is more difficult in the country than in the towns, but it is possible sometimes for all that; in other countries there have been successful strikes, for instance, in the busy seasons, when the landlords and rich farmers are badly in need of hands. If the rural poor are prepared for a strike, if an agreement has long been reached about the general demands, if those demands have been explained in leaflets, or properly explained at meetings, all will stand together, and the landlord will have to give in, or at least put a curb on his greed. If the strike is unanimous and is called during the busy season, the landlord, and even the authorities with their troops, will find it hard to do anything—time will be lost, the landlord will be threatened with ruin, and he will soon become more tractable. Of course, strikes are a new thing, and new things often do not come off well at first. The urban workers, too, did not know how to fight unitedly at first, they did not know what demands to put forward, they simply went out to smash the machines and wreck the factory. But now the workers have learned to conduct a united struggle. Every new job must first be learned. Now the workers understand that at once they can obtain only relief by standing together; meanwhile, the people are learning to put up united resistance and are preparing more and more for the great and decisive struggle. Similarly, the peasants will learn to stand up against the worst robbers, to be united in their demands for some measure of relief and to prepare gradually, persistently and everywhere for the great battle for freedom. The number of class-conscious workers and peasants will grow, and the unions of rural Social-Democrats will become stronger; every case of bondage to the landlord, of extortion on the part of the priest, of police brutality and bureaucratic oppression, will serve to open the eyes of the people, accustom them to putting up united resistance and to the idea that it is necessary to change the political order by force.

At the very beginning of this pamphlet we said that the
urban workers come out into the streets and squares and
publicly demand *freedom*, that they inscribe on their banners and cry: "Down with the autocracy!" The day will
soon come when the urban workers will rise not merely
to march through the streets shouting, but for the great
and final struggle; when the workers will declare as one
man: "We shall secure freedom, or die fighting"; when the
places of the hundreds who are killed and fall in the fight
will be taken by thousands of fresh and still more resolute fighters. And the peasants, too, will then rise all over
Russia and go to the assistance of the urban workers, will
fight to the end for the freedom of the peasants and the
workers. The tsar's hosts will be unable to withstand that
onslaught. Victory will go to the working people, and the
working class will march along the wide, spacious road
to the liberation of all toilers from all oppression. The
working class will make use of freedom to fight for socialism!

### THE PROGRAMME OF THE RUSSIAN SOCIAL-DEMOCRATIC LABOUR PARTY PROPOSED BY THE NEWSPAPER *ISKRA* TOGETHER WITH THE MAGAZINE *ZARYA*[11]

We have already explained what a programme is, why
one is needed, and why the Social-Democratic Party is the
only party that comes out with a clear and definite programme. The programme can be finally adopted only by
the congress of our Party, i.e., the assembly of representatives of all the Party workers. Preparations for such a
congress are now being made by the Organizing Committee. But very many committees of our Party have already
openly declared their agreement with *Iskra*, their recognition of *Iskra* as the leading newspaper. Therefore, before
the congress our draft (proposed) programme can fully
serve as a precise indication of what the Social-Democrats
want, and we consider it necessary to give that draft in
full as an appendix to our pamphlet.

Of course, not every worker will understand everything that is said in the programme without an explanation. Many great Socialists worked on the creation of the teachings of Social-Democracy completed by Marx and Engels; the workers of all countries went through a great deal to acquire the experience that we want to utilize, that we want to use as the basis of our programme. Therefore, the workers must learn the teachings of Social-Democracy in order to understand every word of the programme, *their* programme, *their* banner of the struggle. And the workers are learning and understanding the Social-Democratic programme with particular ease because that programme speaks of what every thinking worker has seen and experienced. Let nobody be deterred by the "difficulty" of understanding the programme at once: the more every worker reads and thinks, the more experience he acquires in the struggle, the more fully will he understand it. But let everybody think over and discuss the *whole* programme of the Social-Democrats, let everybody constantly keep in mind *all that the Social-Democrats want, and what they think about the emancipation* of all the working people. The Social-Democrats want everybody to know clearly and precisely the truth, the whole truth, about what the Social-Democratic Party is.

We cannot here explain the whole programme in detail. A separate pamphlet would be needed for that. We shall merely briefly outline what the programme says and advise the reader to get hold of two pamphlets to use as aids. One pamphlet is by the German Social-Democrat Karl Kautsky, and its title is *The Erfurt Programme*. It has been translated into Russian. The other pamphlet is by the Russian Social-Democrat L. Martov, and its title is *The Worker's Cause in Russia*. Those pamphlets will help the reader to understand the whole of our programme.

Let us now indicate each part of our programme by a separate letter (see programme below) and show what is spoken about in each part.

A) At the very beginning it says that the proletariat all over the world is fighting for its emancipation, and the

Russian proletariat is only a unit of the world army of the working class of all countries.

B) It then goes on to explain the bourgeois order of things in nearly all countries in the world, including Russia: how the majority of the population, working for the landlords and capitalists, live in poverty and want; how the small artisans and peasants are ruined while the big factories grow bigger; how capital crushes the worker and also his wife and children; how the conditions of the working class are growing worse and worse and unemployment and want are increasing.

C) It then speaks of the union of the workers, of their struggle, of the great aim of that struggle: to liberate all the oppressed, to abolish completely all oppression of the poor by the rich. This part also explains why the working class is growing stronger and stronger, why it will certainly defeat all its enemies, all the defenders of the bourgeoisie.

D) Then it explains why Social-Democratic parties have been formed in all countries, how they help the working class to wage its struggle, unite and guide the workers, enlighten them and prepare them for the great struggle.

E) Further on it explains why the conditions of the people in Russia are even worse than in other countries, what a great evil the tsarist autocracy is, why we must first of all overthrow that autocracy and establish popular, elective government in Russia.

F) What improvements must popular elective government bring the whole people? We explain that in our pamphlet, and it is also explained in the programme.

G) Then the programme indicates what improvements for the whole of the working class we must strive to achieve immediately in order to make life easier for it and enable it to fight more freely for socialism.

H) Special reference is made in the programme to those improvements which we must first of all strive to achieve for all the peasants so as to enable the rural poor to wage the class struggle more easily and freely against the rural and the entire Russian bourgeoisie.

I) Lastly, the Social-Democratic Party warns the people not to believe any police or bureaucratic promises or honeyed words, but to fight firmly for the immediate convocation of a free national assembly of deputies.

Written in March 1903
First published in pamphlet form
in May 1903, in Geneva, by the
League of Russian Social-Democrats Abroad

Vol. VI, pp. 325-92

# REPORT ON THE RESOLUTION CONCERNING SUPPORT OF THE PEASANT MOVEMENT DELIVERED AT THE THIRD CONGRESS OF THE R.S.D.L.P.

*April 19 (May 2), 1905*

In view of the statement submitted by seventeen comrades stressing the urgent need to speed up the congress,[12] I shall try to be as brief as possible. Strictly speaking, the question under examination contains no points involving dispute in principle; no such points were advanced even during the Party crisis which abounded in differences of "principle."

Moreover, the draft resolution was published quite some time ago in the newspaper *Vperyod*,[13] and therefore I shall confine myself merely to defending the resolution.

The question of support to the peasant movement actually can be broken down into two issues: 1) the theoretical fundamentals and 2) the practical experience of the Party. The latter will be dealt with by our second reporter, Comrade Barsov, who is well acquainted with the most advanced peasant movement—that in Guria. As regards the theoretical fundamentals involved, it is now a matter of reaffirming slogans already worked out by the Social-Democratic movement as applied to the present peasant movement. This movement is growing and spreading before our very eyes. The government is again resorting to the old attempts to deceive the peasants with fake concessions. This policy of corruption must be countered with the slogans of our Party.

These slogans, I believe, are set forth in the following draft resolution:

"The Russian Social-Democratic Labour Party, as the Party of the class-conscious proletariat, is striving toward the full deliverance of all working people from all and every exploitation and supports all revolutionary movements against the present social and political system. Hence the R.S.D.L.P. most vigorously supports the present peasant movement as well, upholding every revolutionary measure capable of improving the condition of the peasantry, and, to this end, not stopping at the expropriation of the landed estates. Moreover, as a class Party of the proletariat, the R.S.D.L.P. steadfastly works toward independent class organization of the rural proletariat, always remembering that it is its task to explain to them that their interests and those of the peasant bourgeoisie are antagonistic, to explain to them that only the joint struggle of the rural and the urban proletariat against bourgeois society as a whole can lead to the socialist revolution, which alone can really deliver the entire mass of the rural poor from poverty and exploitation.

"As a practical slogan for agitation among the peasantry and a means for imparting the highest degree of consciousness to the present movement, the R.S.D.L.P. proposes the immediate establishment of revolutionary peasant committees to render every support to all democratic reforms and to carry them out in detail. In such committees too the R.S.D.L.P. will seek to promote the independent organization of rural proletarians with a view, on the one hand, to supporting the peasantry as a whole in all their revolutionary democratic actions, and on the other hand, to protecting the true interests of the rural proletariat in their struggle against the peasant bourgeoisie." (*Vperyod*, No. 11.)

This draft has already been discussed in the committee on the agrarian question which the delegates set up before this congress convened in order to prepare for it. In spite of the great variety of views expressed, the discussion brought out a number of salient shades of opinion and it is on these that I shall dwell. According to the draft resolution, the revolutionary measures possible and necessary in the agrarian field essentially amount to "improving the condition of the peasantry." Hence, the resolution clearly expresses the conviction shared by all Social-Democrats that these measures can by no means bring about any transformation of the very foundations of the present social and economic system. In this we differ from the Socialist-Revolutionaries. The revolutionary movement of the peasantry can result in a substantial improvement of their position, but not in capitalism being substituted by another mode of production.

The resolution speaks of not stopping at the expropriation of landed estates. It has been said that this formulation introduces a change in our agrarian programme. I do not agree with this opinion. Of course, the wording may be improved: it is not our Party, but the peasantry that will not stop at expropriation. Our Party supports the peasantry, even when they do not stop at measures of this kind. Instead of expropriation a more limited concept ought to be used—"confiscation," for we are definitely against any payment of compensation. We shall never stop at confiscation of land. But laying aside these isolated corrections, our resolution, as we can see, in no way amends the agrarian programme. All Social-Democratic writers have always expressed the view that the point concerning cut-off lands by no means marks the limits of the peasant movement, by no means curtails or restricts it. Both Plekhanov and myself have declared in the press that the Social-Democratic Party will never dissuade the peasantry from taking revolutionary measures to effect agrarian reforms down to a "black redistribution."[14] Hence we are not amending our agrarian programme. We must now resolutely state our position on the practical issue of support to the peasants to the very end, so as to eliminate any possibility of misunderstanding and misrepresentation. The peasant movement now stands on the order of the day, and the Party of the proletariat must officially declare that it gives this movement its full support and in no way limits its scope.

Further the resolution speaks of the need to pay particular attention to the interests of the rural proletariat and to organize them separately. There is no need to defend

this elementary truth before a gathering of Social-Democrats. The desirability of adding a point on support to agricultural labourers' and peasants' strikes especially during the harvest, haymaking season, etc., was brought up
in the agrarian committee. One cannot of course have
anything against this in principle. Let our practical workers say what they think of the possible significance of
such a point in the immediate future.

The resolution then goes on to deal with the formation
of revolutionary peasant committees.

The idea that the demand for the immediate establishment of revolutionary peasant committees should be made
the central issue in our agitation was developed in greater detail in *Vperyod* No. 15. Even the reactionaries now
talk about "improving the living conditions," but their
way of effecting what they call improvements is the official, bureaucratic way, whereas the Social-Democrats
must of course stand for the revolutionary way. The main
task is to make the peasant movement a politically conscious movement. The peasants have a vague idea of what
they need, but they do not see the connection between the
general political order and their wishes and demands.
Because of this political double-dealers find them easiest
of all to deceive by propounding instead of political changes
economic "improvements" which cannot be realized in
practice without the political changes. Hence the slogan
concerning revolutionary peasant committees is the only
correct one. Unless these committees exercise their revolutionary rights the peasants will never be able to retain
what they are gaining today. The objection has been raised
that here too we are amending the agrarian programme,
which contains no mention of *revolutionary* peasant committees or their tasks in the sphere of democratic changes.
This objection is not justified. We are not amending our
programme, but applying it to the given concrete instance.
Once there is no doubt that peasant committees cannot be anything but revolutionary in the given conditions,
we are not changing the programme but applying it to a
revolutionary moment when we point this out. Our programme declares, for instance, that we recognize the self-

determination of nations; if a concrete situation were to prompt us to declare for the self-determination of a particular nation, for its full independence, this would be applying, not amending the programme. Peasant committees are a flexible institution suitable both in the present conditions and, say, after the establishment of a provisional revolutionary government when these committees would become its organs. It has been said that these committees might turn out to be reactionary, not revolutionary. We, Social-Democrats, however, have never forgotten the dual nature of the peasant or the possibility of a reactionary peasant movement against the proletariat. This is not the issue now; the fact remains that at the present time the peasant committees, set up to sanction land reforms, can only be revolutionary. At the present time the peasant movement is unquestionably revolutionary. It has been said that having seized the land, the peasants will calm down. This is possible. But the autocratic government will not be able to calm down if the peasants seize the land, and this is the crux of the matter. Only a revolutionary government or revolutionary peasant committees can sanction such seizure.

Lastly, the concluding section of the resolution once again defines the stand of the Social-Democrats in the peasant committees, namely, the need to go with the rural proletariat and organize it separately and independently. In the countryside, too, only the proletariat can be the consistently revolutionary class.

First published in 1905 in
*Third Congress of the R.S.D.L.P.*
*Complete Text of Proceedings*
The Publishing House of the
Central Committee, Geneva

Vol. VIII, pp. 368-72

# TWO TACTICS OF SOCIAL-DEMOCRACY IN THE DEMOCRATIC REVOLUTION

## (Excerpts)

### 10. "REVOLUTIONARY COMMUNES" AND THE REVOLUTIONARY-DEMOCRATIC DICTATORSHIP OF THE PROLETARIAT AND THE PEASANTRY

The conference of the new *Iskra*-ists[15] did not keep to the anarchist position into which the new *Iskra* had talked itself (only "from below," not "from below and from above"). The absurdity of admitting the possibility of an insurrection and not admitting the possibility of victory and participation in a provisional revolutionary government was too glaring. The resolution therefore introduced certain reservations and restrictions into the solution of the question proposed by Martynov and Martov. Let us consider these reservations as stated in the following section of the resolution:

"These tactics" ("to remain the party of extreme revolutionary opposition") "do not, of course, in any way exclude the expediency of a partial and episodic seizure of power and the establishment of revolutionary communes in one or another city, in one or another district, exclusively for the purpose of helping to spread the insurrection and of disrupting the government."

That being the case, it means that in principle they admit the possibility of action not only from below, but also from above. It means that the proposition laid down in L. Martov's well-known article in *Iskra* (No. 93) is discarded, and that the tactics of *Vperyod*, i.e., not only "from below," but also "from above," are acknowledged as correct.

Further, the seizure of power (even if partial, episodic, etc.) obviously presupposes the participation not only of Social-Democrats and not only of the proletariat. This follows from the fact that it is not only the proletariat that is interested and takes an active part in a democratic revolution. This follows from the fact that the insurrection is a "popular" one, as is stated in the beginning of the resolution we are discussing, that "non-proletarian groups" (the words used in the conference resolution on the uprising), i.e., the bourgeoisie, also take part in it. Hence, the principle that any participation of Socialists in a provisional revolutionary government jointly with the petty bourgeoisie is treachery to the working class *was thrown overboard by the conference*, which is what *Vperyod* sought to achieve. "Treachery" does not cease to be treachery because the action which constitutes it is partial, episodic, local, etc. Hence, the parallel drawn between the participation in a provisional revolutionary government and vulgar Jaurèsism *was thrown overboard* by the conference, which is what *Vperyod* sought to achieve. A government does not cease to be a government because its power does not extend to many cities but is confined to a single city, does not extend to many districts but is confined to a single district; not because of the name that is given to it. Thus, *the formulation of the principles of this question* which the new *Iskra* tried to give *was discarded by the conference.*

Let us see whether the restrictions imposed by the conference on the formation of revolutionary governments and participation in them, which is now admitted in principle, are reasonable. What difference is there between the concept "episodic" and the concept "provisional," we do not know. We are afraid that this "new" and foreign word is merely a screen for lack of clear thinking. It *seems* "more profound," but actually it is only more obscure and confused. What is the difference between the "expediency" of a partial "seizure of power" in a city or district, and participation in a provisional revolutionary government of the entire state? Do not "cities" include a city like St. Petersburg, where the events of January 9 took place?[16]

Do not districts include the Caucasus, which is bigger than many a state? Will not the problems (which at one time vexed the new *Iskra*) of what to do with the prisons, the police, public funds, etc., etc., confront us the moment we "seize power" in a single city, let alone in a district? No one will deny, of course, that if we lack sufficient forces, if the insurrection is not wholly successful, or if the victory is indecisive, it is possible that provisional revolutionary governments will be set up in separate localities, in individual cities and the like. But what is the point of such an assumption, gentlemen? Do not you yourselves speak in the beginning of the resolution about a "decisive victory of the revolution," about a "victorious popular insurrection"?? Since when have the Social-Democrats taken over the job of the anarchists: to divide the attention and the aims of the proletariat, to direct its attention to the "partial" instead of the general, the single, the integral and complete? While presupposing the "seizure of power" in a city, you yourselves speak of "spreading the insurrection"—to another city, may we venture to think? to all cities, may we dare to hope? Your conclusions, gentlemen, are as unsound and haphazard, as contradictory and confused as your premises. The Third Congress of the R.S.D.L.P. gave an exhaustive and clear answer to the question of a provisional revolutionary government in general. And this answer covers all cases of local provisional governments as well. The answer given by the conference, however, by artificially and arbitrarily singling out a *part* of the question, merely *evades* (but unsuccessfully) the issue as a whole, and creates confusion.

What does the term "revolutionary communes" mean? Does it differ from the term "provisional revolutionary government," and, if so, in what respect? The conference gentlemen themselves do not know. Confusion of revolutionary thought leads them, as very often happens, to *revolutionary phrasemongering*. Yes, the use of the words "revolutionary commune" in a resolution passed by representatives of Social-Democracy is revolutionary phrasemongering and nothing else. Marx more than once condemned such phrasemongering, when "fascinating" terms of the *bygone past* were used to hide the tasks of the future. In such cases a fascinating term that has played its part in history becomes futile and pernicious trumpery, a child's rattle. We must give the workers and the whole people a clear and unambiguous explanation as to *why* we want a provisional revolutionary government to be set up, and *exactly what changes* we shall accomplish, if we exercise decisive influence on the government, on the very morrow of the victory of the popular insurrection which has already commenced. These are the questions that confront political leaders.

The Third Congress of the R.S.D.L.P. gave perfectly clear answers to these questions by drawing up a complete programme of these changes—the minimum programme[17] of our Party. The word "commune," however, is not an answer at all; it only serves to confuse people by the distant echo of a sonorous phrase, or empty rhetoric. The more we cherish the memory of the Paris Commune of 1871, for instance, the less permissible is it to refer to it offhand, without analyzing its mistakes and the special conditions attending it. To do so would be to follow the absurd example of the Blanquists—whom Engels ridiculed —who (in 1874, in their "Manifesto") paid homage to every act of the Commune. What reply will a conferencer give to a worker who asks him about *this* "revolutionary commune" that is mentioned in the resolution? He will only be able to tell him that this is the name, known in history, of a workers' government that was unable to, and could not at that time, distinguish between the elements of a democratic revolution and those of a socialist revolution, that confused the tasks of fighting for a republic with the tasks of fighting for socialism, that was unable to carry out the task of launching an energetic military offensive against Versailles, that made a mistake in not seizing the Bank of France, etc. In short, whether in your answer you refer to the Paris Commune or to some other commune, your answer will be: it was a government *such as ours should not be.* A fine answer indeed! Does it not testify to pedantic moralizing and impotence on the part of a revolutionary who says nothing about the practical programme of the Party and inappropriately begins to give lessons in history in a resolution? Does this not reveal the very mistake we have unsuccessfully been accused of, i.e., confusing a democratic revolution with a socialist revolution, between which none of the "communes" differentiated?

The aim of a provisional government (so inappropriately termed "commune") is declared to be "exclusively" to spread the insurrection and to disrupt the government. Taken in its literal sense, the word "exclusively" eliminates all other aims; it is an echo of the absurd theory of "only from below." Such elimination of other aims is another instance of short-sightedness and lack of reflection. A "revolutionary commune," i.e., a revolutionary government, even if only in a single city, will inevitably have to administer (even if provisionally, "partly, episodically") *all* the affairs of state, and it is the height of folly to bury one's head in the sand. This government will have to enact an eight-hour working-day, establish workers' inspection of factories, institute free universal education, introduce the election of judges, set up peasant committees, etc.; in a word, it will certainly have to carry out a number of reforms. To designate these reforms as "helping to spread the insurrection" would be playing with words and deliberately causing greater confusion in a matter which requires absolute clarity.

---

The concluding part of the new *Iskra*-ists' resolution does not provide any new material for a criticism of the fundamental trends of "Economism"[18] which has revived in our Party, but it illustrates what has been said from a somewhat different angle.

Here is that part:

"Only in one event should Social-Democracy, on its own initiative, direct its efforts towards seizing power and holding it as long as possible—namely, in the event of the revolution spreading to the advanced countries of Western Europe, where conditions for the achievement of socialism have already reached a certain (?) degree of maturity. In that event the limited historical scope of the Russian revolution can be considerably widened and the possibility of entering the path of socialist reforms will arise.

"By framing its tactics in accordance with the view that, during the whole period of the revolution, the Social-Democratic Party will retain the position of extreme revolutionary opposition to all the governments that may succeed one another in the course of the revolution, Social-Democracy will best be able to prepare itself to utilize governmental power if it falls" (??) "into its hands."

The basic idea here is the one that *Vperyod* has repeatedly formulated, stating that we must not be afraid (as is Martynov) of a complete victory for Social-Democracy in a democratic revolution, i.e., of a revolutionary-democratic dictatorship of the proletariat and the peasantry, for such a victory will enable us to rouse Europe, and the socialist proletariat of Europe, after throwing off the yoke of the bourgeoisie, will in its turn help us to accomplish the socialist revolution. But see how this idea is worsened in the new *Iskra*-ists' rendering of it. We shall not dwell on details—on the absurd assumption that power could "fall" into the hands of a class-conscious party which considers seizure of power harmful tactics; on the fact that in Europe the conditions for socialism have reached not a certain degree of maturity, but are already mature; on the fact that our Party programme does not speak of socialist reforms at all, but only of a socialist revolution. Let us take the principal and basic difference between the idea presented by *Vperyod* and that presented in the resolution. *Vperyod* set the revolutionary proletariat of Russia an active aim: to win the battle for democracy and to use this victory for carrying the revolution into Europe. The resolution fails to grasp this connection between our "decisive victory" (not in the new *Iskra* sense) and the revolution in Europe, and therefore it speaks not about the tasks of the proletariat, not about the prospects of *its* victory, but about one of the possibilities in general: "in the event of the revolution spreading.".... *Vperyod* pointedly and definitely indicated—and this was incorporated in the resolution of the Third Congress of the Russian Social-

Democratic Labour Party—how "governmental power" can and must "be utilized" in the interests of the proletariat, bearing in mind what can be achieved immediately, at the given stage of social development, and what must first be achieved as a democratic prerequisite of the struggle for socialism. Here, also, the resolution hopelessly drags behind when it states: "will be able to prepare itself to utilize," but fails to say *how* it will be able, *how* it will prepare itself, and to utilize *for what*? We have no doubt, for instance, that the new *Iskra*-ists may be "able to prepare themselves to utilize" the leading position in the party; but the point is that the way they have gone about such utilization so far, and their preparations for it up till now, do not hold out much hope of possibility being transformed into reality. . . .

*Vperyod* quite definitely stated wherein lies the real "possibility of holding power"—namely, in the revolutionary-democratic dictatorship of the proletariat and the peasantry, in their joint mass strength, which is capable of outweighing all the forces of counter-revolution, in the inevitable concurrence of their interests as regards *democratic* changes. Here, too, the resolution of the conference gives us nothing positive, but merely evades the question. For the possibility of holding power in Russia must be determined by the composition of the social forces in Russia herself, by the circumstances of the democratic revolution which is now taking place in our country. A victory of the proletariat in Europe (and it is still somewhat of a far cry from carrying the revolution into Europe to the victory of the proletariat) will give rise to a desperate counter-revolutionary struggle on the part of the Russian bourgeoisie—yet the resolution of the new *Iskra*-ists does not say a word about this counter-revolutionary force, the importance of which has been appraised in the resolution of the Third Congress of the R.S.D.L.P. If in our fight for a republic and democracy we could not rely upon the peasantry besides the proletariat, the prospect of our "holding power" would be hopeless. But if it is not hopeless, if a "decisive victory of the revolution over tsarism" opens up such a possibility, then we must point to it, we must ac-

tively call for its transformation into reality and issue
practical slogans not only *for the contingency* of the revolution being carried into Europe, but also *for the purpose* of carrying it there. The reference made by the
*khvostist* Social-Democrats to the "limited historical scope
of the Russian revolution" merely serves to cover up their
limited understanding of the aims of this democratic revolution and of the leading role of the proletariat in this
revolution!

One of the objections raised to the slogan of "the revolutionary-democratic dictatorship of the proletariat and
the peasantry" is that dictatorship presupposes a "single
will" (*Iskra*, No. 95), and that there can be no single will
of the proletariat and the petty bourgeoisie. This objection is unsound, for it is based on an abstract, "metaphysi-
cal" interpretation of the term "single will." There can
be a single will in one respect and not in another. The
absence of unity on questions of socialism and in the
struggle for socialism does not preclude singleness of will
on questions of democracy and in the struggle for a republic. To forget this would be tantamount to forgetting
the logical and historical difference between a democratic
and a socialist revolution. To forget this would be tantamount to forgetting the character of the democratic revolution as a revolution of *the whole people*: if it is "of
the whole people" it means that there *is* "singleness of
will" precisely in so far as this revolution satisfies the
common needs and requirements of the whole people.
Beyond the bounds of democracy there can be no question of the proletariat and the peasant bourgeoisie having a single will. Class struggle between them is inevitable; but it is in a democratic republic that this struggle
will be the most thoroughgoing and widespread struggle
of the people *for socialism*. Like everything else in the
world, the revolutionary-democratic dictatorship of the proletariat and the peasantry has a past and a future. Its
past is autocracy, serfdom, monarchy and privilege. In
the struggle against this past, in the struggle against
counter-revolution, "singleness of will" of the proletariat

and the peasantry is possible, for here there is unity of interests.

Its future is the struggle against private property, the struggle of the wage-worker against the employer, the struggle for socialism. Here singleness of will is impossible.* Here our path lies not from autocracy to a republic but from a petty-bourgeois democratic republic to socialism.

Of course, in actual historical circumstances, the elements of the past become interwoven with those of the future, the two paths cross. Wage-labour, with its struggle against private property, exists under the autocracy as well; it is generated even under serfdom. But this does not in the least prevent us from drawing a logical and historical dividing line between the major stages of development. We all draw a distinction between bourgeois revolution and socialist revolution, we all absolutely insist on the necessity of drawing a most strict line between them; but can it be denied that individual, particular elements of the two revolutions become interwoven in history? Have there not been a number of socialist movements and attempts at establishing socialism in the period of democratic revolutions in Europe? And will not the future socialist revolution in Europe still have to do a very great deal that has been left undone in the field of democracy?

A Social-Democrat must never for a moment forget that the proletariat will inevitably have to wage the class struggle for socialism even against the most democratic and republican bourgeoisie and petty bourgeoisie. This is beyond doubt. Hence the absolute necessity of a separate, independent, strictly class party of Social-Democracy. Hence the temporary nature of our tactics of "striking jointly" with the bourgeoisie and the duty of keeping a strict watch "over our ally, as over an enemy," etc. All this is also beyond the slightest doubt. But it would be

---

* The development of capitalism, which is more widespread and rapid where there is freedom, will inevitably put a speedy end to singleness of will; the sooner counter-revolution and reaction are crushed, the sooner will the singleness of will come to an end.

ridiculous and reactionary to deduce from this that we must forget, ignore or neglect these tasks which, although transient and temporary, are vital at the present time. The fight against the autocracy is a temporary and transient task of the Socialists, but to ignore or neglect this task in any way would be tantamount to betraying socialism and rendering a service to reaction. The revolutionary-democratic dictatorship of the proletariat and the peasantry is unquestionably only a transient, temporary aim of the Socialists, but to ignore this aim in the period of a democratic revolution would be downright reactionary.

Concrete political aims must be set in concrete circumstances. All things are relative, all things flow, and all things change. The programme of the German Social-Democratic Party does not contain the demand for a republic. The situation in Germany is such that this question can in practice hardly be separated from the question of socialism (although even as regards Germany, Engels, in his comments on the draft of the Erfurt Programme in 1891, warned against belittling the importance of a republic and of the struggle for a republic). In the Russian Social-Democratic Party the question of eliminating the demand for a republic from its programme and agitation has never even arisen, for in our country there can be no talk of an indissoluble connection between the question of a republic and the question of socialism. It was quite natural for a German Social-Democrat of 1898 not to put the special question of a republic in the forefront, and this evokes neither surprise nor condemnation. But a German Social-Democrat who in 1848 would have left the question of a republic in the shade would have been a downright traitor to the revolution. There is no such thing as abstract truth. Truth is always concrete.

The time will come when the struggle against the Russian autocracy will end and the period of democratic revolution will be over in Russia; then it will be ridiculous to talk about "singleness of will" of the proletariat and the peasantry, about a democratic dictatorship, etc. When that

time comes we shall attend directly to the question of
the socialist dictatorship of the proletariat and deal with
it at greater length. But at present the party of the advanced class cannot but strive most energetically for a
decisive victory of the democratic revolution over tsarism.
And a decisive victory means nothing else than the revolutionary-democratic dictatorship of the proletariat and
the peasantry.


## NOTE

1) We would remind the reader that in the polemics
between *Iskra* and *Vperyod*, the former referred among
other things to Engels' letter to Turati, in which Engels
warned the (future) leader of the Italian reformists not
to confuse the democratic with the socialist revolution.
The impending revolution in Italy—wrote Engels about
the political situation in Italy in 1894—will be a petty-
bourgeois, democratic and not a socialist revolution. *Iskra*
reproached *Vperyod* with having departed from the principle laid down by Engels. This reproach was unjustified,
because *Vperyod* (No. 14) fully acknowledged, on the
whole, the correctness of Marx's theory of the difference
between the three main forces in the revolutions of the
nineteenth century. According to this theory, the following forces take a stand against the old order,
against the autocracy, feudalism, serfdom: 1) the
liberal big bourgeoisie, 2) the radical petty bourgeoisie, 3) the proletariat. The first fights for nothing more
than a constitutional monarchy; the second, for a democratic republic; the third, for a socialist revolution. To
confuse the petty-bourgeois struggle for a complete democratic revolution with the proletarian struggle for a
socialist revolution spells political bankruptcy for a Socialist. Marx's warning to this effect is quite justified.
But it is precisely for this very reason that the slogan
"revolutionary communes" is erroneous, because the very
mistake committed by the communes that have existed in
history is that they confused the democratic revolution

with the socialist revolution. On the other hand, our slogan—a revolutionary-democratic dictatorship of the proletariat and the peasantry—fully safeguards us against
this mistake. While recognizing the incontestably bourgeois nature of the revolution, which is incapable of *directly* overstepping the bounds of a mere democratic revolution, our slogan *pushes forward* this particular revolution
and strives to mould it into forms most advantageous
to the proletariat; consequently, it strives to make the
very most of the democratic revolution in order to attain
the greatest success in the further struggle of the proletariat for socialism.

### 12. WILL THE SWEEP OF THE DEMOCRATIC REVOLUTION BE DIMINISHED IF THE BOURGEOISIE RECOILS FROM IT?

#### *(Excerpt)*

Have you ever considered, gentlemen, what real social
forces determine "the sweep of the revolution"? Let us
leave aside the forces of foreign politics, of international
combinations, which have turned out very favourably for
us at the present time, but which we all leave out of our
discussion, and rightly so, inasmuch as we are concerned
with the question of the internal forces of Russia. Look at
these internal social forces. Aligned against the revolution are the autocracy, the imperial court, the police, the
bureaucracy, the army, and the handful of high nobility.
The deeper the indignation of the people grows, the less
reliable become the troops, and the more the bureaucracy
wavers. Moreover, the bourgeoisie, on the whole, is now
in favour of the revolution, is zealously making speeches
about liberty, holding forth more and more frequently in
the name of the people, and even in the name of the revolution.* But we Marxists all know from theory and from
daily and hourly observation of our liberals, Zemstvo-ists

* Of interest in this connection is Mr. Struve's open letter to
Jaurès, recently published by the latter in *l'Humanité* and by Mr.
Struve in *Osvobozhdeniye*, No. 72.

and *Osvobozhdentsi*[19] that the bourgeoisie is inconsistent, self-seeking, and cowardly in its support of the revolution. The bourgeoisie, in the mass, will inevitably turn towards counter-revolution, towards the autocracy, against the revolution and against the people, as soon as its narrow, selfish interests are met, as soon as it "recoils" from consistent democracy (*and it is already recoiling from it!*). There remain the "people," that is, the proletariat and the peasantry: the proletariat alone can be relied on to march to the end, for it is going far beyond the democratic revolution. That is why the proletariat fights in the front ranks for a republic and contemptuously rejects silly and unworthy advice to take care not to frighten away the bourgeoisie. The peasantry includes a great number of semi-proletarian as well as petty-bourgeois elements. This causes it also to be unstable and compels the proletariat to unite in a strictly class party. But the instability of the peasantry differs radically from the instability of the bourgeoisie, for at the present time the peasantry is interested not so much in the absolute preservation of private property as in the confiscation of the landed estates, one of the principal forms of private property. While this does not make the peasantry become socialist or cease to be petty-bourgeois, it is capable of becoming a whole-hearted and most radical adherent of the democratic revolution. The peasantry will inevitably become such if only the progress of revolutionary events, which is enlightening it, is not checked too soon by the treachery of the bourgeoisie and the defeat of the proletariat. Subject to this condition, the peasantry will inevitably become a bulwark of the revolution and the republic, for only a completely victorious revolution can give the peasantry *everything* in the sphere of agrarian reforms—*everything* that the peasants desire, of which they dream, and of which they truly stand in need (not for the abolition of capitalism as the "Socialist-Revolutionaries"[20] imagine, but) in order to emerge from the mire of semi-serfdom, from the gloom of oppression and servitude, in order to improve their living conditions as much as it is possible to improve them under the system of commodity production.

Moreover, the peasantry is attached to the revolution not only by the prospect of radical agrarian reform but by its general and permanent interests. Even in fighting the proletariat the peasantry stands in need of democracy, for only a democratic system is capable of giving exact expression to its interests and of ensuring its predominance as the mass, as the majority. The more enlightened the peasantry becomes (and since the war with Japan[21] it is becoming enlightened much more rapidly than those accustomed to measure enlightenment by the school standard suspect), the more consistently and determinedly will it favour a thoroughgoing democratic revolution; for, unlike the bourgeoisie, it has nothing to fear from the supremacy of the people, but, on the contrary, stands to gain by it. A democratic republic will become the ideal of the peasantry as soon as it begins to free itself from its naive monarchism, because the enlightened monarchism of the bourgeois stockjobbers (with an upper chamber, etc.) implies for the peasantry the same disfranchisement and the same downtroddenness and ignorance as it suffers from today, only slightly glossed over with the varnish of European constitutionalism.

That is why the bourgeoisie as a class naturally and inevitably strives to come under the wing of the liberal-monarchist party, while the peasantry, in the mass, strives to come under the leadership of the revolutionary and republican party. That is why the bourgeoisie is incapable of carrying the democratic revolution to its consummation, while the peasantry is capable of doing so, and we must exert all our efforts to help it to do so.

It may be objected: but this requires no proof, this is all ABC; all Social-Democrats understand this perfectly well. But that is not so. It is not understood by those who can talk about "the sweep" of the revolution being "diminished" because the bourgeoisie will fall away from it. Such people repeat the words of our agrarian programme that they have learned by rote without understanding their meaning, for otherwise they would not be frightened by the concept of the revolutionary-democratic dictatorship of the proletariat and the peasantry, which inevitably follows from the entire Marxian world outlook and from our programme; otherwise they would not restrict the sweep of the great Russian revolution to the limits to which the bourgeoisie is prepared to go. Such people defeat their abstract Marxian revolutionary phrases by their concrete anti-Marxian and anti-revolutionary resolutions.

Those who really understand the role of the peasantry in a victorious Russian revolution would not dream of saying that the sweep of the revolution would be diminished when the bourgeoisie recoils from it. For, as a matter of fact, the Russian revolution will begin to assume its real sweep, will really assume the widest revolutionary sweep possible in the epoch of bourgeois-democratic revolution, only when the bourgeoisie recoils from it and when the masses of the peasantry come out as active revolutionaries side by side with the proletariat. In order that it may be consistently carried to its conclusion, our democratic revolution must rely on such forces as are capable of paralyzing the inevitable inconsistency of the bourgeoisie (i.e., capable precisely of "causing it to recoil from the revolution," which the Caucasian adherents of *Iskra* fear so much because of their lack of judgement).

*The proletariat must carry to completion the democratic revolution by allying to itself the mass of the peasantry in order to crush by force the resistance of the autocracy and to paralyze the instability of the bourgeoisie. The proletariat must accomplish the socialist revolution by allying to itself the mass of the semi-proletarian elements of the population in order to crush by force the resistance of the bourgeoisie and to paralyze the instability of the peasantry and the petty bourgeoisie.* Such are the tasks of the proletariat, which the new *Iskra*-ists present so narrowly in all their arguments and resolutions about the sweep of the revolution.

Written in June-July 1905
First published as a separate
pamphlet in July 1905 in Geneva
Vol. IX, pp. 60-69 and 78-81

# THE ATTITUDE OF SOCIAL-DEMOCRACY TOWARD THE PEASANT MOVEMENT

The tremendous importance of the peasant movement in the democratic revolution through which Russia is now passing has been repeatedly explained in the entire Social-Democratic press. As is well known, the Third Congress of the R.S.D.L.P. adopted a special resolution on this question in order to define more exactly and to co-ordinate the activities of the whole party of the class-conscious proletariat precisely with regard to the peasant movement of the present day. Despite the fact that the resolution was prepared in advance (the first draft was published in the *Vperyod*, No. 11, March 10 [23], 1905), despite the fact that it was carefully gone over at the Party Congress, which took pains to formulate the views that had already been established throughout the Russian Social-Democratic movement—in spite of all this, the resolution has caused perplexity among a number of comrades working in Russia. The Saratov Committee has unanimously declared this resolution to be unacceptable (see the *Proletary*,[22] No. 10). Unfortunately, the desire we expressed at the time, to receive an explanation of that verdict, has not been satisfied as yet. All we know is that the Saratov Committee has declared the agrarian resolution passed by the new *Iskra* conference also unaccept-able—hence it is what is common to both resolutions that dissatisfies them, and not what distinguishes one from the other.

New material on this question is provided by a letter we have received from a Moscow comrade (issued in the form of a hectographed leaflet). We publish this letter in full:

## An Open Letter to the Central Committee
## and to the Comrades Working in the Rural Districts

Comrades! The regional organization of the Moscow Committee has definitely taken up work among the peasants. The lack of experience in organizing such work, the special conditions prevailing in the rural districts of Central Russia, and also the lack of clarity in the directives contained in the resolutions of the Third Congress on this question and the almost complete absence of material in the periodical and other press on work among the peasantry, compel us to appeal to the Central Committee to send us detailed directives, covering both the principles and the practical questions involved, while we ask you comrades who are doing similar work to acquaint us with the practical knowledge your experience has given you.

We consider it necessary to inform you about the perplexity that has arisen among us upon perusal of the resolution of the Third Congress "on the attitude toward the peasant movement," and about the organizational plan which we are already beginning to apply in our work in the rural districts.

"§ a) To carry on propaganda among the broad strata of the people to the effect that Social-Democracy sets itself the task of giving most energetic support to all the revolutionary measures undertaken by the peasantry that are capable of improving its position, including confiscation of the land belonging to the landlords, the state, the church, the monasteries, and the imperial family" (from the resolution of the Third Congress of the R.S.D.L.P.).

First of all, it is not made clear in this paragraph how the Party organizations will, or should, carry on their propaganda. Propaganda requires, first and foremost, an organization which is very close to those whom it is intended to propagandize. The question as to whether this organization is to be committees consisting of the rural proletariat, or whether other organizational means of conducting oral and written propaganda may be adopted, is left open.

The same may be said of the promise to render energetic support. To render support, and energetic support at that, is also possible only if local organizations exist. The question of "energetic support" seems to us to be extremely hazy in general. Can Social-Democracy support the expropriation of those landlords' estates which are farmed most intensively, employ machinery, cultivate high-grade crops, etc.? The transfer of such estates to petty-bourgeois proprietors, however important it may be to improve their position, would be a step back from the standpoint of the capitalist development of the given estate. In our opinion, we, as Social-Democrats, should have made a reservation on this point of "support": "provided the expropriation of this land and its transfer to peasant (petty-bourgeois) ownership results in a higher form of economic development on these estates."

Further:

"§ d) To strive for the independent organization of the rural proletariat, for its fusion with the urban proletariat under the banner of the Social-Democratic Party, and for the inclusion of its representatives in the peasant committees."

Doubts arise with regard to the latter part of this paragraph. The fact is that the bourgeois democratic organizations, such as the Peasants' Union[23] and reactionary utopian organizations, such as those of the Socialist-Revolutionaries, organize under their banner both the bourgeois and the proletarian elements of the peasantry. By electing our own representatives of the rural proletarian organizations to such "peasant" committees, we shall be contradicting ourselves, our views regarding entering a bloc, etc.

Here, too, we believe, amendments, and very serious ones, are needed.

These are a few general remarks on the resolutions of the Third Congress. It is desirable to have these analyzed as soon and in as great detail as possible.

As regards the plan for a "rural" organization in our Regional Organization, we are obliged to work under conditions which the resolutions of the Third Congress wholly ignore. First of all, we must note that the territory we cover—the Moscow Gubernia and the adjoining uyezds of the neighbouring gubernias—is mainly an industrial area with a relatively undeveloped system of handicraft industries and with a very small section of the population engaged *exclusively* in agriculture. Huge textile mills, each employing 10,000 to 15,000 workers, are interspersed among small factories employing 500 to 1,000 workers and scattered in out-of-the-way hamlets and villages. One would think that under such conditions Social-Democracy would find a most favourable field for its activity here, but facts have proved that such bird's-eye view premises do not stand criticism. Even now, in spite of the fact that some of the factories have been in existence for 40-50 years, the overwhelming majority of our "proletariat" has not become divorced from the land. The "village" has such a strong hold over it, that none of the psychological and other characteristics which a "pure" proletarian acquires in the course of collective work develop among our proletarians. The farming carried on by our "proletarians" is of a peculiar mongrel type. A weaver employed in a factory hires an agricultural labourer to till his patch of land. His wife (if she is not working in the factory), his children, and the aged and invalid members of the family work on this same piece of land, and he himself will work on it when he becomes old or crippled, or is fired for violent or suspicious behaviour. Such "proletarians" can hardly be called proletarians. Their economic status is that of paupers. In ideology they are petty bourgeois. They are ignorant and conservative. From among them "Black-Hundred"[24] elements are recruited. Lately, however, even among them class-consciousness has begun to awaken. Using "pure" proletarians as footholds, we are endeavouring to rouse these ignorant masses from their age-long slumber, and

not without success. The footholds are increasing in number, and in
places are becoming firmer, the paupers are coming under our influence, are beginning to adopt our ideology, both in the factory and
in the village. And we believe that it will not be unorthodox to form
organizations in an environment that is not "purely" proletarian. We
have no other environment, and if we were to insist on orthodoxy and
organize only the rural "proletariat," we would have to dissolve our'
and neighbouring organizations. We know we shall have difficulties
in combating the burning desire to expropriate the arable and other
land neglected by the landlords, or those lands which the holy fa-
thers in hoods and cassocks have not been able to farm properly. We
know that bourgeois democracy, from the "democratic monarchist" faction (such a faction exists in the Ruza Uyezd) down to the "Peasants'" Union, will fight us for influence among the "paupers," but
we shall arm the latter to oppose the former. We shall make use of
all the Social-Democratic forces in the region, both intellectuals and
proletarian workers, to set up and consolidate our Social-Democratic
committees of "paupers." And we shall do this in accordance with
the following plan. In each uyezd centre, or big industrial centre, we
shall set up uyezd committees of the groups that work under the
Regional Organization. In addition to setting up factory committees
in its district, the uyezd committee will also set up "peasant" committees. For reasons of secrecy, these committees should not be large,
and should consist of the most revolutionary and capable pauperized
peasants. In places where there are both factories and peasants, it
is necessary to organize workers and peasants in a single sub-group
committee.

In the first place, such committees should have a clear and exact
idea of local conditions: A) The agrarian relationships: 1) Peasant
allotments, leases, form of tenure (communal, by households, etc.);
2) The local land: a) to whom it belongs; b) the amount of land;
c) what relation the peasants have to this land; d) on what terms
the land is held; 1) labour rent; 2) exorbitant rent for cut-off lands,
etc.; e) indebtedness to kulaks, landlords, etc. B) Imposts, taxes, the
rate of assessment of peasant and landlord lands respectively. C) Migratory and handicraft industries, passports, winter hiring, etc. D)
Local factories and plants: the working conditions in these: 1) wages,
2) working-day; 3) treatment by the management; 4) housing conditions, etc. E) The administration: the Zemstvo chiefs, the village
elder, the clerk, the volost judges, constables, priest. F) The Zemstvo: the councillors representing the peasants, the Zemstvo employees: the teacher, doctor, libraries, schools, tea-shops. G) Volost assemblies: their composition and procedure. H) Organizations: the
Peasant League, Socialist-Revolutionaries, Social-Democrats.

After acquainting itself with all this data, the Peasant Social-
Democratic Committee must get such decisions passed by the village
assemblies as may be necessitated by any abnormal state of affairs.
Simultaneously with this, such a committee must conduct intense
propaganda and agitation for the ideas of Social-Democracy among
the masses, organize circles, impromptu meetings, mass meetings,

8*

distribute leaflets and other literature, collect money for the Party
and keep in touch with the Regional Organization through the uyezd
group.

If we succeed in setting up a number of such committees the success of Social-Democracy will be assured.

Regional Organizer

It goes without saying that we shall not undertake the
task of working out the detailed practical directives to
which the comrade refers: this is a matter for the comrades
on the spot and for the central body in Russia, which is
guiding the practical work. We propose to take the opportunity presented by our Moscow comrade's interesting
letter to explain the resolution of the Third Congress and
the urgent tasks of the Party in general. It is obvious from
the letter that the perplexity caused by the resolution of
the Third Congress is only partly due to theoretical doubts.
It is also due to a *new* problem, which has not arisen before—the question of the interrelation between the "revolutionary peasant committees" and the "*Social-Democratic
committees*" working among the peasants. The very fact
that this question has been raised testifies to the great
progress Social-Democratic work among the peasants has
made. Relatively detailed questions are already being pushed
into the forefront by the practical requirements of "rural"
agitation, which is becoming a fixed feature and assuming
stable, permanent forms. And the author of the letter keeps
forgetting that when he is blaming the congress resolution for lack of clarity, he is, in fact, seeking an answer to
a question which the Party Congress did not raise and
could not have raised.

For instance, the author is not quite right when he says
that both propagation of our ideas and support for the
peasant movement are possible "only" if we have our organizations in the particular localities. Of course, such
organizations are desirable, and as the work increases
they will become necessary; but such work is possible and
necessary even where no such organizations exist. In all
our activities, even when carried on exclusively among
the urban proletariat, we must never lose sight of the
peasant question and must give wide circulation to the

declaration made by the *whole party of the class-conscious proletariat* as represented by the Third Congress, namely, that we support a peasant uprising. The peasants must learn this—from literature, from the workers, from special organizations, etc. The peasants must learn that the Social-Democratic proletariat, in giving this support, will *not stop* at any form of confiscation of the land (i.e., expropriation without compensation to the owners).

The author of the letter raises a theoretical question in this connection, viz., whether the demand for the expropriation of the big estates and their transfer to "peasant, petty-bourgeois ownership" should not be circumscribed by a special reservation. But by proposing such a reservation the author has arbitrarily limited the purport of the resolution of the Third Congress. There is *not a word* in the resolution about the Social-Democratic Party undertaking to support the transfer of the confiscated land to petty-bourgeois proprietors. The resolution states: we support... "including confiscation," i.e., including expropriation without compensation, but the resolution does not in any way decide to whom the expropriated land is to be given. It was not by chance that the question was left open: it is obvious from the articles in the *Vperyod* (Nos. 11, 12, 15) that it was deemed unwise to decide the question in advance. It was stated there, for instance, that under a democratic republic Social-Democracy cannot pledge itself and tie its hands with regard to the nationalization of the land.

Indeed, unlike the petty-bourgeois Socialist-Revolutionaries, we lay the main emphasis *at the present time* on the revolutionary-democratic aspect of the peasant uprising and the special organization of the rural proletariat into a class party. The crux of the question now is not schemes of "Black Redistribution," or nationalization, but that the peasants should recognize the need of and carry out a *revolutionary* break-up of the old order. That is why the Socialist-Revolutionaries emphasize "socialization," etc., while we lay stress on *revolutionary peasant committees*. Without the latter, we say, no reform will amount to anything. With them and supported by them the *victory of the peasant uprising* is possible.

We must assist the peasant uprising in every way, including confiscation of the land, *but certainly not including all sorts of petty-bourgeois schemes.* We support the peasant movement, insofar as it is a revolutionary-democratic movement. We are making ready (making ready at once, immediately) to fight against it insofar as it becomes reactionary and anti-proletarian. The whole essence of Marxism lies in that double task, which only those who do not understand Marxism can vulgarize or compress into a single and simple task.

Let us take a concrete instance. Let us assume that the peasant uprising has been victorious. The revolutionary peasant committees and the provisional revolutionary government (relying, in part, on these very committees) can proceed to the confiscation of any big property. We are in favour of confiscation, as we have already declared. But to whom shall we recommend that the confiscated land be given? On this question we have not tied our hands nor shall we ever do so by declarations like those rashly proposed by the author of the letter. The author of the letter has forgotten that the resolution of the Third Congress speaks of *"purging the revolutionary-democratic content of the peasant movement of all reactionary admixtures"*— that is one point—and, secondly, of the need *"in all cases and under all circumstances for an independent organization of the rural proletariat."* These are our directives. There will always be reactionary admixtures in the peasant movement, and we declare war on them in advance. Class antagonism between the rural proletariat and the peasant bourgeoisie is inevitable, and we reveal it in advance, explain it *and prepare for the struggle on the basis of it.* One of the immediate causes of such struggle may very well be the question: to whom shall the confiscated land be given, and how? We do not gloss over that question, nor do we promise equal distribution, "socialization," etc. What we do say is: we shall fight this out later on, fight again, on a new field and with other allies: then we shall certainly be with the rural proletariat, with the entire working class *against* the peasant bourgeoisie. In practice, this may mean the transfer of the land to the class of small peasant proprietors—wherever big estates based on bondage and feudal servitude still prevail, where there are as yet no material prerequisites for large-scale socialist production; it may mean nationalization—provided the democratic revolution is completely victorious; or the big capitalist estates may be transferred to *workers' associations*; for from the democratic revolution we shall at once, and just in accordance with the measure of our strength, the strength of the class-conscious and organized proletariat, begin to pass to the socialist revolution. We stand for uninterrupted revolution. We shall not stop half-way. The reason we do not now and immediately promise all sorts of "socialization" is just because we know what is actually required for that task, and do not gloss over but reveal the new class struggle that is maturing within the ranks of the peasantry.

At first we support the peasantry in general against the landlords, support it to the end and by all means, including confiscation, and then (or rather not "then," but at the same time) we support the proletariat against the peasantry in general. To try *now* to calculate what the interrelation of forces will be within the peasantry on "the morrow" of the revolution (the democratic revolution) is sheer utopia. Without descending to adventurism or going against our scientific conscience, without striving for cheap popularity, we can and do say *only one thing*: we shall put every effort into assisting the entire peasantry to make the democratic revolution, *in order thereby to make it easier* for us, the Party of the proletariat, to pass on, as quickly as possible, to the new and higher task—the socialist revolution. We hold forth no promises of harmony, equalization or "socialization" as a result of the victory of the *present* peasant uprising—on the contrary, we "promise" a new struggle, new inequality, a new revolution, toward which we are striving. Our doctrine is not as "sweet" as the fairy-tales of the Socialist-Revolutionaries, but let whoever wants to be fed solely on sweets join the Socialist-Revolutionaries; we shall say to such people: good riddance.

In our opinion this Marxist standpoint also settles the question of the committees. In our opinion *there should be no Social-Democratic peasant* committees: if they are Social-Democratic that means they are not purely peasant committees; if they are peasant committees that means they are not purely proletarian, not Social-Democratic committees. A host of people would like to confuse these two, but we are not of their number. Wherever possible we shall strive to set up *our* committees, committees of the *Social-Democratic Labour Party*. They will be joined by peasants, paupers, intellectuals, prostitutes (a worker recently asked us in a letter why not carry on agitation among prostitutes), soldiers, teachers, workers—in short, *all Social-Democrats and none but Social-Democrats*. These committees will conduct the whole of Social-Democratic work, in its entire scope, striving, however, to organize the rural proletariat separately and particularly, for the Social-Democratic Party is the class party of the proletariat. To consider it "unorthodox" to organize the proletariat which had not entirely freed itself from various survivals of the past is a *great mistake* and we would like to think that the corresponding passages of the letter are due simply to a misunderstanding. The urban and industrial proletariat will inevitably be the basic nucleus of our Social-Democratic Labour Party, but we must attract to it, enlighten, and organize all toilers and all the exploited, as is stated in our programme—all without exception: handicraftsmen, paupers, beggars, servants, tramps, prostitutes—of course, subject to the necessary and obligatory condition that they join the Social-Democratic movement and not that the Social-Democratic movement join them, that they adopt the standpoint of the proletariat and not that the proletariat adopt theirs.

The reader may ask—what is the point, then, of having revolutionary peasant committees? Does this mean that they are not necessary? No, they are necessary. Our ideal is: purely Social-Democratic committees in all rural districts, and then agreement between them and *all* the revolutionary-democratic elements, groups, and circles of the peasantry for the purpose of establishing revolutionary committees. There is a perfect analogy here to the independence of the Social-Democratic Labour Party in the cities and its alliance with all the revolutionary democrats for the purpose of insurrection. We are in favour of a peasant uprising. We are absolutely opposed to the mixing and merging of heterogeneous class elements and heterogeneous parties. We hold that for the purpose of insurrection *Social-Democracy* should push forward the *whole* of revolutionary democracy, should assist the *whole* of it to organize, should *march shoulder to shoulder* with it, but without merging with it, to the barricades in the cities and against the landlords and the police in the villages.

Long live the insurrection in town and country against the autocracy! Long live revolutionary Social-Democracy, the vanguard of the entire revolutionary democracy in the present revolution!

*Proletary,* No. 16,
September 14 (1), 1905

Vol. IX, pp. 207-15

# SOCIALISM,
## PETTY-BOURGEOIS AND PROLETARIAN

In Europe, Marxism has at the present time gained complete supremacy over the various other theories of socialism, and the struggle for the realization of the socialist system is waged almost exclusively as a struggle of the working class led by Social-Democratic parties. But this complete supremacy of proletarian socialism, which is based on the teachings of Marxism, was not established all at once, but only after a lengthy struggle with all kinds of backward teachings—with petty-bourgeois socialism, anarchism, and the like. Some thirty years ago Marxism was not yet supreme even in Germany, where, strictly speaking, transitional, mixed, eclectic views varying between petty-bourgeois and proletarian socialism prevailed. And in the Latin countries, in France, Spain, Belgium, the most widespread teachings among the advanced workers were Proudhonism, Blanquism, and anarchism, all of which obviously expressed the point of view of the petty bourgeois, and not the proletarian.

What caused this rapid and complete victory of Marxism during precisely the last few decades? The whole development of modern societies, both in its economic and political aspect, the entire experience of the revolutionary movement and of the struggle of the oppressed classes confirmed more and more the correctness of the Marxist views. The decline of the petty bourgeoisie inevitably brought with it sooner or later the dying away of all kinds of petty-bourgeois prejudices, while the growth of capitalism and the intensified struggle of the classes within capitalist society served as the best propaganda in favour of the ideas of proletarian socialism.

Russia's backwardness naturally explains the great tenacity with which backward theories of socialism persist
in our country. The whole history of Russian revolutionary
thought for the last quarter of a century is a history of the
struggle of Marxism against petty-bourgeois Narodnik
socialism. And whereas the rapid growth and striking successes achieved by the Russian working-class movement
have already secured the victory of Marxism also in Russia, the development of the undoubtedly revolutionary peasant movement—particularly after the famous revolts of
the peasants in Little Russia in 1902—has, on the other
hand, called forth a certain revival of decrepit, senile
Narodism. Hoary Narodism refurbished with fashionable
European opportunism (revisionism, Bernsteinism, criticism of Marx) composes the entire original ideological
stock-in-trade of the so-called Socialist-Revolutionaries.
Therefore, the peasant question is the pivotal point in the
controversies between Marxists, on the one hand, and Narodniks pure and simple as well as Socialist-Revolutionaries, on the other.

To a certain extent Narodism was an integral and consistent teaching. It denied the domination of capitalism in
Russia; it denied that the role of the factory workers was
that of the advanced fighters of the whole proletariat; it
denied the importance of political revolution and bourgeois
political freedom; it preached direct socialist revolution,
with the peasant community and its small-scale farming as
the starting-point. Now only shreds are left of this integral teaching; but if one is to get an intelligent idea of current disputes and not to allow these disputes to sink to the
level of mere squabbles, one must always bear in mind
the general and fundamental Narodnik *sources* of the
errors committed by our Socialist-Revolutionaries.

The man of the future in Russia is the peasant, the Narodniks thought, a view which inevitably sprang from their
belief in the socialist nature of the commune and their dis-
belief in the destiny of capitalism. The man of the future
in Russia is the worker, the Marxists believe, and the development of Russian capitalism, in both agriculture and
industry, confirms their view more and more. The working-

class movement in Russia has now compelled recognition; but with regard to the peasant movement, the gulf between Narodism and Marxism makes itself felt even today in the different ways in which this movement is *understood*. To the Narodnik the peasant movement is, to all intents and purposes, a refutation of Marxism; it is a movement which stands for direct socialist revolution; it recognizes none of the bourgeois political freedoms; it proceeds not from large-scale, but small-scale farming. In a word, to the Narodnik the peasant movement is a real, truly socialist and directly socialist movement. The belief of the Narodniks in the peasant community and Narodnik anarchism fully explain why these views are inevitable.

To the Marxist the peasant movement is not a socialist, but a democratic movement. It is an essential concomitant of the democratic revolution in Russia, as it was in the other countries, a revolution which is bourgeois in its social-economic content. It is not in the least directed against the foundations of bourgeois order, against commodity economy, against capital. On the contrary, it is directed against the old, serf, precapitalist relations in the countryside, and against the ownership of land by landlords, that being the main prop of all the survivals of serfdom. The complete victory of this peasant movement will, therefore, not do away with capitalism, but, on the contrary, will create a wider basis for its development, will accelerate and intensify purely capitalist development. The complete victory of a peasant uprising can only create a bulwark of the democratic-bourgeois republic, in which the struggle of the proletariat against the bourgeoisie will develop for the first time in its purest form.

And so you have two opposite views, which must be clearly understood by everyone who wants to find his way among the abysmal differences in principle between the Socialist-Revolutionaries and the Social-Democrats. According to the one view, the peasant movement is a socialist movement; according to the other, it is democratic-bourgeois. This reveals the ignorance displayed by our Socialist-Revolutionaries when they repeat a hundred times (compare, for instance, No. 75 of *Revolutsionnaya Rossiya* that the orthodox Marxists at this or that time "ignored" (did not want to know anything about) the peasant question. Such gross ignorance can be combated by only one means: repetition of the ABC, exposition of the old consistently-Narodnik views, pointing out a hundred and a thousand times that the real difference is not whether you want to or do not want to take the peasant question into consideration, not whether you recognize or ignore it, but consists in the *different appraisals* of the present-day peasant movement and the present-day peasant question in Russia. Anyone who says that the Marxists "ignore" the peasant question in Russia is, in the first place, an absolute ignoramus, for all the principal works of the Russian Marxists, beginning with Plekhanov's *Our Differences* (published over twenty years ago), were written, in the main, precisely to explain the erroneous nature of the Narodnik views on the peasant question in Russia. In the second place, anyone who argues that the Marxists "ignore" the peasant question shows his desire to evade a complete assessment of the real difference in principle involved: is the present-day peasant movement democratic-bourgeois or not? Is it, objectively considered, directed against the remnants of serfdom or not?

The Socialist-Revolutionaries have never given, and never can give, a clear and exact answer to this question, because they hopelessly confuse the old Narodnik and the modern Marxist view of the peasant question in Russia. It is precisely because the Socialist-Revolutionaries cannot rid themselves of their petty-bourgeois illusions, of the fantastic notions of Narodism in the appraisal of the peasant movement that the Marxists call them supporters of the point of view of the petty bourgeoisie (ideologists of the petty bourgeoisie).

That is why we have to repeat once more: ABC. What is the goal of the peasant movement today in Russia? Land and freedom. What will be the significance of a complete victory of this movement? After obtaining freedom it will abolish the domination of the landlords and officials in the administration of the state. After obtaining the land it will hand over the land of the landlords to the peasants. Will the most complete freedom and the most complete expropriation of the landlords (taking away the land from them) abolish commodity economy? No, it will not. Will the most complete freedom and the most complete expropriation of the landlords abolish individual peasant farming on the communal land or on "socialized" land? No, it will not. Will the most complete freedom and the most complete expropriation of the landlords bridge the deep gulf that divides the rich peasant with his many horses and his many cows from the farm-labourer, the day-labourer, that is, separates the peasant bourgeoisie and the rural proletariat? No, it will not. On the contrary, the more complete the defeat and destruction of the highest *social estate* (the estate of the landlords) the greater will be the *class* enmity between the bourgeoisie and the proletariat. What will be the significance of a complete victory of the peasant uprising, judged by its objective significance? This victory will utterly destroy all remnants of serfdom but will not at all destroy bourgeois management, will not destroy capitalism, nor the division of society into classes, into rich and poor, into bourgeoisie and proletariat. Why is the present-day peasant movement a democratic-bourgeois movement? Because while abolishing the power of the officials and landlords it establishes a democratic system of society, without altering the bourgeois basis of this democratic society, without abolishing the domination of capital. What should be the attitude of the class-conscious worker, the socialist, to the present-day peasant movement? He should support this movement, help the peasants with all the energy he can command, help them to the utmost to cast off entirely the power of both the officials and the landlords. But at the same time he must explain to the peasants that it is not enough to cast off the rule of the officials and landlords. While casting off this rule one must at the same time prepare to abolish the power of capital, the power of the bourgeoisie. And this requires that the true socialist, that is, the Marxist teaching, should be immediately propagated and that the rural proletarians should be united, cemented, organized for the struggle against the peasant bourgeoisie and the bourgeoisie of all Russia. Can the class-conscious worker forget about the struggle for democracy for the sake of the struggle for socialism, or about the struggle for socialism for the sake of the struggle for democracy? No, the class-conscious worker calls himself a Social-Democrat precisely because he has come to understand the relation between the two struggles. He knows there is no other way to socialism than through democracy, through political freedom. He strives, therefore, for the complete and consistent realization of democracy for the sake of attaining the ultimate goal, socialism. Why are the conditions of the struggle for democracy and of the struggle for socialism not alike? Because the workers are bound to have different allies in the two struggles. The democratic struggle is waged by the workers together with part of the bourgeoisie, particularly the petty bourgeoisie. The socialist struggle is waged by the workers against the whole bourgeoisie. The struggle against the officials and landlords can and must be fought together with the whole peasantry, even the well-to-do and middle peasants. But the struggle against the bourgeoisie, and hence also against the well-to-do peasants, can be fought with prospect of success only together with the rural proletariat.

If we bear in mind all these elementary truths of Marxism, an analysis of which the Socialist-Revolutionaries always prefer to fight shy of, it will be easy for us to evaluate the following "latest" objections they have to Marxism.

"Only Allah knows," exclaims *Revolutsionnaya Rossiya* (No. 75), "why it was necessary first to support the peasantry in general against the landlord, and afterwards (that is, at the same time) support the proletariat against the peasantry in general instead of at once supporting the proletariat against the landlords, and what Marxism has to do with it!"

This is the point of view of the most primitive, childishly naive anarchism. Destroying "at once" every manner of exploitation was long the dream of mankind, a dream that lasted many hundreds and even thousands of years. But this dream remained nothing but a dream until the millions of the exploited began to unite all over the world in order to carry on a firm, staunch, and comprehensive struggle to change capitalist society along the line of the natural development of this society. The dream of socialism was converted into a struggle for socialism by millions of people only when the scientific socialism of Marx linked up the aspiration for this transformation with the struggle of a definite class. Without class struggle socialism is an empty word or a naive dream. But what we in Russia see going on before our eyes is two different struggles waged by two different social forces. The proletariat fights the bourgeoisie wherever there are capitalist relations of production (and they exist—for the information of our Socialist-Revolutionaries—even within the peasant community, that is, on the most "socialized" land there is, from their point of view). The peasantry, as a stratum of small landowners, of petty bourgeois, fights against all remnants of serfdom, against the officials and landlords. Only people wholly unacquainted with political economy and the history of revolutions all over the world can fail to see these two different, heterogeneous social wars. To close one's eyes to the heterogeneity of these wars by using the handy words "at once" means to bury one's head in the sand and refuse to make any analysis of reality.

As the view of the old Narodism had ceased to be an integral whole to the Socialist-Revolutionaries, they forgot much even of what the Narodniks themselves had taught. "In helping the peasantry to expropriate the landlords," *Revolutsionnaya Rossiya* writes, *ibid.*, "Mr. Lenin unconsciously assists in the establishment of a petty-bourgeois economy on the ruins of what already are more or less developed forms of capitalist agriculture. Is this not a step back from the point of view of orthodox Marxism?"

Shame on you, gentlemen! Why, you forgot your Mr. V. V.! Consult his *Destiny of Capitalism*, the *Outlines* by Mr. Nikolai—on,[25] and other sources of your wisdom. You will then recall that landlord economy in Russia combines features of capitalism and serfdom. You will then learn that there is a labour-rent system of economy, that direct survival of serf labour. If, in addition, you take a look in so orthodox-Marxian a book as the third volume of Marx's

*Capital* you will learn that the development of serf economy and its conversion into capitalist economy did not and
could not proceed anywhere otherwise than through the
agency of petty-bourgeois peasant economy. You pick too
simple, too discredited a way of making mincemeat of
Marxism: you ascribe to Marxism a view that is so over-
simplified as to be a caricature—direct substitution of
large-scale capitalist economy for large-scale serf economy! You reason: landlord crops are bigger than peasant
crops, hence expropriation of the landlords is a step back.
Such reasoning befits a fourth-grade schoolboy. Just think
a bit, gentlemen; was it not a "step back" when the low-
yield peasant lands were separated from the high-yield
landlord lands at the time of the fall of serfdom?

Modern landlord economy in Russia combines features
of capitalism and serfdom. The present-day struggle of the
peasants against the landlords is, in its objective significance, a struggle against the remnants of serfdom. But
anyone who expects Marxists to try to enumerate every
single instance, weigh it and determine with the exactness
of an apothecary's scale where serfdom ends and pure capitalism begins, would be ascribing to them his own
pedantry. We cannot figure out what part of the price paid
for supplies bought from a small shopkeeper represents
labour value and what part is swindle, etc. Does this
mean, gentlemen, that the theory of labour value has to be
jettisoned?

Modern landlord economy combines features of capitalism and serfdom. From this only pedants can conclude that
it is our duty to weigh, compute, and register every minor
feature in each individual case, according to its particular
social character. From this only utopians can conclude that
it is "pointless" to differentiate between the two heterogeneous social wars. From this the following, and only the
following, conclusion ought to be drawn: that both in our
programme and our tactics we should combine the purely
proletarian struggle against capitalism with the all-democratic (and all-peasant) struggle against serfdom.

The more powerfully the capitalist features are developed
in modern landlord, semi-serf economy the more urgent

is the necessity of immediately organizing the rural proletariat as an independent body, because the sooner will
the purely capitalist or purely proletarian antagonism become apparent whenever a confiscation is made. The more
powerful the capitalist features in landlord economy the
sooner will democratic confiscation give impetus to a real
struggle for socialism—and hence the greater the danger
of a false idealization of the democratic revolution, an
idealization brought about with the aid of the convenient
word "socialization." That is the conclusion that follows
from a confusion of capitalism and serfdom in landlord
economy.

And so the purely proletarian struggle must be combined
but not confused with the all-peasant struggle. We must
support the all-democratic and all-peasant struggle without
in the least fusing with this non-class struggle, without in
the least idealizing it by the use of false catchwords like
socialization, without in the least forgetting even for a
moment the need to organize both the urban *and the rural*
proletariat into the completely independent class party of
Social-Democracy. While upholding the most resolute democracy to the very end this party will not permit itself to
be diverted from its revolutionary course by reactionary
dreams of, and experiments in the creation of "equalitarianism" in commodity economy. The struggle of the
peasants against the landlords is at present revolutionary,
the confiscation of the landlord lands at the present moment of economic and political evolution is in all respects
revolutionary, and we support this revolutionary-democratic measure. But to call this measure "socialization," to deceive oneself and the people with regard to the possibility
of "equalitarian" land tenure under commodity economy is
a reactionary petty-bourgeois utopia, which we leave to
the Socialist-Reactionaries.

*Proletary*, No. 24,
November 7 (October 25),
1905

Vol. IX, pp. 407-15

# THE PROLETARIAT AND THE PEASANTRY

The Congress of the Peasants' Union now in session in Moscow once again places the vital question of the attitude of the Social-Democrats to the peasant movement on the order of the day. This question has always been a vital one for Russian Marxists in defining their programme and tactics. Already in the first draft of the programme of the Russian Social-Democrats, which was printed abroad in 1884 by the Emancipation of Labour group, the peasant question was dealt with as a cardinal issue.

Since then there has not been a single major Marxist work dealing with general questions or a single Social-Democratic printed organ which has not repeated, developed, or applied to definite cases Marxist views and slogans.

Now the peasant movement has become a pressing question not only in the theoretical but also in the most direct practical sense. Our general slogans must now be translated into direct calls addressed by the revolutionary proletariat to the revolutionary peasantry. The time has arrived when the peasantry is coming out as a conscious shaper of a new mode of life in Russia. And the course and outcome of the great Russian revolution depend in tremendous measure on the growth of the peasants' consciousness.

What does the peasantry expect of the revolution? What can the revolution give the peasantry? Every person who engages in political activity, and especially every class-conscious worker, who goes in for politics not in the sense vulgarized by bourgeois politicians, but in the best sense of the word, must answer these two questions.

The peasantry wants land and freedom. There can be no two opinions on this score. All class-conscious workers give their full support to the revolutionary peasantry. All class-conscious workers want the peasantry to receive all the land and full freedom, and are working toward this

9*

end. To demand all the land means not to be satisfied with
any partial concessions and handouts, to strive not for
compromise between the peasantry and the landlords, but
for the abolition of landed estates. The party of the class-
conscious proletariat, the Social-Democrats, have most
vigorously proclaimed this view: at its Third Congress held
in May this year, the R.S.D.L.P. adopted a resolution directly declaring for support of the peasants' revolutionary
demands, *including confiscation* of *all* privately-owned
lands. This resolution clearly shows that the party of class-
conscious workers supports the peasants' demand for all the
land. And in *this* respect the purport of the resolution
adopted at the conference of the other half of our party
fully coincides with that of the resolution passed by the
Third Congress of the R.S.D.L.P.

"Full freedom" means election of officials and other office-holders who administer public and state affairs. "Full
freedom" means the complete abolition of a state administration that is not wholly and exclusively dependent on
the people, that is not elected by the people, responsible to
the people, and within the powers of the people to change.
"Full freedom" means that it is not the people who should
be subordinated to the officials, but the officials who should
be subordinated to the people.

Of course not all peasants fighting for land and freedom
are fully aware of the purport of their struggle and go as
far as to demand a republic. But for all that the democratic trend of the peasants' demands is beyond all doubt.
Hence the peasantry can be certain that the proletariat will
support these demands. The peasants must know that the
red flag that has been raised in the cities is the flag of
struggle not only for the immediate and vital demands of
the industrial and rural workers, but also for the demands of
the millions and tens of millions of small tillers of the soil.

Survivals of serfdom in every possible form and shape
lay to this day a ruthless yoke on the peasant masses as a
whole, and the proletarians under their red flag have declared war on this yoke.

But the red flag not only signifies proletarian support of
the peasants' demands. It also stands for the independent

demands of the proletariat. It stands not only for struggle for land and freedom, but also for struggle against all exploitation of man by man, struggle against the poverty of the masses, against the rule of capital. And it is here that we are faced with the second question: What can the revolution give the peasantry? Many sincere friends of the peasants (the Socialist-Revolutionaries, for instance, among them) ignore this question, do not realize its importance. They think it is sufficient to raise and settle the question of what the peasants want, to get the answer—land and freedom. This is a big mistake. Full freedom, the election of all officials all the way to the head of the state, would not do away with the rule of capital, would not abolish the wealth of the few and the poverty of the masses. Complete abolition of private property in land too would do away with neither the rule of capital nor the poverty of the masses. Even on land belonging to the whole nation, only those with capital of their own, only those who have the implements, livestock, machines, stocks of seed, financial resources in general, etc., will be able to farm independently. And he who has nothing but his hands will inevitably remain a slave of capital even in a democratic republic, even when the land belongs to the whole nation. The idea that "socialization" of land can be effected without socialization of capital, that equalitarian use of land is possible while capital and commodity economy exist, is a delusion. In nearly all countries of Europe socialism has experienced periods when this or some similar delusion has been prevalent. The experience of working-class struggle in all countries has shown in practice how dangerous such a delusion is, and now the Socialist proletarians of Europe and America have completely rid themselves of it.

Thus the red flag of the class-conscious workers signifies, firstly, that we give every support to the peasants' struggle for full freedom and all the land; secondly, it signifies that we do not stop at this, but forge on farther. We are waging besides the struggle for freedom and land a fight for socialism. The fight for socialism is fight against the rule of capital. It is conducted primarily by the wage-workers, who are directly and wholly dependent on capital. As for small holders, some of them own capital of their own and frequently exploit the workers. Hence, not all small peasants will join the ranks of fighters for socialism; but only those do who resolutely and consciously come over to the workers' side against capital, the side of public property against private property.

That is why the Social-Democrats say they are fighting together with the entire peasantry against the landlords and officials, besides which they—the urban and rural proletarians together—are fighting against capital. The struggle for land and freedom is a democratic struggle. The struggle to abolish the rule of capital is a socialist struggle.

Let us then send our fervent greetings to the Peasants' Union, which has decided to stand together and fight staunchly, selflessly and inflexibly for full freedom and all the land. These peasants are true democrats. We must explain to them patiently and consistently where their views on the tasks of democracy and socialism are erroneous, regarding them as allies with whom we are united by the great common struggle. These peasants are truly revolutionary democrats with whom we must and shall carry on the fight for the complete victory of the present revolution. We give our fullest support to the plan for a general strike and the decision to rise together the next time, with the urban workers and all the peasant poor acting in unison. All class-conscious workers will exert every effort to help carry out this plan. Yet no alliance, even with the most honest and determined revolutionary democrats, will ever make the proletarians forget the still greater and more important goal they have set themselves—the fight for socialism, for the complete abolition of the rule of capital, for the emancipation of all working people from every kind of exploitation. Forward, workers and peasants, to joint struggle for land and freedom! Forward, proletarians, united by international Social-Democracy, to the fight for socialism!

*Novaya Zhizn*, No. 11,
November 12, 1905
Vol. X, pp. 22-25

# REVISION OF THE AGRARIAN PROGRAMME
## OF THE WORKERS' PARTY

*(Excerpt)*

### IV. THE AIMS OF OUR AGRARIAN PROGRAMME

The question of the agrarian programme of the R.S.D.L.P. would become considerably clearer if we were to try setting it forth in the shape of simple and clear advice which the Social-Democrats should give to the proletariat and peasantry in the period of the democratic revolution.

The first piece of advice is bound to be this: all efforts must be directed to ensuring the full victory of the peasant uprising. Unless this victory is achieved, there cannot be any serious talk of "taking away the land" from the landlords or of establishing a truly democratic state. There is only one slogan that can urge the peasants to rise: confiscation of all landed estates (and by no means alienation in general or expropriation in general without full clarity on the question of compensation), moreover, confiscation by the peasant committees pending the convocation of the constituent assembly.

Any other advice (including Maslov's[26] slogan of "alienation" and his whole municipalization scheme) would amount to urging the solution of the problem not by insurrection, but through a deal with the landlords, a deal with the reactionary central authority; not by revolutionary means, but through bureaucratic channels, for the most democratic regional and Zemstvo organizations cannot but be bureaucratic in comparison with the revolutionary peasant committees, which must at once and on the spot settle accounts with the landlords and assume rights subject to the sanction of a national constituent assembly.

The second piece of advice is bound to be this: without a thorough democratization of the political system, without the establishment of the republic and the realization in practice of government by the people, there can be no question of retaining the gains of the peasant uprising or taking any other step forward. We must formulate this advice of ours to the workers and peasants particularly clearly and precisely, so as to preclude the possibility of the slightest uncertainty, ambiguity, misrepresentation, tacit acceptance of anything so absurd as the possibility of abolishing landlordism while the central authority remains reactionary. And hence, while vigorously propagating our political advice, we must say to the peasant: having taken the land, you must forge ahead, otherwise you will inevitably be defeated and thrown back by the landlords and the big bourgeoisie. It is impossible to gain possession of the land and hold it without further political gains, without dealing another and still more decisive blow at private ownership of land in general. In politics, as in public life as a whole, not to forge ahead means to be thrown back. Either the bourgeoisie, grown stronger as a result of the democratic revolution (which naturally strengthens it), will deprive both the workers and the masses of peasants of all their gains, or the proletariat and the peasant masses will forge their way ahead. And this implies the republic and undivided government by the people. This implies, provided the republic is achieved, the nationalization of all land as the maximum possible of achievement in the bourgeois-democratic revolution and the natural and essential step from the victory of bourgeois democracy toward the beginning of a genuine battle for socialism.

The third and last piece of advice: build up your own organization, you proletarians and semi-proletarians of town and country. Do not place your faith in any petty proprietors, even though they may be small ones, or work themselves. Do not repose your hopes in small farmholds while commodity production remains. The closer the victory of the peasant uprising, the nearer the time when the peasant proprietors will turn against the proletariat, the more pressing the need for an independent proletarian organization, the more energetically, insistently, resolutely, and loudly must we urge a complete socialist revolution. We shall support the peasant movement to the end, but we must remember that this is a movement of another class, *not* of the class which can and will carry out the socialist revolution. Because of this we leave aside the question of what to do with the land in the sense of its distribution as the object of husbandry, for within the framework of the bourgeois society, this question can be decided, and will be decided, only by the proprietors, big and small. We are interested wholly (and after the victory of the peasant uprising will be interested almost exclusively) in the question of what the rural proletariat is to do. We are concerned, and shall continue to concern ourselves, mainly with this question, leaving the ideologists of the petty bourgeoisie to exercise their imagination on equalitarian land tenure and the like. Our reply to this, the fundamental question of the new, bourgeois-democratic Russia is: the rural proletariat must organize independently together with the urban proletariat in order to fight for a complete socialist revolution.

Consequently, our agrarian programme should consist of three basic parts: firstly, a formulation of the most resolute call to revolutionary action on the part of the peasantry against landlord land tenure; secondly, a precise definition of the next step the movement can and must take to consolidate the gains of the peasants and to pass over from the victory of democracy to the direct struggle of the proletariat for socialism; thirdly, an exposition of the proletarian class aims of the party, which confront us all the more imperatively and demand clear formulation all the more insistently as the victory of the peasant uprising approaches.

Maslov's programme does not provide the solution for a single one of the basic tasks which the R.S.D.L.P. must now solve. It does not advance a slogan that could set the peasant movement on the road to victory, now, without delay, in this epoch of the most anti-democratic state; it does not give an exact definition of the political reforms necessary for the completion and consolidation of the agrarian reforms; it does not indicate the measures that have to be taken in the field of land reform when the fullest and most consistent democracy is achieved; it does not set forth the proletarian stand of our Party in regard to all bourgeois-democratic reforms. This programme defines neither the prerequisites of the "first step" nor the tasks of the "second step"; instead it mixes up everything in one tangle, beginning with the transfer of lands belonging to the royal family to a non-existent "democratic state" and down to the transfer of the landlord holdings into the hands of democratic municipalities for fear of the non-democratic character of the central authority! Being non-revolutionary as regards its practical significance at the present moment and based on anticipation of a completely artificial and completely incredible deal with a semi-reactionary central authority, this programme cannot serve as a guide to a workers' party, no matter which of the possible and conceivable courses of development the democratic revolution in Russia may take.

To sum up, the only correct programme in the conditions of the democratic revolution is this: we must demand at once, and without any limiting reservations, confiscation of the landlord holdings and the establishment of peasant committees.* This demand is a revolutionary one and advantageous from the viewpoint of both the proletariat and the peasantry under all, even the worst, conditions. This demand will inevitably bring about the collapse of the police state and strengthening of democracy.

But confiscation is not enough. In the period of the democratic revolution and the peasant uprising we can by no

---

* Like X, Maslov "sees a contradiction in the fact that we demand abolition of estates and the establishment of peasant committees, that is, committees of a particular estate. Actually the contradiction is only a seeming one: to abolish estates the 'dictatorship' of the lowest, oppressed estate is required, just as the dictatorship of the proletariat is necessary for the abolition of classes in general, the proletariat as a class included. Our entire agrarian programme aims at the abolition of serf and estate traditions in the sphere of agrarian relations, and to bring this about one can appeal only to the lowest estate, to those who are oppressed by these survivals of the serf system." Lenin, "Reply to X," p. 29.

means unconditionally reject nationalization of the land. It is only necessary to qualify this demand by definite stipulation of the political system in the absence of which nationalization might be detrimental to the proletariat and peasantry.

Such a programme would be complete and comprehensive. It would provide for the absolute maximum that can in general be envisaged in any bourgeois-democratic revolution. It would not tie the Social-Democrats' hands, allowing as it does for either distribution or nationalization depending on the political situation. In no case would it cause a rift between the peasantry and the proletariat as champions of democracy.* It would set forth now, immediately, in the present political conditions of police-autocratic rule, slogans that are unquestionably revolutionary and capable of revolutionizing these conditions; moreover, it would advance further demands in the event of the complete victory of the democratic revolution, i.e., in the event of a situation when the consummation of the democratic revolution opens new prospects and poses new tasks.

It is absolutely necessary to give in the programme an exact definition of our specifically proletarian stand in regard to the democratic agrarian revolution as a whole. We need not be reluctant to do so on the grounds that this should go into the resolution on tactics, or that it is a repetition of what has been said in the preamble to the programme.

It is worth sacrificing strict thematic division into programme and tactical issues for the sake of making our position clear and elucidating it to the masses.

We now submit a corresponding draft of the agrarian programme drawn up by the majority of the Agrarian

---

* In order to preclude any idea that the workers' party is seeking to impose reform projects of any kind on the peasantry without regard for its desires, without regard for the independent movement within the peasantry, *Variant A* is appended to the draft programme. This variant, instead of advancing the direct demand of nationalization, first declares that the Party will support the striving of the revolutionary peasantry for abolition of private property in land.

Commission (the Agrarian Commission was appointed by the Joint Central Committee of the R.S.D.L.P. to draft a new agrarian programme).

## V. DRAFT AGRARIAN PROGRAMME

With a view to abolishing the survivals of serfdom which place a heavy burden directly on the peasants, and in the interest of unhampered development of the class struggle in the countryside, the Party demands:

1) confiscation of all church, monastery, appanage, state, crown, and landlord lands;

2) establishment of peasant committees to abolish at once every trace of landlord authority and privilege and to take actual charge of the confiscated lands pending the institution of a new system of land tenure by the national constituent assembly;

3) abolition of the poll-tax and all other duties now levied on the peasantry as a poll-tax-paying estate;

4) repeal of all laws restricting the rights of the peasant to dispose of his land;

5) empowering of elected people's judges to reduce excessive rents and to annul enslaving contracts.

If the decisive victory of the present revolution in Russia fully ensures government by the people, i.e., establishes a republic and a completely democratic state system, the Party will* work for the abolition of private property in land and the transfer of all land to common ownership by the whole people.

Moreover, the Russian Social-Democratic Labour Party, whenever and whatever democratic agrarian reforms are carried out, makes it its aim steadfastly to strive for independent class organization of the rural proletariat, to explain to them the irreconcilable antagonism of their in-

---

\* Variant A:
    ... the party will support the striving of the revolutionary peasantry for abolition of private property in land and work for the transfer of all land to state ownership.

terests and the interests of the peasant bourgeoisie, to
warn them against illusory faith in the small-holding
system, which can never, so long as commodity production exists, do away with the poverty of the masses, and,
finally, to point to the need for a complete socialist revolution as the only way to abolish all poverty and all exploitation.


Written in the second half of
March 1906
Published early in April 1906
as a separate pamphlet by the
Nasha Mysl Publishers

Vol. X, pp. 167-74

# CONCLUDING SPEECH ON THE AGRARIAN QUESTION DELIVERED AT THE FOURTH (UNITY) CONGRESS OF THE R.S.D.L.P.

I submit two basic premises: 1) the peasants will never want municipalization; 2 )without a democratic republic, without fully guaranteed government by the people, without elections of officials, municipalization is harmful. To develop these premises, I shall dwell first on the more serious objections raised to nationalization. Undoubtedly, one of these more serious objections is that made by Comrade Plekhanov. Comrade Plekhanov said literally this—I wrote down his words: "Under no circumstances can we support nationalization." This is an erroneous view. I take it upon myself to declare that if the peasant revolution really takes place in our country and if the political revolution accompanying it leads to the establishment of a genuinely democratic republic, Comrade Plekhanov will find it possible to support nationalization, and that if the coming revolution in Russia really were to bring about the democratic republic, the entire situation, both domestic and international, would impel us to go on to nationalization. If, on the other hand, this condition is not created, then, too, municipalization will prove a fiction; it could be realized only as a new form of compensation to the landlords. Comrade John uses the term alienation instead of confiscation, and as could be seen from his speech, he uses this term not by chance; yet the term comes straight from the Constitutional Democrats, it can imply anything under the sun, and it is fully in agreement with the compensation scheme projected by the Constitutional Democrats. Let us proceed further. Comrade Plekhanov asked what guarantee there was against restoration. I do not think that this question has a close and direct bearing on the programme we are examining, but since it has been raised, it has to be answered definitely and unequivocally. If we have in mind a real, fully effective economic guarantee against restoration, i.e., a guarantee that would create the economic conditions that would preclude restoration, then we have to say: the only guarantee against restoration is socialist revolution in the West; there can be no other guarantee in the real and full meaning of the word. Without this condition, if the question is solved in any other way (municipalization, distribution of land, etc.), restoration is not only possible, but inevitable. I would put it this way: the Russian revolution has enough forces of its own to be victorious, but not enough under any circumstances to retain and consolidate its gains. It cannot do this unless there is a socialist revolution in the West; without this prerequisite restoration is inevitable irrespective of whether you have municipalization, nationalization or a distribution of the land, for the petty proprietor, whatever the forms of ownership and property, will support restoration. After the complete victory of the democratic revolution the petty proprietor will inevitably turn against the proletariat as soon as all the common enemies of the proletariat and the petty proprietors have been swept aside—namely, the capitalists, landlords, finance bourgeoisie, etc. Our democratic republic has no reserve to fall back on except the socialist proletariat in the West, and in this connection we must not ignore the fact that classical bourgeois revolution in Europe, and by that I mean the great French revolution in the eighteenth century, proceeded in an international situation entirely different from that in which the Russian revolution is taking place. France at the end of the eighteenth century was surrounded by feudal and semi-feudal states. Twentieth-century Russia, which is carrying out a bourgeois revolution, is surrounded by countries in which the socialist proletariat stands fully prepared on the threshold of its final conflict with the bourgeoisie. If such relatively insignificant developments as the October 17 promise by the

tsar of freedom in Russia greatly spurred on the proletarian movement in Western Europe—if the St. Petersburg report on the notorious constitutional manifesto was
enough to make the Austrian workers come out in the
streets at once, to set off a series of demonstrations and
armed clashes in the leading industrial cities of Austria,
one can well imagine how the international socialist proletariat would react if they learned not of a promise of
freedom in Russia, but of the actual realization of that
freedom and the complete victory of the revolutionary
peasantry. If we raise the question of guarantees against
restoration from another angle, that is, if we speak of a
relative and conditional guarantee against restoration,
we must say this: the only conditional and relative
guarantee against restoration is that the revolution be
carried out with the utmost resolve, that it be carried out
directly by a revolutionary class, with the participation
of the fewest possible intermediaries, opportunists and
conciliators of all kinds, that this revolution be really
carried to its consummation; if this is done my project
provides the maximum guarantees against restoration.

In my project the peasant committees are advanced as a
direct lever and the most desirable form of the revolutionary peasant movement. When translated into simple
language, the peasant committees mean calling upon the
peasants to deal with the officialdom and the landlords
themselves, directly and without delay, in the most decisive manner. To speak of peasant committees means
urging a people oppressed by survivals of serfdom and
police rule to deal with these survivals in a "plebeian"
manner, as Marx put it. This premise of a revolution
carried to completion and resulting in the election of
officials by the people reminded Comrade Plekhanov of
anarchism, which is so distasteful to him, as to all the rest
of us, yet it is most curious that the election of officials by
the people could even suggest anarchism; it is most
curious that at a time like the present the question of popular election of officials should or could elicit a smile
from any Social-Democrat, with the exception perhaps of
Bernstein. Just now we are living through a time when

this slogan—election of officials by the people—acquires the most direct, tremendous practical significance. All our activity, propaganda and agitation among the peasant masses must consist in large measure of the propaganda, dissemination and popularization of this very slogan. To advocate the peasant revolution, to speak in any serious-ness of the agrarian revolution and at the same time not to speak of the need for real democracy, that is, of the election of officials by the people for one thing, constitutes a crying contradiction. The accusation of anarchism on this score merely reminds me of the German Bernsteinians, who recently engaging in polemics with Kautsky levelled this charge against him.

We must tell the peasant directly and definitely: if you want to carry the agrarian revolution to completion, you must do the same with the political revolution; without carrying the political revolution to consummation there will be either no agrarian revolution of any permanence or none at all. Without a complete democratic revolution, without the election of officials by the people, we shall have either agrarian revolts or agrarian reforms after the Con-stitutional-Democrat pattern. We shall not have anything worthy of the resounding words used by Plekhanov: peasant revolution. Further. Municipalization opens up a wide arena for class struggle, Plekhanov said; I have tried to repeat this assertion of his as literally as possible, and I must emphatically declare that this assertion is utterly *wrong*—wrong from both the political and econom-ic standpoints. Provided the other conditions are equal, the municipality and municipal land ownership afford an un-questionably narrower arena for class struggle than the nation as a whole, than nationalization of the land. Nationalization of the land in a democratic republic would create definitely the broadest field for class struggle—the broadest possible field that is in general conceivable under capitalism. Nationalization means abolition of absolute rent, reduction of the price of grain, maximum freedom of competition and freedom for the penetration of capital into agriculture. Municipalization, on the contrary, narrows down the nation-wide class struggle by not freeing all relations of production in agriculture from absolute rent and by substituting partial demands for our general demand; at any rate municipalization tends to cover up the class struggle. From this point of view the question raised by Plekhanov can be settled in only one way. From this point of view municipalization is absolutely unacceptable. Municipalization means narrowing down and covering up the class struggle.

Plekhanov's next objection concerns the question of seizure of power. He discovered this issue in the draft of my agrarian programme, and I must say that the idea of the revolutionary peasantry taking over power really is contained in my draft agrarian programme; yet it would be the greatest of mistakes to reduce this idea to the Narodnaya Volya[27] view on seizure of power. In the seventies and the eighties, when the Narodnaya Volya cultivated the idea of seizure of power, they constituted only a group of intellectuals, for there was no really wide mass revolutionary movement. Seizure of power was then a desire expressed or a catchword advanced by a handful of intellectuals, and not an inevitable further step of an already developing mass movement. Today, after October, November, and December 1905,[28] after the broad masses of the working class, semi-proletarian elements, and the peasantry have demonstrated to the world forms of revolutionary movement it has not seen for a long time, today, after outbreaks of popular revolutionary struggle for power in Moscow, the South and in the Baltic area—to reduce the idea of conquest of political power by the revolutionary people to the Narodnaya Volya pattern today would mean lagging behind a full twenty-five years, deleting a whole momentous period, from the history of Russia. Plekhanov said: do not fear the agrarian revolution. Yet this fear of the revolutionary peasantry capturing power is nothing but fear of the agrarian revolution. The agrarian revolution is a meaningless phrase if its victory is not understood to mean conquest of power by the revolutionary people. Unless the latter condition is complied with, it will not be an agrarian revolution, but either a peasant insurrection or agrarian reforms of the Constitutional-

Democrat type.[29] To wind up the examination of this point, I shall only remind you that even the resolution submitted by the comrades of the minority which was printed in No. 2 of *Partiiniye Izvestia* says that the task now looming up before us is one of wresting power from the hands of the government.

The expression "popular initiative" which I believe does not occur in our resolutions but which, if we are to rely on Comrade Plekhanov's memory, I used in my speech, strikes him as a reminder of our old acquaintances from the Narodnaya Volya and the Socialist-Revolutionaries. This revival of memories on the part of Comrade Plekhanov seems to me to be an instance of his being twenty-five years late again. Remember what happened in Russia in the last quarter of 1905: strikes, soviets of workers' deputies, insurrections, peasant committees, railway committees, etc. —all this testifies precisely to the popular movement passing over to the form of insurrection, all this reveals what unquestionably are embryonic forms of organs of revolutionary power, and when I spoke about popular initiative, I had something very definite and concrete in mind; I was referring to these historic days of the Russian revolution, I was describing this very method of not only fighting against the old power, but of employing revolutionary power as an instrument of this struggle, a method first employed by the broad masses of Russian workers and peasants in the memorable days of October and December. If our revolution is to be buried, so are these embryonic forms of revolutionary peasants' and workers' power; but if you are not merely doing lip service to the peasant revolution, if we shall really have an agrarian revolution in the true sense of the word, we shall undoubtedly see a repetition of the October and December events on an incomparably broader scale. A revolutionary power, not of intellectuals, not of a group of conspirators, but of the workers and peasants has already existed in Russia— realized in practice in the course of our revolution. It was crushed owing to the victory of the reaction, yet if we have real grounds to be certain that there will be a revolutionary upsurge, we cannot but look forward to the rise, development and triumph of new, still more resolute organs of revolutionary power with still closer bonds with the peasantry and the proletariat. Hence, Plekhanov resorted to the absurd and threadbare "Narodnaya Volya" bogey only to evade analyzing the forms of the movement in the October-December days.

Finally, let us examine the question of how flexible my programme is and how firmly it stands on its feet. I believe that in this respect too my agrarian programme is the most satisfactory of all. What is to be done if things go badly with the revolution? What is to be done if all the "if's" set forth in my draft are not realized and it will prove impossible to carry our democratic revolution to consummation? In that case we undoubtedly shall have to reckon with the conditions of peasant agriculture and peasant land tenure that exist already now. In this connection I refer to such a factor of prime importance as leasing of land. For, assuming that things might go badly with the revolution, that it might not be carried to the end, we would unquestionably have to reckon with this factor remaining unabolishable, and for this eventuality too—this possibility of all the allegedly utopian "if's" not being taken care of—I have set forth the tasks of the Party more fully, more precisely and far more soberly than Comrade Maslov. Thus, my programme contains practical slogans applicable to both the present conditions of peasant farming and peasant land tenure and the most favourable prospects of further development of capitalism. Comrade John tried to joke at my expense, saying that I have in my programme too many programmes, inasmuch as both confiscation and lease figure in it and the two are mutually exclusive; the joke fell flat because confiscation of landlord estates does not exclude leasing of land, which can take place under peasant ownership as well. Hence, Comrade Plekhanov erred all the more when he advanced his particularly spectacular argument against me. It is not hard, he claimed, to write a programme with a view to the best possible outcome. Anybody can write such a programme, but just try writing one for an eventuality when the ideal conditions will be lacking. And I declare in answer to this argument that precisely in case the revolution takes the worst possible course or leads to the worst possible outcome, my programme, which proclaims the confiscation of landed estates and provides for issues such as leaseholds, will prove to be a particularly sober and particularly well-founded programme, whereas Comrade John's draft, completely ignoring these worst possible conditions, i.e., conditions when real political democracy has not been achieved, offers us nothing but municipalization, and municipalization without popular election of officials, without the abolition of a standing army, etc., presents just as great and even greater danger than nationalization. That is why I insist on advancing these "if's" which were so unfairly condemned by Plekhanov.

The peasants, then, will not accept municipalization. Comrade Kartvelov has said that in the Caucasus the peasants, while fully agreeing with the Socialist-Revolutionaries, want to know whether they would have the right to sell the land they get as a result of division of holdings or socialization. Quite right, Comrade Kartvelov! Your observation fully conforms with the interests of the peasants in general and the peasants' understanding of their interests, but it is just because the peasants will look upon any agrarian reform from the viewpoint of whether they will have the right to sell the additional land they get that they will unquestionably be against municipalization, against Zemstvozation.[30] To this day the peasants associate the Zemstvo with the Zemstvo chief, and they have far greater justification to do so than the august Constitutional-Democrat professors of law who sneer at peasant ignorance can imagine. Hence it is necessary, absolutely necessary, to speak of popular election of officials before speaking of municipalization. At the present moment, however, when this democratic demand has not been realized, one can speak only of confiscation in general, or of the division of land. Hence, so as to simplify the basic issue before this congress, I shall do this: inasmuch as Comrade Borisov's programme has a number of features in common with my programme, and is based on division of land, not nationalization, I shall withdraw my programme and leave it for the congress to declare for division or municipalization. If you reject division, or perhaps it will be more correct to say "when" you reject division, I shall of course have to withdraw my draft once and for all as having no chance of success; if you accept division, I shall move my programme in full as an amendment to Comrade Borisov's draft. In reply to the accusations that I am forcing nationalization on the peasants, I want to remind you that my programme includes "*Variant A*" which makes it clear that there is no question whatsoever of imposing anything on the peasants against their will. Hence, putting Borisov's draft to the vote first instead of mine essentially changes nothing and only makes it easier and simpler for us to ascertain the real will of the congress. In my opinion, municipalization is erroneous and harmful; division is erroneous but not harmful.

I shall dwell briefly on this difference. The "divisionists" interpret the facts correctly, but they do not remember what Marx said about the old materialism: "The philosophers have only interpreted the world in various ways; the point, however, is to change it."[31] The peasant speaks of "God's land, the people's land, nobody's land." The "divisionists" tell us that he does not mean this, that he has something else in mind. What the peasants really want, they say, is nothing but additional land, an extension of his petty farmhold and nothing more. All this is absolutely true. Our differences with the "divisionists," however, do not end, but begin here. We must make use precisely of these words of the peasants in our propaganda, in spite of the fact that they are economically utterly unsound or meaningless. You say you want everybody to have the use of the land? You want to give the land to the people? That is all very well, but what does giving the land to the people mean? Who disposes of the public wealth and public property? The officialdom, the Trepovs.[32] Do you want to turn the land over to Trepov and the officialdom? No. Any peasant will tell you that he does not want to give the land to them. Or would you prefer to give it to the Petrunkeviches and Rodichevs[33] who might be sitting in the municipal governments? No. The peasant most likely would not want to turn the land over to these gentlemen. Hence, we explain to the peasants, in order that the peasants should gain from the land being turned over to the nation, it is necessary to secure the election of all officials without exception by popular vote. Consequently, the project I have put forward calling for nationalization provided the democratic republic is fully ensured charts just the right line of action for our propagandists and agitators; it shows them clearly and graphically that the peasants' demands regarding the land must be made to serve as the groundwork for political propaganda, propaganda for a republic in particular. For instance, the peasant Mishin, who was chosen for the Duma[34] as deputy from the peasants of Stavropol, brought with him a mandate from his electors in the electoral college which has been printed in full in the *Russkoye Gosudarstvo*. This document demands the abolition of the Zemstvo officialdom, the organization of grain elevators and the transfer of all land to the state. The demand for such a transfer is undoubtedly a reactionary delusion, for the state in present-day as well as in tomorrow's constitutional Russia is a state subordinated to a police and military despotism, but for all that we must not simply reject it as a pernicious delusion; we must "seize" upon it in order to explain to Mishin and others like him how things really stand. We must tell Mishin and others like him that the demand for the transfer of the land to the state expresses, though very ineptly, an idea of great importance and value to the peasants. Transfer of the land to the state can be very useful to the peasants and will be very useful to them only when the state has become a fully democratic republic, when all officials without exception are elected by popular vote, the standing army has been abolished, etc. It is for these reasons that I believe that if you reject nationalization, you will inevitably cause our practical workers, propagandists and agitators to commit the same mistakes as we gave rise to with our erroneous cut-off land programme in 1903. At that time a narrower interpretation was given of our position than the authors of the point had had in mind, and now, too, rejection of nationalization and substitution of the demand for division instead, not to speak of the completely muddled idea of municipalization, will inevitably lead to such a succession of mistakes on the part of our practical workers, propagandists and agitators, as would very soon make us regret having adopted a "divisionist" or municipalization programme.

I shall conclude by repeating once more my two basic theses: firstly, that the peasants will never want municipalization; secondly, that municipalization without the democratic republic, without popular election of officials, can only do harm.

"Minutes of the Unity Congress
of the R.S.D.L.P., Stockholm,
1906," 1907, Moscow

Vol. X, pp. 253-62

# THE LAND QUESTION IN THE DUMA

The initial act of the Constitutional Democrats in the Duma was to compile an address in reply to the speech from the throne. What they drew up was a timid plea, not a demand. Their second "act" was to pass over in silence to current business when their deputation was told it was inacceptable. This was a still more timid thing to do. Now a third thing has come up—the debate on the land question, which has been put on the Duma order of the day.

All workers should follow this question particularly closely. Most of all it affects the mass of the peasants. And it is the peasants who are now the principal and practically the only allies the workers have in the revolution. Moreover, the land question will show especially clearly whether the Constitutional Democratic Party, which calls itself the party of popular freedom, truly furthers this cause.

What is it that the people, i.e., the whole peasantry primarily, want? The peasantry want land. Everybody knows this. The peasants demand that all the land in the country should belong to them. They want to overthrow the yoke of the landlords and officials. To take the land away from the landlords so that they should not be able to force the muzhik to work for them, that is, perform what is essentially old-time serf labour, and to deprive the officials of power so that they should not lord it over the common people—this is what the peasants want. And the workers must help the peasants both in the fight for the land and in raising the land question in a direct, clear and absolutely definite manner.

The land question is one in which it is particularly easy to confuse and muddle the issue. It is simple enough to de-

clare that the peasants are entitled to receive allotments
and at the same time stipulate conditions for the granting
of these allotments that would make it of no benefit whatever for the peasants. If the allotments are to be granted
again by the officials, if the liberal landlords will once
again appear in the role of some sort of *"miroviye posredniki,"* if the old autocratic government is to decide what
is "reasonable" compensation, the peasants, instead of ben-
efiting by it, will find themselves fooled, as they did in
1861, find a new noose slipped around their necks. Hence
the class-conscious workers must most energetically explain to the peasants that in the land question they must
be particularly cautious and distrustful. The question of
compensation for land and the question of what authority
will issue the land "grants" assume enormous importance
in the present situation. In the matter of compensation one
can tell at once and unerringly who stands for the peasants and who for the landlords, as well as who is vacillating between the two. The Russian peasant knows—and
only too well—what compensation means. This issue offers
a splendid instance of the divergence of interests between
the peasants and the landlords. Hence, the Unity Congress
of the R.S.D.L.P. was quite right in changing the word
"alienation" in the original draft of the agrarian programme to "confiscation" (that is, alienation without compensation).

In the issue of what authority is to grant the land allotments the interests of the peasants and the officialdom differ just as sharply as the interests of the peasants and
the landlords do in the matter of compensation. The socialist workers must therefore work particularly persistently
to make the peasants see how important it is that the
old government should not handle the land question. Let
the peasants know that they will not benefit from any land
reform carried out by the old authority. Fortunately on
this issue too the Unity Congress of the R.S.D.L.P. essentially achieved unanimity, for the congress resolution unconditionally declares for support of revolutionary action
on the part of the peasantry. True, the congress in our opinion made a mistake by not directly stating that the land

reform is the very thing that can be entrusted only to a *fully* democratic state authority, only to officials elected by the people, responsible to the people, and subject to replacement by the people. But we shall dwell in greater detail on this another time.

Two principal agrarian programmes will be submitted to the Duma. The Constitutional Democrats who have the upper hand in the Duma want both to satisfy the landlords and to spare the peasants. They are agreed to compulsory alienation of the bulk of the landed estates, but, firstly, advocate the payment of compensation to the landlords, and secondly, stand for a liberal-bureaucratic and not a revolutionary-peasant solution of the problem of ways and means of carrying out the land reform. As always, the Constitutional Democrats in their agrarian programme wriggle between the landlords and the peasants, between the old government and popular freedom.

The Trudovaya or peasant group[35] have not yet fully defined their agrarian programme. All the land must belong to the toiling people—but on the question of compensation, as on that of the old government, still not a word. We shall have occasion enough to discuss this programme when it becomes more clearly defined.

The bureaucratic government naturally will not hear of any agrarian reform, not even that proposed by the Constitutional Democrats. The bureaucratic government, headed as it is by the richest landlord officials owning as often as not tens of thousands of dessiatins of land each, "will sooner accept the Moslem faith" (as one witty writer put it) than permit any compulsory alienation of landed estates. In a word, any *"solution"* of the agrarian question by the Duma will actually not be a solution at all, but merely a proclamation, a declaration of demands. The Constitutional Democrats will again put forth timid pleas instead of proud and courageous, honest and frank demands such as might be expected of the people's representatives. Let us hope that the Trudovaya group will at least this time take their own stand fully independent of the Constitutional Democrats.

As for the socialist workers, a particularly great task now faces them. They must broaden their organization in general and their ties with the peasants in particular by every means in their power. The full importance of the question of compensation and the issue of whether the land reform can be allowed to remain in the hands of the old government must be explained to the peasants on as wide a scale and as clearly, thoroughly and exhaustively as possible. Every effort must be made to ensure that the alliance of the socialist proletariat and the revolutionary peasantry should stand firm and strong by the inevitably approaching time when the present political crisis will finally come to a head. It is this alliance, and only this alliance, that can guarantee the successful solution of the question of "all the land" for the peasants and full freedom and undivided power for the people.

*Volna*, No. 15,
May 12, 1906

Vol. X, pp. 382-84

# THE LAND QUESTION
## AND THE FIGHT FOR FREEDOM

The land question is being debated in the Duma. Two principal solutions have been offered to the problem by the Constitutional Democrats and the "Trudoviks," or peasants' deputies.

As regards these offered solutions the Unity Congress of the R.S.D.L.P. quite correctly declared in its resolution on the attitude to be taken toward the peasant movement: "The bourgeois parties are seeking to make use of the peasant movement and to subordinate it to themselves—some (the Socialist-Revolutionaries) with an utopian middle-class socialist aim, others (the Constitutional Democrats) with the aim of preserving to a certain extent large-scale private land ownership and at the same time of weakening the revolutionary movement by partial concessions to the property instincts of the peasantry."

Let us examine the significance of this resolution adopted by the Social-Democratic congress. The Constitutional Democrats are a semi-landowning party. A great many liberal landlords belong to it. It seeks to uphold the interests of the landlords, making only those *concessions* to the peasants which it cannot avoid. The Constitutional Democrats are out to safeguard as much as possible large-scale private land ownership and do not agree to complete alienation of all landed estates in favour of the peasantry. Advocating the payment of compensation for the land by the peasants, that is, the *purchase* by the peasants of estate lands through the agency of the state, the Constitutional Democrats seek to turn the upper strata of the peasantry into a "Party of Order." The fact is that whatever the compensation arrangements and however "fair" the prices set, the payments are bound to be easier for the well-to-do peasants and weigh down heavily on the poor peasants. No matter what rules concerning com-

munal compensation, etc., are put down on paper, actually the land is bound to remain in the hands of those
who can afford to pay for it. That is why the purchase of
land amounts to strengthening the position of the rich
peasants at the expense of the poor, to splitting the peasantry and thereby weakening its struggle for full freedom and all the land. Purchase amounts to *enticing* the
more prosperous peasants to desert the cause of freedom
for the camp of the *old government.* Acquisition of land
through payment of compensation to the landlord means
buying one's release from the fight for freedom; it means
using money to induce part of the fighters for freedom
to side with the enemies of freedom. The well-to-do peasant who has acquired land by paying compensation to the
landowner becomes a petty landlord himself and will find
it particularly easy to side for good with the old, landlord-bureaucratic government.

Hence the Social-Democratic congress was absolutely
right in declaring that the Constitutional Democratic
Party (which is a semi-landowning party) is advocating
measures that *weaken* the revolutionary movement, that is,
the fight for freedom.

Now let us see how the "Trudoviks" or peasant deputies in
the Duma propose to solve the land question. So far they
have not formulated their views with full clarity. They
stand somewhere half-ways between the Constitutional
Democrats and the Socialist-Revolutionaries (the party of
Narodnik Socialists), between alienation of part of the
land with compensation (as proposed by the Constitutional
Democrats) and confiscation of all land (as proposed by
the Socialist Revolutionaries), though they are shifting more
and more away from the former and closer to the latter.

Was the Social-Democratic congress correct in appraising
the Socialist-Revolutionaries as a bourgeois party whose
aims are the aims of utopian middle-class socialism?

Take the latest land reform project offered by the Socialist Revolutionaries which was printed yesterday in
their newspaper *Narodny Vestnik* (No. 9). It provides
for the abolition of all private ownership of land and
"universal equal use of the land." Why do the Socialist-

Revolutionaries advocate equality in the use of land? Because they want to do away with the difference between the rich and the poor. This is a socialist wish. All Socialists want the same thing. But there are different kinds of socialism. There is even a clerical socialism, just as there are middle-class socialism and proletarian socialism.

The petty proprietor's dream of abolishing the difference between the rich and the poor is middle-class socialism. It envisages the possibility of making all people "equal" petty proprietors, neither poor nor rich. Middle-class socialism drafts projects of laws on universal equal utilization of the land. In reality, however, poverty and want cannot be abolished in the way the petty proprietor would like. There can be no equal *use* of the land so long as the power of money, the power of capital, exists. No laws in the world can do away with inequality and exploitation so long as market economy continues to exist, so long as money reigns and capital retains its power. Only the organization of large-scale planned public economy, with the ownership of all land, the factories and instruments of production vested in the working class, can put an end to all exploitation. Hence, proletarian socialism (Marxism) exposes all the groundless hopes fostered by middle-class socialism that "equalitarian" petty economy is possible and that in general petty economy can be preserved under capitalism.

The class-conscious proletariat gives every support to the peasants' struggle for all the land and for full freedom, but at the same time it warns them against false hopes of all kinds. With the help of the proletariat, the peasants can completely overthrow the power of the landlords, they can wipe out every vestige of landlord landownership and the landlord-bureaucratic state. They can even put an end to private ownership of land in general. All such measures would be of tremendous benefit to the peasantry and the working class alike, to the entire people. The interests of the working class require that it render the most solid support to the peasants' struggle. But the most complete overthrow of the power of the landlords and the officialdom would not in any way undermine the power of capital. It is only in a society free of landlord and bureaucratic rule that the outcome of the great final struggle between the proletariat and the bourgeoisie, the struggle for a socialist society, can be decided.

This is why the Social-Democrats resolutely oppose the treacherous programme advanced by the Constitutional Democrats and warn the peasants against pinning false hopes on "equality." To win the present battle for land and freedom, the peasants must act completely independently of the Constitutional Democrats. They must not allow themselves to be carried away by debates on all kinds of land-tenure projects. So long as power remains in the hands of the old autocratic, landlord-bureaucratic government, all these projects concerning "labour norms," "equalitarianism," etc., are a waste of time. The peasants' fight for the land can only be weakened by the mass of points and rules contained in these projects, which the old government will either scrap completely or turn into a new means for deceiving the peasant. The "land-tenure projects" make it harder rather than easier for the peasants to understand how they really can gain possession of the land. These projects obscure the issue of the old authority of the bureaucratic government by petty chicanery. They muddle up people's minds with pipe dreams about benevolent rulers when in reality the old savage rulers with their unbridled violence remain. Stop playing with your paper "land-tenure projects," gentlemen—the peasants will settle the land question easily enough when the impediment of the old government is done away with—better give all your attention to the peasants' struggle for the complete elimination of all such impediments.

Written May 19 (June 1), 1906
Printed May 20, 1906, in the
newspaper *Volna*, No. 22

Vol. X, pp. 402-05

# THE AGRARIAN QUESTION AND THE FORCES
## OF THE REVOLUTION

The newspaper *Trudovoi Narod*, the mouthpiece of the Trudoviks and members of the Peasants' Union, has assessed the alignment of forces in the Duma on the land question, that "life and death question" for the peasantry.

"The Trudoviks (100), Popular Socialists (14), and Socialist-Revolutionaries (34), *148 in all*, may act together in the land question to uphold the interests of the working people. Assuming that the Social-Democrats (64) too will join them on many points of the land question, the *total will come to 212*.

"All these will be opposed by the Constitutional Democrats (91), the Polish deputies (46), Independents (52), the October group, and Moderates (32), *221 in all*.

"Thus there is a preponderance of votes against. And we have counted neither the Moslems (30) nor the Cossacks (17); it is likely that at the very best half of them will side with the Left and the other half with the Right. In any case there are more votes against the Trudovik land law than for it."

The enumeration omits the Monarchists (22), but including them would only bear out the conclusion arrived at by the Trudoviks.

This conclusion is of interest in two respects: firstly, it throws light on the fundamental question of the alignment of social forces in the present Russian revolution, and secondly, it helps to clarify the significance of the Duma and parliamentary action for the liberation movement.

All Social-Democrats are convinced that for social and economic content the revolution under way is a *bourgeois* revolution. This means that it is proceeding on the basis of capitalist relations of production, and that it will inevitably result in a further development of these very relations of production. To put it more simply still: the

entire economy of society will *remain* under the domination of the market, under the domination of money, even
after the broadest *freedom* has been achieved and the peasants have won a complete victory in their fight for the
*land*. The fight for land and freedom is a fight for the conditions of existence of bourgeois society, for *capital* will
continue to dominate in the most democratic republic and
irrespective of how the transfer of "all the land to the
people" is effected.

Such a view may seem strange to anyone not familiar
with Marxist theory. Yet it is not hard to see that it is
the correct view—one need but recall the Great French Revolution and its outcome, the history of the "free lands" in
America,[36] and so on.

The Social-Democrats by no means wish to minimize the
tasks of the present revolution or belittle its significance
by calling it a bourgeois revolution. On the contrary.
The struggle of the working class against the capitalist
class cannot develop on a wide enough scale and end in
victory unless the older historical enemies of the proletariat
are overthrown.

Hence, the principal task of the proletariat at the present moment is to win the broadest freedom and bring
about the most complete destruction of landlord (feudal)
land tenure. Only by doing this, only by completely
smashing the old, semi-feudal society by democratic action,
can the proletariat rise to its full stature as an independent class, lay full emphasis on its specific, i.e., socialist
tasks as distinct from the democratic tasks common to
"all the oppressed," and secure for itself the most favourable conditions for free, sweeping, intensified struggle for
socialism. If the bourgeois-democratic liberation movement stops half-way, if it is not carried to consummation,
the proletariat would have to spend a great deal more of
its strength on general democratic, i.e., bourgeois-democratic, tasks than on its own proletarian class tasks, i.e.,
socialist tasks.

But can the socialist proletariat carry out the bourgeois
revolution independently and as the leading force? Does

not the very concept "bourgeois revolution" imply that it can be effected only by the bourgeoisie?

The Mensheviks often fall into this error. Yet this view is a caricature of Marxism. A liberation movement that is bourgeois in social and economic content is not a bourgeois movement as regards its motive forces. It is not the bourgeoisie, but the proletariat and the peasantry that can be the motive force. Why is this possible? Because the proletariat and the peasantry suffer even more than the bourgeoisie from the survivals of serfdom, because they are in greater need of freedom and abolition of the landlord yoke. For the bourgeoisie, on the contrary, complete victory presents a threat, since the proletariat will make use of full freedom against the bourgeoisie, and the fuller the freedom and the more completely the power of the landlords has been destroyed, the easier it will be for the proletariat to do so.

Hence the bourgeoisie strives to stop the bourgeois revolution half-ways, when freedom has been only half won, by a deal with the old government and the landlords. This striving springs from the class interests of the bourgeoisie. It was manifested so clearly already in the German bourgeois revolution of 1848 that the Communist Marx directed the spearhead of proletarian policy against the "compromising" (the expression is Marx's) liberal bourgeoisie.

Our Russian bourgeoisie is still more cowardly, and our proletariat far more class-conscious and better organized than the German in 1848. In our country complete victory of the bourgeois-democratic movement is possible only in spite of the "compromising" liberal bourgeoisie, only in the event of the mass of the democratic peasantry following the proletariat in the struggle for full freedom and all the land.

The Second Duma offers still more striking confirmation of this view. Even the peasants have now realized that the liberal bourgeoisie, the Constitutional Democrats, belong to the Right, and the peasants and the workers to the Left. True, the Trudoviks, Popular Socialists,[37] and Socialist-Revolutionaries constantly vacillate between the bourgeoisie and the proletariat, and as often as not are *in reality* political *hangers-on* of the liberals (the voting for Golovin, the "tactics of silence," agreement to refer the budget to a commission,[38] etc., etc.). This vacillation is not accidental. It springs from the class nature of the petty bourgeoisie.

Why must the Constitutional Democrats be included in the Right line-up in a question as pressing as the land question? Because the Constitutional-Democrat agrarian policy is essentially a *landlord* policy. The "compulsory alienation" advocated by the Constitutional Democrats is actually *compulsion of the peasants by the landlords to undertake ruinous* compensation payments, for in fact both the amount of these payments and the tax rates *will be determined by the landlords*, inasmuch as the landlords and officials will constitute the majority in the local land committees (in the First Duma the Constitutional Democrats were opposed to the election of these committees by universal ballot), and in central all-Russian legislation the landlords will have the upper hand through the Council of State, etc. The "liberalism" of the Constitutional Democrats is the liberalism of a bourgeois lawyer who *mediates* between the peasant and the landlord but does it *in favour of the landlord.*\*

Let us pass over to the second question. The Constitutional Democrats and other elements of the Right constitute the majority in the Duma. "*What is the way out?*" *Trudovoi Narod* asks. The answer is simple: the "way out" is to rise above purely parliamentary logomachy.

This would be necessary even if the Left had a majority

---

\* In view of what the *Rech* said about the landlord affiliations of the Constitutional Democrats being only a platform catchword, we must add this: of the 79 unmistakable Constitutional Democrats we counted in the well-known book *Members of the Second State Duma* (St. Petersburg, 1907), *20 are landlords.* Let us mention *Tuchkov, Boguslavsky, Bychkov,* Bakunin, *Rodichev, Bogdanov,* Salazkin, *Tatarinov, Stakhovich, Ikonnikov, Savelyev, Dolgorukov, Chelnokov, Golovin,* both *Pereleshins, Volotsky,* Iordansky, Chernosvitov. The underlined are marshals of the nobility, Zemstvo chiefs or chairmen of Zemstvo administrations.

in the Duma, for the Duma is powerless, and the Council of State would *"improve,"* in the interests of the landlords, *any* project passed by the Duma. And it is necessary now —not from any subjective party viewpoint, but in the objective historical sense; *unless this is done*, the land question can be settled *only* in favour of the landlords.

*Nashe Ekho,* No. 7,
April 1, 1907

Vol. XII, pp. 296-99

# THE AGRARIAN PROGRAMME OF SOCIAL-DEMOCRACY IN THE FIRST RUSSIAN REVOLUTION, 1905-1907

*(Excerpt)*

## CONCLUSION

The agrarian question is the basis of the bourgeois revolution in Russia and determines the national peculiarity of this revolution.

The essence of this question is the struggle the peasantry is waging to abolish landlordism and the remnants of serfdom in the agricultural system of Russia, and, consequently, also in all her social and political institutions.

Ten and a half million peasant households in European Russia possess together 75,000,000 dessiatins of land. Thirty thousand, chiefly noble, but partly also upstart, landlords each own over 500 dessiatins—a total of 70,000,000 dessiatins. Such is the main background of the picture. Such are the main reasons for the predominance of feudal landlords in the agricultural system of Russia and, consequently, in the Russian state generally, and in the whole of Russian life. The owners of the latifundia are feudal landlords in the economic sense of the term: the basis of their landownership was created by the history of serfdom, by the history of land grabbing by the nobility throughout the centuries. The basis of their present methods of farming is the labour rent system, i.e., a direct survival of serf labour; it implies cultivation of the land with the implements of the small tillers in an endless variety of ways: winter hiring, annual leases, share-cropping on a 50 per cent basis, labour rent, bondage for debt, bondage for cut-off lands, for the use of forests, meadows, water, and so on and so forth, *ad infinitum*. Capitalist development in Russia has made such strides during the last half century that the retention of serfdom in agriculture has become *absolutely* impossible, and its abolition has assumed the forms of a violent crisis, of a nation-wide revolution. However, the abolition of serfdom in a bourgeois country is possible in two ways.

Serfdom may be abolished by slowly transforming the feudal landlord farms into Junker-bourgeois farms, by transforming the masses of the peasants into landless husbandmen and Knechts, by forcibly keeping the masses down to the pauper standard of living, by the rise of small groups of Grossbauern, of rich bourgeois peasants who inevitably spring up under capitalism from among the peasantry. The Black-Hundred landlords and Stolypin,[39] their Minister, have chosen that path. They have realized that the path for the development of Russia *cannot* be cleared unless the rusty medieval forms of landownership are forcibly broken up. And they have boldly set out to break them up *in the interest of the landlords*. They have thrown overboard the liking which only recently prevailed among the bureaucracy and the landlords for the semi-feudal village community. They have evaded all the "constitutional" laws in order to break it up by force. They have given the kulaks *carte blanche* to rob the peasant masses, to break up the old system of landownership, to ruin thousands of peasant farms; they have handed over the medieval village to be "sacked and plundered" by the owners of rubles. They *cannot* act otherwise if they are to retain their class rule, for they have realized the necessity of adapting themselves to, and not fighting, capitalist development. And in order to preserve their rule they can find no other allies *against* the masses of the peasants than the "upstarts," the Razuvayevs and Kolupayevs.[40] They have no other alternative than to shout to these Kolupayevs: *Enrichissez-vous*!—get rich! We shall create opportunities for you to make a hundred rubles for every one you invest, if only you will help us to save the basis of our rule under the new conditions! That path of development, if it is to be travelled successfully, calls for wholesale, systematic, unbridled *violence* against the peasant masses and against

the proletariat. And the landlord counter-revolution is
hastening to organize that violence all along the line.

The other path of development we have designated the
American path of development of capitalism, in contra-
distinction to the former, the Prussian path. It, too, neces-
sitates the forcible break-up of the old system of landownership; only the stupid philistines of Russian liberalism can dream of the possibility of a painless, peaceful
outcome of the exceedingly acute crisis in Russia.

But this indispensable and inevitable break-up may be
carried out in the interests of the peasant masses and not
of the landlord gang. A mass of free farmers may serve
as a basis for the development of capitalism without any
landlord farming whatsoever, for, *taken as a whole*, the
latter form of farming is economically reactionary, whereas the elements of free farming were *created* among the
peasantry by the preceding economic history of the
country. If capitalist development proceeds along that path
it *should* develop infinitely more broadly, more freely, and
more rapidly as a result of a tremendous growth of the
home market and of a rise in the standard of living, the
energy, initiative, and culture of the *entire* population. And
Russia's gigantic colonization fund, the utilization of
which is greatly hampered by the feudal oppression of the
mass of the peasantry in Russia proper, as well as by the
feudal-bureaucratic approach to agrarian policy—this fund
will provide the economic foundation for a tremendous expansion of agriculture and for increased production both
in volume and in scope.

Such a path of development requires not only the abolition of landlordism. For the rule of the feudal landlords
through the centuries has put its imprint on *all* forms of
landownership in the country, on the peasant allotments as
well as upon the holdings of the settlers in the relatively
free frontier lands: the whole colonization policy of the
autocracy is permeated with the Asiatic interference of a
die-hard bureaucracy, which hampered the free settlement
of the migrants, introduced terrible confusion into the new
agrarian relationships and contaminated the frontier regions with the virus of the feudal bureaucracy of Central

Russia.* Not only is landlordism in Russia medieval, but so also is the peasant allotment system. The latter is in a terrible tangle. It splits up the peasantry into thousands of small units, medieval groups, social categories. It reflects the age-long history of shameless interference in the peasants' agrarian relationships both by the central government and by the local authorities. It confines the peasants, as in a ghetto, in petty medieval associations of a fiscal, tax-extorting character, in associations for the ownership of allotted land, i.e., in the village communities. And Russia's economic development is *actually* pulling the peasantry out of this medieval environment—on the one hand, by giving rise to the renting out and abandonment of allotments and, on the other hand, by creating the system of farming by the free farmers of the future (or by the future Grossbauern of a Junker Russia) *out of the fragments* of the most diversified forms of landownership: personal allotments, rented allotments, purchased property, land rented from the landlord, land rented from the state, and so on.

In order to establish *really* free farming in Russia, it is necessary to "unfence" *all* the land, landlord as well as allotment. The *whole* system of medieval landownership must be broken up and all lands must be made equal for free farmers upon a free soil. The greatest possible facilities must be created for the exchange of holdings, for the free choice of settlements, for rounding off holdings, for the creation of new, free associations instead of the rusty, tax-extorting village community. All the land must be "cleared" of all medieval lumber.

The expression of this economic necessity is the nationalization of the land, the abolition of the private ownership of land, and transfer of *all* the land to the state, which will mark a complete break with feudal relations in the countryside. It is this economic necessity that has turned the *mass* of Russian peasants into supporters of

---

* A. Kaufman, in his *Migration and Colonization* (St. Petersburg, 1905), gives an outline of the history of Russian colonization policy. Like a good "liberal," he shows undue deference to the feudal landlord bureaucracy.

land nationalization. The mass of small-owner tillers declared in favour of nationalization at the congresses of the Peasants' Union in 1905, in the First Duma in 1906, and in the Second Duma in 1907, i.e., during the whole of the first period of the revolution. They did so not because the "village community" has imbued them with certain special "germs," certain special, non-bourgeois "labour principles." On the contrary, they did so because life had urged them to seek *emancipation* from the medieval village community and from the medieval allotment system. They did not do so because they wanted to, or could, build up socialist agriculture, but because they wanted, and now want, to build, were, and now are, in a position to build up really bourgeois small farming, i.e., farming purged to the utmost of *all* the traditions of serfdom.

Thus, it was neither chance nor the influence of this or that doctrine (as some short-sighted people think) that determined this peculiar attitude of the classes fighting in the Russian revolution towards the question of private ownership of land. This peculiar attitude is to be explained by the conditions of the development of capitalism in Russia and by the requirements of capitalism at this stage of its development. All the Black-Hundred landlords, all the counter-revolutionary bourgeoisie (including the Octobrists and the *Constitutional Democrats*) stand for private ownership of land. The whole of the peasantry and the whole of the proletariat are opposed to private ownership of land. The reformist path of creating a Junker-bourgeois Russia necessarily presupposes the preservation of the foundations of the old system of landownership and a slow adaptation of them to capitalism, which would be painful for the masses of the population. The revolutionary path of really overthrowing the old order inevitably demands, as its economic basis, the destruction of all the old forms of landownership, together with all the old political institutions of Russia. The experience of the first period of the Russian revolution has conclusively proved that it can be victorious only as a peasant agrarian revolution, and that the latter cannot completely fulfil its historical mission unless the land is nationalized.

Social-Democracy, as the party of the international proletariat, the party which has set itself world-wide socialist aims, cannot, of course, identify itself with any epoch of any bourgeois revolution, nor can it tie its destiny to this or that outcome of this or that bourgeois revolution. No matter what the outcome may be, we must remain an independent, purely proletarian party, which steadfastly leads the toiling masses to their great socialist goal. We cannot, therefore, undertake to guarantee that any of the gains of the bourgeois revolution will be permanent, because impermanence and inherent contradiction are immanent features of *all* the gains of bourgeois revolutions as such. The "invention" of "guarantees against restoration" can only be the fruit of wrong thinking. We have but one task: to rally the proletariat for the socialist revolution, to support every fight against the old order in the most resolute way, to fight for the best possible conditions for the proletariat in the developing bourgeois society. And it inevitably follows from this that our Social-Democratic programme in the Russian bourgeois revolution can be *only* the nationalization of the land. Like every other *part* of our programme, we must connect it with definite forms and a definite degree of political reform, because the sweep of the political revolution and that of the agrarian revolution cannot but be identical. Like every other part of our programme, we must isolate it strictly from petty-bourgeois illusions, from intelligentsia-bureaucratic babble about "norms," from reactionary talk about strengthening the village communities, or about equal land tenure. The interests of the proletariat do not demand that a special slogan, a special "plan" or "system" be invented for this or that bourgeois revolution, they only demand that the objective conditions for this revolution shall be *consistently* expressed and that these objective, economically unavoidable conditions be purged of illusion and utopias. The nationalization of the land is not only the sole means for completely liquidating medievalism in agriculture, but also the best form of agrarian relationships conceivable under capitalism.

Three circumstances have temporarily diverted the Russian Social-Democrats from this correct agrarian programme. Firstly, P. Maslov, the initiator of "municipalization" in Russia, "corrected" the theory of Marx, repudiated the theory of absolute rent, revived the semi-decayed bourgeois doctrines of the law of diminishing returns, its connection with the theory of rent, etc. The repudiation of absolute rent is tantamount to denying that private land-ownership has any economic significance under capitalism, and, consequently, it inevitably led to the distortion of the Marxist view on nationalization. Secondly, not having before them tangible evidence that the peasant revolution had *begun*, Russian Social-Democrats could not but regard its possibility with caution, because, for the revolution to be victorious, a number of especially favourable conditions and an especially favourable sweep of the revolutionary class-consciousness, energy, and initiative of the masses are required. Having no *experience*, and holding that it· is impossible to invent *bourgeois* movements, the Russian Marxists naturally could not, *before the revolution*, present a correct agrarian programme. But even *after* the revolution had begun, they committed the following mistake: instead of *applying* the theory of Marx to the peculiar conditions prevailing in Russia (Marx and Engels always taught that our theory is· not a dogma, but a *guide to action*), they uncritically repeated the conclusions drawn from the application of Marx's theory to foreign conditions, to a *different* epoch. The German *Social-Democrats*, for instance, have quite naturally abandoned all the old programmes of Marx containing the demand for the nationalization of the land, because Germany has taken final shape as a Junker-bourgeois country, and all movements based on the bourgeois order have become completely obsolete, and there is not, nor can there be, any people's movement for nationalization. The predominance of Junker-bourgeois elements has *actually transformed* the plans for nationalization into a plaything, and even into an instrument of the Junkers for robbing the masses. The Germans are right in refusing even to talk about nationalization. But to apply this conclusion to Russia (as is done in effect by those of our Mensheviks who do not see the connection between municipalization and Maslov's revision of the theory of Marx) reveals an inability to think of the tasks each Social-Democratic party has to perform in specific periods of its historical development.

Thirdly, the municipalization programme obviously reflects the mistaken tactical line of Menshevism in the Russian bourgeois revolution: failure to understand that only "an alliance between the proletariat and the peasantry"* can guarantee its victory, failure to understand the leading role the proletariat plays in the bourgeois revolution, the striving to push the proletariat aside, to adapt it to an incomplete outcome of the revolution, to convert it from the leader into an auxiliary (actually into a labourer and servant) of the liberal bourgeoisie. "Don't get too enthused, adapt yourselves, march slowly forward, working people"—these words, uttered by Narcissus Tuporylov against the "Economists"[41] (=the first opportunists in the R.S.D.L.P.), completely reflect the *spirit* of our present agrarian programme.

Combating the "enthusiasm" of petty-bourgeois socialism must result not in the contraction, but in the expansion, of the sweep of the revolution and of its aims as determined by the proletariat. We must not encourage "regionalism," no matter how strong it may be among the backward sections of the petty bourgeoisie or the privileged peasantry (Cossacks), nor must we encourage the insularity of the different nationalities. No. We must explain to the peasantry the importance of unity if victory is to be achieved, we must advance slogans that will widen the movement, not narrow it, and that will place the responsibility for the *incompleteness* of the bourgeois revolution on the backwardness of the bourgeoisie and not on lack of understanding on the part of the proletariat. We must not "adapt" our programme to "local" democracy; we must not invent rural "municipal socialism," which is absurd and impossible under an undemocratic central government; we must not seek to adjust petty-bourgeois social-

---

* That is how Kautsky expressed it in the *second* edition of his pamphlet, *The Social Revolution.*

ist reformism to the bourgeois revolution, but must concentrate the attention of the masses on the actual conditions for the victory of the revolution as a bourgeois revolution, on the need for achieving not only local, but "central" democracy, i.e., the democratization of the central authorities of the state—and not only democracy in general, but the most complete, highest forms of democracy, for otherwise the peasant agrarian revolution in Russia will become *utopian* in the scientific sense of the term.

And let it not be thought that because the Black-Hundred die-hards are howling and roaring in the Third Duma, because the raging counter-revolution has reached *nec plus ultra* and reaction is committing ferocious acts of political vengeance against the revolutionaries in general and against the Social-Democratic deputies in the Second Duma in particular—let it not be thought because of all this that the present historical moment is "unsuitable" for "broad" agrarian programmes. Such a thought would be akin to the renegacy, despondency, disintegration, and decadence which have spread among wide sections of the petty-bourgeois intellectuals who belong to the Social-Democratic Party, or sympathize with this Party in Russia. The proletariat will only gain if this refuse is thoroughly swept from the ranks of the workers' party. The more savage the reaction the more it actually retards the inevitable economic development and the more effectively it paves the way to a wider upsurge of the democratic movement. And we must take advantage of temporary lulls in mass action in order critically to study the experience of the great revolution, verify it, purge it of dross, and transmit it to the masses as a guide for the impending struggle.

November-December 1907

First printed in 1908, (confiscated); published in 1917 by *Zhizn i Znaniye* as a separate edition

Vol. XIII, pp. 386-94

# WHAT IS HAPPENING IN THE COUNTRYSIDE?

Ex-Minister of Agriculture Yermolov's new book about the "present epidemic of incendiarism in Russia" has given rise to debates in the press. The liberal press has observed that there has been no decrease but rather an increase in fires in the villages after the revolution. The reactionary newspapers have taken up Yermolov's hue and cry about "incendiaries enjoying impunity," the "terror in the villages," and so on. There has been an extraordinary increase in the number of fires in rural localities. For instance, between 1904 and 1907 the figure went up *twofold* in Tambov Gubernia, *two and a half times* in Oryol Gubernia, and *threefold* in Voronezh Gubernia. "The more or less well-to-do peasants," writes the government flunkey *Novoye Vremya*, "want to set up farmsteads and are trying to introduce new farming methods, but are harassed, as if besieged by guerrillas in enemy territory, by a lawless rural element that has run wild. They are burned out and hounded, hounded and burned out until there is nothing left for them to do but abandon everything and run."

An unpleasant admission indeed for the partisans of the tsarist government! For us Social-Democrats the latest information is not lacking in interest as further proof of the falsity of the government claims and the utter impotence of liberal policy.

The revolution of 1905 fully showed that the old order in the Russian countryside is irrevocably doomed by history. Nothing in the world can bolster up this order. How is it then to be changed? The peasant masses gave the answer by their uprisings in 1905 and through their deputies in the First and Second Dumas. The landed estates must be taken away from the landlords without compensation. When 30,000 landlords (headed by Nikolai Romanov) own *70 million* dessiatins of land and 10 million peasant households just about the same amount, the result can be nothing except slavery, abject poverty, ruination and stagnation of the whole of the national economy. Hence the Social-Democratic Labour Party called on the peasants to take revolutionary action. By their mass strikes in 1905 workers all over Russia rallied the peasants and directed their struggle. The liberal plan to "reconcile" the peasants with the landlords through "fair compensation payments" was an empty, contemptible, treacherous trick.

How does the Stolypin government propose to change the old order in the countryside? It wants to speed up the complete ruination of the peasants, to preserve the landed estates, to help an insignificant handful of rich peasants to set up farms and grab as much as possible of the communal land. The government has realized that the mass of the peasants are against it and is trying to find allies among the rich peasants.

Stolypin himself once said that "twenty years of tranquillity" would be needed to carry out the "reform" proposed by the government. By "tranquillity" he means submissiveness on the part of the peasants, the absence of any struggle against violence. Yet without violence committed by the Zemstvo chiefs and other authorities, violence at every step, violence against *tens of millions*— without suppressing the slightest manifestation of independence on the part of these millions, the Stolypin "reform" cannot be carried out. Not even for three years, let alone twenty, has Stolypin been able to bring about "tranquillity," nor will he be able to do so; this is the unpleasant truth of which the tsar's flunkeys have been reminded by the ex-minister's book about fires in the countryside.

The peasants do not and cannot have any other way out of the desperate want, poverty, and death by starvation in which the government has plunged them than mass struggle together with the proletariat to overthrow the tsarist rule. Preparation of the forces of the proletariat for this struggle, the creation, development, and consolidation of proletarian organizations—this is the immediate task of the R.S.D.L.P.

*Rabochaya Gazeta,* No. 2,
December 18 (31), 1910

Vol. XVI, pp. 329-30

# THE PEASANTRY AND THE WORKING CLASS

In the Narodnik newspapers and magazines we often meet with the assertion that the workers and the "working" peasantry belong to the same class.

The utter incorrectness of this view is obvious to anybody who understands that more or less developed capitalist production, i.e., the domination of capital in the market and the transformation by it of the masses of the toilers into wage-workers, predominates in all modern states. The so-called "working" peasant is in fact a *small proprietor*, or a petty bourgeois, who nearly always either hires himself out as a labourer or hires workers. Being a small proprietor, the "working" peasant vacillates in politics, too, between the masters and the workers, between the bourgeoisie and the proletariat.

One of the most striking proofs of this proprietor, or bourgeois, nature of the "working" peasant are statistics on *wage-labour* in agriculture. The bourgeois economists (including the Narodniks) usually praise the "vitality" of small production in agriculture, by which they mean farming without wage-labour. But they do not like precise figures on wage-labour among the peasantry!

Let us examine data collected on this question during the most recent agricultural censuses: the Austrian census of 1902 and the German of 1907.

The more developed a country is, the more extensively is wage-labour employed in agriculture. In Germany, out of a total of 15,000,000 workers in agriculture, it is calculated that 4,500,000, or 30 per cent, are wage-workers, and in Austria, out of a total of 9,000,000, 1,250,000, or about 14 per cent. But even in Austria, if we take farms usually regarded as peasant (or "working" peasant) farms, i.e., those from 2 to 20 hectares (one hectare equals 9/10 dessiatin), we will find wage-labour used on a considerable scale. Farms from 5 to 10 hectares number 383,000; of these 126,000 employ wage-workers. Farms from 10 to 20 hectares number 242,000; of these 142,000, or nearly three-fifths, employ wage-workers.

Thus, small ("working") peasant farming exploits *hundreds of thousands* of wage-workers. The larger the peasant farm, the larger the number of wage-workers employed, side by side with a larger contingent of family workers. For example, in Germany, for every 10 peasant farms, there are:

| Size of farm | Family workers | Wage-workers | Total |
|---|---|---|---|
| 2 to 5 hectares | 25 | 4 | 29 |
| 5 to 10 " | 31 | 7 | 38 |
| 10 to 20 " | 34 | 17 | 51 |

The wealthier peasantry, who have more land and a larger number of "their own" workers in the family, *in addition* employ a larger number of *wage-workers.*

In capitalist society, which is entirely dependent on the market, small (peasant) production on a mass scale is *impossible* in agriculture without the mass employment of wage-labour. The sentimental catchword, "working" peasant, merely deceives the workers by *concealing* this exploitation of wage-labour.

In Austria, about 1,500,000 peasant farms (from 2 to 20 hectares) employ *half a million* wage-workers. In Germany, 2,000,000 peasant farms employ *more than one and a half million* wage-workers.

And what about the smaller farmers? They hire themselves out! They are wage-workers with a plot of land. For example, in Germany there are nearly three and one-third million (3,378,509) farms of less than 2 hectares. Of these, *independent* tillers number *less than half a million*

(474,915), while *wage-workers* number a little less than *two million* (1,822,792)!!

Thus, the very position of the small farmers in modern society inevitably transforms them into petty bourgeois. They are eternally vacillating between the wage-workers and the capitalists. The majority of the peasants live in poverty, are ruined, and become transformed into proletarians, while the minority trail after the capitalists and foster the dependence of the masses of the rural population upon the capitalists. That is why, in all capitalist countries, the peasants, in the main, have up to now remained aloof from the socialist movement of the workers and have joined various reactionary and bourgeois parties. Only an independent organization of the wage-workers which conducts a consistent class struggle can wrest the peasantry from the influence of the bourgeoisie and explain to them the absolute hopelessness of the small producers' position in capitalist society.

In Russia the position of the peasants in relation to capitalism is quite the same as in Austria, Germany, etc. Our "specific feature" is our backwardness: the peasant is still confronted, not with the capitalist, but with the *feudal* big landowner, who is the principal bulwark of the economic and political backwardness of Russia.

*Pravda*, No. 132,
June 11, 1913

Vol. XIX, pp. 179-81

# THE TASKS OF THE PROLETARIAT IN OUR REVOLUTION

## (Draft Platform of the Proletarian Party)
### Excerpt from the Pamphlet

## THE AGRARIAN AND NATIONAL PROGRAMMES

13. At the present moment we cannot say for certain whether a powerful agrarian revolution will develop in the Russian countryside in the near future. We cannot say exactly how profound is the class cleavage within the peasantry, which has undoubtedly grown more profound latterly, between the agricultural labourers, wage-workers, and poor peasants ("semi-proletarians"), on the one hand, and the well-to-do and middle peasants (capitalists and petty capitalists), on the other. Such questions will be, and can be, decided only by actual experience.

But being the party of the proletariat we are unquestionably in duty bound, not only immediately to advance an agrarian (land) programme but also to advocate practical measures which can be immediately realized *in the interests* of the peasant agrarian revolution in Russia.

We must demand the nationalization of *all* the land, i.e., that all the land in the state should become the property of the central state power. This power shall fix the size, etc., of the migration fund, pass legislation for the conservation of forests, for land improvement, etc., and absolutely prohibit any middlemen to interpose themselves between the owner of the land, i.e., the state, and the tenant, i.e., the tiller (prohibit all subletting of land). However, the *disposal* of the land, the determination of the *local regulations* governing ownership and tenure of land, must in no case be placed in the hands of bureaucrats and officials, but exclusively in the hands of the regional and local *Soviets of Peasants' Deputies.*

In order to improve the technique of grain-growing and to increase the output, and in order to develop rational cultivation on a large scale under public control, we must strive within the peasant committees to secure the transformation of every confiscated landed estate into a large model farm controlled by the *Soviets of Agricultural Labourers' Deputies.*

In order to counteract the petty-bourgeois phrasemongering and policy prevailing among the Socialist-Revolutionaries, particularly the idle talk about "consumption" standards or "labour" standards, the "socialization of the land," etc., the Party of the proletariat must make it clear that the small-farming system under commodity production *cannot* save mankind from the poverty and oppression of the masses.

Without necessarily splitting the Soviets of Peasants' Deputies at once, the Party of the proletariat must explain the necessity of organizing separate Soviets of Agricultural Labourers' Deputies and separate Soviets of deputies from the poor (semi-proletarian) peasants, or, at least, of holding regular separate conferences of deputies *of this class status* in the shape of separate groups of parties within the general Soviets of Peasants' Deputies. Otherwise all the honeyed petty-bourgeois talk of the Narodniks regarding the peasants in general will serve as a shield for the deception of the propertyless masses by the well-to-do peasants, who are but one variety of *capitalists.*

To counteract the bourgeois-liberal or purely bureaucratic sermons preached by many Socialist-Revolutionaries and Soviets of Workers' and Soldiers' Deputies, who advise the peasants not to seize the landed estates and not to start the agrarian reform pending the convocation of the Constituent Assembly, the Party of the proletariat must urge the peasants to carry out the agrarian reform at once on their own, and to confiscate the landed estates immediately, upon the decisions of the peasants' deputies in the localities.

At the same time, it is particularly important to insist on the necessity of *increasing* the production of foodstuffs, for the soldiers at the front and for the towns, and on the absolute inadmissibility of causing any damage or injury to livestock, implements, machinery, buildings, etc.

14. As regards the national question, the proletarian Party first of all must advocate the proclamation and immediate realization of complete freedom of secession from Russia for all the nations and peoples who were oppressed by tsarism, or who were forcibly joined to, or forcibly retained within, the boundaries of the state, i.e., annexed.

All statements, declarations, and manifestoes concerning renunciation of annexations, if not accompanied by the realization of the right of secession in practice, are but bourgeois deception of the people, or else pious pettybourgeois wishes.

The proletarian Party strives to create as large a state as possible, for this is to the advantage of the toilers; it strives to bring about a *rapprochement* between nations and the *further fusion* of nations; but it desires to achieve this aim not by violence, but exclusively through a free, fraternal union of the workers and the toiling masses of all nations.

The more democratic the Russian republic is, and the more successfully it organizes itself into a Republic of Soviets of Workers' and Peasants' Deputies, the more powerful will be the force of *voluntary* attraction to such a republic felt by the toiling masses of *all* nations.

Complete freedom of secession, the broadest local (and national) autonomy, and elaborate guarantees of the rights of national minorities—such is the programme of the revolutionary proletariat.

First printed in September 1917
as a separate pamphlet by the
Priboi Publishers

Vol. XXIV, pp. 50-52

# CONGRESS OF PEASANTS' DEPUTIES

A congress of representatives of peasants' organizations and Soviets of Peasants' Deputies who have met to draw up regulations governing the convocation of an All-Russian Soviet of Peasants' Deputies and to set up such Soviets in the localities, has been in session since April 13 in the Taurida Palace.

According to *Dyelo Naroda*,[42] the congress is attended by the representatives of more than 20 gubernias.

So far resolutions have been adopted on the need for the speediest organization of the "peasantry" from bottom to "top." "Soviets of Peasants' Deputies functioning in the various areas" have been recognized as the "best form of organization of the peasantry."

A member of the provisional bureau for the convocation of the present congress, Bykhovsky, has pointed out that a decision to organize the peasantry by setting up an All-Russian Soviet of Peasants' Deputies had been taken by the Moscow Co-operative Congress, which represented an organized membership of twelve million, or a total of fifty million people.

This is an undertaking of enormous importance which must be given every support. If it is carried out without delay, if the peasantry, in spite of Shingaryov,[43] takes all the land into its own hands at once by majority decision and not through "voluntary agreement" with the landlords as he would have it, not only the soldiers, who would receive more bread and meat, but also the cause of freedom would gain by it.

For organization of the peasants, without fail from below, without the officialdom, without the "control and supervision" of the landlords and their hangers-on, is the most reliable, the sole guarantee of the success of the revolution, success of freedom, success in the liberation of Russia from landlord yoke and bondage.

There is no doubt that all the members of our Party, all class-conscious workers, will support in every way the organization of Soviets of Peasants' Deputies, seek to increase their number and consolidate their strength, exert every effort to work inside these Soviets along consistent and strictly proletarian class lines.

To carry on this work, it is necessary to organize separately the proletarian elements (agricultural labourers, day-labourers, etc.) *within* the general peasant Soviets, or (sometimes *and*) set up separate Soviets of Agricultural Labourers' Deputies.

It is not to scatter forces that we propose this; on the contrary, in order to strengthen and broaden the movement, the *very "lowest,"* to use the terminology of the landlords and capitalists, section of society, or more correctly, class, must be aroused.

To advance the movement, it must be freed of the influence of the bourgeoisie; efforts must be made to purge it of the inevitable weaknesses, vacillation, and mistakes of the petty bourgeoisie.

This must be done by means of comradely persuasion, without anticipating events, without hurrying to "consolidate" organizationally that which the representatives of the rural proletarians and semi-proletarians have not as yet fully realized, thought out, understood, and felt *themselves*. But it must be done, and a start must be made at once and everywhere.

The practical demands, slogans, or, more properly, proposals that should be advanced and to which the peasants' *attention* should be drawn, must be immediate, pressing issues dictated by life itself.

The first issue is land. The rural proletarians will support the complete and immediate transfer of *all* land without exception to the whole people, to be taken over immediately by the local committees. But you cannot eat land. The millions of households that have no horses, implements, or seed will gain nothing from the transfer of the land to the "people."

The question of continuing to operate the big farms, whenever there is the slightest possibility of doing so, as large-scale enterprises, directed by agricultural experts and the Soviets of Agricultural Labourers' Deputies and using the best machines, seeds, and most efficient farming methods, must be discussed and practical measures taken without delay.

We cannot conceal from the peasants and still less from the rural proletarians and semi-proletarians the fact that small farming under the conditions of commodity economy and capitalism *cannot* free humanity of mass pauperism, that it is necessary to *think* about going over to large-scale farming conducted for the public account and to *launch out along these lines at once*, teaching the masses and *learning from the masses* what practically expedient measures can be taken to effect such a transition.

Another most important, most pressing question is state organization and administration. It is not enough to advocate democracy, not enough to proclaim it and decree it, not enough to entrust its implementation to the people's "representatives" in representative institutions. Democracy must be *built* at once, from below, through the initiative of the masses themselves, through their effective participation *in all* phases of state activity, without "supervision" from above, without a bureaucracy.

Replacement of the police, the bureaucracy, and the standing army with universal arming of the whole people, a universal *militia* consisting of the whole people, not excluding the women, is a practical matter that can and must be undertaken at once. The more initiative, variety, daring, and ingenuity the masses contribute to this, the better. Not only the rural proletarians and semi-proletarians, but probably nine-tenths of the entire peasantry will follow us if we explain our proposal clearly, simply, understandably, drawing on living examples and the lessons of real life. We propose:

—not to allow any restoration of the police;

—not to allow any restoration of the absolute powers of officials who in practice cannot be removed from office and who belong to the landlord or capitalist class;

—not to allow any restoration of a standing army separated from the people, for such an army is the surest guarantee that attempts of all kinds will be made to stamp out freedom and return to the monarchy;

—to instruct the people, down to the rank and file, in the art of government not only in theory but in practice, by beginning to make use of the experience of the masses, at once and everywhere.

Democracy from below, democracy without an official-dom, without a police, without a standing army; public service by an armed *militia* consisting of the whole people—this is a guarantee of freedom which neither tsars nor blustering generals nor capitalists can take away.

*Pravda*, No. 34,
April 16, 1917

Vol. XXIV, pp. 138-41

# RESOLUTION OF THE SEVENTH (APRIL) ALL-RUSSIAN CONFERENCE OF THE R.S.D.L.P. (B.) ON THE AGRARIAN QUESTION

The existence of landlord ownership of land in Russia is the material mainstay of the power of the feudal landlords and a pledge of the possibility of the restoration of the monarchy. This system of land ownership inevitably condemns the overwhelming mass of the population of Russia, the peasantry, to pauperism, bondage, and a downtrodden existence, and the entire country to backwardness in every sphere of life.

Peasant land ownership in Russia, both in the case of allotted land (communal and homestead) and of private land (leased or purchased), is fettered from top to bottom, and all around, by old semi-feudal ties and relationships, by the division of the peasants into categories inherited from the time of serfdom, by interspersed holdings, and so forth. The necessity of breaking down these antiquated and injurious partitions, of "unenclosing" the land, and of reconstructing all the relations of land ownership and agriculture so as to adjust them to the new conditions of Russian and world economy, forms the material basis of the desire of the peasantry for the nationalization of *all* the land in the state.

Whatever the petty-bourgeois utopias in which all Narodnik parties and groups array the struggle of the peasant masses against feudal landlord ownership of land and against all the feudal fetters which enmesh all land ownership and land tenure in Russia generally—in itself that struggle is an expression of a thoroughly bourgeois-democratic, undoubtedly progressive, and economically essential striving resolutely to break all those fetters.

Nationalization of the land, while it is a bourgeois measure, provides the greatest amount of freedom for the class struggle and divests land tenure of all non-bourgeois accessories to the utmost degree possible and conceivable in a capitalist society. Moreover, nationalization of the land, representing as it does the abolition of private ownership of land, would in practice deal such a mighty blow to the private ownership of all means of production in general that the Party of the proletariat must assist such a reform in every possible way.

On the other hand, the well-to-do peasants of Russia have long ago evolved the elements of a peasant bourgeoisie, and the Stolypin agrarian reform[44] has undoubtedly strengthened, multiplied, and fortified these elements. At the other pole of the rural population, the agricultural wage-workers, the proletarians, and the mass of semi-proletarian peasantry, who stand close to the proletarians, have likewise become strengthened and multiplied.

The more determined and consistent the break-up and elimination of the landed estates and the more determined and consistent the bourgeois-democratic agrarian reform in Russia in general, the more vigorous and speedy will be the development of the class struggle of the agricultural proletariat against the well-to-do peasantry (the peasant bourgeoisie).

The fate and the outcome of the Russian revolution will depend on whether the urban proletariat succeeds in securing the following of the rural proletariat, together with the mass of rural semi-proletarians, or whether this mass follows the peasant bourgeoisie, which is gravitating towards an alliance with Guchkov and Milyukov, with the capitalists and landlords, and the counter-revolution in general—unless the incipient proletarian revolution in Europe exercises a direct and powerful influence on our country.

In view of this class situation and relation of forces the conference resolves that:

1) The Party of the proletariat will fight with all its might for the immediate and complete confiscation of all

landed estates in Russia (and also appanage lands, church lands, crown lands, etc., etc.);

2) The Party will vigorously advocate the immediate transfer of all lands to the peasantry organized in Soviets of Peasants' Deputies, or in other organs of local self-government elected in a really democratic way and entirely independent of the landlords and officials;

3) The Party of the proletariat demands the nationalization of all the land in the state; nationalization, which signifies the transfer of the right of ownership of all land to the state, vests the right of administering the land in local democratic institutions;

4) The Party must, on the one hand, wage a determined struggle against the Provisional Government, which, both through Shingaryov as its mouthpiece and by its collective utterances, is trying to force the peasants to come to "voluntary agreement with the landlords," i.e., is trying virtually to impose upon them a reform which suits the interests of the landlords, and is threatening the peasants with punishment for "unauthorized action," that is, with the use of violence by a minority of the population (the landlords and capitalists) against the majority. On the other hand, the Party must wage a determined struggle against the petty-bourgeois vacillations of the majority of the Narodniks and the Menshevik Social-Democrats, who are advising the peasants not to take all the land pending the convocation of the Constituent Assembly;

5) The Party advises the peasants to take the land in an organized way, not allowing the slightest damage to property, and taking measures to increase production;

6) Any agrarian reform in general can be successful and durable only provided the whole state is democratized, i.e., provided, on the one hand, the police, the standing army, and the actually privileged bureaucracy are abolished, and provided, on the other, there exists a system of broad local self-government wholly exempt from supervision and tutelage from above;

7) The separate and independent organization of the agricultural proletariat must be undertaken immediately and everywhere, both in the form of Soviets of Agricultural

Labourers' Deputies (as well as of separate Soviets of deputies of the semi-proletarian peasantry), and in the form
of proletarian groups or fractions within the general Soviets of Peasants' Deputies, in all local and municipal
government bodies, etc., etc.;

8) The Party must support the initiative of those peasant committees which in a number of localities in Russia
are handing over the livestock and agricultural implements of the landlords to the peasantry organized in those
committees, to be used in a socially regulated manner for
the cultivation of all the land;

9) The Party of the proletariat must advise the rural
proletarians and semi-proletarians to strive to convert
every landed estate into a fair-sized model farm to be
conducted for the public account by the Soviets of Agricultural Labourers' Deputies under the direction of agricultural experts and with the application of the best technique.

*Pravda*, No. 45,
May 13 (April 30), 1917

Vol. XXIV, pp. 257-60

## OPEN LETTER TO THE DELEGATES
## TO THE ALL-RUSSIAN
## CONGRESS OF PEASANTS' DEPUTIES

Comrades peasants' deputies,

The Central Committee of the Russian Social-Democratic Labour Party (Bolsheviks), to which I have the honour to belong, wanted me to represent our Party at the peasant congress, but illness has prevented me from carrying out this mission. I therefore take the liberty of addressing this open letter to you in order to greet the all-Russian association of the peasantry and briefly to point out the deep-going differences existing between our Party and the party of the Socialist-Revolutionaries and the Menshevik Social-Democrats.

These deep-going differences concern the three most important questions: the land, the war, and state organization.

All the land must belong to the people. All the landed estates must be turned over to the peasants without compensation. This is clear. The dispute here is whether or not the peasants in the various localities should take the land at once, without paying any rent to the landlords or waiting for the Constituent Assembly.

Our Party believes that they should, and advises the peasants locally to take over all the land without delay, and to do it in as organized a way as possible, under no circumstances allowing damage to property and exerting every effort to increase the production of grain and meat since the troops at the front are in dire straits. In any case, although the final decision on how to dispose of the land will be made by the Constituent Assembly, a preliminary settlement now, at once, in time for the spring sowing, can be made only by local institutions, inasmuch as our Provisional Government, which is a government of the landlords and capitalists, is putting off the convocation of the Constituent Assembly and so far has not even appointed a date for it.

Only local institutions are able preliminarily to take charge of the land. The fields must be planted to crops. The majority of the peasants in the various localities are perfectly capable of making use of the land in an organized way, of ploughing and putting it all under crops. This is essential if the supply of food to the soldiers at the front is to be improved. Hence to wait for the Constituent Assembly is out of the question. We by no means deny the right of the Constituent Assembly finally to institute public ownership of the land and to regulate its disposal. In the meantime, however, right now, this spring, the peasants themselves must decide locally what to do with it. The soldiers at the front can and should send delegates to the villages.

Further. For all the land to pass over to the working people, a close alliance of the urban workers and the poorest peasants (semi-proletarians) is essential. Unless such an alliance is formed, the capitalists cannot be defeated. And if they are not defeated, no transfer of the land to the people will deliver it from poverty. You cannot eat land, and without money, without capital, there is no way of obtaining implements, livestock, or seed. The peasants must trust not the capitalists or the rich muzhiks (who are capitalists too), but only the urban workers. Only in alliance with the latter can the poorest peasants ensure that the land, the railways, the banks, and the factories become the property of all working people; if this is not done, the transfer of the land to the people cannot alone abolish want and pauperism.

Workers in certain localities in Russia are already beginning to establish their supervision (control) over the factories. Such control by the workers is beneficial to the peasants, for it will result in higher production and cheaper products. The peasants must give every support to such initiative on the part of the workers and not believe the slander which the capitalists spread against the workers.

The second question is the question of the war.

The present war is a war of conquest. It is being waged by the capitalists of all countries with predatory aims, to increase their profits. To the working people this war does not and cannot under any circumstances bring anything but death, suffering, destruction, and savagery. That is why our Party, the Party of class-conscious workers and the poorest peasants, vigorously and unconditionally condemns this war, refuses to justify the capitalists of the one country as against the capitalists of another, refuses to support the capitalists of any country whatever, and is working for the speediest termination of the war through the overthrow of the capitalists in all countries, through the workers' revolution in all countries.

In the new Provisional Government we now have, there are ten ministers belonging to the landlord and capitalist parties and six to the Narodnik (Socialist-Revolutionary) and Menshevik Social-Democratic parties. We are convinced that the Narodniks and Mensheviks have made a grave and fatal mistake by entering the capitalist government and in general agreeing to support it. Men like Tsereteli and Chernov are hoping to induce the capitalists to bring the present predatory war to an earlier and more honourable end. But these leaders of the Narodnik and Menshevik parties are making a mistake: they are actually helping the capitalists to prepare an offensive by the Russian troops against Germany, that is, to drag out the war, to add to the unprecedentedly enormous sacrifices the Russian people have made in the war.

We are convinced that the capitalists in all countries are deceiving the people by promising an early and just peace when they are actually prolonging the war of conquest. The Russian capitalists, who controlled the old Provisional Government and continue to control the new one, did not even wish to publish the secret plunder agreements ex-tsar Nikolai Romanov concluded with the capitalists of Britain, France, and other countries with the object of seizing Constantinople from the Turks and taking away Galicia from the Austrians, Armenia from the Turks, and so on. The Provisional Government has confirmed these agreements.

Our Party maintains that these agreements are just as criminal and predatory as the treaties the German brig-and-capitalists and their brigand-emperor Wilhelm have with their allies.

The workers' and peasants' blood must not be shed for the sake of such plunderous aims of the capitalists.

This criminal war must be brought to the speediest end, *not* by a separate peace with Germany, *but by a universal peace*, not by a capitalist peace, but by a peace of the working masses *against* the capitalists. There is only one way to achieve this: by the transfer of all state power wholly into the hands of the Soviets of Workers', Soldiers', and Peasants' Deputies both in Russia and in other countries. Only such Soviets will be able really to prevent the capitalists from deceiving the peoples, to prevent the capitalists from prolonging the war.

I now come to the third and last of the questions I have mentioned: the question of state organization.

Russia must become a democratic republic. Even the majority of the landlords and capitalists, who have always stood for the monarchy but now see that the people of Russia will on no account allow it to be restored, are in agreement with this. The capitalists now have directed all their efforts at making the Russian republic as much like a monarchy as possible so that it might be changed back into a monarchy with the least difficulty (this has happened time and again in many countries). For this purpose the capitalists want to preserve the bureaucracy standing *above* the people, to preserve the police and the standing army separated from the people and commanded by non-elective generals and other officers. And the generals and other officers, unless they are elected, will almost invariably be landlords and capitalists. This we know if only from the experience of all the republics in the world.

Our Party, the Party of class-conscious workers and the poorest peasants, is therefore working for a democratic republic of another kind. We want a republic where there

13*

is no police that browbeats the people; where all officials, from top to bottom, are elected and subject to recall whenever the people demand it, and paid salaries not higher than the wages of a good worker; where all army officers are similarly elective and where the standing army separated from the people and subordinated to classes alien to the people is replaced by the armed people, a universal, popular militia.

We want a republic where all state power, from the bottom to the top, belongs wholly and exclusively to the Soviets of workers', soldiers', peasants', and other deputies.

The workers and peasants are the majority of the population. The power must belong to them, not to the landlords or the capitalists.

The workers and peasants are the majority of the population. The power and the functions of administration must belong to *their Soviets*, not the bureaucracy.

Such are our views, comrades peasant deputies. We are firmly convinced that experience will soon show the broadest masses of the people how erroneous is the policy of the Narodniks and Mensheviks. Experience will soon show the masses that compromise with the capitalists cannot save Russia, which, like Germany and other countries, is standing on the brink of disaster, cannot save the war-tormented peoples. The transfer of all state power directly to the majority of the population alone can save the peoples.

Petrograd, May 7, 1917

Published May 24 (11), 1917, in
the newspaper *Soldatskaya
Pravda*, No. 19

Vol. XXIV, pp. 335-39

# DRAFT RESOLUTION ON THE AGRARIAN QUESTION SUBMITTED TO THE FIRST ALL-RUSSIAN CONGRESS OF PEASANTS' DEPUTIES

1) All landed estates and privately owned lands, as well as appanages, church lands, etc., are to be turned over immediately to the people without any compensation.

2) The peasantry must in an organized manner, through their Soviets of Peasants' Deputies, immediately take over all the land in their localities, for the purpose of its economic exploitation, without, however, in any way prejudicing thereby the final establishment of land regulations by the Constituent Assembly or by the All-Russian Council of Soviets, should the people decide to entrust the central power of the state to such a Council of Soviets.

3) Private property in land generally must be abolished, i.e., the ownership of the whole land shall be vested solely in the whole people, while the disposal of the land shall be entrusted to the local democratic institutions.

4) The peasants must reject the advice of the capitalists and landlords and of their Provisional Government to come to "an agreement" with the landlords in each locality as to the immediate disposal of the land; the disposal of all the land must be determined by the organized decision of the majority of the local peasants, and not by an agreement between the majority, i.e., the peasants, and the minority, and an insignificant minority at that, i.e., the landlords.

5) Not only the landlords are fighting and will continue to fight with every means at their disposal against the transfer of the landed estates to the peasants without compensation, but also the capitalists, who wield tremendous power not only because of their money, but because of

their influence on the as yet unenlightened masses through
the newspapers, the numerous officials, employees, etc.,
accustomed to the domination of capital. Hence, the transfer without compensation of all the landed estates to the
peasantry cannot be effected completely and secured unless the confidence of the peasant masses in the capitalists
is destroyed, unless a close alliance is established between
the peasantry and the city workers, and unless the state
power is completely taken by the Soviets of workers', soldiers', peasants', and other deputies. Only a state power
which is in the hands of such Soviets, and which governs
the state not through a police, or a bureaucracy, or a
standing army separated from the people, but through a
popular, universal armed militia of workers and peasants,
can guarantee the realization of the above-mentioned agrarian reforms, which are being demanded by the entire
peasantry.

6) Agricultural labourers and poorest peasants, i.e.,
such as for the lack of sufficient land, cattle, and implements secure their livelihood partly by working for hire,
must make every effort to organize themselves independently into separate Soviets, or into separate groups within
the general Peasants' Soviets, in order to defend their interests against the rich peasants, who inevitably strive to
form an alliance with the capitalists and landlords.

7) As a result of the war, Russia, like all other belliger-
ent countries, as well as many neutral (non-belligerent)
countries, is being threatened by economic dislocation, disaster, and famine because of the shortage of hands, coal,
iron, etc. Only if the Workers' and Peasants' Deputies assume control and supervision over the entire production
and distribution of goods can the country be saved. It is
therefore necessary to proceed immediately to arrange
agreements between Soviets of Peasants' Deputies and Soviets of Workers' Deputies regarding the exchange of
grain and other rural products for implements, footwear,
clothing, etc., without the intermediary of the capitalists,
who must be removed from the management of the factories. With the same purpose in view, the peasants' committees must be encouraged to take over the livestock and

implements of the landlords, such livestock and implements to be used in common. Similarly, the conversion of
all large landed estates into model farms must be encouraged, the land to be cultivated collectively with the
aid of the best implements under the direction of agricultural experts and in accordance with the decisions of the
Soviets of Agricultural Labourers' Deputies.

Written before May 17 (30),
1917
First published in 1917 in the
pamphlet *Material on the
Agrarian Question*, Priboi Publishers.

Vol. XXIV, pp. 445-47

# THE NEED FOR A RURAL WORKERS' UNION
## IN RUSSIA

### FIRST ARTICLE

One highly important question that must be raised at the all-Russian trade-union conference now in session in Petrograd is the establishment of an all-Russian union of *rural workers*.

All classes in Russia are organizing. Only the class which is the most exploited and the poorest of all, the most disunited and the most crushed, the agricultural wage-workers of Russia, seems to have been forgotten. In some non-Russian border territories, in the Latvian area, for instance, there are organizations of agricultural wage-workers. The vast majority of the Great Russian and Ukrainian gubernias have no class organizations of the rural proletariat.

It is indisputably the prime duty of the vanguard of the proletarians of Russia, the industrial workers' trade unions, to come to the aid of their brothers, the rural workers. The difficulties involved in organizing the rural workers are manifestly enormous, as is borne out also by the experience of all other capitalist countries.

All the more necessary is it then to make use with the utmost speed and vigour of political freedom in Russia and establish at once an all-Russian union of rural workers. The body that can and must do this is the trade-union conference. The more experienced, more developed, more class-conscious representatives of the proletariat gathered at this conference are the people who can and must issue a call to the rural workers, urging the latter to join them in the ranks of the independently organizing proletarians, the ranks of their trade unions. It is the wage-workers at the factories who must take the initiative and make use of the trade-union cells, groups, and branches spread all over Russia to awaken the rural worker to independent life and active participation in the struggle to improve his position, to uphold his class interests.

It may seem to many, and perhaps to most at the present moment, that with the peasantry organizing all over Russia and declaring for abolition of private property in land and for its "equal" use, this is not the time to establish a rural workers' union.

Quite the contrary. This is precisely the time when it is particularly and urgently imperative to do this. Those who share the proletarian class point of view can have no doubt as to the correctness of the proposition which the Bolsheviks advanced and the Mensheviks accepted at the Stockholm Congress of the Russian Social-Democratic Labour Party in 1906, and which has ever since been included in the programme of the R.S.D.L.P. This proposition is:

"The Party, *whenever* and *whatever* democratic agrarian reforms are carried out, makes it its aim *steadfastly* to strive for *independent class* organization of the *rural proletariat*, to explain to them the irreconcilable antagonism of their interests and the interests of the peasant bourgeoisie, to warn them against illusory faith in the small-holding system, which can never, so long as commodity production exists, do away with the poverty of the masses, and, finally, to point to the need for a complete socialist revolution as the only way to abolish all poverty and all exploitation."

No class-conscious worker, no member of a trade union, denies the correctness of these propositions. To carry them out, inasmuch as it is a question of *independent class organization of the rural proletariat*, is something precisely the trade unions must do.

We hope that at this revolutionary time, when the striving to express themselves, to chart their own path, to see to it that life is not shaped anew without the workers themselves independently deciding issues pertaining to labour, is making itself felt among the working masses in general and the workers in particular—that at this time the trade unions will not confine themselves to narrow craft interests and forget their weaker brothers, the rural workers, but will exert all their energy to help the latter by founding a union of the rural workers of Russia.

In the next article we shall try to outline some practical steps in this direction.

## SECOND ARTICLE

In the previous article we dealt with the significance of a rural workers' union in Russia as a matter of principle. Here we shall touch upon certain practical aspects of the question.

A union of the rural workers of Russia should unite all who are engaged largely or mainly, *or even part time*, as wage-workers at agricultural enterprises.

Whether or not it will be necessary to subdivide such unions into those of pure agricultural workers and those of part-time wage-workers experience will tell. At any rate, this is not the essential thing. What is essential is that the fundamental class interests of *all* who sell their labour power are identical and that the union of *all* who even partly gain their livelihood by hiring out to "strangers" is absolutely necessary.

The wage-workers in the cities, those who work at factories and mills, are bound by thousands and millions of ties with the wage-workers in the countryside. A call issued by the former to the latter cannot remain unheeded. But it is not only a matter of issuing such a call. The urban workers have far more experience, knowledge, means, and strength. *Part of this strength* must be used to *help* the rural workers to *get on their feet*.

All organized workers should give one day's wages to promoting and strengthening the unity of the wage-workers of town and country. A definite part of this sum ought to be the urban workers' contribution to advancing class organization of the rural workers. This fund should cover the expense of putting out the most popular kind of leaflets, of publishing a rural workers' newspaper, even a weekly one to begin with, and of sending at least a few agitators and organizers to the countryside in order *to establish at once* unions of agricultural wage-labourers in the various localities.

Only the experience gained by such unions themselves will help to find the correct path for developing this work further. The prime task of each such union must be improvement of the conditions of those who sell their labour power to agricultural enterprises, winning of higher wages, better housing conditions, better food, etc.

A most determined war must be declared on the preconceived notion that the coming abolition of private property in land can "give land" to every farm-hand and day-labourer and undermine the very foundations of wage-labour in agriculture. This is a preconceived notion and an extremely pernicious one at that. The abolition of private property in land is a tremendous and unquestionably progressive reform that undoubtedly corresponds to the interests of economic development and the interests of the proletariat, a reform which every wage-worker will support heart and soul, but it in no way does away with wage-labour.

You cannot eat land. You cannot farm without livestock, implements, seed, a reserve of produce, or money. To rely on "promises," whoever they may emanate from, that the wage-workers in the villages will be "helped" to acquire cattle, implements, etc., would be the worst kind of mistake, unforgivable naiveté.

The basic rule, the first commandment of any trade-union movement is not to rely on the "state," to rely only on the *strength of your own class*. The state is an organization of the ruling class.

Do not rely on promises—rely only on the unity and consciousness of your class!

Hence it must be made the task of the rural workers' trade union from the very outset not only to fight for the improvement of the workers' conditions in general, but in particular *to defend their interests as a class* in the course of the forthcoming great land reform.

"Farm-hands must be placed at the disposal of the volost committees," the peasants and the Socialist-Revolutionaries often reason. The agricultural wage-worker class holds the very opposite view: the volost committees must be placed at the disposal of the "hands"! The position of the master and the position of the wage-worker thus stand out clearly defined.

"The land must belong to the whole people." This is correct. *But the people are divided into classes.* Every worker knows, sees, feels, experiences the truth of this fact which the bourgeoisie deliberately seeks to conceal and the *petty bourgeois always forgets.*

Alone the poor man is helpless. No "state" will help the rural wage-worker, the farm-hand, the day-labourer, the poor peasant, the semi-proletarian *if he does not help himself.* The first step in this direction is independent class organization of the rural proletariat.

We hope that the all-Russian trade-union conference will undertake this most energetically, issue a call to all Russia, stretch out a helping hand, the mighty hand of the organized vanguard of the proletariat, to the proletarians of the countryside.

*Pravda*, Nos. 90 and 91, July 7
(June 24) and July 8 (June
25), 1917

Vol. XXV, pp. 103-107

# FROM A PUBLICIST'S DIARY

## THE PEASANTS AND THE WORKERS

*The Izvestia of the All-Russian Soviet of Peasants' Deputies*, No. 88, of August 19, carries an exceedingly interesting article which should be regarded as a basic document by every Party propagandist and agitator who has anything to do with the peasantry and by every class-conscious worker who is going to the countryside or comes in contact with it.

This article is entitled "Model Mandate Compiled on the Basis of 242 Mandates Submitted by Local Deputies to the First All-Russian Congress of Peasants' Deputies Held in Petrograd in 1917."

It would be most desirable for the Soviet of Peasants' Deputies to publish as detailed information as possible about all these mandates (if it is absolutely impossible to print them all in full, which of course would be the very best thing). For instance, it would be particularly necessary to give a full list of the gubernias, uyezds, and volosts, showing how many mandates have been received from each locality, when they were compiled or delivered, and to analyze at least the basic demands so that one could tell whether the various points differ according to areas; whether such questions as abolition of private property rights to all *peasant* lands, periodic redistribution of land, prohibition of wage-labour, confiscation of the landlords' implements and livestock, etc., etc., are put differently in, say, areas with homestead and communal land ownership, areas with Great Russian and non-Russian populations, central areas and outlying ones, areas that never had serfdom, and so on. No scientific study of the extraordinarily valuable material contained in the peasant mandates is

possible without such detail. And we Marxists must exert
every effort to make a scientific study of the facts that un-
derlie our policy.

In the absence of better material, and so long as it has
not been proved factually incorrect in one or another respect, the *summary of the mandates* (as we shall call the
"model mandate") remains the only material of its kind
which, we repeat, must absolutely be placed in the hands
of every member of our Party.

The first part of the summary is devoted to general
political principles, demands of political democracy; the
second, to the land question. (It is to be hoped that the
All-Russian Soviet of Peasants' Deputies or some other
body will summarize the peasants' mandates and resolutions concerning the war.) Without dwelling in detail on
the first part, we shall note only two points in it, § 6, demanding the election of all office-holders, and § 11, calling
for the abolition of the standing army once the war is over.
These points bring the political programme of the peasants
*closest of all* to the programme of the Bolshevik Party.
Basing ourselves on these points, we must point out and
prove through all our propaganda and agitation that the
Menshevik and Socialist-Revolutionary leaders are traitors
not only to socialism, but also to democracy, inasmuch as
in Kronstadt, for instance, contrary to the will of the population and the principles of democracy, and to please the
capitalists, they upheld the office of a commissar subject
to *approval* by the government, that is, an office not purely
elective. In the District Dumas of Petrograd and other
municipal institutions the Socialist-Revolutionary and
Menshevik leaders, contrary to the principles of democracy, are fighting the Bolshevik demand for the immediate institution of a workers' militia with a view to
going over to a universal popular militia later on.

According to the summary, the land demands of the
peasantry are primarily abolition of all types of private
ownership of land, including the peasants' lands, without
compensation; transfer of lands on which high-level scientific farming is practised to the state or the communities;
confiscation of all the livestock and implements on the

confiscated lands (peasants with little land are not included) and their transfer to the state or the communities; no
hired labour to be permitted; distribution of land among
the toilers on an equality basis, with periodical redistribu-
tions, and so on. In the transition period pending the convocation of the Constituent Assembly, the peasants
demand *immediate* enactment of laws prohibiting the
purchase and sale of land, abolition of laws concerning
separation from the community, individual farmholds,[45]
etc., laws on the protection of forests, fisheries, etc., on
abolition of long-term and revision of short-term leases,
and so on.

One need not ponder long over these demands to see
the utter impossibility of their realization *in alliance* with
the capitalists, without a complete break with them, without waging the most determined and ruthless struggle against the capitalist class, without overthrowing its
rule.

The Socialist-Revolutionaries are deceiving themselves
and the peasantry precisely by assuming and spreading
the idea that such reforms, or *similar* reforms, are possible
without overthrowing the rule of the capitalists, without
all state power being transferred to the proletariat, without the poorest peasantry supporting the most resolute,
revolutionary measures of a proletarian state power
against the capitalists. The significance of the appearance
of a Left wing among the "Socialist-Revolutionaries" lies
precisely in the fact that it proves there is a growing
awareness of this deception within this party.

Indeed, confiscation of all privately-owned land means
the confiscation of hundreds of millions of capital belonging to the banks to whom the greater part of this land is
mortgaged. Is any measure of the kind possible without
the revolutionary class overcoming the capitalist resistance by revolutionary means? Moreover, what is in question here is the most highly centralized capital of all, bank
capital, which is bound by billions of threads with all the
nerve centres of the capitalist economy of a huge country
and which can be defeated only by the no less centralized
might of the urban proletariat.

Further, take the transfer to the state of highly-efficient farms. Is it not obvious that the "state" capable of taking them over and running them really in the interests of the working people and not the officials and the very same capitalists can only be the proletarian revolutionary state?

The confiscation of stud farms, etc., and then of all live-stock and implements, is something more than raining one giant blow after another at private property in the means of production. It means taking stride after stride toward socialism, for the transfer of *livestock and implements* "into the exclusive use of the state or a community" signifies the need for large-scale, socialist agriculture or at least so-cialist control over united small farms, socialist regula-tion of their economy.

And what about "not permitting" hired labour? This is an empty phrase, helpless, unreasoned, and naive wishful thinking on the part of downtrodden petty proprietors who do not see that capitalist industry as a whole would come to a standstill if there were no reserve army of wage-labour in the countryside, that it is impossible "not to per-mit" wage-labour in the villages when it is allowed in the cities, and finally that "not to permit" wage-labour means nothing else but a step toward socialism.

Here we come to the fundamental question of the atti-tude of the workers to the peasants.

A mass Social-Democratic workers' movement has been in existence in Russia for more than twenty years (if we count from the great strikes of 1896). Throughout this long span of time, through two great revolutions, the issue of whether the working class is to lead the peasants for-ward, to socialism, or whether the liberal bourgeoisie is to drag them back, to conciliation with capitalism, can be traced through the entire political history of Russia.

The opportunist wing of Social-Democracy has always been guided in its reasoning by this astute formula: *since* the Socialist-Revolutionaries are petty bourgeois, "we" discard their middle-class utopian views on socialism *for the sake of* bourgeois rejection of socialism. Marxism is neatly substituted by Struvism, and Menshevism slithers down to playing the part of a Constitutional-Democrat flunkey that seeks to "reconcile" the peasants to rule by the bourgeoisie. Tsereteli and Skobelev, hand in hand with Chernov and Avksentyev, busy signing the Constitutional Democrats' reactionary landlord decrees in the name of "revolutionary democracy"—such is the latest and most striking manifestation of this role of a flunkey.

Revolutionary Social-Democracy, which never has refrained from criticism of the petty-bourgeois illusions of the Socialist-Revolutionaries, and *never entered into any bloc* with them except *against* the Constitutional Democrats, works unremittingly *to wrest* the peasants away from Constitutional-Democrat influence and opposes to the middle-class utopian view of socialism not liberal conciliation with capitalism, but the revolutionary proletarian road to socialism.

Now, when the war has speeded up developments to an extraordinary degree, aggravated the crisis of capitalism to the extreme, and faced the peoples with the necessity of choosing without delay between destruction and immediate determined strides toward socialism—at this time the full depth of the gulf between semi-liberal Menshevism and revolutionary-proletarian Bolshevism is revealed clearly in the practical question of what action the tens of millions of peasants should take.

Accept the rule of capital *because* "we" are not yet ripe for socialism, the Mensheviks tell the peasants, substituting, incidentally, the abstract question of "socialism" in general for the concrete question of whether it is at all possible to heal the wounds inflicted by the war without decisive strides toward socialism.

Accept capitalism, *because* the Socialist-Revolutionaries are petty-bourgeois utopians, the Mensheviks tell the peasants and rally together with the Socialist-Revolutionaries to support the Constitutional-Democrat government....

And the Socialist-Revolutionaries, beating their breast, assure the peasants that they are opposed to any peace with the capitalists, that they have never regarded the Russian revolution as a bourgeois revolution—and *because of this* enter into a bloc *precisely* with the opportunist Social-Democrats and rally to support precisely a bourgeois government.... The Socialist-Revolutionaries sign all programmes advanced by the peasantry, even the most revolutionary, only not to carry them out, but to pigeonhole them, only to deceive the peasants with empty promises, while actually pursuing a policy of conciliation with the Constitutional Democrats in the coalition government for months.

This crying, practical, direct, palpable betrayal of the peasants' interests by the Socialist-Revolutionaries radically changes the situation. We must take this change into account. It is not enough to conduct agitation against the Socialist-Revolutionaries only in the old way, the way we did in 1902-03 and 1905-07. It is not enough to expose theoretically the petty-bourgeois illusions of "socialization of land," "equal use of land," "not permitting hired labour," etc.

That was on the eve of the bourgeois revolution, or before the bourgeois revolution had been completed, and the task consisted primarily in carrying it on to the overthrow of the monarchy.

Now the monarchy has been overthrown. The bourgeois revolution has been completed insofar as Russia has become a democratic republic with a government consisting of Constitutional Democrats, Mensheviks and Socialist-Revolutionaries. And the war in the past three years has advanced us a good thirty years ahead, imposed upon Europe universal labour service and the compulsory syndication of enterprises, caused hunger and unprecedented devastation in the leading countries, and made steps toward socialism imperative.

Only the proletariat and the peasantry can overthrow the monarchy—this was the fundamental premise of our class policy at that time. And this premise was the correct one. February and March 1917 once again confirmed this.

Only the proletariat, leading the poorest peasantry (the semi-proletarians, as our programme puts it), can end the war with a democratic peace, heal the wounds it has inflicted, and initiate the steps toward socialism which have become absolutely necessary and *urgent*—this is premise of our class policy today.

Hence the conclusion: the emphasis in our propaganda and agitation against the Socialist-Revolutionaries must be shifted to the fact that they have betrayed the peasants. They represent not the mass of peasant poor, but a minority of well-to-do farmers. They are leading the peasantry not toward alliance with the workers, but to alliance with the capitalists, i.e., subordination to them. They have bartered the interests of the working and exploited masses for ministerial seats, for a bloc with the Mensheviks and the Constitutional Democrats.

History, accelerated by the war, has forged so far ahead that the old formulas have acquired new content. "Not permitting hired labour" was formerly *only* an empty phrase bandied about by the petty-bourgeois intellectual. In the life of today it means something entirely different: the millions of peasant poor in their 242 mandates declare that they want hired labour abolished, but they do not know how to do it. We know how. We know that this can be done only in alliance with the workers, under the workers' leadership, against the capitalists, not through conciliation with them.

Such are the changes that must be introduced now in the basic line of our propaganda and agitation against the Socialist-Revolutionaries, the basic line we pursue in addressing the peasantry.

The Socialist-Revolutionary Party has betrayed you, comrades peasants. It has betrayed the hovels and gone over to the side of the palaces, if not the palaces of the monarch, then the palaces where the Constitutional Democrats, those mortal enemies of the revolution and the peasant revolution in particular, sit in the same government with the Chernovs, Peshekhonovs, and Avksentyevs.

Only the revolutionary proletariat, only the vanguard that unites it, the Party of the Bolsheviks, can *actually* carry out the programme of the peasant poor which is set forth in the 242 mandates. For the revolutionary proletariat is *really* forging on toward the abolition of wage-labour along the only correct path, through the overthrow of capital and not through prohibition of the employment of hired labour, not by "not permitting" the hiring of

14*

hands. The revolutionary proletariat is really forging on toward confiscation of land, implements, agricultural technical enterprises, toward what the peasants want and what the Socialist-Revolutionaries *cannot* give them.

Such is the change that must now be made in the basic line pursued by the worker in addressing the peasant. We workers can and will give you what the peasant poor want and are searching for without always knowing where and how to find it. We workers are upholding our own interests and at the same time the interests of the vast majority of the peasants *against the capitalists*, while the Socialist-Revolutionaries, allying themselves with the capitalists, are betraying these interests.

\*    \*    \*

Let us recall what Engels said on the peasant question shortly before his death. He stressed that Socialists have no intention whatever of expropriating the small peasants, and that the advantages of mechanized socialist agriculture will be made clear to them only by the *force of example.*

The war has now confronted Russia in practice with a problem of precisely this order. There is a shortage of implements. They must be confiscated, and the highly efficient farms "must not be divided up."

The peasants have begun to realize this. Need has compelled them to do so. The war has compelled them, for there are no implements to be had anywhere. What there is must be thriftily husbanded. And large-scale farming means saving of labour through the use of implements as well as in many other respects.

The peasants want to keep their small farms, to set equal standards for all, and to make readjustments on an equality basis from time to time. ... Let that be so. No intelligent Socialist will part ways with the peasant poor because of this. If the land is confiscated, that *means* that the domination of the banks has been undermined, if the implements are confiscated, that *means* that the domination of capital has been undermined—and in that case, *provided the proletariat rules in the centre*, provided political power is taken over by the proletariat, the rest will come about *of itself* as a result of the "force of example," prompted by practical developments as such.

The crux of the matter lies in political power passing into the hands of the proletariat. When that has taken place, everything that is essential, basic, fundamental in the programme set out in the 242 mandates *will become feasible*. Life itself will show with what amendments it will be carried out. This is not an urgent issue. We are not doctrinaires. Our theory is no dogma, but a guide to action.

We do not claim that Marx or the Marxists know the road to socialism to the last concrete detail. To claim anything of the kind would be absurd. What we know is the direction of this road, we know what class forces follow it; the concrete, practical details will be revealed only by the *experience of the millions* when they take things into their own hands.

Have confidence in the workers, comrades peasants, and break with the capitalists! Only in close alliance with the workers *can* you begin to realize in practice the programme set forth in the 242 mandates. Allied with the capitalists and led by the Socialist-Revolutionaries, you will never live to see *a single* determined, resolute step in the spirit of this programme.

When in alliance with the urban workers, waging a ruthless struggle against capital, you *begin* to realize the programme of the 242 mandates, the whole world will come to your and our assistance and the success of the programme—not as it is formulated at present, but as regards its substance—will be ensured. When that happens, the domination of capital and wage slavery will come to an end. That will be the beginning of the era of socialism, the era of peace, the era of the working people.

*Rabochy*, No. 6,
September 11 (August 29),
1917

Vol. XXV, pp. 253-60

# REPORT ON THE LAND AT THE
## SECOND ALL-RUSSIAN CONGRESS
## OF SOVIETS OF WORKERS' AND SOLDIERS' DEPUTIES

*October 26 (November 8), 1917*

We maintain that the revolution has proved and demonstrated how important it is that the land question should be put clearly. The outbreak of the armed uprising, the second, the October Revolution, clearly proves that the land must be turned over to the peasants. The government that has been overthrown and the compromising parties of the Mensheviks and Socialist-Revolutionaries committed a crime when they kept postponing the settlement of the land question on various pretexts and thereby brought the country to economic dislocation and a peasant revolt. Their talk about riots and anarchy in the countryside sounds false, cowardly, and deceitful. Where and when have riots and anarchy been provoked by wise measures? If the government had acted wisely, and if their measures had met the needs of the poor peasants, would there have been unrest among the peasant masses? But all the measures of the government, approved by the Avksentyev and Dan Soviets,[46] went counter to the interests of the peasants and compelled them to revolt.

Having provoked the revolt, the government raised a hue and cry about riots and anarchy, for which they themselves were responsible. They were going to crush it by blood and iron, but were themselves swept away by the armed uprising of the revolutionary soldiers, sailors, and workers. The first duty of the government of the workers' and peasants' revolution must be to settle the land question, which can pacify and satisfy the vast masses of poor peasants. I shall read to you the clauses of a decree your Soviet Government must issue. In one of the clauses of this decree is embodied the Mandate to the Land Committees, compiled from 242 mandates from local Soviets of Peasants' Deputies.

## DECREE ON THE LAND

1) Landlord ownership of land is abolished forthwith without any compensation.

2) The landed estates, as also all appanage, monasterial, and church lands, with all their livestock, implements, buildings and everything pertaining thereto, shall be placed at the disposal of the volost land committees and the uyezd Soviets of Peasants' Deputies pending the convocation of the Constituent Assembly.

3) All damage to confiscated property, which henceforth belongs to the whole people, is proclaimed a grave crime to be punished by the revolutionary courts. The uyezd Soviets of Peasants' Deputies shall take all necessary measures to assure the observance of the strictest order during the confiscation of the landed estates, to determine the size of estates, and the particular estate subject to confiscation, to draw up exact inventories of all property confiscated and to protect in the strictest revolutionary way all agricultural enterprises transferred to the people, with all buildings, implements, livestock, produce stocks, etc.

4) The following peasant Mandate, compiled by the *Izvestia of the All-Russian Soviet of Peasants' Deputies* from 242 local peasant mandates and published in No. 88 of the *Izvestia* (Petrograd, No. 88, August 19, 1917), shall serve everywhere to guide the implementation of the great land reforms until a final decision on the latter is taken by the Constituent Assembly.

5) The land of ordinary peasants and ordinary Cossacks shall not be confiscated.

## PEASANT MANDATE ON THE LAND

"The land question in its full scope can be settled only by the popular Constituent Assembly.

"The most equitable settlement of the land question is to be as follows:

"1) *Private ownership of land shall be abolished for ever*; land shall not be sold, purchased, leased, mortgaged, or otherwise alienated.

"All land, whether *state, appanage, crown, monasterial, church, factory, primogenitary, private, public, peasant, etc., shall be alienated without compensation* and become the property of the whole people, and pass into the use of all those who cultivate it.

"Persons who suffer by this property revolution shall be deemed to be entitled to public support only for the period necessary for adaptation to the new conditions of life.

"2) All mineral wealth, e.g., ore, oil, coal, salt, etc., as well as all forests and waters of state importance, shall pass into the exclusive use of the state. All the small streams, lakes, woods, etc., shall pass into the use of the communities, to be administered by the local self-government bodies.

"3) Lands on which *high-level scientific* farming is practised, e.g., orchards, plantations, seed plots, nurseries, hothouses, etc., *shall not be divided up, but shall be converted into model farms*, to be turned over for exclusive use *to the state or to the communities,* depending on the size and importance of such lands.

"Household land in towns and villages, with orchards and vegetable gardens, shall be reserved for the use of their present owners, the size of the holdings, and the size of tax levied for the use thereof, to be determined by law.

"4) Stud farms, government, and private pedigree stock and poultry farms, etc., shall be confiscated and become the property of the whole people, and pass into the exclusive use of the state or a community, depending on the size and importance of such farms.

"The question of compensation shall be examined by the Constituent Assembly.

"5) All livestock and farm implements of the confiscated estates shall pass into the exclusive use of the state or a community, depending on their size and importance, and no compensation shall be paid for this.

"The farm implements of peasants with little land shall not be subject to confiscation.

"6) The right to use the land shall be accorded to all citizens of the Russian state (without distinction of sex) desiring to cultivate it by their own labour, with the help of their families, or in partnership, but only as long as they are able to cultivate it. The employment of hired labour is not permitted.

"In the event of the temporary physical disability of any member of a village community for a period of up to two years, the village community shall be obliged to assist him for this period by collectively cultivating his land until he is again able to work.

"Peasants who, owing to old age or ill-health, are permanently disabled and unable to cultivate the land personally, shall lose their right to the use of it, but, in return, shall receive a pension from the state.

"7) Land tenure shall be on an equality basis, i.e., the land shall be distributed among the toilers in conformity with a labour standard or a consumption standard, depending on local conditions.

"There shall be absolutely no restriction on the forms of land tenure: household, farm, communal, or co-operative, as shall be decided in each individual village and settlement.

"8) All land, when alienated, shall become part of the national land fund. Its distribution among the toilers shall be in charge of the local and central self-government bodies, from democratically organized village and city communities, in which there are no distinctions of social rank, to central regional government bodies.

"The land fund shall be subject to periodical redistribution, depending on the growth of population and the increase in the productivity and the scientific level of farming.

"When the boundaries of allotments are altered, the original nucleus of the allotment shall be left intact.

"The land of the members who leave the community shall revert to the land fund; preferential right to such land shall be given to the near relatives of the members who have left, or to persons designated by the latter.

"The cost of fertilizers and improvements put into the land, to the extent that they have not been fully used up at the time an allotment is returned to the land fund, shall be compensated.

"Should the available land fund in a particular district prove inadequate for the needs of the local population, the surplus population shall be settled elsewhere.

"The state shall take upon itself the organization of resettlement and shall bear the cost thereof, as well as the cost of supplying implements, etc.

"Resettlement shall be effected in the following order: landless peasants desiring to resettle, then members of the community who are of vicious habits, deserters, and so on, and, finally, by lot or by agreement."

The entire contents of this Mandate, as expressing the absolute will of the vast majority of the class-conscious peasants of all Russia, is proclaimed a provisional law, which, pending the convocation of the Constituent Assembly, shall be carried into effect as far as possible immediately, and as to certain of its provisions with due gradualness, as shall be determined by the uyezd Soviets of Peasants' Deputies.

Voices are being raised here that the decree itself and the Mandate were drawn up by the Socialist-Revolutionaries. What of it? Does it matter who drew them up? As a democratic government, we cannot ignore the decision of the rank and file of the people, even though we may disagree with it. In the fire of experience, applying the decree in practice, and carrying it out locally, the peasants will themselves realize where the truth lies. And even if the peasants continue to follow the Socialist-Revolutionaries, even if they give this party a majority in the Constituent Assembly, we shall still say—what of it? Life is the best teacher and it will show who is right. Let the peasant solve this problem from one end and we shall solve it from the other. Life will oblige us to draw together in the general stream of revolutionary creative work, in the elaboration of new state forms. We must be guided by experience; we must allow complete freedom to the creative faculties of the masses. The old government, which was overthrown by armed uprising, wanted to settle the land question with the help of the old, unchanged tsarist bureaucracy. But instead of solving the question, the bureaucracy only fought the peasants. The peasants have learnt something during the eight months of our revolution; they want to settle all land questions themselves. We are therefore opposed to all amendments to this draft law. We want no detail in it, for we are writing a decree, not a programme of action. Russia is vast, and local conditions vary. We trust that the peasants themselves will be able to solve the problem correctly, properly, better than we could do it. Whether they do it in our spirit or in the spirit of the programme of the Socialist-Revolutionaries is not the point. The point is that the peasants should be firmly assured that there are no more landlords in the countryside, that they themselves must decide all questions, and that they themselves must arrange their own lives. (*Loud applause.*)

*Izvestia of the Central Executive Committee,* No. 209, October 28, 1917, and *Pravda,* No. 171, November 10 (October 28), 1917

Vol. XXVI, pp. 225-29

# REPLY TO INQUIRIES FROM PEASANTS

In reply to numerous inquiries from peasants, be it known that all power in the country henceforth belongs wholly to the Soviets of Workers', Soldiers', and Peasants' Deputies. The workers' revolution has won in Petrograd and Moscow and is winning everywhere else in Russia. The Workers' and Peasants' Government ensures the alliance of the mass of the peasants, the poorest peasants, the majority of the peasants, with the workers against the landlords, against the capitalists.

Hence the Soviets of Peasants' Deputies, primarily the uyezd and then the gubernia Soviets, are from now on, pending the convocation of the Constituent Assembly, vested with full governmental authority in their localities. Landlord ownership of land has been *abolished* by the Second All-Russian Congress of Soviets. A decree on land has already been issued by the present Provisional Workers' and Peasants' Government. In conformity with this decree all landed estates pass over wholly and in their entirety to the Soviets of Peasants' Deputies.

The volost land committees must at once take over the administration of all landed estates, instituting the strictest accounting, maintaining perfect order and safeguarding with utmost strictness the former landlord property, which henceforth is the property of the whole people and which the people themselves must therefore protect.

All rulings of the volost land committees issued with the approval of the uyezd Soviets of Peasants' Deputies have the force of *law* and must be carried out unconditionally and without delay.

The Workers' and Peasants' Government appointed by the Second All-Russian Congress of Soviets has been named the Council of People's Commissars.

The Council of People's Commissars calls upon the peasants to take all power into their own hands in their respective localities. The workers give their full, undivided, all-round support to the peasants, are getting the production of machines and implements started, and ask the peasants to help by delivering grain.

*V. Ulyanov (Lenin)*,
Chairman of the Council of People's
Commissars

Petrograd,
November 5, 1917

*Izvestia of the Central Executive Committee*, No. 219, November 8, 1917

Vol. XXVI, pp. 263-64

# DRAFT RESOLUTION

## FOR THE EXTRAORDINARY ALL-RUSSIAN CONGRESS
## OF SOVIETS OF PEASANTS' DEPUTIES

The Peasants' Congress fully and in every way supports the law (decree) on land of October 26, 1917, approved by the Second All-Russian Congress of Soviets of Workers' and Soldiers' Deputies and published by the Council of People's Commissars as the provisional Workers' and Peasants' Government of the Russian republic. The peasants' congress declares its firm and unshakable resolve to uphold the realization of this law, calls upon all peasants to support it unanimously and to carry it out themselves in the localities without delay, and also to elect to all and every responsible post and office only people who have proved not in words but in deeds their complete devotion to the interests of the working and exploited peasants, their readiness and ability to uphold these interests against whatever resistance the landlords, capitalists, and their supporters or accomplices may offer.

The peasants' congress also declares that it is convinced that the full implementation of all the measures constituting the law on land is possible only if the workers' socialist revolution which began on October 25 is successful, for only the socialist revolution can secure the transfer of the land to the working peasantry without compensation, the confiscation of the landlords' implements, full protection of the interests of agricultural wage-workers together with the immediate commencement of the unconditional abolition of the entire system of capitalist wage-slavery, proper, planned distribution of the products of both agriculture and industry among the various regions and the inhabitants of the country, control over the

banks (without such control the people will not be the
masters of the land even with the abolition of private property in land), all-round assistance precisely to the toilers and the exploited on the part of the state, etc.

Therefore the peasants' congress, fully supporting the
revolution of October 25, and supporting it precisely as
a socialist revolution, declares its unswerving resolve to
carry out, with due gradualness but without the slightest
vacillation, measures aimed at the socialist transformation
of the Russian republic.

A necessary condition for the victory of the socialist
revolution, which alone can secure the lasting triumph
and full implementation of the law on land, is the close
alliance of the working, the exploited and toiling peasantry with the working class—the proletariat—in all the
advanced countries. In the Russian republic the entire
organization and administration of the state from top to
bottom must henceforth be based on such an alliance. Rejecting all and every attempt, direct and indirect, overt
and covert, to return to a course doomed by life itself,
to the course of conciliation with the bourgeoisie and the
proponents of bourgeois policy, this alliance alone can
ensure the victory of socialism the world over.

*Izvestia of the Central Executive
Committee,* No. 226, November
15, 1917

Vol. XXVI, pp. 290-91

# ALLIANCE BETWEEN THE WORKERS
## AND THE TOILING AND EXPLOITED PEASANTS

### A LETTER TO *PRAVDA*

Today, Saturday, November 18, in the course of a speech I made at the Peasants' Congress I was publicly asked a question to which I forthwith replied. It is essential that this question and my reply should immediately be made known to all the reading public, for while formally speaking only in my own name, I was actually speaking in the name of the whole Bolshevik Party.

The matter was as follows.

Touching on the question of an alliance between the Bolshevik workers and the Left Socialist-Revolutionaries, whom many peasants at present trust, I argued in my speech that this alliance *can* be an "honest coalition," an honest alliance, for there is *no* radical divergence of interests between the wage-workers and the toiling and exploited peasants. Socialism is *fully* able to satisfy the interests of both. *O n l y* socialism can satisfy their interests. Hence the possibility and neccesity for an "honest coalition" between the proletarians and the toiling and exploited peasantry. On the contrary, a "coalition" (alliance), between the toiling and exploited classes, on the one hand, and the bourgeoisie, on the other, *c a n n o t* be an "honest coalition" because of the radical divergence of interests between these classes.

Imagine, I said, that there is a majority of Bolsheviks and a minority of Left Socialist-Revolutionaries in the government, or even, let us assume, only one Left Socialist-Revolutionary—the Commissar of Agriculture. Could the Bolsheviks practise an honest coalition under such circumstances?

They could; for, while they are irreconcilable in their fight against the counter-revolutionary elements (including the Right Socialist-Revolutionary and the defencist), the Bolsheviks would be obliged to *abstain* from voting on questions which concern purely Socialist-Revolutionary points in the land programme approved by the Second All-Russian Congress of Soviets. Such, for instance, would be the principle of equal land tenure and the redistribution of land among the small owners.

By abstaining from voting on such a point the Bolsheviks would not be changing their programme one jot. For, given the victory of socialism (workers' control over the factories, to be followed by their expropriation, the nationalization of the banks, and the creation of a Supreme Economic Council for the regulation of the entire economic life of the country)—given that, the workers *would be obliged* to agree to the transitional measures proposed by the small toiling and exploited peasants, provided such measures were *not detrimental* to the cause of socialism. Even Kautsky, when he was still a Marxist (1899-1909), frequently admitted—I said—that the measures of transition to socialism cannot be identical in countries with large-scale and in countries with small farming.

We Bolsheviks would be obliged to abstain from voting when such a point was being decided in the Council of People's Commissars or in the Central Executive Committee, for if the Left Socialist-Revolutionaries (as well as the peasants who support them) agreed to workers' control, to the nationalization of the banks, etc., equal land tenure would be only one of the measures of *transition* to complete socialism. For the proletariat to *impose* such transitional measures would be absurd; it is obliged, in the interests of the victory of socialism, to *yield* to the small toiling and exploited peasants in the choice of these transitional measures, for they could do no *harm* to the cause of socialism.

Thereupon, a Left Socialist-Revolutionary (it was Comrade Feofilaktov, if I am not mistaken) asked me the following question:

".How would the Bolsheviks act if in the Constituent

Assembly the peasants wanted to pass a law on equal land tenure, while the bourgeoisie were opposed to the peasants and the decision depended on the Bolsheviks?"

I replied: under such circumstances, when the cause of socialism would be ensured by the introduction of workers' control, the nationalization of the banks, etc., the alliance between the workers and the toiling and exploited peasants would oblige the Party of the proletariat to vote for the peasants and against the bourgeoisie. The Bolsheviks, in my opinion, would be entitled when the vote was being taken to make a declaration of dissent, to place on record their non-agreement, etc., but to abstain from voting under such circumstances would be to betray their allies *in the fight for socialism* because of a difference with them on a partial issue. The Bolsheviks would never betray the peasants in such a situation. Equal land tenure and like measures *c a n n o t* prejudice socialism if the power is in the hands of a Workers' and Peasants' Government, if workers' control has been introduced, the banks nationalized, a workers' and peasants' supreme economic body set up to direct (regulate) the *e n t i r e* economic life of the country, and so forth.

Such was my reply.

Written November 18 (December 1), 1917
Published in *Pravda* No. 194.
December 2 (November 19), 1917

Vol. XXVI, pp. 298-300

## ON THE FAMINE

### (A Letter to the Workers of Petrograd)

Comrades, the other day your delegate, a Party comrade, a worker in the Putilov Works, called on me. This comrade drew a detailed and extremely harrowing picture of the famine in Petrograd. We all know that the food situation is just as acute in a number of the industrial gubernias, that famine is knocking just as cruelly at the door of the workers and the poor generally.

And side by side with this we observe an orgy of profiteering in grain and other food products. The famine is not due to the fact that there is no grain in Russia, but to the fact that the bourgeoisie and the rich generally are putting up a last decisive fight against the rule of the toilers, against the state of the workers, against the Soviet power, on this most important and acute of issues, the issue of bread. The bourgeoisie and the rich generally, including the rural rich, the kulaks, are thwarting the grain monopoly; they are disrupting the distribution of grain undertaken by the state for the purpose and in the interests of supplying bread to the whole of the population, and in the first place to the workers, the toilers, the needy. The bourgeoisie are disrupting the fixed prices, they are profiteering in grain, they are making a hundred, two hundred and more rubles' profit on every pood of grain; they are disrupting the grain monopoly and the proper distribution of grain by resorting to bribery and corruption and by deliberately supporting everything tending to destroy the power of the workers, which is endeavouring to put into effect the prime, basic, and root principle of socialism: "He who does not work, neither shall he eat."

"He who does not work, neither shall he eat"—every toiler understands that. Every worker, every poor, and even middle peasant, everybody who has suffered need in his lifetime, everybody who has ever lived by his own labour, is in agreement with this. Nine-tenths of the population of Russia are in agreement with this truth. In this simple, elementary, and perfectly obvious truth lies the basis of socialism, the indefeasible source of its strength, the indestructible pledge of its final victory.

But the whole point of the matter is that it is one thing to subscribe to this truth, to swear one's allegiance to it, to give it verbal recognition, but it is quite different to be able to put it into effect. When hundreds of thousands and millions of people are suffering the pangs of hunger (in Petrograd, in the non-agricultural gubernias, and in Moscow) in a country where millions upon millions of poods of grain are being concealed by the rich, the kulaks, and the profiteers—in a country which calls itself a Socialist Soviet Republic—there is something to which every conscious worker and peasant must give the most serious and profound thought.

"He who does not work, neither shall he eat"—how is this to be put into effect? It is as clear as daylight that in order to put it into effect we require, firstly, a state grain monopoly, i.e., the absolute prohibition of all private trade in grain, the compulsory delivery of all surplus grain to the state at a fixed price, the absolute prohibition of all hoarding and concealment of surplus grain, no matter by whom. Secondly, we require the strictest registration of all grain surpluses, and faultless organization of the transportation of grain from places of abundance to places of shortage, and the building up of reserves for consumption, for processing, and for seed. Thirdly, we require a just and proper distribution of bread, controlled by the workers' state, the proletarian state, among all the citizens of the state, a distribution which will permit of no privileges and advantages for the rich.

One has only to reflect ever so slightly on these conditions for coping with the famine to see the abysmal stupidity of the contemptible anarchist windbags, who deny the necessity of a state power (and, what is more, a power ruthless in its severity towards the bourgeoisie and ruthlessly firm towards disorganizers of government) for the transition from capitalism to communism and for the ridding of the working people from all forms of oppression and exploitation. It is at this moment, when our revolution has directly, concretely, and practically approached the tasks involved in the realization of socialism—and therein lies its inestimable merit—it is at this moment, and exactly in connection with this most important of issues, the issue of bread, that the need becomes absolutely clear for an iron revolutionary rule, for a dictatorship of the proletariat, for the organization of the collection of food products, their transportation, and distribution on a mass, national scale, taking into account the requirements of tens and hundreds of millions of people, calculating the conditions and the results of production for a year and many years ahead (for there are sometimes years of crop failure, sometimes land improvements essential for increasing grain crops require years of work, and so forth).

Romanov and Kerensky left to the working class a country utterly impoverished by their predatory, criminal, and most burdensome war, a country picked clean by Russian and foreign imperialists. Bread will suffice for all only if we keep the strictest account of every pood, only if every pound is distributed absolutely evenly. There is also an acute shortage of bread for machines, i.e., fuel: the railroads and factories will come to a standstill, unemployment and famine will bring ruin on the whole nation, if we do not bend every effort to establish a strict and ruthless economy of consumption and proper distribution. We are faced by disaster, it has drawn terribly near. An intolerably severe May will be followed by a still more severe June, July, and August.

Our state grain monopoly exists in law, but in practice it is being thwarted at every step by the bourgeoisie. The rural rich, the kulak, the parasite who has been robbing the whole neighbourhood for decades, prefers to enrich himself by profiteering and illicit distilling: that is so advantageous for his pocket, while he throws the blame for the famine on the Soviet power. That, too, is the line of the political defenders of the kulak—the Constitutional Democrats, the Right Socialist-Revolutionaries, and the Mensheviks—who are overtly and covertly "working" against the grain monopoly and against the Soviet power. The party of the spineless, i.e., the Left Socialist-Revolutionaries, are displaying their spinelessness here too: they are yielding to the covetous howls and outcries of the bourgeoisie, they are crying out against the grain monopoly, they are "protesting" against the food dictatorship, they are allowing themselves to be intimidated by the bourgeoisie, they are afraid to fight the kulak, and are hysterically tossing hither and thither, recommending that the fixed prices be raised, that private trading be permitted, and so forth.

This party of the spineless reflects in politics something akin to what takes place in ordinary life when the kulak incites the poor peasants against the Soviets, bribes them by, say, letting some poor peasant have a pood of grain not for six, but for three rubles, so that the poor peasant, thus corrupted, may himself "make a bit" by profiteering, "turn a penny" by selling that pood of grain at a profiteering price of one hundred and fifty rubles, and himself become a decrier of the Soviets, which have prohibited private trading in grain.

Whoever is capable of reflecting, whoever is desirous of reflecting ever so little, will see clearly what line this fight has taken.

Either the advanced and class-conscious workers triumph and unite around themselves the poor peasant masses, establish rigorous order, a mercilessly severe rule, a genuine dictatorship of the proletariat—either they compel the kulak to submit, and institute a proper distribution of food and fuel on a national scale;

—or the bourgeoisie, with the help of the kulaks, and with the indirect support of the spineless and muddleheaded (the anarchists and the Left Socialist-Revolutionaries), overthrow the Soviet power and set up a Russo-German or a Russo-Japanese Kornilov,[47] who will present the peo-

ple with a sixteen-hour working-day, two ounces of bread
per week, mass shooting of workers and torture in dun-
geons, as has been the case in Finland and the Ukraine.

Either—or.

There is no middle course.

The situation of the country is desperate in the extreme.

Whoever reflects upon political life cannot but see that the
Cadets, the Right Socialist-Revolutionaries, and the Mensheviks are coming to an understanding as to who would
be "pleasanter," a Russo-German or a Russo-Japanese
Kornilov, as to who would crush the revolution more effectively and reliably, a crowned or a republican Kornilov.

It is time all class-conscious and advanced workers
came to an understanding. It is time they bestirred themselves and realized that every minute's delay may spell
ruin to the country and ruin to the revolution.

Half-measures will be of no avail. Complaining will
lead us nowhere. Attempts to secure bread or fuel "in
retail fashion," "each man for himself," i.e., for his "own"
factory, his "own" workshop, are only increasing the disorganization and facilitating for the profiteers their selfish, filthy, and shady work.

That is why, comrades, workers of Petrograd, I have
taken the liberty of addressing this letter to you. Petrograd is not Russia. The Petrograd workers are only a
small part of the workers of Russia. But they are one
of the best, the advanced, most class-conscious, most revolutionary, most steadfast detachments of the working
class and of all the working people of Russia, and one
of the least liable to succumb to empty phrases, to spineless despair and to the intimidation of the bourgeoisie.
And it has frequently happened at critical moments in
the life of nations that even small advanced detachments
of advanced classes have carried the rest after them, have
fired the masses with revolutionary enthusiasm, and have
accomplished tremendous historic feats.

"There were forty thousand of us at the Putilov Works,"
the delegate from the Petrograd workers said to me. "But
the majority of them were 'temporary' workers, not proletarians, an unreliable, flabby lot. Fifteen thousand are

now left, but these are proletarians, tried and steeled in the fight."

That is the sort of vanguard of the revolution—in Petrograd and throughout the country—that must sound the call, must *rise in their mass*, must understand that the salvation of the country is in their hands, that from them is demanded a heroism no less than that which they displayed in January and October 1905 and in February and October 1917, that a great "*crusade*" must be organized against the grain profiteers, the kulaks, the parasites, the disorganizers, and bribe-takers, a great "*crusade*" against the violators of strictest state order in the collection, transportation, and distribution of bread for the people and bread for the machines.

The country and the revolution can be saved only by the mass effort of the advanced workers. We need tens of thousands of advanced and steeled proletarians, class-conscious enough to explain matters to the millions of poor peasants all over the country and to assume the leadership of these millions, tempered enough to ruthlessly cast out of their midst and shoot all who allow themselves to be "seduced"—as indeed happens—by the seducements of profiteering and turn from fighters for the cause of the people into robbers; we need politicians steadfast enough and devoted enough to the revolution to bear in an organized way all the hardships of the *crusade* into every corner of the country for the establishment of order, for the consolidation of the local organs of Soviet power, and for the exercise of control in the localities over every pood of grain and every pood of fuel.

It is rather more difficult to do this than to display heroism for a few days without leaving one's accustomed place, without joining in a crusade, confining oneself to a spasmodic uprising against the idiot fiend Romanov or the fool and braggart Kerensky. Heroism displayed in prolonged and persevering organizational work on a national scale is immensely more difficult than, but at the same time immensely superior to, heroism displayed in an uprising. But the strength of working-class parties, the strength of the working class always lay in that it looks

danger boldly, squarely and openly in the face, that it
does not fear to admit danger and soberly weigh the forces
in its "own" camp and in "the other" camp, the camp of
the exploiters. The revolution is progressing, developing,
and growing. The tasks we face are also growing. The struggle is broadening and deepening. Proper distribution of
bread and fuel, their procurement in greater quantities
and keeping of very strict account and control of them
*by the workers* on a national scale—that is the real and
chief prelude to socialism. That is no longer a "general
revolutionary" task but a *communist* task, a task which
requires that the working people and the poor engage
capitalism in a decisive battle.

And this battle is worth giving all one's strength to
it; its difficulties are great, but so is the cause of the
abolition of oppression and exploitation for which we are
fighting.

When the people are starving, when unemployment is
becoming ever more terrible, anyone who conceals an ex-
tra pood of grain, anyone who deprives the state of a
pood of fuel is an out-and-out criminal.

At such a time—and for a truly communist society, it
is always true—every pood of grain and fuel is veritably
sacred, much more so than the sacred things which priests
use to confuse the minds of fools, promising them the
kingdom of heaven as a reward for slavery on earth. And
in order to rid this genuinely sacred thing of every rem-
nant of the "sacredness" of the priests, we must *take possession of it practically*, we must achieve its proper distribution *in practice*, we must collect the whole of it without
exception, every particle of surplus grain must be brought
into the state stores, *the whole country must be swept
clean* of concealed or ungarnered grain surpluses, we need
the firm hand of the worker to harness every effort, to increase the output of fuel and to secure the greatest economy of it and the greatest efficiency in the transportation and consumption of fuel.

We need a mass "crusade" of the advanced workers to
every centre of production of grain and fuel, to every important centre where they are brought and distributed; a

mass "crusade" to increase the intensity of work tenfold, to assist the local organs of Soviet power in the matter of accounting and control, and to eradicate profiteering, graft, and slovenliness by armed force. This is not a new task. History, properly speaking, is not advancing new tasks—all it is doing is to increase the size and scope of the old tasks as the scope of the revolution, its difficulties, and the greatness of its world-historic aim, increase.

One of the greatest and indefeasible accomplishments of the October Revolution—the Soviet revolution—is that the advanced worker, *as the leader* of the poor, *as the leader* of the toiling masses of the countryside, *as the builder of the state of the toilers*, has "gone among the people." Petrograd and other proletarian centres have given thousands upon thousands of their best workers to the countryside. The detachments of fighters against the Kaledins and Dutovs, and the food detachments, are nothing new. Only the proximity of disaster, the acuteness of the situation compel us to do *ten times more* than before.

When the worker became the vanguard leader of the poor he did not thereby become a saint. He led the people forward, but he also became infected with the diseases of petty-bourgeois disintegration. The fewer the detachments of best organized, of most class-conscious, and most disciplined and steadfast workers were, the more frequently did these detachments degenerate, the more frequently did the small-proprietor instincts of the past triumph over the proletarian-communist consciousness of the future.

Having begun the communist revolution, the working class cannot instantly discard the weaknesses and vices inherited from the society of landlords and capitalists, the society of exploiters and parasites, the society based on the filthy selfishness and personal gain of a few and the poverty of the many. But the working class can vanquish the old world—*and in the end will certainly and inevitably vanquish it*—with its vices and weaknesses, if against the enemy are brought ever greater detachments of workers, ever more enlightened by experience and tempered by the hardships of the struggle.

Such and only such is the state of affairs in Russia today. Single-handed and disunited we shall not be able to cope with famine and unemployment. We need a mass "crusade" of advanced workers to every corner of this vast country. We need ten times more *iron detachments* of the proletariat, class-conscious, and boundlessly devoted to communism. Then we shall triumph over famine and unemployment. Then we shall advance the revolution to be the real prelude to socialism, and then too we shall be in a position to conduct a victorious war of defence against the imperialist vultures.

May 22, 1918                                              *N. Lenin*

*Pravda*, No. 101,
May 24, 1918

Vol. XXVII, pp. 355-62

# DRAFT OF A TELEGRAM TO ALL SOVIETS OF DEPUTIES CONCERNING THE ALLIANCE OF WORKERS AND PEASANTS

The Committees of Poor Peasants[48] are necessary to fight the kulaks, the rich, the exploiters, who shackle the working peasants. But between the kulaks, who are a small minority, and the poor or semi-proletarians there is the stratum of the middle peasants. Soviet power has never declared or conducted any struggle against them. Any contrary steps or measures are to be condemned most vigorously and must be stopped. The socialist government is bound to pursue a policy of agreement with the middle peasantry. Soviet power has time and again shown by its actions that it is firmly resolved to pursue this policy. The most important of such actions are the adoption by a Communist (Bolshevik) majority of the Law on the Socialization of the Land[49] and its strictly faithful enforcement, followed by the trebling of grain prices (decree... of August, 1918). The purport of the decree on agricultural machinery,[50] etc., is the same. The policy set forth above is to be strictly followed by all.

Written August 16, 1918
First published in 1931

Vol. XXVIII, p. 41

## SPEECH DELIVERED TO DELEGATES
## FROM THE COMMITTEES
## OF POOR PEASANTS OF MOSCOW REGION

*November 8, 1918*

Comrades, the organization of the poor peasants faces us as the most important problem in our work of internal construction, and even in our whole revolution.

The aim of the October Revolution was to wrench the mills and factories from the hands of the capitalists so as to make the means of production the property of the whole people, and to reconstruct agriculture on socialist lines by handing over all the land to the peasants.

The first half of this aim was much more easy to accomplish than the second. In the cities, the revolution dealt with large-scale industry in which hundreds of thousands of workers are engaged. The mills and factories belonged to a small number of capitalists, with whom the workers had no difficulty in coping. The workers had already gained experience in their long struggle against the capitalists, which had taught them to act concertedly, resolutely, and in an organized way. Moreover, it was not necessary to divide up the mills and factories; all that was required was that all production should be made to serve the interests of the working class and the peasantry and that the products of labour should not fall into the hands of the capitalists.

But the case is entirely different with the land. Here, in order to secure the victory of socialism a number of transitional measures are required. To transform a vast number of small-scale peasant farms into large-scale production is something that cannot be done immediately.

Agriculture, which hitherto has been conducted on individual lines, cannot immediately be socialized and transformed into large-scale state enterprises, the products of which would be equally and justly distributed among the whole of the working people under a system of universal and equal labour service. It is impossible, of course, to achieve this immediately, or in a short space of time.

While the workers of the mills and factories in the cities have already succeeded in completely overthrowing the capitalists and casting off the yoke of exploitation, in the agricultural districts the real fight against exploitation has only just begun.

After the October Revolution we smashed the landlord and deprived him of his land. But that did not end the struggle in the agricultural districts. The conquest of the land, like every other conquest by the toilers, can be permanent only when it is based on the independent action of the toilers themselves, on their own organization, on their endurance and revolutionary determination.

Did the toiling peasants have this organization?

Unfortunately not; and that is the root cause, the reason why the struggle is so difficult.

Peasants who do not employ the labour of others, who do not profit at the expense of others, will, of course, always be in favour of the land being divided among everybody equally, they will always be in favour of everybody working, of the possession of land not serving as a basis of exploitation, and of numerous land holdings not therefore becoming concentrated in single hands. But it is different with the kulaks and the parasites who grew rich on the war, who took advantage of the famine to sell grain at fabulous prices, who concealed grain in expectation of higher prices, and who are now striving in every way to grow rich on the misfortunes of the people and on the hunger of the poor peasants and the workers in the cities.

They, the kulaks and parasites, are enemies no less formidable than the capitalists and landlords. And if the kulaks are not dealt with, if we do not cope with the parasites, the return of the tsar and the capitalists is inevitable.

The experience of every revolution that has hitherto occurred in Europe offers striking corroboration of the fact that revolution is inevitably doomed if the peasants do not throw off the domination of the kulaks.

Every European revolution ended in failure because the peasants could not cope with their enemies. In the cities the workers overthrew their kings (in England and France they executed their kings several centuries ago; it was only we who were late with our tsar), yet after a certain interval the old order was restored. That was because in those days even in the cities there was no large-scale industry which could unite millions of workers in the mills and factories and consolidate them into an army powerful enough to withstand the onslaught of the capitalists and the kulaks even without the support of the peasants.

The poor peasants were unorganized, fought the kulaks badly, and as a result the revolution was defeated even in the cities.

But now the situation is different. During the last two hundred years large-scale production has developed so powerfully and has covered all the countries with such a network of huge mills and factories employing thousands and tens of thousands of workers that now everywhere in the cities large cadres have been created of organized workers, the proletariat, who constitute a force strong enough to achieve final victory over the bourgeoisie, the capitalists.

In former revolutions the poor peasants had nowhere to turn for support in their difficult struggle against the kulaks.

The organized proletariat—which is stronger and more experienced than the peasantry (it gained that experience in earlier struggles)—is now in power in Russia and is in possession of all the means of production, the mills, the factories, the railways, ships, etc.

The poor peasants now possess a reliable and powerful ally in their struggle against the kulaks. The poor peasants know that the city is behind them, that the proletariat will help them, is in fact already helping them with every means in its power. That has been shown by recent events.

You remember, comrades, in what a dangerous situation the revolution was in July of the present year. The Czechoslovak revolt[51] was spreading, the food shortage in the cities was becoming increasingly acute and the kulaks in the villages were becoming more and more insolent and more and more violent in their attacks on the cities, the Soviet government, and the poor peasants.

We called on the poor peasants to organize. We proceeded to form committees and to organize workers' food detachments. The Left Socialist-Revolutionaries raised a revolt. They declared that the Committees of Poor Peasants consisted of idlers and that the workers were robbing the toiling peasants of grain.

And we replied that they were defending the kulaks, who realized that the Soviet government could be fought not only by arms but also by starvation. They talked about "idlers." And we asked, "But why has any particular individual become an 'idler,' why has he deteriorated, why is he impoverished, and why has he taken to drink? Was it not because of the kulaks?" The kulaks, like the Left Socialist-Revolutionaries, raised an outcry against "idlers," but they themselves were raking in grain, concealing it and profiteering in the desire to grow rich on the hunger and sufferings of the workers.

The kulaks were squeezing the poor peasants dry. They were deriving advantage from the labour of others, at the same time crying, "Idlers!"

The kulaks awaited the Czechoslovakians impatiently. They would most willingly have enthroned a new tsar, in order to continue their exploitation with impunity, in order to continue to dominate the farm-labourer, and to continue to grow rich.

And salvation was wholly due to the fact that the village united with the city, that the proletarian and semi-proletarian elements of the countryside (i.e., those who do not employ the labour of others) started a campaign against the kulaks and the parasites together with the city workers.

In order to achieve this unity a great deal had particularly to be done in connection with the food situation. The working-class population of the cities was suffering severely from hunger, but the kulak said: "I shall hold back my grain a little longer, perhaps they will pay more."

The kulaks, of course, were in no hurry; they had money in plenty; they say themselves that they have accumulated Kerensky notes by the pound weight.

But people who at a time of famine are capable of concealing and hoarding grain are vicious criminals. They must be fought as the worst enemies of the people.

And this fight in the country districts we have begun.

The Mensheviks and the Socialist-Revolutionaries tried to frighten us by asserting that in organizing the Committees of Poor Peasants we were causing a split among the peasants. But what does not causing a split among the peasants mean? It means leaving them to the mercy of the kulak. But that is exactly what we do not want, and we therefore decided to cause a split among the peasants. We said: true, we are losing the kulaks; that misfortune cannot be concealed (*laughter*); but we shall win millions of poor peasants who will come over to the side of the workers. (*Applause.*)

And that is exactly what is taking place. The split among the peasants only served to show more clearly who are poor peasants, who are middle peasants not employing the labour of others, and who are parasites and kulaks.

The workers have helped and are helping the poor peasants in their struggle against the kulaks. In the civil war which has broken out in the countryside the workers are on the side of the poor peasants, as they were when they passed the Socialist-Revolutionary law on the socialization of the land.

We Bolsheviks were opposed to the law on the socialization of the land. Yet we signed it, because we did not wish to go counter to the will of the majority of the peasantry. The will of the majority is binding on us always, and to oppose the will of the majority is to betray the revolution.

We did not want to force on the peasants the idea that the equal division of the land was useless, an idea which was alien to them. We consider it better if the toiling peasants themselves, as a result of their own experience and their own suffering, came to realize that equal division was nonsense. Only then would we be able to ask them what, then, was the way of escape from the ruin and kulak domination that follow from the division of the land.

Division of the land was all very well as a beginning. Its purpose was to show that the land was being taken from the landlords and handed over to the peasants. But that is not enough. The solution lies only in social cultivation of the land.

You did not realize this at the time, but you are being led to this conviction by force of experience. Salvation from the disadvantages of small-scale farming lies in communes, cultivation by artels, or peasant associations. That is the way to raise and improve agriculture, to economize forces and to combat the kulaks, parasites, and exploiters.

We were well aware that the peasants live rooted to the soil. The peasants fear innovations, they cling tenaciously to old habits. We knew that the peasants would come to believe in the benefits of any particular measure only when their own intelligence led them to understand and appreciate those benefits. And that is why we helped to divide the land, although we realized that this was not the solution.

But now the poor peasants themselves are coming to agree with us. Experience is teaching them that while ten ploughs, say, are required when the land is divided into one hundred separate holdings, a smaller number of ploughs suffices under communal farming because the land is not divided up so minutely. A commune permits a whole artel, or association, to make improvements in agriculture which are beyond the capacity of individual small owners, and so forth.

16—1928

Of course, not everywhere will it be possible to proceed to social cultivation of the land immediately. The kulaks will resist it in every way—ay, and frequently the peasants themselves will stubbornly resist the introduction of communal principles in agriculture. But the more the peasants become convinced by example and by their own experience of the advantages of communes, the more successfully will matters progress.

In this respect the Committees of Poor Peasants will play an extremely important part. Committees of Poor Peasants must cover the whole of Russia. For a long time, the development of the Committees of Poor Peasants has been proceeding intensively. The other day a Congress of Committees of Poor Peasants of the Northern Region was held in Petrograd. In place of the seven thousand representatives expected, twenty thousand actually appeared, and the hall assigned for the purpose was unable to seat all present. The situation was saved by the fine weather, which made it possible to hold the meeting on the square outside the Winter Palace.

This congress showed that the civil war in the countryside is being properly understood: the poor peasants are uniting and have formed solid ranks against the kulaks, the rich, and the parasites.

The Central Committee of our Party has drawn up a plan for the reformation of the Committees of Poor Peasants which will be submitted for the approval of the Sixth Congress of Soviets. We have decided that the Committees of Poor Peasants and the Soviets in the rural districts must not exist separately, for otherwise there will be squabbling and too much useless talk. We shall merge the Committees of Poor Peasants with the Soviets, we shall turn the Committees of Poor Peasants into Soviets.

We know that the kulaks sometimes worm their way even into the Committees of Poor Peasants. If this continues the poor peasants will have the same sort of attitude towards the Committees of Poor Peasants as they had towards the kulak Soviets of Kerensky and Avksentyev. A change of name will fool nobody. It is therefore proposed to hold new elections to the Committees of Poor Peasants. Only those who do not exploit the labour of others, who do not make the hunger of the people a source of plunder, who do not profiteer on grain surpluses and do not conceal them will be entitled to vote in the elections to the Committees of Poor Peasants. There must be no place for kulaks and parasites in the proletarian Committees of Poor Peasants.

The Soviet government has decided to assign one thousand million rubles to a special fund for the improvement of agriculture.[52] All existing communes and all new communes will receive monetary and technical assistance.

We shall send trained experts if they are required. Although the majority of them are counter-revolutionary, the Committees of Poor Peasants will be able to harness them and they will work for the people no worse than they formerly worked for the exploiters. And generally our intellectuals have already become convinced that they will not overthrow the workers' government by sabotage and by wilful damage to work.

Foreign imperialism also has no terrors for us. Germany has already burnt her fingers in the Ukraine. In place of the sixty million poods of grain which Germany hoped to carry off from the Ukraine, she got only nine million poods; and, in addition, she got Russian Bolshevism, for which she cherishes no particular sympathies. (*Thunderous applause.*) The British should take care the same thing does not happen to them, and we can say to them: "Beware, friends, you don't choke yourselves!" (*Laughter and applause.*)

But the danger for us continues to exist as long as our brothers abroad have not everywhere risen. And we must therefore continue to organize and consolidate our Red Army. The poor peasants should be particularly concerned in this matter, for they can carry on their domestic activities only under the protection of our army.

Comrades, the transition to the new form of agriculture may perhaps proceed slowly, but the beginnings of communal farming must be carried into practice unswervingly.

16*

The fight against the kulaks must be fought energet-ically; no deals must be made with them.

We can work together with the middle peasants, and together with them fight the kulaks. We have nothing against the middle peasants. They are, perhaps, not So-cialists, and never will be Socialists, but experience will teach them the advantages of the social cultivation of the land and the majority of them will not resist.

To the kulaks we say: we have nothing against you either, but hand over your surplus grain, do not profiteer and do not exploit the labour of others. Until that is done we shall wage ruthless war on you.

We are taking nothing from the toilers; but those who employ hired labour, who grow rich at the expense of oth-ers, we shall expropriate completely. (*Stormy applause.*)

*Bednota*, No. 185,
November 10, 1918

Vol. XXVIII, pp. 152-58

# VALUABLE ADMISSIONS BY PITIRIM SOROKIN

*Pravda* carries today a remarkably interesting letter by Pitirim Sorokin, to which the special attention of all Communists should be drawn. In this letter, which was printed in the *Izvestia of the North Dvina Executive Committee*, Pitirim Sorokin announces that he is leaving the Party of the Right Socialist-Revolutionaries and resigning as member of the Constituent Assembly. The motives of the author of the letter are that he finds it difficult to provide effective political recipes, not only for others, but even for himself, and that therefore he "renounces all politics." Pitirim Sorokin writes: "The past year of revolution has taught me one truth: politicians may make mistakes, politics may be socially useful, but may also be socially harmful, whereas work in the sphere of science and public education is always useful and is always needed by the people...." The letter is signed: "Pitirim Sorokin, lecturer in the St. Petersburg University and the Psycho-Neurological Institute, former Member of the Constituent Assembly and former Member of the Party of Socialist-Revolutionaries."

This letter is noteworthy in the first place because it is an extremely interesting "human document." We do not often meet with such sincerity and frankness as are displayed by P. Sorokin in admitting the mistakenness of his politics. In practically the majority of cases politicians who become convinced that the line they have been pursuing is erroneous try to conceal their change of front, to hush it up, to "invent" more or less extraneous motives, and so on. A frank and honest admission of one's political error is in itself an important political act. Pitirim Sorokin is wrong when he says that work in the sphere of science "is always useful." For mistakes are made even in this sphere, and there are examples even in Russian literature of the obstinate advocacy of, for instance, reactionary philosophical views by people who are not conscious reactionaries. On the other hand, a frank declaration by a prominent person—i.e., a person who has occupied a responsible political post known to the people at large—that he is renouncing politics *is also politics*. An honest confession of a political error may be of great political benefit to many people if the error was shared by whole parties which at one time enjoyed influence over the masses.

The political significance of Pitirim Sorokin's letter is very great precisely at the present moment. It is a "lesson" which we all should seriously ponder over and learn thoroughly.

It is a truth long known to every Marxist that in every capitalist society the only *decisive* forces are the proletariat and the bourgeoisie, while all social elements occupying a position between these classes and coming within the economic category of the petty bourgeoisie *inevitably* vacillate between these decisive forces. But there is an enormous gulf between academic recognition of this truth and the ability to draw the conclusions that follow from it in the complex conditions of practical reality.

Pitirim Sorokin is representative of an extremely broad public and political current, the Menshevik-Socialist-Revolutionary current. That this is a single current, that the difference between the Mensheviks and the Socialist-Revolutionaries in their attitude towards the struggle of the bourgeoisie and the proletariat is insignificant, is especially convincingly and strikingly borne out by the events in the Russian revolution since February 1917. The Mensheviks and the Socialist-Revolutionaries are varieties of petty-bourgeois democrats—that is the economic essence and fundamental political characteristic of the current in question. We know from the history of the advanced countries how frequently this current in its early stages assumes a "socialist" hue.

The question arises: what was it that several months ago so forcibly repelled the representatives of this current from the Bolsheviks, from the proletarian revolution, and what is it that is now inducing them to shift from hostility to neutrality? It is quite obvious that the cause of this shift was, firstly, the collapse of German imperialism in connection with the revolution in Germany and other countries and the exposure of Anglo-French imperialism, and, secondly, the dispelling of bourgeois-democratic illusions.

Let us deal with the first cause. Patriotism is one of the most deeply ingrained of sentiments, inculcated by the fact that separate fatherlands have existed for hundreds and thousands of years. One of the most pronounced, one might say exceptional, difficulties of our proletarian revolution is the fact that it was obliged to pass through a phase of extreme departure from patriotism, the phase of the Peace of Brest-Litovsk.[53] The bitterness, resentment, and violent indignation provoked by this peace were easy to understand and it goes without saying that we Marxists could expect only the class-conscious vanguard of the proletariat to appreciate the truth, namely, that we were making and were obliged to make great national sacrifices for the sake of the supreme interests of the world proletarian revolution. There was no source from which ideologists who are not Marxists and the broad masses of the toilers who do not belong to the proletariat trained in the long school of strikes and revolution could derive either a firm conviction that the revolution was maturing, or an unreserved devotion to it. At best, our tactics appeared to them a fantastic, fanatical, and adventurist sacrifice of the real and most obvious interests of hundreds of millions for the sake of an abstract, utopian, and dubious hope of something that might occur in other countries. And the petty bourgeoisie, owing to its economic position, is more patriotic than either the bourgeoisie or the proletariat.

*But it turned out as we had foretold.*

German imperialism, which had seemed to be the only enemy, collapsed. The German revolution, which had appeared to be a "dream-farce" (to use Plekhanov's expression), became a fact. Anglo-French imperialism, which the fantasy of the petty-bourgeois democrats pictured as a friend of democracy and a protector of the oppressed, turned out to be a savage beast, which imposed on the German Republic and the peoples of Austria terms worse than those of Brest, a savage beast which used armies of "free" republicans—French and American—as gendarmes, butchers, and throttlers of the independence and freedom of small and weak nations. Anglo-French imperialism was exposed by world history with ruthless thoroughness and frankness. The facts of world history demonstrated to the Russian patriots, who formerly would hear of nothing that was not to the direct advantage (as formerly understood) of their country, that the transformation of our Russian revolution into a socialist revolution was not a dubious venture but a necessity, *for there was no other* alternative: Anglo-French and American imperialism will *inevitably* destroy the independence and freedom of Russia *if* the world socialist revolution, world Bolshevism, does not triumph.

Facts are stubborn things, as the English say. And during recent months we have witnessed facts that signify a most momentous turning-point in world history. These facts are compelling the petty-bourgeois democrats of Russia, in spite of their hatred of Bolshevism, a hatred inculcated by the history of our internal Party struggle, to turn from hostility to Bolshevism, first to neutrality towards and then to support of Bolshevism. The objective conditions which repelled these democratic patriots from us most strongly have now vanished. The objective conditions that have set in in the world now *compel* them to turn towards us. Pitirim Sorokin's change of front is by no means fortuitous, but rather the symptom of an inevitable change of front on the part of a *whole class*, of the whole petty-bourgeois democracy. Whoever fails to reckon with this fact and to take advantage of it is not a Marxist but a bad Socialist.

Furthermore, faith in "democracy" *in general* as a universal panacea, and failure to understand that this democracy is *bourgeois* democracy, historically limited in its usefulness and its necessity, have for decades and centuries held particularly strong sway over the petty bourgeoisie of all countries. The big bourgeois is case-hardened; he knows that under capitalism a democratic republic, like every other form of state, is nothing but a machine for the suppression of the proletariat. The big bourgeois *knows* this from his most intimate acquaintance with the real leaders and with the most profound (and therefore frequently the most concealed) springs of *every* bourgeois state machine. The petty bourgeois, owing to his economic position and his conditions of life generally, is less able to appreciate this truth, and even cherishes the illusion that a democratic republic implies "pure democracy," "a free people's state," the non-class or supra-class rule of the people, a pure manifestation of the will of the people, and so on and so forth. The tenacity of these prejudices of the petty-bourgeois democrat is inevitably due to the fact that he is farther removed from the acute class struggle, the bourse, and "real" politics; and it would be absolutely un-Marxist to expect that these prejudices can be eradicated very rapidly by propaganda alone.

But world history is moving with such furious rapidity, is smashing everything customary and established with a hammer of such immense weight and by crises of such unparalleled intensity, that the most tenacious prejudices are giving way. The naive belief in a Constituent Assembly and the naive habit of contrasting "pure democracy" with "proletarian dictatorship" took shape naturally and inevitably in the mind of the "democrat in general." But the experiences of the Constituent Assembly supporters in Arkhangelsk, Samara, Siberia, and the South could not but destroy even the most tenacious of prejudices. The idealized democratic republic of Wilson *proved* in practice to be a form of the most rabid imperialism, of the most shameless oppression and suppression of weak and small nationalities. The average "democrat" in general, the Menshevik and the Socialist-Revolutionary, thought: "How can we even dream of some allegedly superior type of state, some Soviet government? God grant us even an or-

dinary democratic republic!" And, of course, in "ordinary," comparatively peaceful times he could have kept on
cherishing this "hope" for many a long decade.

But now the course of world events and the bitter lessons derived from the alliance of all the Russian monarchists with Anglo-French and American imperialism are
proving *in practice* that a democratic republic is a bourgeois-democratic republic, which has already become antiquated from the point of view of the problems which imperialism has placed on the agenda of history. They show
that there is no *other* alternative: *either* Soviet government
triumphs in every advanced country in the world, *or* the
most reactionary imperialism triumphs, the most savage imperialism, which is throttling the small and weak peoples
and reinstating reaction all over the world—Anglo-American imperialism, which has perfectly mastered the art of
using the form of a democratic republic.

One or the other.

There is no middle course. Until quite recently this view
was regarded as the blind fanaticism of the Bolsheviks.
*But it turned out to be true.*

If Pitirim Sorokin has resigned as member of the Constituent Assembly, it is not without reason; it is a symptom of a change of front on the part of a whole class, the
petty-bourgeois democracy. A split among this class is
inevitable: one section will come over to our side, another
section will remain neutral, while a third will deliberately
join forces with the monarchist Constitutional Democrats,
who are selling Russia to Anglo-American capital and seeking to crush the revolution with the aid of foreign bayo-
nets. One of the most urgent tasks of the present day is
to take into account and make use of the turn among the
Menshevik and Socialist-Revolutionary democrats from
hostility to Bolshevism, first to neutrality and then to support of Bolshevism.

Every slogan the Party addresses to the masses is bound
to outlive its time, to remain valid for many even when
the conditions which rendered it necessary have changed.
That is an unavoidable evil, and it is impossible to ensure
the correctness of Party policy unless we learn to combat

and overcome that evil. The period in our proletarian revolution in which the differences with the Menshevik and
Socialist-Revolutionary democrats were particularly acute
was a historically necessary period. It was impossible
to avoid waging a vigorous struggle against these democrats when they swung to the camp of our enemies and set
about restoring a *bourgeois and imperialist* democratic
republic. Many of the slogans of this struggle have now
become frozen and petrified and *prevent* us from properly
assessing and taking effective advantage of the new period, in which a change of front has begun among these
democrats, a change in our direction, not a fortuitous
change, but one rooted deep in the conditions of the international situation.

It is not enough to encourage this change of front and
amicably greet those who are making it. A politician who
knows what he is working for must learn to *bring about*
this change of front among the various sections and
groups of the broad mass of petty-bourgeois democrats if
he is convinced that serious and deep-going historical reasons for such a turn exist. A revolutionary proletarian must
know whom to suppress and with whom—and when and
how—to conclude an agreement. It would be ridiculous
and foolish to refrain from employing terror against and
suppressing the landlords and capitalists and their henchmen, who are selling Russia to the foreign imperialist
"allies." It would be farcical to attempt to "convince" or
generally to "psychologically influence" them. But it
would be equally foolish and ridiculous—if not more so—
to insist only on tactics of suppression and terror in relation to the petty-bourgeois democrats when the course of
events is compelling them to turn in our direction.

And the proletariat encounters these democrats everywhere. Our task in the rural districts is to destroy the
landlord and smash the resistance of the exploiter and the
kulak profiteer. For this purpose we can safely rely *only*
on the semi-proletarians, the "poor peasants." But the
middle peasant is not our enemy. He vacillated, is vacillating, and will continue to vacillate. The task of influencing the vacillators *is not identical* with the task of over-

throwing the exploiter and defeating the active enemy. The task at the present moment is to come to an agreement with the middle peasant, while not for a moment renouncing the struggle against the kulak and at the same time relying solely on the poor peasant, for a turn in our direction on the part of the middle peasants is now inevitable owing to the causes enumerated above.

This applies also to the handicraftsman, the artisan, and the worker whose conditions are most petty bourgeois or whose views are most petty bourgeois, and to many office workers and army officers, and, in particular, to the intellectuals generally. It is an unquestionable fact that there often are instances in our Party of inability to make use of this change of front among them and that this inability can and must be overcome.

We already have the firm support of the vast majority of the proletarians organized in the trade unions. We must know how to win over the least proletarian and most petty-bourgeois sections of the *toilers*, who are turning towards us, to include them in the general organization and to subject them to the general proletarian discipline. The slogan of the moment here is not to fight these sections, but to win them over, to be able to influence them, to convince the waverers, to make use of those who are neutral, and, by mass proletarian influence, to educate those who are lagging behind or who have only very recently begun to free themselves from "Constituent Assembly" or "patriotic-democratic" illusions.

We already have sufficiently firm support among the toiling masses. This was particularly strikingly borne out by the Sixth Congress of Soviets. We are not afraid of the bourgeois intellectuals, but we shall not for a moment relax the struggle against the deliberate saboteurs and Whiteguards among these intellectuals. But the slogan of the moment is to make use of the change of attitude towards us which is taking place among them. There still remain plenty of the worst representatives of the bourgeois intelligentsia who have wormed themselves into Soviet positions. To cast them out, to replace them by intellectuals who yesterday were our convinced enemies and today are only neutral is one of the most important tasks of the present moment, the task of every active Soviet functionary who comes into contact with the "intelligentsia," of every agitator, propagandist, and organizer.

Of course, like every other political action in a complex and rapidly changing situation, agreement with the middle peasant, with the worker who was a Menshevik yesterday and with the office worker or intellectual who was a saboteur yesterday, takes skill to achieve. The whole point is not to rest content with the skill we have acquired by previous experience, but *under all circumstances to go on, under all circumstances to strive for something bigger,* under all circumstances to proceed from simpler tasks to more difficult tasks. Otherwise, no progress whatever is possible and in particular no progress is possible in socialist construction.

The other day I was visited by representatives from a congress of delegates of credit co-operative societies. They showed me one of their congress resolutions protesting *against the merger* of the Credit Co-operative Bank with the People's Bank of the Republic. I told them that I stood for agreement with the middle peasantry and highly valued even the beginnings of a change in attitude from hostility to neutrality towards the Bolsheviks on the part of the co-operators, but the basis for an agreement could be created only by their consent to the complete merger of their special bank with the united Bank of the Republic. The representatives of the congress thereupon replaced their resolution by another, which they had the congress adopt, and in which everything hostile to the merger was deleted; *but... but* what they proposed was a plan for a *special* "credit union" of co-operators, which in fact differed in no way from a special bank! That was ridiculous. Only a fool, of course, will be deceived by verbal retouchings. But the "failure" of one such ... "attempt" will not affect our policy in the least; we have pursued and will pursue a policy of agreement with the co-operators, the middle peasants, at the same time suppressing every attempt to change the *line* of the Soviet government and of Soviet socialist construction.

Vacillation on the part of the petty-bourgeois democrats is inevitable. It was enough for the Czechoslovaks to win a few victories for these democrats to fall into a panic, to begin to spread panic, to hasten to the side of the "victors," and be ready to greet them servilely. Of course, it must not be forgotten for a moment that now too any partial success of, let us say, the Anglo-American-Krasnov[54] Whiteguards would be enough for vacillation to begin in the other direction, panic will increase and cases of the dissemination of panic, of treachery, and desertion to the imperialists, and so on and so forth, will be multiplied.

We are aware of that. We shall not forget it. The purely proletarian basis we have won for Soviet power, which is supported by the semi-proletarians, will remain firm and enduring. Our ranks will not falter, our army will not waver—that we already know from experience. But when profound world historic changes bring about an inevitable turn in our direction among the mass of non-Party, Menshevik, and Socialist-Revolutionary democrats, we must learn and shall learn to make use of this change of front, to encourage it, to induce it among the various groups and strata, to do everything possible to reach agreement with these elements and thus facilitate the work of socialist construction and ease the burden of grievous economic dislocation, ignorance, and incompetence which are delaying the victory of socialism.

Written November 20, 1918
Printed November 21, 1918, in
*Pravda*, No. 252

Vol. XXVIII, pp. 165-73

# SPEECH DELIVERED AT THE FIRST ALL-RUSSIAN CONGRESS
## OF LAND DEPARTMENTS,
## COMMITTEES OF POOR PEASANTS AND COMMUNES

*December 11, 1918*

*(Loud applause rising to an ovation. All rise)* Comrades, the composition of this congress, in my opinion, is in itself an indication of the profound change that has taken place and the great progress we, the Soviet Republic, have made in the work of socialist construction, in particular in the sphere of agricultural relations, which are of the utmost importance to our country. The present congress embraces representatives of the Land Departments, the Committees of Poor Peasants, and the agricultural communes, a combination which shows that within a short space of time, within a single year, our revolution has made great strides in reconstructing those relations whose reconstruction presents the greatest difficulties, relations which in all previous revolutions constituted the greatest hindrance to the cause of socialism, and which must be most profoundly reconstructed in order to ensure the triumph of socialism.

The first stage, the first period in the development of our revolution after October, was mainly devoted to defeating the common enemy of the peasantry as a whole, namely, the landlords.

Comrades, you are all very well aware of the fact that even the February Revolution—the revolution of the bourgeoisie, the revolution of the compromisers—promised the peasants this defeat of the landlords, and that this promise was not fulfilled. It was only the October Revolution, only the victory of the working class in the cities, only Soviet

government that enabled the whole of Russia, from end to
end, to be cleared of that ulcer, the heritage of the old feudal system, the old feudal exploitation, the large landed
estates and the oppression exercised by the landlords over
the peasantry as a whole, over all the peasants without
distinction.

This fight against the landlords was one in which all
the peasants were bound to engage, and actually did engage. This fight united the poor toiling peasants, who do
not live by exploiting the labour of others. But it also united the most prosperous and even wealthy section of the
peasantry, which cannot get along without hired labour.

As long as our revolution was occupied with this task,
as long as we had to exert every effort in order that the
power of the landlords might really be swept away and
entirely abolished by the independent movement of the
peasants aided by the movement of the city workers, the
revolution was a general revolution of the peasants and
could therefore not go beyond bourgeois limits.

It had still not touched the more powerful and more
modern enemy of all toilers—capital. It therefore threatened to end half-way, as was the case with the majority of
the revolutions in Western Europe, in which a temporary
alliance of the urban workers and the whole of the peasantry succeeded in sweeping away the monarchy and the
survivals of medievalism, in sweeping away the landed
estates and the power of the landlords more or less thoroughly, but never succeeded in undermining the actual
foundations of the power of capital.

And it was this much more important and much more
difficult task that our revolution began to tackle in the
summer and autumn of the present year. The tide of counter-revolutionary uprisings which rose in the summer of
the present year—when the attack of the West-European
imperialists, of their Czechoslovak hirelings, on Russia was
joined by all the exploiting and oppressing elements in
Russian life—inspired a new spirit and new life in the peasants.

All these revolts in practice united the European imperialists, their Czechoslovak hirelings, and all those who in

Russia remained on the side of the landlords and capitalists in a desperate struggle against the Soviet power. And they were followed by the revolt of all the village kulaks.

The peasantry ceased to be united. The peasants, who had fought like one man against the landlords, split into two camps: the camp of the poor toiling peasants, who, side by side with the workers, continued steadfastly to strive for the realization of socialism and proceeded from fighting the landlords to fighting capital, the power of money, and the use of the great agrarian reform in the interests of the kulaks—and the camp of the more wealthy peasants. This struggle, which finally severed the property-owning and exploiting classes from the revolution, placed our revolution completely on those socialist lines on which the urban working class so firmly and determinedly desired to place it in October, but along which it can never successfully direct the revolution if it does not meet with enlightened, determined, and solid support in the rural districts.

Herein lies the significance of the revolution which took place in the summer and autumn of the present year even in the most remote and out-of-the-way villages of Russia, a revolution which was not spectacular, not as striking and obvious as the revolution of October of last year, but the significance of which is incomparably deeper and greater.

The formation of the Committees of Poor Peasants in the rural districts marked a turning-point and showed that the working class of the cities, which in October had united with the whole of the peasantry to smash the principal enemy of free, toiling and socialist Russia, the landlords, had advanced from this task to a much more difficult and historically superior and truly socialist task—to carry the conscious socialist struggle also into the rural districts, to awaken the peasants as well. The great agrarian revolution, the proclamation in October of the abolition of private property in land, the proclamation of the socialization of the land, would inevitably have remained a revolution only on paper had not the urban workers roused to life the rural proletariat, the poor peasants, the toiling peasants, who constitute the vast majority, who, like the middle peasants, do not exploit the labour of others and are not inter-

ested in exploitation, and who therefore are capable of
progressing, and have already progressed, beyond the joint
struggle against the landlords to the general proletarian
struggle against capital, against the power of the exploiters—who rely on the power of money and movable property—progressed from sweeping Russia clear of the landlords to the task of establishing a socialist system.

This step, comrades, was an extremely difficult one. Regarding this step, those who doubted the socialist character of our revolution prophesied that we would inevitably
fail. Yet it is on this step that the whole cause of socialist
construction in the agricultural districts now depends. The
formation of the Committees of Poor Peasants, the wide
network of these committees which has spread all over
Russia, their transformation, which is now about to take
place, and which in part has already begun, into fully competent rural Soviets of Deputies, the duty of which will be
to give effect in the rural districts to the fundamental principles of Soviet organization—the power of the toilers—
therein lies the genuine pledge that we have not confined
ourselves to the tasks to which ordinary bourgeois-democratic revolutions in West-European countries confined
themselves. Having destroyed the monarchy and the medieval power of the landlords, we are now passing over to
the work of genuine socialist construction. In the rural
districts this is the most difficult but at the same time most
important work. It is most thankful work. In the fact that
we have aroused the consciousness of the toiling section
of the peasants, in the fact that they have been finally severed from the interests of the capitalist class by a wave of
capitalist revolts, in the fact that the toiling peasants in
the Committees of Poor Peasants and the Soviets, which
are now being reformed, are joining forces more and more
closely with the urban workers—in this we see the sole,
yet true and undoubtedly abiding pledge that the cause of
socialist development in Russia has now been placed on a
firmer foundation. It has now acquired a basis also among
the vast masses of the agricultural rural population.

It cannot be denied that in a peasant country like Russia socialist construction is a very difficult thing. It can-

not be denied that it was comparatively easy to sweep away an enemy like tsarism, like the landlords, like the landed estates. That task could be accomplished in the centre in a few days; it could be accomplished all over the country in a few weeks. But, by its very nature, the task we are now tackling can be accomplished only by extremely persistent and protracted effort. Here we shall have to fight, step by step and inch by inch. We shall have to fight for the achievement of a new, socialist Russia; we shall have to fight for the social cultivation of the land.

And it goes without saying that a revolution of this kind, the transition from small, individual peasant farms to the social cultivation of the land, will require considerable time and can in no case be accomplished instantly.

We know very well that in countries where small-peasant economy prevails the transition to socialism cannot be effected except by a series of gradual preliminary stages. In the light of this, the first aim set by the October Revolution was merely to overthrow and destroy the power of the landlords. The February fundamental law on the socialization of the land, which, as you know, was passed by the unanimous vote both of the Communists and of those participants in Soviet government who did not share the point of view of the Communists, was at the same time an expression of the conscious will of the vast majority of the peasants and a proof of the fact that the working class, the workers' Communist Party, aware of their task, are persistently and patiently advancing towards the new socialist construction—advancing by a series of gradual measures, by awakening the toiling section of the peasantry, and forging ahead only in step with this awakening, only in the measure that the peasantry is independently organized.

We fully realize that such vast upheavals in the lives of tens of millions of people as the transition from small individual peasant farming to the joint cultivation of the land, affecting as they do the most deep-going roots of life and habits, can be accomplished only by long effort, and can in general be accomplished only when necessity compels people to reshape their lives.

17*

And now, after a long and desperate war all over the world, we clearly discern the beginnings of a socialist revolution all over the world. This necessity has been created even for the most backward of countries and—irrespective of any theoretical views or socialist doctrines—is impressing most forcefully on everybody that it is impossible to live in the old way.

When the country has suffered such tremendous ruin and collapse, when we see this collapse spreading all over the world, when we see the achievements of culture, science, and technology gained by mankind in the course of many centuries swept away in these four years of criminal, destructive, and predatory war, and the whole of Europe, and not merely Russia alone, returning to a state of barbarism—in the face of these facts, the broad masses, and particularly the peasantry, who perhaps have suffered most from this war, are coming clearly to realize that tremendous efforts are required, that every ounce of energy must be exerted in order to get rid of the aftermath of this accursed war which has left us nothing but ruin and want. It is impossible to live in the old way, in the way we lived before the war. And the waste of human toil and effort associated with individual, small-scale peasant farming can no longer be tolerated. The productivity of labour would be doubled or trebled, the saving of human labour in agriculture and human economy in general would be doubled or trebled if a transition were made from this disunited, small-scale production to social production.

The impoverishment bequeathed us by the war simply does not allow us to restore the old small-scale peasant form of production. Not only have the mass of the peasants been awakened by the war, not only has the war shown them what marvels of technique now exist and how these marvels have been adapted for the extermination of human beings, but it has provoked the thought that these marvels of technique must be used primarily to reshape the form of production which is the most common in the country, in which the greatest number of people are engaged, but which at the same time is most backward—agriculture. Not only has this idea been provoked, but people have been

made to realize by the monstrous horrors of modern war-
fare what forces modern technique has created, how these
forces are wasted in frightful and senseless war, and that
these very forces of technique are the only means of salvation from these horrors. It is our obligation and duty
to use them to place the most backward form of production—agriculture—on new lines, to reshape it, and to transform it from a form of production conducted in the old, unenlightened way into a form of production based on science and technical achievements. The war has made people
realize this much more than any of us can imagine. But
besides this the war has also made it impossible to restore
production in the old way.

Those who cherish the hope that after this war the pre-
war situation can be restored, that the old system and methods of production can be resumed, are mistaken—and
are coming to realize their mistake more and more every
day. The war has resulted in such frightful impoverishment that individual small farms now possess neither
draught animals nor implements. We can no longer tolerate such a dissipation of the labour of the people. The
toiling, poor peasants, who have borne the greatest sacrifices for the revolution and have suffered most from the
war, did not take the land from the landlords in order that
it should fall into the hands of new kulaks. The very facts
of life are now compelling these toiling peasants to face
the question of turning to the social cultivation of the land
as the only means of restoring the culture that has now
been ruined and destroyed by the war, and as the only
means of escaping from the state of ignorance, downtroddenness, and oppression to which the whole mass of the
agricultural population was condemned by capitalism—the
ignorance and oppression which permitted the capitalists
to inflict the war on mankind for four years and from
which the toilers of all countries are resolving with revolutionary energy and fervour to rid themselves at all costs.

These, comrades, are the conditions that had to be created on a world scale for this most difficult and at the same
time most important socialist reform, this most important
and fundamental socialist measure, to be placed on the

order of the day, and in Russia it has been placed on the order of the day. The formation of the Committees of Poor Peasants and this Joint Congress of Land Departments, Committees of Poor Peasants and agricultural communes, taken in conjunction with the struggle which took place in the agricultural districts in the summer and autumn of the present year, go to show that very wide sections of the toiling peasantry have been awakened, and that the peasantry itself, the majority of the toiling peasants, are striving toward social cultivation of the land. Of course, I repeat, we must tackle this great reform gradually. Nothing can be done here in a hurry. But I must remind you that the fundamental law on the socialization of the land, the adoption of which the very next day after the revolution of October 25, at the very first session of the first organ of Soviet power, the Second All-Russian Congress of Soviets, was a foregone conclusion, not only abolished private property in land for ever, not only did away with landlord property, but also stipulated, incidentally, that farm property, draught animals, and farm implements which passed into the possession of the people and of the toiling peasants should also become public property and cease to be the private property of individual farms. And on the fundamental question of our present aims, of the way we desire the land to be disposed of and what we call on the supporters of the Soviet government, the toiling peasants, to do in this respect, Article 11 of the law on the socialization of the land which was adopted in February 1918 states that the aim is to develop collective farming in agriculture, as being the most advantageous from the point of view of economy of labour and products, at the expense of individual farming and with the aim of passing over to a socialist system of production.

Comrades, when we passed this law complete unanimity and agreement did not exist between the Communists and the other parties. On the contrary, we passed this law when the Soviet government consisted of a union of the Communists and the Party of Left Socialist-Revolutionaries, who did not share the communist views. Nevertheless, we arrived at a unanimous decision, to which we adhere to this

day, remembering, as I repeat, that the transition from individual farming to the social cultivation of the land cannot be effected all at once, and that the struggle which developed in the cities was simpler. In the cities thousands
of workers were confronted by one capitalist, and it did not
require much effort to remove him. The struggle which developed in the rural districts, however, was much more
complex. At first there was the general assault of the peasants on the landlords; at first there was the complete abolition of the power of the landlords in such a way that it
could never be restored again. This was followed by a
struggle among the peasants themselves, among whom
new capitalists arose in the shape of the kulaks, in the
shape of the exploiters and profiteers, who used their surplus grain to enrich themselves at the expense of the starving non-agricultural parts of Russia. Here a new struggle
had to be fought, and you know that in the summer of this
year this struggle led to the outbreak of a number of revolts. We do not say of the kulak as we do of the landlord
and capitalist that he must be deprived of all his property.
What we say is that we must break the kulak's resistance
to indispensable measures, such as the grain monopoly,
which he is violating in order to enrich himself by selling
grain surpluses at profiteering prices, while the workers
and peasants in the non-agricultural areas are suffering
the torments of starvation. And our policy here was to
wage a struggle as merciless as that waged against the
landlords and the capitalists. But there also remained the
question of the attitude of the poor section of the toiling
peasantry to the middle peasantry. Our policy in relation
to the middle peasant always was to form an alliance with
him. He is no enemy of Soviet institutions; he is no enemy
of the proletariat and socialism. He will, of course, vacillate and will consent to adopt socialism only when he sees
by definite and convincing example that it is necessary.
The middle peasant, of course, cannot be convinced by
theoretical arguments or by agitational speeches; and we
do not count on doing so. But he can be convinced by the
example and the solid front of the toiling section of the
peasantry. He can be convinced by an alliance of the toil-

ing peasantry with the proletariat. And here we count on
a prolonged and gradual process of persuasion and on a
number of transitional measures which will embody the
agreement of the proletarian socialist section of the population, the agreement of the Communists—who are conducting a resolute fight against capital in all its forms—with
the middle peasantry.

It is because we realize this state of affairs, because we
realize that the task confronting us in the agricultural district is incomparably more difficult, that we are tackling
the question in the way it was tackled in the law on the
socialization of the land. You know that this law proclaimed the abolition of private property in land and introduced the equal division of land. You know that enforcement
of this law was begun in this spirit, and that it has been
put into effect in the majority of agricultural districts. Yet
at the same time the law contains, with the unanimous
consent both of Communists and of people who at that time
did not yet share communist views, the thesis I have just
read to you, which declares that our common task and our
common aim is the transition to socialist production, to
collective land tenure and social cultivation of the land.
As the period of construction progresses, both the peasants
who have already settled on the land and the prisoners of
war who are now returning in hundreds of thousands and
millions, worn and exhausted from captivity, are coming
to realize more and more clearly the vast scope of the work
that must be performed in order to restore agriculture and
emancipate the peasant for ever from his old neglected,
downtrodden, and ignorant state. It is becoming more and
more clear to them that the only permanent way of escape,
one that will bring the masses of the peasants nearer to
a cultured life and place them in a position of equality with
other citizens, is the social cultivation of the land. And the
Soviet government is now systematically striving by gradual measures to bring about this social cultivation of the
land. It is in order to bring about the social cultivation of
the land that communes and state farms are being formed.
The importance of such a form of farming is pointed
out in the law on the socialization of the land. In the sec-

tion of the law which sets forth who is entitled to the use of the land, you will find that among the persons and institutions entitled to use the land the first place is given to the state, the second to public organizations, the third to agricultural communes, and the fourth to agricultural co-operative societies. I again draw your attention to the fact that these fundamental theses of the law on the socialization of the land were laid down when the Communist Party was carrying out not only its own will, when it made deliberate concessions to those who in one way or another expressed the mind and will of the middle peasantry. We made such concessions, and are still making them. We concluded and are concluding an agreement of this kind because the transition to the collective form of agriculture, to the social cultivation of the land, to state farms, to communes, cannot be accomplished all at once; it demands the exercise of stubborn and persistent influence by the Soviet government. The Soviet government has assigned one thousand million rubles for the improvement of agriculture on condition that social cultivation of the land be adopted. This law shows that we desire to influence the mass of middle peasants rather by the force of example, by inviting them to improve their methods of husbandry, and that we count only on the gradual influence of such measures to bring about this profound and most important revolution in agricultural production in Russia.

The alliance of the Committees of Poor Peasants, agricultural communes, and Land Departments we have at the present congress shows us, and fully assures us, that the matter has now been put on the right lines, on a truly socialist scale, by this transition to the social cultivation of the land. By steady and systematic work along these lines an increase in the productivity of labour must be secured. For this purpose we must adopt the best agricultural methods and enlist the agronomical forces of Russia so that we may be able to work the best organized farms, which hitherto have served as a source of enrichment for individuals, as the source of a revival of capitalism, as the source of a new bondage and a new enslavement of wage-labourers, but which now, under the law on the socialization of the land and the complete abolition of private property in land, must serve as a source of agricultural knowledge and culture and of increased productivity for the millions of toilers. This alliance of the urban workers with the toiling peasantry, the formation of the Committees of Poor Peasants and the new elections to them as Soviet institutions are evidence that agricultural Russia has now entered on a path which is being taken by one West-European state after another, later than us, but more surely. It was much harder for them to start the revolution, because their enemy was not a rotten autocracy, but a highly cultured and united capitalist class. But you know that this revolution has begun. You know that the revolution has not been confined to Russia, and that our chief hope, our chief support, is the proletariat of the more advanced countries of Western Europe, and that this chief support of the world revolution has been set in motion. And we are firmly convinced, and the course of the German revolution has shown it in practice, that in those countries the transition to socialist farming, the use of more advanced agricultural techniques and the union of the toiling agricultural population will proceed more rapidly and easily than in our country.

In alliance with the workers of the cities and with the socialist proletariat of the whole world, the toiling peasants of Russia can now be certain that they will overcome all their adversities, beat off the attacks of the imperialists, and accomplish that without which the emancipation of the toilers is impossible, viz., the social cultivation of the land, the gradual but steady transition from small individual farms to the social cultivation of the land. (*Loud, prolonged applause.*)

*Pravda,* No. 272,
December 14, 1918

Vol. XXVIII, pp. 314-25

# DRAFT PROGRAMME OF THE R.C.P. (B.)
## *(Excerpt)*

### AGRARIAN SECTION OF THE PROGRAMME

Soviet power, having completely abolished private property in land, has already passed over to the implementation of a whole series of measures aimed at the organization of large-scale socialist agriculture. The most important of these measures are the organization of state farms, i.e., large socialist farms, encouragement of agricultural communes, i.e., voluntary associations of tillers of the land for large-scale farming in common, and societies as well as co-operatives for public cultivation of land; cultivation by the state of all uncultivated lands, whomever they may belong to; mobilization by the state of all agricultural specialists for energetic measures to raise efficiency in farming, etc.

Regarding all these measures as the only way to raise productivity of agricultural labour, which is absolutely imperative, the R.C.P. seeks to carry them out as fully as possible, to extend them to the more backward regions of the country, and to take further steps in this direction.

Inasmuch as the antithesis between town and country is one of the root-causes of the economic and cultural backwardness of the countryside, one which in a period of so deep a crisis as the present confronts both town and country with the direct threat of degradation and ruin, the R.C.P. regards the eradication of this antithesis as one of the basic tasks in the building of communism and, alongside the above measures, considers it necessary extensively and systematically to enlist industrial workers in communist organization of agriculture, to promote the activities of the nation-wide "Workers' Auxiliary Committee" set up with this in view by the Soviet power, and so on.

In all its work in the countryside the R.C.P. will continue to rely on the proletarian and semi-proletarian sections of the rural population, primarily organizing them into an independent force, setting up committees of poor peasants, party cells in the villages, a specific type of trade unions for rural proletarians and semi-proletarians, etc., exerting every effort to bring them closer to the urban proletariat and wresting them away from the influence of the rural bourgeoisie and petty-property interests.

In regard to the kulaks, the rural bourgeoisie, it is the policy of the R.C.P. to wage a resolute struggle against their exploiter-predilections, to suppress their resistance to Soviet, communist, policy.

In regard to the middle peasantry it is the policy of the R.C.P. gradually and systematically to enlist them in the work of socialist construction. The Party aims to distinguish between them and the kulaks, to attract them to the side of the working class by a considerate attitude toward their needs, combating their backwardness by ideological persuasion, not by coercion, seeking in all cases affecting their vital interests to reach practical agreement with them, and making concessions in defining ways of effecting socialist reforms.

First published in 1930

Vol. XXIX, pp. 119-20

# REPORT ON WORK IN THE RURAL DISTRICTS DELIVERED AT THE EIGHTH CONGRESS OF THE R.C.P. (B.)

### March 23, 1919

(*Prolonged applause*) Comrades, I must apologize for having been unable to attend all the meetings of the committee elected by the congress to consider the question of work in the rural districts. My report will therefore be supplemented by the speeches of comrades who took part in the work of the committee from the very beginning. The committee finally drew up theses which were turned over to a commission and which will be reported on to you. I should like to dwell on the general significance of the question as it confronts us following the work of the committee and as, in my opinion, it now confronts the whole Party.

Comrades, it is quite natural that as the proletarian revolution develops we have to put in the forefront now one now another of the most complex and important problems of social life. It is perfectly natural that in a revolution which affects, and is bound to affect, the deepest foundations of life and the broadest masses of the population, not a single party, not a single government, no matter how close it may be to the masses, can possibly embrace all phases of life *at once*. And if we now have to deal with the question of work in the rural districts, and in connection with this question to give prominence to the position of the middle peasantry, there is nothing strange or abnormal in this from the standpoint of the development of the proletarian revolution in general. It is natural that the proletarian revolution had to begin with the fundamental relation between two hostile classes, the proletariat and the bourgeoisie. The principal task was to transfer the power to the working class, to secure its dictatorship, to overthrow the bourgeoisie and to deprive it of the economic sources of its power, which are undoubtedly a hindrance to all socialist construction in general. Acquainted as we were with Marxism, no one of us has ever for a moment doubted the truth that, owing to the very economic structure of capitalist society, the deciding factor in that society can be either the proletariat or the bourgeoisie. We now see many former Marxists—from the Menshevik camp, for example—who assert that in a period of decisive struggle between the proletariat and the bourgeoisie *democracy in general* can prevail. This is what is said by the Mensheviks, who have come to a complete agreement with the Socialist-Revolutionaries. As though it is not the bourgeoisie itself that creates or abolishes democracy as it finds most convenient for itself! And since that is so, there can be no question of democracy in general at a time of acute struggle between the bourgeoisie and the proletariat. It is astonishing how rapidly these Marxists, or pseudo-Marxists—our Mensheviks, for example—expose themselves, and how rapidly their true nature, the nature of petty-bourgeois democrats, comes to the surface.

Marx all his life fought most of all the illusions of petty-bourgeois democracy and bourgeois democracy. Marx scoffed most of all at empty talk of freedom and equality, when it serves as a screen for the freedom of the workers to starve to death, or the equality of one who sells his labour power with the bourgeois who allegedly freely purchases the labour of the former in the open market as from an equal, and so forth. Marx explains this in all his economic works. It may be said that the whole of Marx's *Capital* is devoted to explaining the truth that *the basic forces of capitalist society are, and can only be, the bourgeoisie and the proletariat*—bourgeoisie, as the builder of this capitalist society, as its leader, as its motive force, and the proletariat, as its grave-digger and as the only force capable of replacing it. One can hardly find a single chapter in any of Marx's works that is not devoted to this. One might say that all over the world the Socialists of the Second International have vowed and sworn to the workers time out of number that they understand this truth. But when matters reached the stage of the real and moreover decisive struggle for power between the proletariat and the bourgeoisie, we find that our Mensheviks and Socialist-Revolutionaries, like the leaders of the old socialist parties all over the world, forgot this truth and began to repeat in a purely automatic way the philistine phrases about democracy in general.

Attempts are sometimes made to lend these words what is considered to be greater force by speaking of "the dictatorship of democracy." That is sheer nonsense. We know perfectly well from history that the dictatorship of the democratic bourgeoisie meant nothing but the suppression of the insurgent workers. That has been the case ever since 1848—at any rate, not later, and isolated examples may be found even earlier. History shows that it is precisely in a bourgeois democracy that a most acute struggle between the proletariat and the bourgeoisie proceeds widely and freely. We have had occasion to convince ourselves of this truth in practice. And the measures taken by the Soviet Government since October 1917 were distinguished by their firmness on all fundamental questions precisely because we have never departed from this truth and have never forgotten it. The issue of the struggle for supremacy waged against the bourgeoisie can be settled only by the dictatorship of one class—the proletariat. Only the dictatorship of the proletariat can defeat the bourgeoisie. Only the proletariat can overthrow the bourgeoisie. And only the proletariat can secure the following of the masses in the struggle against the bourgeoisie.

However, it by no means follows from this—it would be a profound mistake to think it does—that in further building communism, when the bourgeoisie has been overthrown and political power is already in the hands of the proletariat, we can continue to carry on without the participation of the middle, intermediary elements.

It is natural that at the beginning of the revolution—the proletarian revolution—the whole attention of its active participants should be concentrated on the main and fun-

damental thing, the supremacy of the proletariat and the securing of that supremacy by a victory over the bourgeoisie
—making it certain that the bourgeoisie cannot return to
power. We are well aware that the bourgeoisie still enjoys
the advantages derived from the wealth it possesses in
other countries or even the monetary wealth it sometimes
possesses in our own country. We are well aware that there
are social elements who are more experienced than proletarians and who aid the bourgeoisie. We are well aware
that the bourgeoisie has not abandoned the idea of returning to power and has not ceased attempting to restore its
supremacy.

But that is by no means all. The bourgeoisie, which puts
forward most insistently the principle "my country is
wherever it is good for me," and which, as far as money is
concerned, has always been international—*the bourgeoisie internationally is at present still stronger than we are.*
Its supremacy is being rapidly undermined, it is being
confronted with such facts as the Hungarian revolution
—about which we were happy to inform you yesterday and
are today receiving confirming reports—and it is beginning to understand that its supremacy is shaky. It no longer enjoys freedom of action. But now, if one takes into
account the material means on the world scale, we cannot
help admitting that in the material respect the bourgeoisie is at present still stronger than we are.

That is why nine-tenths of our attention and our practical activities were devoted, and had to be devoted, to
this fundamental question—the overthrow of the bourgeoisie, the establishment of the power of the proletariat and
the elimination of every possibility of the return of the
bourgeoisie to power. That is absolutely natural, legitimate,
and unavoidable, and very much in this respect has been
successfully accomplished.

Now, however, we must put on the order of day the question of other strata of the population. We must—and this
was our unanimous conclusion in the agrarian committee,
and on this, we are convinced, all Party workers will
agree, because we merely summed up the results of their

observations—we must now put on the order of day *the question of the middle peasantry* in its full magnitude.

Of course, people will be found who, instead of reflecting on the course of our revolution, instead of pondering over the tasks now confronting us, instead of all this will make every step of the Soviet government a butt of derision and criticism of the type we here heard from those gentlemen, the Mensheviks and the Right Socialist-Revolutionaries. These people have still not understood that they must make a choice between us and the bourgeois dictatorship. We have displayed great patience, even indulgence, towards these people. We shall allow them to enjoy our indulgence once more. But in the very near future we shall set a limit to our patience and indulgence, and if they do not make their choice, we shall tell them in all seriousness to go to Kolchak.[55] (*Applause.*) We do not expect particularly brilliant intellectual ability from such people. (*Laughter.*) But it might have been expected that after experiencing the bestialities of Kolchak they ought to understand that we are entitled to demand that they should choose between us and Kolchak. If during the first few months that followed the October Revolution there were many naive people who were stupid enough to believe that the dictatorship of the proletariat was something transitory and fortuitous, today even the Mensheviks and the Socialist-Revolutionaries ought to understand that there is something logically necessary in the struggle that is being waged before the onslaught of the whole international bourgeoisie.

Only two forces, in fact, have arisen: the dictatorship of the bourgeoisie and the dictatorship of the proletariat. Whoever has not learnt this from Marx, whoever has not learnt this from the works of all the great Socialists, has never been a Socialist, understood nothing about socialism, and has only called himself a Socialist. We are allowing these people a short space for reflection and demand that they make their decision. I have mentioned them because they are now saying or will say: "The Bolsheviks have raised the question of the middle peasants; they want to make advances to them." I am very well aware that considerable space is given in the Menshevik press to arguments of this kind, and even far worse. We ignore such arguments, we never attach importance to the jabber of our adversaries. People who are still capable of running to and fro between the bourgeoisie and the proletariat may say what they please. We are following our own road.

Our road is determined above all by considerations of class forces. A struggle is developing in capitalist society between the bourgeoisie and the proletariat. As long as that struggle has not ended we shall give our keenest attention to fighting it out to the end. It has not yet been brought to the end. In that struggle much has already been accomplished. The hands of the international bourgeoisie are now no longer free. The best proof of this is that the Hungarian proletarian revolution has taken place. It is therefore clear that our constructive work in the rural districts has already gone beyond the limits to which it was confined when everything was subordinated to the fundamental demand of the struggle for power.

This constructive work passed through two main phases. In October 1917 we seized power *together with the peasantry as a whole*. This was a bourgeois revolution, inasmuch as the class struggle in the rural districts had not yet developed. As I have said, the real proletarian revolution in the rural districts began only in the summer of 1918. Had we not succeeded in stirring up this revolution our work would have been incomplete. The first stage was the seizure of power in the cities and the establishment of the Soviet form of government. The second stage was one which is fundamental for all Socialists and without which Socialists are not Socialists, namely, to single out the proletarian and the semi-proletarian elements in the rural districts and to weld them with the urban proletariat in order to wage the struggle against the bourgeoisie in the countryside. This stage is also in the main completed. The organizations we originally created for this purpose, the Committees of Poor Peasants, had become so consolidated that we found it possible to replace them by properly elected Soviets, i.e., to reorganize the village Soviets so as to make them the organs of class rule, the or-

gans of proletarian power in the rural districts. Such measures as the law on socialist agrarian measures and measures for transition to socialist agriculture,[56] which was
passed not very long ago by the Central Executive Committee and with which everybody, of course, is familiar,
sum up our experience from the standpoint of our proletarian revolution.

The main thing, the prime and basic task of the proletarian revolution, we have already accomplished. And precisely because we have accomplished it, a more complicated problem has come to the fore—*our attitude towards the
middle peasantry*. And whoever thinks that the fact that
this problem is being brought to the fore is in any way
symptomatic of a weakening of the character of our government, of a weakening of the dictatorship of the proletariat, that it is symptomatic of a change, however partial, however minute, in our basic policy, completely fails
to understand the aims of the proletariat and the aims of
the communist revolution. I am convinced that there are
no such people in our Party. I only wanted to warn the
comrades against people not belonging to the workers'
party who will talk in this way, not because it follows from
any system of ideas, but merely to spoil things for us and
to help the Whiteguards—or, to put it more simply, to incite against us the middle peasant, who is always vacillating, who cannot help vacillating, and who will continue
to vacillate for a fairly long time to come. In order to incite the middle peasant against us they will say: "See, they
are making advances to you! That means they have taken
your revolts to heart, they are beginning to wobble," and
so on and so forth. All our comrades must be armed
against agitation of this kind. And I am certain that they
will be armed—provided we succeed now in having this
question treated from the standpoint of the class struggle.

It is perfectly obvious that this fundamental problem—
*how precisely to define the attitude of the proletariat to-
wards the middle peasantry*—is a more complex but no less
urgent problem. Comrades, from the theoretical point of
view, which has been mastered by the vast majority of the
workers, this question presents no difficulty to Marxists.

18*

I will remind you, for instance, that in Kautsky's book on the agrarian question, written at a time when he was still correctly expounding the teachings of Marx and was regarded as an indisputed authority in this field, he states in connection with the transition from capitalism to socialism that the task of a Socialist party *is to neutralize the peasantry*, i.e., to see to it that in the struggle between the proletariat and the bourgeoisie the peasant should remain neutral and should not be able to give active assistance to the bourgeoisie against us.

Throughout the extremely long period of the rule of the bourgeoisie, the peasants supported the power of the latter; they sided with the bourgeoisie. This will be understood if one considers the economic strength of the bourgeoisie and the political instruments of its rule. We cannot count on the middle peasant coming over to our side immediately. But if we pursue a correct policy, after a time these vacillations will cease and the peasant will be able to come over to our side.

It was Engels—who together with Marx laid the foundations of scientific Marxism, that is, the teachings by which our Party has always guided itself, and particularly in time of revolution—who already established the division of the peasantry into small peasants, middle peasants, and big peasants, and this division holds good for the vast majority of European countries even at the present day. Engels said: "Perhaps it will not be necessary to suppress even the big peasantry by force everywhere." And that we might at any time use violence in relation to the middle peasants (the small peasant is our friend), that thought never occurred to any sensible Socialist. That is what Engels said in 1894, a year before his death, when the agrarian question came to the fore. This point of view expresses a truth which is sometimes forgotten, but with which we are all in theory agreed. In relation to the landlords and the capitalists our aim is complete expropriation. *But we shall not tolerate any violence towards the middle peasantry.* Even in regard to the rich peasants we do not say as resolutely as we say with regard to the bourgeoisie: absolute expropriation of the rich peasants and the kulaks. This distinction is observed in our programme. We say: the resistance and the counter-revolutionary efforts of the rich peasant must be suppressed. That is not complete expropriation.

The basic distinction that determines our attitude towards the bourgeoisie and the middle peasant—complete expropriation of the bourgeoisie and an alliance with the middle peasant who does not exploit others—this basic line is accepted by everybody in theory. But this line is not consistently followed in practice; they have not yet learnt to follow it in the localities. When, after having overthrown the bourgeoisie and consolidated its own power, the proletariat started from various angles to create a new society, the question of the middle peasant came to the fore. Not a single Socialist in the world denied that the building of communism would take different courses in countries where large-scale agriculture prevails and in countries where small-scale agriculture prevails. That is an elementary truth, an ABC. And from this truth it follows that as we approach the problems of communist construction our principal attention must to a certain extent be concentrated precisely on the middle peasant.

Much will depend on how we define our attitude towards the middle peasant. Theoretically, that question has been solved; but we know perfectly well from our own experience that there is a difference between solving a problem theoretically and putting that solution into practical effect. We are now directly confronted with that difference, which was so characteristic of the Great French Revolution, when the French Convention launched into sweeping measures but did not possess the necessary base of support in order to put them into effect, and did not even know on what class to rely in order to put any particular measure into effect.

Our position is an infinitely more fortunate one. Thanks to a whole century of development, we know on which class we are relying. But we also know that the practical experience of that class is extremely inadequate. The fundamental aim was clear to the working class and the workers' party—to overthrow the power of the bourgeoisie and to transfer power to the workers. But *how* was that to be done? Everyone remembers with what difficulty and at the cost of how many mistakes we passed from workers' control to workers' management of industry. And yet that was work within our own class, within the proletarian midst, with which we had always had to deal. But now we are called upon to define our attitude towards a new class, a class the urban worker does not know. We have to determine our attitude towards a class which has no definite and stable position. The proletariat in its mass is in favour of socialism, the bourgeoisie in its mass is opposed to socialism. It is easy to determine the relations between these two classes. But when we pass to a stratum like the middle peasantry we find that *it is a class that vacillates*. The middle peasant is partly a property-owner and partly a toiler. He does not exploit other toilers. For decades the middle peasant defended his position with the greatest difficulty, he suffered the exploitation of the landlords and the capitalists, he bore everything. Yet he is a property-owner. Our attitude towards this vacillating class therefore presents enormous difficulties. In the light of more than a year's experience, in the light of more than six months' proletarian work in the rural districts, and in the light of the fact that class differentiation in the rural districts has already taken place, we must most of all beware here lest we are too hasty, lest we are clumsily theoretical, lest we regard what is in process of being accomplished, but has not yet been realized, as already accomplished. In the resolution which is being proposed to you by the commission elected by the committee, and which will be read to you by a subsequent speaker, you will find sufficient warning against this.

From the economic point of view, it is obvious that we must help the middle peasant. Theoretically, there is no doubt of this. But because of our habits, our level of culture, the inadequacy of the cultural and technical forces we are in a position to place at the disposal of the rural districts, and because of the impotent manner in which we often approach the rural districts, comrades quite often resort to coercion and thus spoil everything. Only yesterday a comrade gave me a pamphlet entitled *Instructions and Regulations on Party Work in the Nizhni-Novgorod Gubernia*, issued by the Nizhni-Novgorod Committee of the Russian Communist Party (Bolsheviks), and in this pamphlet, for example, I find on p. 41: "The whole burden of the extraordinary tax decree must be placed on the shoulder of the village kulaks and profiteers and *the middle element of the peasantry generally*." Well, well! These people have indeed "understood." This is either a printer's error—and it is intolerable that such printer's errors should be permitted—or a piece of rushed, hasty work, which shows how dangerous all haste is in this matter. Or—and this is the worst surmise of all, one I would not like to make with regard to the Nizhni-Novgorod comrades—they have simply failed to understand. It may very well be that it is an oversight.

We have in practice cases like the one related by a comrade in the commission. He was surrounded by peasants, and every one of them asked: "Tell me, am I a middle peasant or not? I have two horses and one cow. I have two cows and one horse," etc. And this agitator, who tours the uyezds, is expected to possess an infallible thermometer with which to gauge every peasant and say whether he is a middle peasant or not. To do that one must know the whole history of the given peasant's farm, his relation to higher and lower groups—and we cannot know that accurately.

Considerable practical ability and knowledge of local conditions are required here. And we do not possess this yet. One need not be ashamed to confess it; it must be admitted frankly. We were never utopians and never imagined that we would build the communist society with the immaculate hands of immaculate Communists, born and educated in an immaculately communist society. That is a nursery tale. We have to build communism from the debris of capitalism, and only the class which has been steeled in the struggle against capitalism can do that. The proletariat, as you are very well aware, is not free from the shortcomings and weaknesses of capitalist society. It is fighting for socialism, but at the same time it is fight-

ing its own shortcomings. The best and foremost section
of the proletariat, which carried on a desperate struggle
in the cities for decades, was in a position to acquire in
the course of that struggle the culture of the city and of
life in the capital; and to a certain extent it did acquire
it. You know that even in advanced countries the rural
districts were condemned to ignorance. Of course, we shall
raise the level of culture in the rural districts, but that will
be a work of many, many years. That is what our comrades
everywhere are forgetting and what is being strikingly
brought home to us by every word uttered by people who
come from the rural districts; not by the intellectuals who
work here, not by the officials—we have listened to them a
lot—but by people who have in practice observed the work
in the rural districts. It was these opinions that we found
particularly valuable in the agrarian committee. These
opinions will be particularly valuable now—I am convinced of that—for the whole Party congress, for they
come not from books, and not from decrees, but from
experience.

All this obliges us to work for the purpose of introducing the greatest possible clarity into our attitude toward
the middle peasant. This is very difficult, because *such
clarity does not exist in reality.* Not only is this problem
unsolved, it is unsolvable, if you want to solve it *immediately and all at once.* There are people who say: "There was
no need to write so many decrees." They blame the Soviet
government for setting about writing decrees without
knowing how they were to be put into effect. These people,
as a matter of fact, do not realize that they are sinking to
the Whiteguard position. If we had expected that life in
the rural districts could be completely changed by writing hundreds of decrees, we would have been absolute
idiots. But if we had refrained from indicating in decrees
the road that must be followed, we would have been traitors to socialism. These decrees, while in practice they
could not be carried into effect fully and immediately,
played an important part for propaganda. While formerly
we carried on our propaganda by means of general truths,
*we are now carrying on our propaganda by our work.* That

is also preaching, but it is preaching by action—only not action in the sense of isolated sallies of some upstarts, at which we scoffed so much in the era of the anarchists and the socialism of the old type. Our decree is a call, but not the old call: "Workers, arise and overthrow the bourgeoisie!" No, it is a call to the masses, it calls them to practical work. *Decrees are instructions which call for practical work on a mass scale.* That is what is important. Let us assume that decrees do contain much that is useless, much that in practice cannot be put into effect; but they contain material for practical action, and the purpose of a decree is to teach practical steps to the hundreds, thousands, and millions of people who hearken to the word of the Soviet government. This is a trial in practical action in the sphere of socialist construction in the rural districts. If we treat matters in this way we shall acquire a good deal from the sum total of our laws, decrees, and ordinances. We shall not regard them as absolute injunctions which must be put into effect instantly and at all costs.

We must avoid everything that in practice may tend to encourage individual abuses. In places careerists and adventurers have attached themselves to us like leeches, people who call themselves Communists and are deceiving us, and who have wormed their way into our ranks because the Communists are now in power, and because the more honest government employees refused to come and work with us on account of their retrograde ideas, while careerists have no ideas, and no honesty. These people, whose only aim is to make a career, resort in the localities to coercion, and imagine they are doing a good thing. But in fact the result of this at times is that the peasants say: "Long live the Soviet power, but *down with the kommunia!*" (i.e., communism). These are not imaginary cases; they are taken from real life, from the reports of comrades in the localities. We must not forget what enormous damage is always caused by lack of moderation, by all rashness, and haste.

We had to hurry and, by taking a desperate leap, to get out at any cost of the imperialist war, which had brought us to the verge of collapse. We had to make most desperate efforts to crush the bourgeoisie and the forces that were threatening to crush us. All this was necessary, without this we could not have triumphed. But if we were to act in the same way towards the middle peasant it would be such idiocy, such stupidity, it would be so ruinous to our cause, that only provocateurs could deliberately act in such a way. The aim here must be an entirely different one. Here our aim is not to smash the resistance of obvious exploiters, to defeat and overthrow them—which was the aim we previously set ourselves. No, now that this main purpose has been accomplished, more complicated problems arise. You cannot create anything here by coercion. *Coercion applied to the middle peasantry would cause untold harm.* This stratum is a numerous one, it consists of millions of individuals. Even in Europe, where it nowhere achieves such strength, where technology and culture, city life and railways are tremendously developed, and where it would be easiest of all to think of such a thing, nobody, not even the most revolutionary of Socialists, has ever proposed adopting measures of coercion towards the middle peasant.

When we were taking power we relied on the support of the peasantry as a whole. At that time the aim of all the peasants was the same—to fight the landlords. But their prejudice against large-scale farming has remained to this day. The peasant thinks: "A large farm, that means I shall again be a farm-hand." That, of course, is a mistake. But the peasant's idea of large-scale farming is associated with a feeling of hatred and the memory of how the landlords used to oppress the people. That feeling still remains, it has not yet died.

We must particularly stress the truth that here, by the very nature of the case, coercive methods can accomplish nothing. The economic task here is an entirely different one. Here there is no upper layer that can be cut off, leaving the foundation and the building intact. That upper layer which in the cities was represented by the capitalists does not exist here. *Here coercion would ruin the whole cause.* What is required here is prolonged educational work. We have to give the peasant, who not only in our country but all over the world is a practical man and a realist, concrete examples to prove that the "kommunia" is the best possible thing. Of course, nothing will come of it if hasty individuals flit down to a village from a city, come there, chat about, stir up a number of intellectual-like and at times unintellectual-like squabbles, and then quarrel with everyone and go their way. That sometimes happens. Instead of evoking respect, they evoke ridicule, and deservedly so.

On this question we must say that we do encourage communes, but they must be so organized *as to gain the confidence of the peasants*. And until then we are pupils of the peasants and not their teachers. Nothing is more stupid than when people who know nothing about agriculture and its specific features, people who rush to the village only because they have heard of the advantages of socialized farming, are tired of city life and desire to work in rural districts—when such people regard themselves as teachers of the peasants in every respect. *Nothing is more stupid than the very idea of applying coercion in economic relations with the middle peasant.*

The aim here is not to expropriate the middle peasant but to bear in mind the specific conditions in which the peasant lives, to learn from the peasant methods of transition to a better system, *and not to dare to give orders!* That is the rule we have set ourselves. (*General applause.*) That is the rule we have endeavoured to set forth in our draft resolution, for in that respect, comrades, we have indeed sinned a great deal. We are by no means ashamed to confess it. We were inexperienced. Our very struggle against the exploiters was taken from experience. If we have sometimes been condemned on account of it, we can say: "Messieurs the capitalists, you have only yourselves to blame. If you had not offered such savage, senseless, insolent, and desperate resistance, if you had not joined in an alliance with the world bourgeoisie, the revolution would have assumed more peaceful forms." Now that we have repulsed the savage onslaught on all sides, we can change to other methods, because we are acting not as a study circle, but as a Party which is leading the millions.

The millions cannot immediately understand a change of course, and so it frequently happens that blows aimed at the kulaks fall on the middle peasants. That is not surprising. It must only be understood that this is due to historical conditions which have now been outlived and that the new conditions and the new tasks in relation to this class demand a new psychology.

Our decrees on peasant farming are in the main correct. We have no grounds for renouncing a single one of them, or for regretting a single one of them. But if the decrees are right, *it is wrong to impose them on the peasantry by force*. That is not contained in a single decree. They are right inasmuch as they indicate the roads to follow, inasmuch as they call to practical measures. When we say, "Encourage associations," we are giving instructions which must be tested many times before the final *form* in which to put them into effect is found. When it is stated that we must strive to gain the peasants' voluntary consent, it means that they must be persuaded, and persuaded by practical deeds. They will not allow themselves to be convinced by mere words, and they are perfectly right in that. It would be a bad thing if they allowed themselves to be convinced merely by reading decrees and agitational leaflets. If it were possible to reshape economic life in this way, such reshaping would not be worth a brass farthing. It must first be proved that such association is better, people must be united in such a way that they become actually united and are not at odds with each other—it must be proved that association is advantageous. That is the way the peasant puts the question and that is the way our decrees put it. If we have not been able to achieve that so far, there is nothing to be ashamed of and we must admit it frankly.

We have so far accomplished only the fundamental task of every socialist revolution—that of defeating the bourgeoisie. That in the main has been accomplished, although an extremely difficult half-year is beginning in which the imperialists of the world are making a last attempt to crush us. We can now say without in the least exaggerating that *they themselves understand that after this half-*

*year their cause will be absolutely hopeless.* Either they
take advantage now of our state of exhaustion and defeat
us, an isolated country, or we emerge victorious not merely in regard to our country alone. In this half-year, in
which the food crisis has been aggravated by a transport
crisis, and in which the imperialist powers are endeavouring to attack us on several fronts, our situation is extremely
difficult. But *this is the last difficult half-year.* We must
continue to mobilize all our forces in the struggle against
the external enemy, who is attacking us.

But when we speak of the aims of our work in the rural
districts, in spite of all the difficulties, and in spite of the
fact that our experience has been wholly concerned with
the immediate task of crushing the exploiters, we must remember, and never forget, that our aims in the rural districts, in relation to the middle peasant, are entirely different.

All the class-conscious workers—from Petrograd, Ivano-
vo-Voznesensk, or Moscow—who have been to the rural
districts related examples of how a number of misunder-
standings which appeared to be irremovable, and a number of conflicts which appeared to be very serious, were
removed or mitigated when intelligent working-men came
forward and spoke, not in the language of books, but in
a language understood by the muzhiks, when they spoke
not as commanders who take the liberty of giving orders
without knowing anything of rural life, but as comrades,
explaining the situation and appealing to their sentiments
as toilers against the exploiters. And by such comradely
explanation they accomplished what could not be accomplished by hundreds of others who conducted themselves
like commanders and superiors.

That is the spirit that permeates the resolution we are
now submitting to your attention.

I have endeavoured in my brief report to dwell on the
underlying principles, on the general political significance
of this resolution. I have endeavoured to show—and I
should like to think that I have succeeded—that from the
point of view of the interests of the revolution as a whole
we are making no change of policy, we are not changing

the line. The Whiteguards and their henchmen are shouting, or will shout, that we are. Let them shout. We do not care. We are developing our aims in a most consistent manner. We must transfer our attention from the aim of suppressing the bourgeoisie to the aim of arranging the life of the middle peasant. We must live in peace with him. In a communist society the middle peasants will be on our side only when we alleviate and ameliorate their economic conditions. If tomorrow we could supply one hundred thousand first-class tractors, provide them with fuel, provide them with drivers—you know very well that this at present is sheer fantasy—the middle peasant would say: "I am for the kommunia" (i.e., for communism). But in order to do that we must first defeat the international bourgeoisie, we must compel them to give us these tractors, or so develop our productive forces as to be able to provide them ourselves. That is the only correct way to pose this question.

The peasant needs the industry of the towns; he cannot live without it, and it is in our hands. If we set about the task properly, the peasant will be grateful to us for bringing him these products, these implements and this culture from the towns. They will be brought to him not by exploiters, not by landlords, but by his fellow-toilers, whom he values very highly, but values in a practical manner, for the actual help they give, at the same time rejecting—and quite rightly rejecting—all domineering and "orders" from above.

First help, and then endeavour to win confidence. If you set about this task correctly, if every step taken by every one of our groups in the uyezds, the volosts, the food detachments, and in every other organization is made properly, if every step of ours is carefully checked from this point of view, we shall gain the confidence of the peasant, and only then shall we be able to proceed farther. What we must now do is to help him and advise him. This will not be the orders of a commander, but the advice of a comrade. The peasant will then be entirely on our side.

This, comrades, is what is contained in our resolution, and this, in my opinion, must become the decision of the congress. If we adopt this, if it serves to determine the work of all our Party organizations, we shall cope with the second great task confronting us.

We have learnt how to overthrow the bourgeoisie, how to suppress it, and we are proud of the fact. But how to regulate our relations with the millions of middle peasants, in what way to win their confidence, that we have not yet learnt—and we must frankly admit it. But we have understood the task, we have set it, and we say in all confidence, with full knowledge and determination, that we shall cope with this task—and then socialism will be absolutely invincible. (*Prolonged applause.*)

Published in *The Eighth Congress of the Russian Communist Party (Bolsheviks). Verbatim Report,* The Kommunist Publishing House, Moscow 1919

Vol. XXIX, pp. 175-91

# RESOLUTION OF THE EIGHTH CONGRESS OF THE R.C.P. (B.) ON THE ATTITUDE TO THE MIDDLE PEASANTS

Concerning work in the countryside, the Eighth Congress, basing itself on the Party programme adopted on March 22, 1919, and fully supporting the law already promulgated by the Soviet government on socialist agrarian measures and measures for the transition to socialist agriculture, recognizes as a matter of particular importance at the present time a stricter adherence to the line of the Party in relation to the middle peasantry, namely, a more considerate attitude toward its needs, the ending of arbitrary action on the part of local authorities, and efforts toward agreement with it.

1) To confuse the middle peasants with the kulaks and to extend to them in one or another degree measures directed against the kulaks is to violate most flagrantly not only all the decrees of the Soviet government and its entire policy, but also all the basic principles of communism, according to which agreement between the proletariat and the middle peasantry in the period of decisive struggle waged by the proletariat to overthrow the bourgeoisie is one of the conditions for painless transition to abolition of all exploitation.

2) The middle peasantry, which has comparatively strong economic roots owing to the lagging of agricultural techniques behind the industrial even in the leading capitalist countries, not to speak of Russia, will continue to exist for quite a long time after the beginning of the proletarian revolution. Therefore, the tactics of the functionaries of the Soviets in the villages, as well as of Party work-

ers, must envisage a long period of co-operation with the middle peasantry.

3) The Party must see to it without fail that all functionaries of the Soviets in the countryside have a clear and thorough grasp of the axiom of scientific socialism that the middle peasantry are not exploiters, for they do not profit by the labour of others. Such a class of small producers cannot lose by socialism, but, on the contrary, will gain a great deal from the overthrow of the yoke of capital which exploits it in a thousand different ways even in the most democratic republics.

The entirely correct policy of the Soviet power in the countryside thus ensures alliance and agreement between the victorious proletariat and the middle peasantry.

4) While encouraging co-operatives of all kinds as well as agricultural communes of middle peasants, representatives of Soviet power must not allow the slightest coercion being used in setting them up. Only those associations are worth while which have been set up by the peasants themselves on their own initiative, and the benefits of which they have verified in practice. Undue haste in this matter is harmful, for it can only strengthen prejudices against innovations among the middle peasants.

Representatives of Soviet power who permit themselves to employ not only direct but even indirect compulsion to bring peasants into communes must be brought strictly to account and removed from work in the countryside.

5) All arbitrary requisitioning, i.e., requisitioning not in conformity with the exact provisions of laws issued by the central authority, must be ruthlessly punished. The congress insists on the strengthening of control in this respect on the part of the People's Commissariat of Agriculture, People's Commissariat of Home Affairs, and the All-Russian Central Executive Committee.

6) At the present time the extreme dislocation which has been caused in all countries of the world by the four years of imperialist war in the predatory interests of the capitalists and which has become particularly acute in Russia places the middle peasants in a difficult position.

In view of this, the law issued by the Soviet government on the emergency tax, as distinct from the laws issued by all the bourgeois governments in the world, makes a point of laying the burden of the tax wholly on the kulaks, the inconsiderable number of representatives of the peasant exploiters who particularly enriched themselves during the war. The middle peasantry, on the contrary, must be taxed with utmost moderation, so that the sum levied should be fully within their means and not burdensome to them.

The Party demands in any case leniency towards the middle peasantry in collecting the emergency tax, even if this may reduce the total revenue.

7) The socialist state must extend the widest possible aid to the peasantry, mainly by supplying the middle peasants with products of urban industries and especially improved agricultural implements, seed and diverse materials in order to raise efficiency in agriculture and ensure improvement of the peasants working and living conditions.

If the present economic dislocation does not allow the immediate and full implementation of these measures, it remains the duty of local Soviet authorities to explore all possible ways of rendering the poorest and middle peasants real aid of every kind that would support them at the present difficult moment. The Party finds it necessary to assign for this purpose a large state fund.

8) In particular efforts must be made really to carry out in full the law issued by the Soviet government which requires of state farms, agricultural communes, and all other similar associations that they render immediate and all-round assistance to the middle peasants in their neighbourhood. Only on the basis of such actual assistance is it possible to achieve agreement with the middle peasantry. Only in this way can and must its confidence be won.

The congress draws the attention of all Party workers to the need to carry out at once in practice all the demands set forth in the agrarian section of the Party programme, namely:

a) regulation of the use of land by the peasants (elimination of scattered holdings, strip farming, etc.), b) supply of improved seeds and artificial fertilizers to the peasants, c) improvement of the breeds of the peasants' cattle, d) spreading of agronomical knowledge, e) agronomical assistance to the peasants, f) repair of the peasants' farm implements at repair shops belonging to the Soviets, g) organization of stations hiring out implements, experimental stations, model fields, etc., h) improvement of the peasants' land.

9) Peasants' co-operative associations with the object of increasing agricultural production, and especially of processing farm produce, improvement of the peasants' land, support of handicrafts industries, etc., must be accorded extensive aid, both financial and organizational, by the state.

10) The congress goes on record that it should be remembered that neither the decisions of the Party nor the decrees of Soviet power have ever deviated from the line of agreement with the middle peasantry. Thus, in the cardinal matter of organization of Soviet power in the countryside, for instance, a circular letter signed by the Chairman of the Council of People's Commissars and the People's Commissar of Food was issued when the Committees of Poor Peasants were established, pointing to the need to include in these committees also representatives of the middle peasantry. When the Committees of Poor Peasants were abolished, the All-Russian Congress of Soviets again pointed to the need to include representatives of the middle peasants in the volost Soviets. The policy of the Workers' and Peasants' Government and the Communist Party must in the future too be permeated by this spirit of agreement between the proletariat and the poorest peasantry on the one hand, and the middle peasantry, on the other.

Published in *The Eighth Congress of the Russian Communist Party (Bolsheviks). Verbatim Report*. The Kommunist Publishing House, Moscow, 1919

Vol. XXIX, pp. 193-96

# ON THE CANDIDACY OF M. I. KALININ FOR THE POST OF CHAIRMAN OF THE ALL-RUSSIAN CENTRAL EXECUTIVE COMMITTEE

## Speech at twelfth session of the All-Russian Central Executive Committee

### *March 30, 1919*

Comrades! To find a person who could fully take the place of Comrade Yakov Mikhailovich Sverdlov is an exceedingly difficult task, for it is next to impossible for any one man to be at once a leading Party worker, moreover one who knows the history of the Party, and an excellent judge of people capable of choosing leading functionaries of the Soviets. It would be impossible to expect any one comrade to assume all the functions that Comrade Sverdlov took care of alone—on this score there were no two opinions when candidacies were discussed in the Party—and hence we shall have to entrust the various functions to whole boards that will meet from day to day and direct the different spheres of work. As regards the chairman, here we must have in mind his being an exponent of the line of the Party in relation to the peasantry.

You know that our approach to the middle peasants as set forth at the Party congress introduces no change in our policy in general. The tasks we have outlined in regard to the middle peasants must be carried out once our initial task—suppression of the bourgeoisie—has been solved. The question of the attitude to the middle peasants is more of a problem for us than for our comrades in Europe, and we have to see to it that the Soviet state is headed by a comrade who can demonstrate that our decision on this score will really be carried out.

I believe that we can and must find a comrade who will devote himself wholly to carrying out the line of the leading Party in regard to the middle peasants. We know that at present the problem of collecting information on what is taking place in the various parts of the country and communicating with them is particularly acute. We know that owing to the dislocation of transport facilities and the continuation of civil war, which at times disrupts contact between the centre and entire regions, not to speak of separate gubernias—we know that under the circumstances this problem demands special attention.

We know that we can solve this problem if we find a comrade with the necessary experience and knowledge of the life of the middle peasants, and I believe that the candidacy advanced in today's papers meets all these requirements. This is the candidacy of Comrade Kalinin.

Here we have a comrade who has spent nearly twenty years in Party work. He is a peasant from Tver Gubernia, who has been in close contact with peasant farming and has constantly renewed and freshened this contact. Petrograd workers have witnessed for themselves his ability to approach wide sections of the working masses uninitiated in Party policies; where other propagandists and agitators failed to find the right, comradely approach to them, Comrade Kalinin succeeded. At the present time all this is especially important. Of course, the middle peasantry as a whole, all the best elements in it, are rendering us the resolute support we need to overcome all difficulties and stamp out the revolt of the rural kulaks followed by an insignificant minority of the rural masses. We know that our main task in a small peasant country is to ensure an indissoluble alliance between the workers and the middle peasants. Our agrarian measures—complete abolition of landlord landownership and resolute assistance to the middle peasants—have already produced results, and in the course of the past year the number of middle peasants has increased owing to them. But in the localities quite often people have been appointed to administrative posts who were incapable of coping with their tasks.

There have been cases of abuses, but this is not our fault. We know that we have done everything we could to enlist the intelligentsia, but political differences interfered. We know that the epoch of bourgeois parliamentarism has ended, that the sympathy of the workers of the whole world is with the Soviet power, and that the victory of the Soviet power is inevitable, no matter how the bourgeoisie may kill leaders of the proletariat, as they are doing in Germany. The sum total of their experience will inevitably bring the intelligentsia finally into our ranks, and we shall acquire the material with the aid of which we can govern. We shall see to it that alien elements who have attached themselves to the Soviet power are removed— indeed, their presence is one cause of dissatisfaction which we are not reluctant to recognize as legitimate. We must pay the maximum of attention to combating this evil. At the Party congress we firmly decided to make this line of action obligatory for all functionaries.

As we go over to socialist agriculture, we must declare that we see no other way to realize it than through a series of comradely agreements with the middle peasants. We must give our maximum attention to them.

We know also that comrades who bore the brunt of the work in the period of the revolution and were completely engrossed in this work, were unable to approach the middle peasants as they should have, failed to avoid making mistakes, and each of these mistakes was seized upon by the enemies; each of these mistakes gave rise to certain doubts and complicated matters as regards the middle peasant's attitude toward us.

That is why it is very important for us here to find a comrade possessing the qualities I have mentioned. We must help him with our organizational experience, so that the middle peasants should see that the top spokesman of the whole Soviet Republic is one of their own, that the decision of our Party calling for a proper approach to the middle peasant and declaring our resolve to examine, study, and verify every step we make in the light of the experience we have gained—that this decision should not remain on paper.

We know that the numbers of our allies are growing, that they will increase many times over in the next few months, but for the time being the burden rests wholly on our country, which is in an extreme state of ruination and poverty. The load is more than the middle peasant can carry. We must go to him and do everything we can, we must make him understand and show him in practice that we are firmly resolved to carry out the decisions of our Party congress.

That is why the candidacy of a comrade like Comrade Kalinin ought to have the unanimous support of us all. His candidacy will enable us practically to organize a whole series of direct contacts between the top spokesman of Soviet power and the middle peasants; it will help to bring us closer to them.

This aim cannot be achieved at once, but we have no doubt that the decision we propose to make will be the correct one, though we know that we have little practical experience in this respect. Let the top spokesman of the Soviet Republic himself be the first, with our joint assistance, to acquire this experience, to accumulate the full measure of knowledge, verify things, and we can be certain that we shall solve the task facing us, that Russia will become not only the model of a country where the dictatorship of the proletariat has been realized firmly and the bourgeoisie ruthlessly suppressed—this we have already accomplished—but also the model of a country where the relations between the urban workers and the middle peasants are ordered satisfactorily, on the basis of comradely support and our new experience. And this is one of the main guarantees of the complete victory of the proletarian revolution.

That is why I take it upon myself to recommend to you this candidacy—the candidacy of Comrade Kalinin.

Résumé published April 1, 1919
in the newspaper *Izvestia of the
All-Russian Central Executive
Committee*, No. 70
First printed in full in 1932

Vol. XXIX, pp. 209-12

# ON THE MIDDLE PEASANTS

## (A Speech Recorded for a Gramophone Record)

The principal question now facing the Party of Communists and one that drew the most attention at the last Party congress is the question of the middle peasants.

It is natural that the first question people usually ask is what is a middle peasant.

It is natural that Party comrades have told us time and again that they had been asked in the villages what is meant by a middle peasant. To this we reply that the middle peasant is a peasant who does not exploit the labour of others, does not live off the labour of others, in no way makes use of the fruits of the labour of others, but works himself and lives by his own labour.

There were fewer such peasants under capitalism than now, for the majority then lived in abject poverty, and only an insignificant minority then as now consisted of the kulaks, the exploiters, the rich peasants.

The number of middle peasants has been increasing ever since private property in land was abolished. And the Soviet power has firmly decided under all circumstances to establish with them relations of perfect peace and concord. Understandably enough, the middle peasant cannot at once side with socialism, since he firmly persists in what he is accustomed to, regards all innovations with caution, wants to make sure in practice what it is that he is urged to do, and hesitates to change his mode of life before he is certain that such a change is necessary.

Precisely because of this we must know and remember and live up to the principle that Communist workers who go to the villages are duty bound to seek comradely relations with the middle peasants, to establish comradely relations with them, and to remember that a toiler who does not exploit the labour of others is a comrade to the worker and that a voluntary alliance marked by complete sincerity and trust can and must be reached with him. All measures proposed by the Communist government should be regarded only as advice pointing the way to the middle peasant, as suggestions to go over to a new way of life.

Only joint work in the course of which these measures are verified in practice, the mistakes contained in them checked, possible errors prevented, and agreement reached with the middle peasant—only such work will secure the alliance of the workers and peasants. This alliance is the main source of strength, the main bulwark of Soviet power; it is a guarantee that the cause of socialist transformation, of victory over capital, of abolition of all exploitation, is carried by us to its triumphant consummation.

Delivered at the end of March
1919

Vol. XXIX, pp. 222-23

# FOREWORD TO THE SPEECH "ON DECEPTION OF THE PEOPLE WITH SLOGANS OF FREEDOM AND EQUALITY"

The question I dealt with in my speech at the conference on extra-scholastic education on May 19, namely, the question of equality in general and the equality of the worker and the peasant in particular, is undoubtedly one of the most pressing and "painful" questions of our time, and one that touches upon the most deep-seated prejudices of the petty bourgeois, the petty proprietor, the petty commodity-owner, every philistine and nine-tenths of the intelligentsia (including the Menshevik and Socialist-Revolutionary intelligentsia).

Just think of it, how monstrous it is to deny the equality of the worker and the peasant! Of course, this is something all the friends of the capitalists, all of their hangers-on, and the Mensheviks and Socialist-Revolutionaries first of all, are trying to seize upon in order to "irritate" the peasant, to "stir him up," to incite him against the workers, against the Communists. Such attempts are inevitable, but since they are founded on lies, they are doomed to ignominious failure.

Peasants are sober-minded, business-like, practical people. Things must be explained to them in a practical light, through simple, everyday examples. Is the peasant who has a surplus of grain justified in hiding this surplus until prices soar to exorbitant, profiteering levels, without any regard for the workers who are going hungry? Or is the state authority, which is in the hands of the workers, justified in taking over all surplus grain not at profiteering, money-grubbing, hold-up prices, but at a fixed price set by the state?

That is how the question stands. This is the entire essence of the issue. To avoid facing this essence frauds of all kinds who are working, like the Mensheviks and Socialist-Revolutionaries, for the capitalists, for the return of undivided power to them, are resorting to empty phrasemongering about "equality" and the "unity of the working-man's democracy."

The peasant must make his choice:

either free trade in grain, which means speculation in grain, freedom for the rich to grow richer, freedom for the poor to be pauperized and to starve, return of undivided power to the landlords and capitalists, dissolution of the alliance of the peasants and the workers,

or delivery of grain surpluses at a fixed price to the state, i.e., the united workers' authority, which means alliance of the peasants with the workers completely to do away with the bourgeoisie, to eliminate any possibility of its rule being restored.

Such is the choice.

The rich peasants, the kulaks, will choose the first alternative; they will want to try their luck in alliance with the capitalists and landlords against the workers, against the poor, but such peasants are the minority in Russia. The majority of the peasants will prefer an alliance with the workers against the restoration of capitalist rule, against "freedom for the rich to grow richer," against "freedom for the poor to starve," against deceitful camouflage of this accursed capitalist "freedom" (freedom to starve to death) with flowery words about "equality" (the equality of the well-fed, who have a surplus of grain, and the starving).

Our task is to fight the cunning capitalist deceit which the Mensheviks and the Socialist-Revolutionaries practise by means of resounding and flowery phrasemongering about "freedom" and "equality."

Peasants! Unmask the wolves in sheep's clothing who eulogize "freedom," "equality," and "unity of the working man's democracy" and in doing so actually champion the "freedom" of the landlord to oppress the peasants, the "equality" of the wealthy capitalist and the worker or the semi-starved peasant, the "equality" of the well-fed man who hides his surplus grain and the worker who is tormented by hunger and unemployment because the country has been ruined by war. Such wolves in sheep's clothing are the working people's worst enemies; whether they call themselves Mensheviks, Socialist-Revolutionaries, or Independents they are in reality friends of the capitalists.

"The worker and the peasant are equal as toilers, but the well-fed grain speculator is not the equal of the hungry toiler. . . . We are fighting only to uphold the interests of labour, taking grain away from the speculator, not from the toiler. . . . We seek agreement with the middle peasant, the peasant who works himself"—this is what I said in my speech, this is the *crux* of the matter, this is the real truth which the resounding phrase-slinging about "equality" is designed to conceal. Moreover, the vast majority of the peasants know that this is the truth, that the *workers' state* fights the speculators and the rich while rendering every assistance to the working people and the poor, whereas *both the landlord state* (under a monarchy) *and the capitalist state* (under the freest and most democratic republic) has always and everywhere, in all countries, *helped the rich to rob the working people, helped the speculators and the rich to grow richer at the expense of the poor who are pauperized more and more.*

This is a truth every peasant knows. And hence the greater their awareness, the sooner and more resolutely the majority of the peasants will make their choice and declare for alliance with the workers, for agreement with the workers' government, against the landlord or capitalist state; for Soviet power against the "Constituent Assembly" or the "democratic republic"; for agreement with the Bolsheviks, Communists, against any support to the capitalists, Mensheviks and Socialist-Revolutionaries!

\* \* \*

To the "educated" gentlemen, to the Democrats, Socialists, Social-Democrats, Socialist-Revolutionaries, etc., we say: you all pay lip-service to the "class struggle," but actually you close your eyes to it precisely at a time when it is growing especially acute. And to do that means to side with capital, with the bourgeoisie, against the working people.

He who recognizes the class struggle must also recognize that in a bourgeois republic, even in the freest and most democratic bourgeois republic, "freedom" and "equality" never were, nor could they be, anything but an expression of the equality and freedom of the *commodity-owners*, the equality and freedom of *capital*. Marx, in all of his writings and especially in his *Capital* (which you all recognize *in words*), made this clear thousands of times; he ridiculed the abstract conception of "freedom and equality" and vulgarizers like Bentham who closed their eyes to the facts, and he revealed the material roots of these abstractions.

Under the bourgeois system (i.e., as long as private property in land and in the means of production persists) and under bourgeois democracy, "freedom and equality" remain purely formal, signifying in practice *wage-slavery* for the workers (who are formally free and equal) and the *undivided rule of capital*, the oppression of labour by capital. This is the ABC of socialism, my learned gentlemen—and you have forgotten it.

It follows from this ABC that during the proletarian revolution, when the class struggle has sharpened to the point of civil war, only fools and traitors will seek to get away with empty talk about "freedom," "equality" and "unity of the working-man's democracy." Actually everything depends on the outcome of the struggle between the proletariat and the bourgeoisie, and the intermediate, middle classes (including the entire petty bourgeoisie, and hence the entire peasantry) inevitably vacillate between the two camps.

What is in question is which of the main forces, the proletariat or the bourgeoisie, these intermediate sections will join. There *cannot be* any other alternative; he who has not understood this from reading Marx's *Capital* has understood nothing in Marx, understood nothing in socialism, but is in fact a philistine and a petty bourgeois who blindly follows in the wake of the bourgeoisie. On the other hand, he who has understood all this, will not allow himself to be deceived by empty phrases about "freedom" and "equality," but will think and speak of *practical things*, that is, of the concrete conditions for a *rapprochement* between the peasants and the workers, their *alliance* against the capitalists, *agreement* between them against the exploiters, the rich and the speculators.

The dictatorship of the proletariat is not the end of class struggle but its continuation in new forms. The dictatorship of the proletariat is class struggle waged by a proletariat which has been victorious and has taken political power in its hands against a bourgeoisie that has been defeated but not destroyed, a bourgeoisie that has not vanished, not ceased to offer resistance, but that has intensified its resistance. The dictatorship of the proletariat is a specific form of class alliance between the proletariat, the vanguard of the working people, and the numerous non-proletarian sections of the working people (petty bourgeoisie, small proprietors, the peasantry, the intelligentsia, etc.), or the majority of these strata, an alliance against capital, an alliance whose aim is the complete overthrow of capital, complete suppression of the resistance offered by the bourgeoisie as well as of attempts at restoration on its part, an alliance for the final establishment and consolidation of socialism. It is a specific kind of alliance which takes shape in a specific situation, namely, a situation marked by fierce civil war; it is an alliance between firm supporters of socialism and its vacillating allies, sometimes "neutrals" (in which case instead of an agreement on struggle the alliance becomes an agreement on neutrality); an alliance between economically, politically, socially, and spiritually different classes. Only the corrupt heroes of the corrupt "Berne" or yellow International,[57] people like Kautsky, Martov, and Co., can evade examination of the concrete forms, conditions, and tasks of this alliance by resorting to vague phrasemongering about "freedom," "equality," and "unity of the working-man's democracy," that is, to fragments from the ideological baggage of the era of commodity economy.

                                                    *N. Lenin*

June 23, 1919


Printed in the pamphlet:
N. Lenin, *Two Speeches at the
First All-Russian Conference on
Extra-scholastic Education*, Moscow, 1919

Vol. XXIX, pp. 347-51

## LETTER TO THE WORKERS
## AND PEASANTS IN CONNECTION WITH
## THE VICTORY OVER KOLCHAK

Comrades, the Red troops have liberated the entire Urals from Kolchak and have begun the liberation of Siberia. The workers and peasants of the Urals and Siberia are enthusiastically welcoming the Soviet power, for it is sweeping away with an iron besom all the landlord and capitalist scum who ground down the people with exactions, humiliations, floggings, and the restoration of tsarist oppression.

Our general delight, our joy at the liberation of the Urals and the entry of the Red troops into Siberia should not be allowed to lull us into a sense of security. The enemy is still far from being destroyed. He has not even been definitely broken.

Every effort must be made to drive Kolchak and the Japanese together with the other foreign marauders out of Siberia, and an even greater effort is needed to destroy the enemy so as to prevent him from starting his marauding activities again and again.

How is that to be achieved?

The harrowing experience of the Urals and Siberia, as well as the experience of all countries which have been through the torments of the four years of imperialist war, must not be without its lessons for us.

*Here are the five chief lessons* which all workers and peasants, all working people, must draw from this experience so as to ensure themselves against a repetition of the calamities of the rule of Kolchak.

*First lesson.* In order to defend the power of the workers and peasants from the marauders, that is, from the landlords and capitalists, we need a powerful Red Army. We have proved—not by words but by actual deeds—that we are capable of creating it, that we have learned to direct it and to defeat the capitalists notwithstanding the lavish assistance in the way of arms and equipment they are receiving from the richest countries in the world. The Bolsheviks have proved that by actual deeds. All workers and peasants—if they are class-conscious—must place their faith in them, not on the strength of their word (for to believe a man on the strength of his word is foolish), but on the strength of the experience of millions upon millions of people in the Urals and Siberia. The problem of combining the arming of the workers and peasants with the commanding by ex-officers, who for the most part sympathize with the landlords and capitalists, is a most difficult one. It can be solved only given splendid organizing ability, strict and conscious discipline, and the confidence of the broad masses in the leading stratum, the workers' commissars. This most difficult problem the Bolsheviks have solved: cases of treachery on the part of ex-officers are very numerous, nevertheless the Red Army not only is in our hands, but has learned to defeat the generals of the tsar and the generals of Britain, France, and America.

Consequently, everyone who seriously wishes to rid himself of the rule of Kolchak must devote all his energies, means and ability without reservation to the task of building up and strengthening the Red Army. Obey all the laws on the Red Army and all orders conscientiously and scrupulously, support discipline in it in every way, and help the Red Army, each to the best of his ability—such is the prime, fundamental, and principal duty of every class-conscious worker and peasant who does not want the rule of Kolchak.

Fear unruly partisanism, the arbitrary actions of isolated detachments, disobedience towards the central authorities like the plague, for that spells doom. And the Urals, Siberia, and the Ukraine have demonstrated that.

He who does not unreservedly and selflessly assist the Red Army, or support order and discipline in it with all his might, is a traitor and treasonmonger, a supporter of the rule of Kolchak, and should be exterminated without mercy.

With a strong Red Army we shall be invincible. Without a strong army we shall inevitably fall victim to Kolchak, Denikin, and Yudenich.[58]

*Second lesson.* The Red Army cannot be strong without large state stocks of grain, for without them it is impossible to move an army freely or to train it properly. Without them we cannot maintain the workers who are producing for the army.

Every class-conscious worker and peasant must know and remember that the chief reason now for the insufficiently swift and stable successes of our Red Army is precisely the shortage of state stocks of grain. He who does not give his surpluses of grain to the state is helping Kolchak, he is a traitor and betrayer of the workers and peasants and is responsible for the unnecessary death and suffering of tens of thousands of workers and peasants in the Red Army.

Rogues and profiteers and utterly ignorant peasants argue in this way: better sell my grain for a free price, I will get far more for it that way than the fixed price paid by the state.

But the whole point is that free sale promotes profiteering; a few get rich, only the wealthy are sated, while the working masses go hungry. We saw that in practice in the richest grain-bearing districts of Siberia and the Ukraine.

With the free sale of grain capital triumphs, while labour starves and suffers.

With the free sale of grain the price rises to thousands of rubles per pood, money loses its value, a handful of profiteers benefit while the people grow poorer.

With the free sale of grain the government granaries are empty, the army is powerless, industry dies, and the victory of Kolchak and Denikin is inevitable.

Only the rich, only the worst enemies of the Workers' and Peasants' Government are consciously in favour of the free sale of grain. Those who out of ignorance are in favour of the free sale of grain should learn to understand from the example of Siberia and the Ukraine why the free sale of grain means victory for Kolchak and Denikin.

There are still unenlightened peasants who argue as follows: let the state first give me in exchange for my grain good wares at pre-war prices, then I will give up my surplus grain, otherwise I will not. And by this sort of argument the rogues and supporters of the landlords often hoodwink the unenlightened peasants.

It should not be difficult to understand that the workers' state which the capitalists thoroughly devastated by four years of a predatory war for the sake of Constantinople, and which the Kolchaks and Denikins are now devastating again by way of revenge with the help of the capitalists of the whole world—it should not be difficult to understand that such a state cannot at this moment supply the peasants with goods, for industry is at a standstill. There is no food, no fuel, no industry.

Every sensible peasant will agree that the surplus grain must be given to the starving worker as a loan on condition of receiving industrial products in return.

That is the way it is now. All class-conscious and sensible peasants, all except the rogues and profiteers will agree that *all surplus grain without exception* must be turned over to the workers' state as a loan, because then the state will restore industry and supply industrial products to the peasants.

But will the peasants trust the workers' state enough to loan their surplus grain to it?—we may be asked.

Our reply is: firstly, the state gives a bond for the loan in the shape of currency. Secondly, all peasants know by experience that the workers' state, that is, the Soviet power, helps the working people and fights the landlords and capitalists. That is why the Soviet power is called workers' and peasants' power. Thirdly, the peasants have no other alternative: either they trust the worker or they trust the capitalist; they give their confidence and a loan either to the workers' state or to the capitalist state. There is no other alternative either in Russia or in any country in the world. The more conscious the peasants become, the firmer do they stand by the workers, and the more resolute are they in their decision to help the workers' state in every way so as to make the return of the power of the landlords and capitalists impossible.

*Third lesson.* If Kolchak and Denikin are to be completely destroyed the strictest revolutionary order must be maintained, the laws and instructions of the Soviet government must be sacredly observed, and it must be seen to it that they are obeyed by all.

Kolchak's victories in Siberia and the Urals have been a clear example to all of us that the least disorder, the slightest infraction of the laws of the Soviet power, the slightest laxity or negligence at once serves to strengthen the landlords and capitalists and makes for their victory. For the landlords and capitalists have not been destroyed and do not consider themselves vanquished; every intelligent worker and peasant sees, knows, and realizes that they have only been beaten and have gone into hiding, are lying low, very often disguising themselves by a "Soviet" "protective" colouring. Many landlords have wormed their way into state farms, and capitalists into various "chief administrations" and "centres," acting the part of Soviet officials; they are watching every step of the Soviet government for it to make a mistake or show weakness, so as to overthrow it, to help the Czechoslovaks today and Denikin tomorrow.

Everything must be done to track down these bandits, these landlords and capitalists who are lying low, and to ferret them out, *no matter what guise they take*, to expose them and punish them ruthlessly, for they are the worst foes of the working people, skilful, shrewd, and experienced, who are patiently waiting for an opportune moment to set a conspiracy going; they are saboteurs, who stop at no crime to injure the Soviet regime. We must be merciless towards these enemies of the working people, towards the landlords, capitalists, saboteurs, and Whites.

And in order to be able to catch them we must be skilful, careful, and class-conscious, we must watch out most attentively for the least disorder, for the slightest deviation from the conscientious observance of the laws of the Soviet power. The landlords and capitalists are strong not only because of their knowledge and experience and the assistance they get from the richest countries in the world, but also because of the force of habit and the ignorance of the broad masses, who want to live in the "good old way" and do not realize how essential it is that the laws of the Soviet power be strictly and conscientiously observed.

The slightest lawlessness, the slightest infraction of Soviet order is a *loophole*, of which the foes of the working people take immediate advantage, a *starting-point* for Kolchak and Denikin victories. It would be criminal to forget that the Kolchak affair began with a slight carelessness towards the Czechoslovaks, with a slight insubordination on the part of certain regiments.

*Fourth lesson.* It is criminal to forget not only that the Kolchak affair began with trifles but also that the Mensheviks ("Social-Democrats") and S.-R.s ("Socialist-Revolutionaries") assisted its birth and directly supported it. It is time we learned to judge political parties not by their words, but by their deeds.

The Mensheviks and Socialist-Revolutionaries call themselves Socialists, but they are actually *helpers of the Whites*, helpers of the landlords and capitalists. This was proved in practice not only by isolated facts, but by two big periods in the history of the Russian revolution: 1) the Kerensky period, and 2) the Kolchak period. Both times the Mensheviks and Socialist-Revolutionaries while professing to be "Socialists" and "democrats," actually played the role of *helpers of the Whiteguards*. Are we then going to be so foolish as to believe them now that they are proposing that we permit them again to "have a try," and call that permission a "united socialist (or democratic) front"? After the Kolchak affair, can there still be peasants, except for few isolated individuals, who do not realize that a "united front" with the Mensheviks and Socialist-Revolutionaries means union with helpers of Kolchak?

It may be objected that the Mensheviks and Socialist-Revolutionaries have realized their mistake and renounced all alliance with the bourgeoisie. But that is not true. In the first place, the Right Mensheviks and Socialist-Revolutionaries have not even renounced such an alliance, and there is *no* definite line of demarcation from these "Rights." There is no such line through the fault of the "Left" Mensheviks and Socialist-Revolutionaries; for while verbally "condemning" their "Rights," even the best of the Mensheviks and Socialist-Revolutionaries, in spite of all they say, are actually *impotent* compared with them. Secondly, what even the best of the Mensheviks and Socialist-Revolutionaries advocate are actually *Kolchak* ideas which assist the bourgeoisie and Kolchak and Denikin and help to mask their filthy and bloody capitalist deeds. These ideas are: a people's government, universal, equal, and direct suffrage, a constituent assembly, freedom of the press, and the like. All over the world we see capitalist republics which precisely by this lie of "democracy" justify capitalist rule and wars for the enslavement of colonies. In our own country we see that Kolchak, Denikin, Yudenich, and any other general readily hand out such "democratic" promises. Can we trust a man who on the strength of verbal promises helps a known bandit? The Mensheviks and Socialist-Revolutionaries, all without exception, help known bandits, the world imperialists, embellishing *their* power, *their* campaign against Russia, *their* rule, and *their* policy with pseudo-democratic slogans. All the Mensheviks and Socialist-Revolutionaries offer us an "alliance" on condition that we make concessions to the capitalists and their leaders, Kolchak and Denikin; as, for example, that we "renounce terror" (when against us is being applied the terror of the multi-millionaires of the whole Entente, of the whole alliance of the richest countries, which are engineering plots in Russia), or that we open the road to free trade in grain, and so on. What these "conditions" of the Mensheviks and Socialist-Revolutionaries boil down to is this: we, the Mensheviks and Socialist-Revolutionaries, are wavering towards the capitalists, and we want a "united front" with the Bolsheviks, whom the capitalists are fighting, taking advantage of every concession! No, Messieurs, the Mensheviks and Socialist-Revolutionaries, look no more in Russia for people capable of believing you. In Russia the enlightened workers and peasants now re-

alize that the Mensheviks and Socialist-Revolutionaries
are helpers of the Whiteguards, some deliberately and
maliciously, others unwittingly and because they persist
in their old mistakes; but they are helpers of the Whiteguards nevertheless.

*Fifth lesson.* If Kolchak and his ilk are to be destroyed
and not allowed to raise their heads again, all peasants
must unhesitatingly make their choice in favour of the
workers' state. Some people (especially the Mensheviks
and the Socialist-Revolutionaries—all of them, even the
"Lefts" among them) are trying to scare the peasants
with the bogey of the "dictatorship of one party," the Party
of Bolsheviks, Communists.

The peasants have learned from the Kolchak affair not
to be afraid of this bogey.

Either the dictatorship (i.e., the iron rule) of the landlords and capitalists, or the dictatorship of the working
class.

There is no middle course. The scions of the aristocracy,
the wretched intellectuals and the small masters, badly
educated on bad books, dream of a middle course. There
is no middle course anywhere in the world, nor can there
be. Either the dictatorship of the bourgeoisie (masked by
ornate Socialist-Revolutionary and Menshevik phraseology
about a people's government, a constituent assembly, liberties, and the like), or the dictatorship of the proletariat.
He who has not learned this from the whole history of the
nineteenth century is a hopeless idiot. And we in Russia
have all seen how the Mensheviks and the Socialist-Revolutionaries dreamed of a middle course under Kerensky
and under Kolchak.

To whom were these dreams of service? Whom did they
assist? Kolchak and Denikin. Those who dream of a middle course are helpers of Kolchak.

In the Urals and Siberia the workers and peasants had
the opportunity to compare the dictatorship of the bourgeoisie with the dictatorship of the working class. The
dictatorship of the working class is being exercised by the
Bolshevik Party, the Party which as far back as 1905 and

even earlier merged with the entire revolutionary proletariat.

Dictatorship of the working class means that the workers' state will unhesitatingly suppress the landlords and
capitalists and the renegades and traitors who help these
exploiters, and will vanquish them.

The workers' state is an implacable enemy of the landlord and capitalist, of the profiteer and swindler, an enemy
of private ownership of land and capital, an enemy of the
power of money.

The workers' state is the only loyal friend helping the
working people and the peasantry. No wavering towards
capital, an alliance of the working people to fight it,
*workers' and peasants' power, Soviet power*—that is what
the "dictatorship of the working class" means *in practice.*

The Mensheviks and the Socialist-Revolutionaries want
to scare the peasants with these words. They won't succeed. After Kolchak, the workers and peasants even in the
deepest backwoods realize that these words mean *precisely
that without which there can be no salvation from Kolchak.*

Down with the waverers, with the spineless ones, who
are erring in the direction of helping capital and have
been captivated by the slogans and promises of capital! An
implacable fight against capital, and an alliance of the
working people, an alliance of the peasants and the working class—that is the last and most important lesson of
the Kolchak affair.

*N. Lenin*

August 24, 1919

*Pravda,* No. 190,
August 28, 1919

Vol. XXIX, pp. 511-18

# ECONOMICS AND POLITICS IN THE ERA
## OF THE DICTATORSHIP OF THE PROLETARIAT

I had intended in connection with the second anniversary of Soviet government to write a small pamphlet
dealing with the subject indicated in the title. But owing
to the rush of everyday work I have been unable so far to
get beyond preliminary preparations for certain of the sections. I have therefore decided to essay a brief, summarized exposition of what, in my opinion, are the most essential ideas on the subject. A summarized exposition, of
course, possesses many disadvantages and shortcomings.
Nevertheless, a short magazine article may perhaps
achieve the modest aim in view, which is to present the
problem and the groundwork for its discussion by the
Communists in the various countries.

1

Theoretically, there can be no doubt that between capitalism and communism there lies a definite transition period. It cannot but combine the features and properties of
both these forms of social economy. This transition period
cannot but be a period of struggle between moribund capitalism and nascent communism—or, in other words, between capitalism which has been defeated but not destroyed
and communism which has been born but which is still
very feeble.

The necessity for a whole historical era distinguished by
these features of a transition period should be obvious not
only to Marxists, but to every educated person who is in
any degree acquainted with the theory of development. Yet

all the talk on the subject of the transition to socialism
which we hear from present-day representatives of petty-
bourgeois democracy (and such, in spite of their spurious
socialist label, are all the representatives of the Second
International, including such individuals as MacDonald,
Jean Longuet, Kautsky, and Friedrich Adler) is marked by
complete obliviousness to this obvious truth. Petty-bourgeois democrats are distinguished by an aversion to class
struggle, by the hope of managing without a class struggle, by an endeavour to smooth over and reconcile, to take
the edge off sharp corners. Such democrats therefore either
avoid recognizing any necessity for a whole historical
period of transition from capitalism to communism or regard it as their duty to concoct schemes for reconciling the
two contending forces, instead of leading the struggle of
one of these forces.

2

In Russia, the dictatorship of the proletariat must inevitably differ in certain specific features from that in the
advanced countries, owing to the very great backwardness and petty-bourgeois character of our country. But the
basic forces—and the basic forms of social economy—are
the same in Russia as in any capitalist country, so that
these specific features can relate only to what is not most
important.

These basic forms of social economy are capitalism,
petty commodity production, and communism. The basic
forces are the bourgeoisie, the petty bourgeoisie (particularly the peasantry), and the proletariat.

The economic system of Russia in the era of the dictatorship of the proletariat represents a struggle of the first
steps of labour communistically united—on the scale of a
single vast state—against petty commodity production
and capitalism, the capitalism which still persists and
which arises anew on the basis of petty commodity production.

In Russia, labour is united communistically insofar as,
firstly, private ownership of the means of production has

been abolished, and, secondly, the proletarian state power is organizing large-scale production on state-owned land and in state-owned enterprises on a national scale, is distributing labour power among the various branches of production and the various enterprises, and is distributing large quantities of articles of consumption belonging to the state to the working people.

We say "the first steps" of communism in Russia (so spoken of also in the programme of our Party adopted in March 1919), because all these conditions have been only partially achieved in our country, or, to put it otherwise, the achievement of these conditions is only in its early stages. We accomplished instantly, at one revolutionary blow, all that can be instantly accomplished in general: for instance, on the first day of the dictatorship of the proletariat, October 26 (November 8), 1917, private ownership of land was abolished without compensation to the big landowners; the big landowners were expropriated. Within the space of a few months practically all the big capitalists, owners of mills and factories, joint-stock companies, banks, railways, and so forth, were expropriated, also without compensation. The state organization of large-scale production in industry and the transition from "workers' control" to "workers' administration" of factories, mills, and railways—this, by and large, has already been accomplished; but in relation to agriculture it has only just begun ("state farms," i.e., large farms organized by the workers' state on state-owned land). Similarly, we have only just begun the organization of various forms of cooperative societies of small husbandmen as a transition from petty commodity agriculture to communist agriculture.* The same must be said of the state organization of the distribution of products in place of private trade, i.e., the state procurement and delivery of grain to the cities

---

* The number of "state farms" and "agricultural communes" in Soviet Russia amounts to approximately 3,536 and 1,961 respectively, and the number of agricultural artels to 3,696. Our Central Statistical Board is at present making an exact census of all state farms and communes. The results will begin to become available in November 1919.

and of industrial products to the countryside. Available statistical data on this subject will be given below.

Peasant farming continues to be petty commodity production. Here we have an extremely broad and very profoundly and firmly rooted basis for capitalism. On this basis capitalism persists and arises anew in a bitter struggle with communism. The forms of this struggle are bag-trading and profiteering, as against state procurement of grain (and other products) and state distribution of products in general.

3

In illustration of these abstract theoretical propositions, we shall cite concrete data.

According to the figures of Komprod (the People's Commissariat of Food), state procurements of grain in Russia between August 1, 1917, and August 1, 1918, amounted to about 30,000,000 poods, and in the following year to about 110,000,000 poods. During the first three months of the next campaign (1919-20) procurements will presumably total about 45,000,000 poods, as against 37,000,000 poods for the same period (August-October) in 1918.

These figures obviously speak of a slow but steady improvement in the state of affairs from the point of view of the victory of communism over capitalism. This improvement is being achieved in spite of the difficulties without world parallel, caused by the civil war, which the Russian and foreign capitalists are organizing, harnessing all the forces of the strongest powers in the world.

Therefore, in spite of the lies and slanders of the bourgeoisie of all countries and of their open or masked henchmen (the "Socialists" of the Second International), one thing remains beyond dispute, viz., that from the point of view of the basic economic problem of the dictatorship of the proletariat, the victory of communism over capitalism in our country is assured. Throughout the world the bourgeoisie is raging and fuming against Bolshevism and is organizing military expeditions, plots, etc., against the Bolsheviks, just because it fully realizes that our success in reconstructing the social economy is inevitable, provided we are not crushed by military force. And its attempts to crush us in this way are not succeeding.

The extent to which we have already vanquished capitalism in the short time we have had at our disposal, and amidst the incredible difficulties under which we have had to work, will be seen from the following summarized figures. The Central Statistical Board has just prepared for the press data regarding the production and consumption of grain, not for the whole of Soviet Russia, but for twenty-six of her gubernias.

The results are as follows:

| 26 gubernias of Soviet Russia | Population in millions | Production of grain (excluding seed and fodder) | Grain delivered by: | | Total amount of grain at disposal of population | Grain consumption per capita of population in poods |
|---|---|---|---|---|---|---|
| | | | Commissariat of Food | Profiteers | | |
| | | | in millions of poods | | | |
| Producing gubernias Urban 4.4 | | — | 20.9 | 20.6 | 41.5 | 9.5 |
| Rural 28.6 | | 625.4 | — | — | 481.8 | 16.9 |
| Consuming gubernias Urban 5.9 | | — | 20.0 | 20.0 | 40.0 | 6.8 |
| Rural 13.8 | | 114.0 | 12.1 | 27.8 | 151.4 | 11.0 |
| Total (26 gubernias) | 52.7 | 739.4 | 53.0 | 68.4 | 714.7 | 13.6 |

Thus, approximately half the amount of grain supplied to the cities is provided by the Commissariat of Food and the other half by profiteers. This same proportion is revealed by a careful survey, made in 1918, of the food consumed by city workers. It should be borne in mind that for bread supplied by the state the worker pays *one-tenth* of what he pays the profiteer. The profiteering price for bread is *ten times* greater than the state price. That is what is revealed by an accurate study of workers' budgets.

4

If one carefully reflects on the figures quoted, one finds
that they present an exact picture of the fundamental
features of Russia's present-day economy.

The working people have been emancipated from their
age-old oppressors and exploiters, the landlords and capitalists. This step in the direction of real freedom and real
equality, a step which for its extent, its size, its rapidity,
is without parallel in the world, is ignored by the followers
of the bourgeoisie (including the petty-bourgeois democrats), who when they talk of freedom and equality mean
parliamentary bourgeois democracy, which they falsely declare to be "democracy" in general, or "pure democracy"
(Kautsky).

But the working people are concerned only with real
equality and real freedom (freedom from the landlords and
capitalists), and that is why they stand so firmly for Soviet government.

In this peasant country, those who were the first to gain,
to gain most, and gain immediately from the dictatorship of
the proletariat were the peasants as a whole. The peasant
in Russia starved under the landlords and capitalists.
Throughout the long centuries of our history, the peasant
never had the opportunity of working for himself: he
starved while surrendering hundreds of millions of poods
of grain to the capitalists, for the cities and for foreign
delivery. The peasant *for the first time* worked for himself
and *fed better than the city dweller* under the dictatorship
of the proletariat. For the first time the peasant saw real
freedom—freedom to eat his bread, freedom from starvation. In the distribution of the land, as we know, equality
has been established to the maximum: in the vast majority
of cases the peasants are dividing the land according to
the number of "mouths" to feed.

Socialism means the abolition of classes.

In order to abolish classes it is necessary, firstly, to
overthrow the landlords and capitalists. This part of our
task has been accomplished, but it is only a part, and moreover, *not* the most difficult part. In order to abolish classes

it is necessary, secondly, to abolish the difference between working-man and peasant, *to make them all workers*. This cannot be done all at once. This task is incomparably more difficult and will of necessity be a protracted one. It is not a problem that can be solved by overthrowing a class. It can be solved only by the organizational reconstruction of the whole social economy, by a transition from individual, disunited, petty commodity production to large-scale social production. This transition must of necessity be extremely protracted. It may only be delayed and complicated by hasty and incautious administrative and legislative measures. It can be accelerated only by affording such assistance to the peasant as will enable him immensely to improve his whole agricultural technique, to reform it radically.

In order to solve the second and most difficult part of the problem, the proletariat, after having defeated the bourgeoisie, must unswervingly conduct its policy towards the peasantry along the following fundamental lines: the proletariat must separate, demarcate the peasant toiler from the peasant owner, the peasant worker from the peasant huckster, the peasant who labours from the peasant who profiteers.

In this demarcation lies the *whole essence* of socialism.

And it is not surprising that the Socialists who are Socialists in word but petty-bourgeois democrats in deed (the Martovs, the Chernovs, the Kautskys, and so on) do not understand this essence of socialism.

The demarcation we here refer to is very difficult, for in actual life all the features of the "peasant," however diverse they may be, however contradictory they may be, are fused into one whole. Nevertheless, demarcation is possible; and not only is it possible, it inevitably follows from the conditions of peasant economy and peasant life. The toiling peasant has for ages been oppressed by the landlords, the capitalists, the hucksters, and profiteers and by *their* state, including even the most democratic bourgeois republics. Throughout the ages the toiling peasant has educated himself to hate and loathe these oppressors and exploiters, and this "education," engendered by the conditions of life, *compels* the peasant to seek for an alliance with the workers against the capitalist and against the profiteer and trader. Yet at the same time, economic conditions, the conditions of commodity production, inevitably turn the peasant (not always, but in the vast majority of cases) into a huckster and profiteer.

The statistics quoted above reveal a striking difference between the peasant toiler and the peasant profiteer. That peasant who during 1918-19 delivered to the hungry workers of the cities 40,000,000 poods of grain at fixed state prices, who delivered this grain to the state agencies in spite of all the shortcomings of the latter, shortcomings which are fully realized by the workers' government, but which are unavoidable in the first period of the transition to socialism—that peasant is a toiling peasant, a comrade on an equal footing with the socialist worker, his most faithful ally, his kin brother in the fight against the yoke of capital. Whereas that peasant who clandestinely sold 40,000,000 poods of grain at ten times the state price, taking advantage of the need and hunger of the city worker, deceiving the state, and everywhere increasing and creating deceit, robbery, and fraud—that peasant is a profiteer, an ally of the capitalist, a class enemy of the worker, an exploiter. For whoever possesses a surplus of grain gathered from land belonging to the whole state with the help of implements in which in one way or another is embodied the labour not only of the peasant but also of the worker and so on, whoever possesses a surplus of grain and profiteers in that grain is an exploiter of the hungry worker.

You are violators of freedom, equality, and democracy—they shout at us on all sides, pointing to the inequality of the worker and the peasant under our Constitution, to the dispersal of the Constituent Assembly, to the forcible confiscation of surplus grain, and so forth. We reply: never in the world has there been a state which has done so much to remove the actual inequality, the actual lack of freedom from which the toiling peasant has suffered for centuries. But we shall never recognize equality with the peasant profiteer, just as we do not recognize "equality" between the exploiter and the exploited, between the sated and the hungry, nor the "freedom" of the former to rob the latter.

And those educated people who refuse to recognize this difference we shall treat as Whiteguards, even though they may call themselves democrats, Socialists, Internationalists, Kautskys, Chernovs, or Martovs.

- 5

Socialism means the abolition of classes. The dictatorship of the proletariat has done all it could to abolish classes. But classes cannot be abolished all at once.

And classes *remain* and *will remain* in the era of the dictatorship of the proletariat. The dictatorship will become unnecessary when classes disappear. Without the dictatorship of the proletariat they will not disappear.

Classes have remained, but in the era of the dictatorship of the proletariat *every* class has undergone a change, and the relations between the classes have also changed. The class struggle does not disappear under the dictatorship of the proletariat; it merely assumes different forms.

Under capitalism the proletariat was an oppressed class, a class bereft of all ownership in the means of production, the only class which stood directly and completely opposed to the bourgeoisie, and therefore the only one capable of being revolutionary to the very end. Having overthrown the bourgeoisie and won political power, the proletariat has become the *ruling* class; it holds the power of state, it has the disposal of the means of production that have already been socialized; it guides the wavering and intermediary elements and classes; it crushes the enhanced energy of resistance of the exploiters. All these are *specific* tasks of the class struggle, tasks which the proletariat formerly did not set itself, and could not have set itself.

The class of exploiters, the landlords, and capitalists, has not disappeared and cannot disappear all at once under the dictatorship of the proletariat. The exploiters have been smashed, but not destroyed. They still have an international base in the form of international capital, a branch of which they represent. They still retain a part of certain means of production, they still have money, they still have vast social connections. Just because they have been defeated, their energy of resistance has increased a hundred-

and thousandfold. The "art" of state, military, and economic administration gives them a superiority, and ·a very
great superiority, so that their importance is incomparably
greater than their numerical strength among the population would warrant. The class struggle waged by the overthrown exploiters against the victorious vanguard of the
exploited, i.e., the proletariat, has become incomparably
more bitter. And it cannot be otherwise in the case of a
revolution, if this concept is not replaced (as it is by all the
heroes of the Second International) by reformist illusions.

Lastly, the peasantry, like the petty bourgeoisie in general, occupies a half-way, intermediary position even
under the dictatorship of the proletariat: on the one hand,
it represents a fairly large (and in backward Russia, a
vast) mass of toilers, united by the common interest of
the toilers to emancipate themselves from the landlord and
the capitalist; on the other hand, it represents disunited
small proprietors, property-owners, and traders. Such an
economic position inevitably gives rise to vacillation between the proletariat and the bourgeoisie. And in view of
the acute form which the struggle between these latter has
assumed, in view of the incredibly severe break-up of all
social relations, and in view of the great attachment precisely of the peasants and the petty bourgeoisie generally
to the old, the routine, and the unchangeable, it is only
natural that we should inevitably find them swinging
from one side to the other, that we should find them wavering, changeable, uncertain, and so on.

The task of the proletariat in relation to this class—or
to these social elements—is to guide it, to strive to establish its influence over it. The proletariat must lead the
vacillating and unstable along with it.

If we compare all the basic forces or classes and their
interrelations, as modified by the dictatorship of the proletariat, we shall realize how unutterably nonsensical and
theoretically stupid is the common petty-bourgeois idea
shared by all representatives of the Second International,
that the transition to socialism is possible "by means of
democracy" in general. The fundamental source of this error lies in the prejudice inherited from the bourgeoisie that

"democracy" is something absolute and not concerned with classes. As a matter of fact, democracy itself passes into an entirely new phase under the dictatorship of the proletariat, while the class struggle rises to a higher level and dominates over each and every form.

General talk about freedom, equality, and democracy is in fact but a stereotyped repetition of concepts which are only a cast from the relations of commodity production. To attempt to solve the concrete problems of the dictatorship of the proletariat by means of such general talk is to accept the theories and principles of the bourgeoisie all along the line. From the point of view of the proletariat, the question can be put only in the following way: freedom from the oppression of which class? equality of which class with which? democracy based on private property, or on a struggle for the abolition of private property?—and so forth.

Long ago Engels in his *Anti-Dühring* explained that the concept equality is a cast from the relations of commodity production and becomes a prejudice if equality is not understood to mean the *abolition of classes*. This elementary truth regarding the distinction between the bourgeois democratic and the socialist conception of equality is constantly being forgotten. But if it is not forgotten, it becomes obvious that by overthrowing the bourgeoisie the proletariat takes the most decisive step towards the abolition of classes, and that in order to complete the process the proletariat must continue its class struggle, making use of the apparatus of state power and employing various methods of combating, influencing, and bringing pressure to bear on the overthrown bourgeoisie and the vacillating petty bourgeoisie.

(To be continued)

30. X. 1919

*Pravda*, No. 250,
November 7, 1919

Vol. XXX, pp. 87-96

# SPEECH DELIVERED AT THE FIRST ALL-RUSSIAN CONFERENCE
## ON PARTY WORK IN THE COUNTRYSIDE

*November 18, 1919*

Comrades, unfortunately I have not been able to take part in the conference you have arranged, that is, in this conference on work in the countryside. Hence I shall have to limit myself to some general, basic considerations, and I am certain that you will be able gradually to apply these general considerations and fundamental principles of our policy to the various tasks and practical questions that come up before you.

The question of our work in the countryside is now, strictly speaking, the basic question of socialist construction in general, for as regards work among the proletariat and the question of uniting its forces, we can safely say that in the course of two years of Soviet power communist policy has not only taken definite shape but has unquestionably achieved lasting results. At first we had to fight a lack of understanding of the common interest among the workers, to fight various manifestations of syndicalism when the workers of certain factories or certain branches of industry tended to place their own interests, the interests of their factory or industry, above the interests of society. We had to and still have to fight a lack of discipline in the sphere of the new organization of labour. I believe you all remember the major stages through which our policy has passed, when, as we advanced more and more workers to new posts, we gave them an opportunity to become acquainted with the tasks facing us, with the general mechanism of government. Now the organization of the communist activity of the proletariat and the entire policy of the Communists have acquired a finished, lasting form, and I am certain that we are on the right path, progress along which is fully ensured.

As regards work in the countryside, the difficulties here are undoubtedly great, and we raised this question in its full scope at the Eighth Congress of the Party as one of the most important issues. In the countryside as well as in the towns we can base ourselves only on the representatives of the working and exploited masses, only those who bore under capitalism the whole burden of the landlord and capitalist yoke. Of course, since the time when the conquest of power by the workers enabled the peasants, by abolishing private property, to sweep away the power of the landlords with one blow, the peasants, dividing up the land, have given effect to the fullest equality and thus considerably improved the cultivation of the soil, raising it to a level above the average. It goes without saying, however, that we could not achieve everything we would have wished in this respect, for as long as the land is tilled by individual peasants it would take a tremendous quantity of material means to provide each with sufficient seed, livestock, and implements. Moreover, even if our industry were to achieve extraordinary progress in increasing the production of agricultural machines, even if we were to imagine all our wishes realized, we can easily see that to supply each small peasant with sufficient means of production is impossible and most irrational since it would mean a terrific scattering of means; only joint, artel, co-operative labour can help us to emerge from the blind alley in which the imperialist war drove us.

The mass of the peasants, who were the most downtrodden under capitalism owing to their economic position, find it hardest of all to believe in the possibility of sharp changes and transitions. His experience with Kolchak, Yudenich, and Denikin compels the peasant to be especially cautious in regard to his gains. All peasants know that the permanence of their gains is not finally guaranteed, that their enemy—the landlord—has not yet been destroyed, but has gone into hiding and is waiting for his friends, the international capitalist brigands, to come to his aid. And although international capital is becoming weaker from day to day and our international position has greatly improved in the recent period, we must say, if we soberly weigh all the circumstances, that international capital is still undoubtedly stronger than we are. It no longer can openly wage war against us—its wings have already been clipped. Indeed, all these gentlemen have latterly begun to say in the bourgeois press of Europe: "One is likely to get bogged down in Russia, perhaps it is better to make peace with her." That is the way it always is—when the enemy is beaten, he begins talking peace. We have told these gentlemen, the imperialists of Europe, time and again that we agree to make peace, but they continued to dream of enslaving Russia. Now they have realized that their dreams are not fated to come true.

The international millionaires and multi-millionaires are still stronger than we are. The peasants too see perfectly well that the Yudenich, Kolchak, and Denikin attempts to seize power were financed by the imperialists of Europe and America. And the mass of the peasants know very well what the slightest weakness will cost them. The vivid memory of the rule of the landlords and capitalists makes the peasants reliable supporters of Soviet power. With each passing month the stability of the Soviet power is growing and political consciousness increasing among the peasants who formerly toiled and were exploited and themselves experienced the full weight of the landlord and capitalist yoke.

Things, of course, are different with the kulaks, with those who themselves hired workers, made money by usury, enriched themselves at the expense of the labour of others. These in the mass side with the capitalists and are dissatisfied with the revolution that has taken place. And we must clearly realize that we still have a long and stubborn fight to wage against this group of peasants. But between the peasants who shouldered the full load of the landlord and capitalist yoke and those who themselves exploited others there is a mass of middle peasants. Here lies our most difficult task. Socialists have always pointed out that the transition to socialism will raise this difficult problem—the attitude of the working class to the middle peasantry. Here we must expect from the Communists more than from anyone else a serious understanding and intelligent approach to this complicated and difficult task, without trying to solve it with one blow.

The middle peasants are undoubtedly accustomed to farming each for himself. These are peasant proprietors, and although they have no land as yet, although private property in land has been abolished, they remain proprietors, primarily because this group of peasants remain in possession of food products. The middle peasant produces more food than he needs for himself, and since he has surplus grain he becomes the exploiter of the hungry worker. Herein lies the main task and the main contradiction. The peasant as a toiler, as a man who lives by his own labour, as one who bears the yoke of capitalism, sides with the worker. But the peasant as a proprietor with a surplus of grain is accustomed to regarding it as his property which he can sell freely. Yet to sell grain surpluses in a hunger-ridden country means to become a speculator, an exploiter, for the starving man will give everything he has for bread. It is here that the biggest and hardest battle has to be fought, a battle which demands of all of us representatives of Soviet power, and especially the Communists working in the countryside, the greatest attention and most serious thought to the issue at hand and the way to approach it.

We have always said that we do not seek to force socialism on the middle peasant, and the Eighth Congress of the Party fully confirmed this. The election of Comrade Kalinin as Chairman of the All-Russian Central Executive Committee was prompted by the need to build the closest of bonds between the Soviet power and the peasantry. Thanks to Comrade Kalinin our work in the countryside has gained considerable momentum. The peasant is now undoubtedly in a position to keep in closer contact with the Soviet government through Comrade Kalinin, who represents the supreme authority of the Soviet Republic. In this way we said in effect to the middle peasant: "There

can be no question of forcibly imposing socialism on anyone." But we must make him understand this, we must
know how to tell him this in a language the peasant understands best of all. Here we must rely only on the force of
example, successfully organize public farming. To give an
example of artel, co-operative labour we must first successfully organize such farming ourselves. The movement
for setting up agricultural communes and co-operatives
has acquired tremendous scope in these past two years.
But, looking at things soberly, we must say that a great
many of the comrades who tackled the organization of
communes started to farm without sufficient knowledge of
the economic conditions of peasant life. Hence the tremendous number of mistakes resulting from undue haste and
wrong approach to the question that have had to be recti-
fied. Time and again the old exploiters, former landlords,
wormed their way into the Soviet farms. They no longer
dominate there, but they themselves have not been elimi-
nated. It is necessary either to squeeze them out or put
them under the control of the proletariat.

This is a task that confronts us in all spheres of life. You
have heard of the series of brilliant victories won by the
Red Army. In it there are tens of thousands of old colo-
nels and officers of other ranks. If we had not accepted
them in our service, made them serve us, we could not
have created an army. And in spite of the treachery of
some military experts, we have defeated Kolchak and
Yudenich, and are winning on all fronts. The reason for
this is that thanks to the existence in the Red Army of
communist cells which conduct propaganda and agitation
carrying a tremendous impact, the small number of old
officers find themselves in such an evironment, under such
a tremendous pressure from the Communists, that the
majority of them are unable to break away from the bounds
of communist organization and propaganda with which we
have surrounded them.

Communism cannot be built without a reserve of knowledge, technique, and culture, and this reserve is in the
hands of bourgeois specialists. Most of these are not sym-
pathizers of Soviet power, yet without them we cannot

build communism. They must be surrounded with an atmosphere of comradeship, a spirit of communist work and won over to the side of the Workers' and Peasants' Government.

Among the peasants there have been frequent manifestations of extreme distrust and resentment in regard to state farms, even complete rejection of them; we do not want state farms, they say, for you can find the old exploiters there. We have told them: if you are unable to organize farming along new lines yourself, you have to employ the services of old specialists; otherwise there is no way out of poverty. Those of the old experts who violate the decisions of the Soviet government, we shall weed out ruthlessly just as we do in the Red Army; the struggle goes on, and a ruthless struggle at that. But we shall make the majority work as we want them to.

This is a difficult, complex task, a task that cannot be solved at one blow. Here conscious working-class discipline and closer contact with the peasants are needed. The peasants must be shown that we are not blind to any of the abuses that take place in the state farms, but at the same time we tell them that scientists and technicians must be enlisted in the service of public farming, for petty farming will not bring deliverance from want. And we shall do what we are doing in the Red Army—we may take a hundred beatings, but the hundredth-and-first time we defeat all our enemies. But to do this, work in the countryside must proceed by joint efforts, smoothly, in the same strict, orderly way as it has proceeded in the Red Army and as it is proceeding in other fields of economy. We shall slowly and steadily prove to the peasants the superiority of publicly-owned farming.

This is the struggle we must wage in the state farms, this is where the difficulty of transition to socialism lies, and it is thus that Soviet power can be really and finally consolidated. When the majority of the middle peasants come to see that unless they ally themselves with the workers they are helping Kolchak and Yudenich, that in all the world only the capitalists remain with them—the capitalists, who hate Soviet Russia and for years to come will

repeat their efforts to restore their power—even the most
backward middle peasants will realize that either they
must forge ahead in alliance with the revolutionary workers toward full freedom or, if they vacillate even in the
slightest, the enemy, the old capitalist exploiter, will gain
the upper hand. Victory over Denikin is not enough to destroy the capitalists once and for all. This is something we
all must realize. We know full well that they will try time
and again to throw the noose around Soviet Russia's neck.
Hence the peasant has no choice; he must help the workers,
for the slightest hesitation will give the victory to the landlords and the capitalists. It is our prime and basic task to
help the peasants understand this. The peasant who lives
by his own labour is a loyal ally of Soviet power, and the
worker regards such a peasant as his equal, the workers'
government does everything it can for him, indeed there
is no sacrifice the Workers' and Peasants' Government is
not ready to make to satisfy the needs of such a peasant.

But the peasant who makes use of the surplus grain he
possesses to exploit others is our enemy. To satisfy the basic needs of a hungry country is a duty to the state. Yet
far from all peasants realize that free trade in grain is a
crime against the state. "I have raised this grain, it is my
product, and I have a right to do business with it," the
peasant reasons out of habit, as he used to. But we say
*this is a crime against the state.* Free trade in grain means
enriching oneself by means of this grain, and this signifies
return to the old, to capitalism. This we shall not allow; on
this issue we shall fight at all costs.

In the transition period we shall carry out state purchases of grain, and appropriate grain surpluses. We know
that only this will enable us to do away with want and
hunger. The vast majority of the workers suffer hardship
because of improper distribution of grain; to distribute it
properly, the peasants must meet their state grain assessment quotas strictly, conscientiously, and without fail. Here
the Soviet power can make no concessions. This is not a
matter of the workers' government fighting the peasants,
but an issue involving the very existence of socialism, the
existence of Soviet power. We cannot give the peasants

goods now, for there is a shortage of fuel and railway traffic is being held up. We must start with the peasants lending the workers grain, not at profiteering but fixed prices, so that the workers can revive production. Every peasant will agree to this if it is a question of an individual worker dying from starvation before his eyes. But when millions of workers are in question, they do not understand this and the old habits of speculation gain the upper hand.

Prolonged and persistent struggle against such habits, agitation and propaganda, explanatory work, checking up on what has been done—these are the components of our policy toward the peasantry.

We must render every support to the toiling peasant, treat him as an equal, without the slightest attempt to impose anything on him by force—that is our first task. Our second task is to wage an unswerving struggle against speculation, huckstering, ruination.

When we began to build the Red Army, we had only separate, scattered groups of partisans to start with. Lack of discipline and unity resulted in many unnecessary sacrifices, but we overcame these difficulties and built up a Red Army millions strong in place of the partisan detachments. If we were able to do this in the brief period of two years, and in such a difficult and hazardous field as the military sphere, we are all the more certain that we can achieve similar results in all spheres of economic endeavour.

I am certain that this problem too—that of the proper attitude of the workers to the peasantry, of the correct food policy—one of the most difficult though it is, we shall solve and win in this field as well a victory such as we won at the front.

*Pravda*, No. 259,
November 19, 1919

Vol. XXX, pp. 122-29

# SPEECH DELIVERED AT THE FIRST CONGRESS OF AGRICULTURAL COMMUNES AND AGRICULTURAL ARTELS

## *December 4, 1919*

Comrades, I am very glad to greet your first congress of agricultural communes and agricultural artels on behalf of the government. Of course, from all the activities of the Soviet government you know what tremendous significance we attach to the communes, artels, and all organizations generally that aim at transforming and gradually assisting the transformation of small, individual, peasant farming into social, co-operative, or artel farming. You are aware that the Soviet government has long ago assigned a fund of one thousand million rubles to assist efforts of this kind. The "Statute on Socialist Agrarian Measures" particularly stresses the significance of communes, artels, and all enterprises for the common cultivation of the land, and the Soviet government is exerting every effort in order that this law shall not remain on paper only, and that it shall really produce the benefits it is intended to produce.

The importance of all enterprises of this kind is tremendous, because if the old, poverty-stricken peasant husbandry remained unchanged there could be no question of building up a stable socialist society. Only if we succeed in proving to the peasants in practice the advantages of common, collective, co-operative, artel cultivation of the soil, only if we succeed in helping the peasant by means of co-operative or artel farming, will the working class, which holds the state power, be really able to convince the peasant of the correctness of its policy and to secure the real and durable following of the millions of peasants. It is therefore impossible to exaggerate the importance of every measure intended to encourage co-operative, artel forms of agriculture. We have millions of individual farms in our country, scattered and dispersed throughout remote rural districts. It would be absolutely absurd to attempt to reshape these farms in any rapid way, by issuing an order or bringing pressure to bear from without. We fully realize that we can influence the millions of small peasant farms only gradually and cautiously and only by a successful practical example. For the peasants are far too practical and cling far too tenaciously to the old methods of agriculture to consent to any serious change merely on the basis of advice or the indications contained in books. That is impossible and it would be absurd. Only when it is proved in practice, by experience comprehensible to the peasants, that the transition to the co-operative, artel form of agriculture is essential and possible, shall we be entitled to say that in this vast peasant country, Russia, an important step towards socialist agriculture has been taken. Consequently, the vast importance that attaches to communes, artels, and co-operative farms lays on all of you tremendous state and socialist obligations and naturally compels the Soviet government and its representatives to treat this question with especial attention and caution.

In our law on socialist agrarian measures it is stated that we consider it the absolute duty of all co-operative, artel, agricultural enterprises not to isolate and sever themselves from the surrounding peasant population, but to make it their duty to afford them assistance. This is stipulated in the law, it is repeated in the rules of all the communes, artels, and co-operatives; it is constantly stressed in the instructions and rulings of our Commissariat of Agriculture and of all organs of the Soviet government. But the whole point is to find a really practical method of putting this into effect. I am still not convinced that we have overcome this principal difficulty. And I should like your congress, at which practical workers in collective farming from all parts of Russia have the opportunity of sharing their experience, to put an end to all doubts and to prove that we are mastering, are beginning to master in practice, the task of consolidating the artels, co-operative farms, and communes and every form of enterprise for collective and common farming generally. But in order to prove this, real *practical* results are required.

When we read the rules of the agricultural communes, or books devoted to this question, it might appear that we devote too much space in them to propaganda and the theoretical justification of the necessity of organizing communes. Of course, that is necessary, for without detailed propaganda, without explaining the advantages of co-operative agriculture, and without repeating this idea thousands and thousands of times we cannot expect interest to be aroused among the broad masses of peasants and a practical test to be undertaken of the methods of carrying it into effect. Of course, propaganda is necessary, and there is no need to fear repetition, for what may appear to us to be repetition is most likely for hundreds and thousands of peasants not repetition, but a truth revealed for the first time. And if it should occur to us that we are devoting too much attention to propaganda, it must be said that we ought to devote a hundred times more attention to it. And when I say this, I mean it in the sense that if we go to the peasant with general explanations of the advantages of organizing agricultural communes, and at the same time are unable in actual fact to point to the practical advantage that will accrue to him from co-operative, artel farms, he will not have the slightest confidence in our propaganda.

The law says that the communes, artels, and co-operative farms must assist the surrounding peasant population. But the state, the workers' government, is providing a fund of one thousand million rubles for the purpose of assisting the agricultural communes and artels. And, of course, if any commune were to assist the peasants out of this fund I am afraid it would only arouse ridicule among the peasants. And it would be absolutely justified. Every peasant will say: "It goes without saying that if you are getting a fund of one thousand million rubles it means nothing to you to throw a little our way." I am afraid the peasant will only jeer, for he regards this matter very attentively and very distrustfully. The peasant has been accustomed for centuries to expect only oppression from the state power, and he is therefore in the habit of regarding everything that comes from the state with suspicion. And if the assistance given by the agricultural communes to the peasants will be given merely for the purpose of fulfilling the letter of the law, such assistance will be not only useless but harmful. For the name "agricultural commune" is a great one; it is associated with the conception of communism. It will be a good thing if the communes in practice show that they are indeed seriously working for the improvement of peasant husbandry; that will undoubtedly increase the authority of the Communists and the Communist Party. But it has frequently happened that the communes have only succeeded in provoking a negative attitude among the peasantry, and the word "commune" has even at times become a call to fight communism. And this happened not only when stupid attempts were made to drive the peasants into the communes by force. The absurdity of this was so obvious that the Soviet government long ago forbade it. And I hope that if isolated examples of such coercion are to be met with now, they are very few, and that you will take advantage of the present congress to see to it that the last trace of this outrage is swept from the face of the Soviet Republic, and that the surrounding peasant population may not be able to point to a single instance in support of the old opinion that membership of a commune is in one way or another associated with coercion.

But even if we eliminate this old shortcoming and completely obliterate this outrage it will still be only a small fraction of what has to be done. For the necessity of the state helping the communes will still remain, and we would not be Communists and believers in introducing socialist economy if we did not give state aid to every kind of collective agricultural enterprise. We are obliged to do so for the added reason that it is in accordance with all our aims, and because we know that these co-operatives, artels, and collective organizations are innovations, and if support is not given them by the working class in power they will not take root. In order that they should take root, and in view of the fact that the state is affording them monetary and every other kind of support, we must see to it that they do not provoke the ridicule of the peasants. What we must be most

careful about is that the peasants should not say of the com-
munards and members of artels and co-operatives that they
are state pensioners, that they differ from the peasants only
by the fact that they are receiving privileges. If we are to
give land and subsidies for construction purposes out of the
thousand-million-ruble fund, any fool will live somewhat
better than the ordinary peasant. What is there communistic
here, the peasant will ask, and where is the improvement?
What are we to respect them for? If you pick out a few
score, or a few hundred individuals and give them a thousand million, of course they will work.

Such an attitude on the part of the peasants is most to
be feared, and I should like to draw the attention of the comrades assembled at the congress to this question. It must be
solved practically, so as to enable us to say that we have not
only averted this danger, but have also found means whereby the peasant will not be led to think in this way, but
will, on the contrary, find in every commune and artel something which the state power is assisting, will find in them
new methods of agriculture which show their advantages
over the old methods not by books and speeches (that is
not worth much) but in practice. That is why the problem
is so difficult to solve, and that is why it is hard for us, who
have only dry figures before us, to judge whether we have
proved in practice that every commune and every artel is
really superior to every enterprise of the old system and
that the workers' government is here helping the peasant.

I think that, practically, it would be very desirable for the
solution of this problem if you, who have a practical acquaintance with a number of neighbouring communes, artels, and co-operatives, worked out the methods of exercising real and practical control over the carrying out of the
law which demands that the agricultural communes should
give assistance to the surrounding population; over the way
the transition to socialist agriculture is being put into effect
and what concrete forms it is taking in each commune, artel,
and co-operative farm; how it is actually being put into practice, how many co-operatives and communes are in fact putting it into practice, and how many are only preparing to
do so; how many cases have been observed when the com-

munes have given assistance, and what character this assistance bears—philanthropic or socialist.

If out of the aid given them by the state the communes and artels set aside a portion for the peasants, that will only give the peasant grounds for believing that it is merely a case of being helped by kind-hearted people, but not by any means proof of a transition to a socialist system. The peasants have for ages been accustomed to regard such "kind-hearted people" with suspicion. We must know how to keep a check on the way this new social order has manifested itself, by what methods it is being proved to the peasants that co-operative, artel cultivation of the soil is better than individual peasant cultivation of the soil, and that is better *not* because of state aid. We must be able to show the peasants the practical realization of this new order even *without* state aid.

Unfortunately, I shall not be able to attend your congress to the end, and I shall therefore be unable to take part in elaborating these methods of control. But I am certain that with the aid of the comrades in charge of our Commissariat of Agriculture you will succeed in finding these methods. I read with great satisfaction an article by the People's Commissar of Agriculture, Comrade Sereda, in which he stressed that the communes and co-operatives must not isolate themselves from the surrounding peasant population but must endeavour to improve the latter's husbandry. A commune must be so organized as to serve as a model, and so that the neighbouring peasants should feel attracted to it. We must be able to set them a practical example of how to assist people who are conducting their husbandry under these severe conditions, which are marked by a goods shortage and by general dislocation. In order to define the practical methods of effecting this, extremely detailed instructions must be drawn up, which should enumerate all forms of assistance that can be given to the surrounding peasant population, which should ask each commune what it has done to help the peasants, and which should indicate the methods whereby each of the existing two thousand communes and nearly four thousand artels may become a nucleus capable of strengthening the conviction in the peas-

22—1928

ants that collective agriculture, as a transition to socialism, is a beneficial thing, and not a whimsy or the ravings
of a disordered mind.

I have already said that the law requires the communes
to render assistance to the surrounding peasant population.
We could not express ourselves otherwise in the law,
or give any practical instructions in it. It was our
business to establish the general principle, and to count
on enlightened comrades in the localities scrupulously
applying the law and being able to find a thousand
ways of applying it practically in the concrete economic conditions of each given locality. But, of course,
every law can be evaded, even under a pretence of
observing it. And so the law on assisting the peasants, if it
is applied unscrupulously, may become a mere game, and
lead to results quite contrary to those intended.

The communes must develop in such a way that, by contact with them and by the economic help they give, the conditions of peasant husbandry will begin to change, and that
every commune, artel, and co-operative be able to make the
beginnings of an improvement in these conditions and put
it into effect, thereby proving to the peasants in practice
that this change can only be beneficial for them.

Naturally, you may think that we shall be told that in order to improve husbandry we need conditions that differ
from the present conditions of economic dislocation caused
by the four years of imperialist war and the two years of
civil war forced on us by the imperialists. With such conditions as now exist in our country, how can one think of
any widespread improvement of farming—God grant that
we may carry on somehow and do not die of starvation!

If doubts of this kind are expressed, it will be only natural. But if I had to reply to such objections, I would say:
assume that owing to the disorganization of economic life,
to economic dislocation, goods shortage, poor transport and
the destruction of cattle and implements, an extensive improvement of agriculture cannot be effected. But there is
no doubt that a certain, not extensive, improvement is possible in a number of individual cases. But let us assume
that even this cannot be done. Does that mean that the com-

munes cannot produce changes in the life of the surrounding peasants and cannot prove to the peasants that collective agricultural enterprises are not an artificial hothouse growth, but a new form of assistance to the toiling peasantry on the part of the workers' government, and an aid to the toiling peasantry in its struggle against the kulaks? I am convinced that even if the matter is regarded in this way, even if we grant the impossibility of effecting improvements under the present conditions of economic disruption, nevertheless, if there are conscientious Communists in the communes and the artels, a very great deal may be accomplished.

To bear this out, I would refer to what in our cities has been called subbotniks. This is the name given to work performed gratis by the city workers, over and above what is demanded from every worker, and devoted for the space of several hours to some public need. The subbotniks were initiated originally in Moscow by the workers of the Moscow-Kazan Railway. One of the appeals of the Soviet government pointed out that the Red Army men at the front are making unprecedented sacrifices, and that, in spite of all the hardships they are obliged to undergo, they are gaining unprecedented victories over our enemies, and at the same time stated that we can clinch our victories only if such heroism and such self-sacrifice are displayed not only at the front, but also in the rear. The Moscow workers responded to this appeal by organizing subbotniks. There can be no doubt that the workers of Moscow are undergoing greater hardship and want than the peasants. If you were to acquaint yourselves with their conditions of life and were to ponder over the fact that in spite of these incredibly hard conditions they were able to organize subbotniks, you would agree that no reference to arduous conditions can serve as an excuse for not accomplishing what can be achieved under any conditions by applying the method of the Moscow workers. Nothing helped so much to enhance the prestige of the Communist Party in the towns, to increase the respect of the non-Party workers for the Communists, as these subbotniks when they ceased to be isolated instances and when the non-Party workers

22*

saw in practice that the members of the governing Communist Party have obligations and duties, and that the Communists admit new members to the Party not in order that they may enjoy the advantages connected with the position of a governing party, but that they may set an example of real communist labour, i.e., labour performed gratis. Communism is the highest stage in the development of socialism, when people work because they realize the necessity of working for the common good. We know that we cannot establish a socialist order now—God grant that it may be established in our country in our children's time, or perhaps in our grandchildren's time. But we say that the members of the governing Communist Party assume the greater burden of the difficulties in the fight against capitalism, mobilize the best Communists for the front, and demand of such as cannot be used for this purpose that they take part in subbotniks.

By organizing these subbotniks, which have become widespread in every large industrial city, participation in which the Party now demands from every one of its members, punishing non-fulfilment even by expulsion from the Party —by applying this method in the communes, artels, and co-operatives, you can, and must, even under the very worst conditions, bring it about that the peasant shall regard every commune, artel, and co-operative as an association which is distinguished not by the fact that it receives state subsidies, but by the fact that within it are gathered some of the best representatives of the working class, who not only preach socialism for others, but are themselves capable of realizing it; who are capable of showing that even under the worst conditions they can conduct their husbandry in a communist manner and help the surrounding peasant population in every possible way. No reservations are possible on this question, no excuses can be permitted, such as the goods shortage, or absence of seed, or loss of cattle. This will be a test which, at all events, will enable us to say definitely to what extent the difficult task we have taken on ourselves has been mastered in practice.

I am certain that this general meeting of representatives of communes, co-operatives, and artels will discuss this and will realize that the application of this method will really serve as a powerful instrument for the consolidation of the communes and the co-operatives, and will achieve such practical results that nowhere in Russia will there be a single case of hostility towards the communes, artels, and co-operatives on the part of the peasants. But that is not enough. What is required is that the peasants should be sympathetic towards them. For our part, we representatives of the Soviet government will do everything in our power to help to bring this about and to see to it that state assistance from the thousand-million-ruble fund, or from other sources, shall be forthcoming only in cases when closer relations between the toiling communes or artels and the life of the surrounding peasants have actually been established. Unless these conditions are fulfilled, we consider any assistance given to the artels and the co-operatives not only useless, but definitely harmful. Assistance given by the communes to the surrounding peasants must not be regarded as assistance which is merely given out of superfluity; this assistance must be socialist assistance, i. e., it must enable the peasants to replace their isolated, individual farming by co-operative farming. And this can be done only by the subbotnik method of which I have here spoken.

If you learn from the experience of the city workers, who, although living in conditions immeasurably worse than those of the peasants, initiated the movement for subbotniks, I am certain that, with your general and unanimous support, we shall bring about a situation when each of the several thousand existing communes and artels will become a genuine nursery for communist ideas and views, a practical example to the peasants showing them that, although it is still a small and feeble growth, it is nevertheless not an artificial, hothouse growth, but a true growth of the new socialist system. Only then shall we gain a lasting victory over the old ignorance, impoverishment, and want, and only then will the difficulties we meet in our future course hold out no terrors for us.

*Pravda*, Nos. 273 and 274,
December 5 and 6, 1919
Vol. XXX, pp. 173-82

# PRELIMINARY DRAFT OF THESES
## ON THE AGRARIAN QUESTION

### (For the Second Congress of the Communist International)

Comrade Marchlewski gives an excellent explanation in his article of the reasons why the Second International—it has now become the yellow International—failed not only to define the tactics of the revolutionary proletariat on the agrarian question, but even to state that question properly. Comrade Marchlewski then goes on to set forth the fundamentals of the Third International's communist agrarian programme.

A general resolution on the agrarian question can (and, I think, should) be drafted on these fundamentals for the Communist International Congress which will meet on July 15, 1920.

The following is a preliminary draft of such a resolution:

1) Only the urban and industrial proletariat, led by the Communist Party, can liberate the working masses of the countryside from the yoke of capital and big landlordism, from ruin and imperialist wars, which must inevitably break out again and again if the capitalist system is preserved. There is no salvation for the working masses of the countryside except in alliance with the Communist proletariat, and unless they give the latter devoted support in its revolutionary struggle for the overthrow of the yoke of the land lords (big landowners) and the bourgeoisie.

On the other hand, the industrial workers cannot fulfil their epoch-making mission of emancipating mankind from the yoke of capital and from wars if they concern themselves exclusively with their narrow craft, their narrow trade interests, and smugly confine themselves to attaining an improvement in their own, sometimes tolerable and petty-bourgeois, conditions.

This is just what happens in many advanced countries to the "labour aristocracy" which forms the base of the supposedly Socialist Parties of the Second International, and which in reality represents the bitter enemies and betrayers of socialism, petty-bourgeois chauvinists and agents of the bourgeoisie within the labour movement. The proletariat is a really revolutionary class and acts in a really socialist manner only when it comes out and acts as the vanguard of all the toilers and the exploited, as their leader in the struggle for the overthrow of the exploiters; but this cannot be done unless the class struggle is carried into the countryside, unless the rural working masses are united around the Communist Party of the urban proletariat, and unless they are trained by the proletariat.

2) The rural working and exploited masses, whom the urban proletariat must lead into the struggle, or, at all events, win over, are represented in all capitalist countries by the following classes:

First, the agricultural proletariat, wage-labourers (by the year, season, or day), who obtain their livelihood by working for hire in capitalist agricultural enterprises. The organization of this class (political, military, trade-union, co-operative, cultural, educational, etc.) independently and separately from other groups of the rural population, the conduct of intense propaganda and agitation among this class, and the winning of its support for Soviet government and the dictatorship of the proletariat constitute the *fundamental* task of the Communist Parties in all countries.

Second, the semi-proletarians, or dwarf peasants, i.e., those who obtain their livelihood partly as wage-labourers in agricultural and industrial capitalist enterprises and partly by working their own, or rented, plots of land, which provide only a part of the means of subsistence for their families. This group of the rural working population is very numerous in all capitalist countries; its existence and special position are obscured by the representatives of the bourgeoisie and by the yellow "Socialists" belonging to the Sec-

ond International, partly by deliberately deceiving the workers and partly by blindly submitting to the routine of petty-bourgeois views and confusing this group with the general
mass of the "peasantry." This bourgeois method of deceiving the workers is most to be observed in Germany and in
France, but also in America and other countries. If the work
of the Communist Party is properly organized, this group
will become its assured supporter; for the lot of these semi-
proletarians is a very hard one and they stand to gain enormously and immediately from Soviet government and the
dictatorship of the proletariat.

Third, the small peasantry, i.e., the small tillers, who hold,
either as owners or as tenants, small plots of land which
enable them to meet the requirements of their families and
their farms without hiring outside labour. This stratum, as
such, undoubtedly stands to gain by the victory of the proletariat which will bring it immediate and full: (a) relief from
the necessity of paying rent or a share of the crop (for example, the métayers, share croppers, in France, also in Italy and other countries) to the big landowners; (b) relief
from mortgages; (c) relief from the numerous forms of oppression by, and dependence on, the big landowners (forest
lands and their use, etc.) and (d) immediate assistance for
their farms on the part of the proletarian state (use of the
agricultural implements and part of the buildings on the
big capitalist farms expropriated by the proletariat, the
immediate transformation by the proletarian state of the
rural co-operative societies and agricultural associations
from organizations which under capitalism serve above all
the rich and middle peasants into organizations that will primarily assist the poor, i.e., the proletarians, semi-proletarians, small peasants, etc.), and many other forms of assistance.

At the same time the Communist Party must clearly realize that in the period of transition from capitalism to communism, i.e., in the period of the dictatorship of the proletariat, this stratum, or, at all events, part of it, will inevitably sway towards unrestricted freedom of trade and the
free enjoyment of the rights of private property; for, consisting already of sellers (although in a small way) of articles

of consumption, this stratum had been corrupted by profit-eering and proprietary habits. However, if a firm proletarian policy is pursued, and if the victorious proletariat deals very resolutely with the big landowners and the big peasants, the vacillation of this stratum cannot be considerable and cannot alter the fact that, on the whole, it will side with the proletarian revolution.

3) Together, the three groups enumerated constitute the majority of the rural population in all capitalist countries. Therefore, the success of the proletarian revolution is fully assured, not only in the towns but in the countryside as well. The opposite view is widespread; but it only persists, firstly, because of the deception systematically practised by bourgeois science and statistics, which do everything to obscure both the wide gulf that separates the above-mentioned classes in the countryside from the exploiters, the landlords and capitalists, and the wide gulf that separates the semi-proletarians and small peasants from the big peasants; it persists, secondly, because of the inability and unwilling-ness of the heroes of the yellow Second International and of the "labour aristocracy" in the advanced countries, which has been corrupted by imperialist privileges, to conduct genuinely proletarian revolutionary work of propaganda, agitation and organization among the rural poor; the atten-tion of the opportunists was and is wholly concentrated on inventing theoretical and practical compromises with the bourgeoisie, including the big and middle peasants (which are dealt with below), and not on the revolutionary over-throw of the bourgeois government and the bourgeoisie by the proletariat; it persists, thirdly, because of the obstinate refusal to understand—so obstinate as to be equivalent to a prejudice (connected with all the other bourgeois-democrat-ic and parliamentary prejudices)—a truth which has been fully proved by Marxist theory and fully corroborated by the experience of the proletarian revolution in Russia, viz., although all the three above-enumerated categories of the rural population—which in all, even the most advanced, countries are incredibly downtrodden, disunited, crushed, and doomed to semi-barbarous conditions of existence—are economically, socially, and culturally interested in the vic-

tory of socialism, they are capable of giving resolute support to the revolutionary proletariat only *after* the latter has won political power, only *after* it has resolutely dealt with the big landowners and capitalists, only *after* these downtrodden people see *in practice* that they have an organized leader and champion, strong and firm enough to assist and lead them and to show them the right path.

4) By "middle peasants," in the economic sence, are meant small tillers who also hold, either as owners or tenants, small plots of land, but such, firstly, as, under capitalism, provide them, as a general rule, not only with a meagre subsistence for their families and the bare minimum needed to keep up the farm, but also with the possibility of securing a certain surplus, which, at least in good years, may be converted into capital; and, secondly, fairly frequently (for example, one farm out of two or three) resort to the hire of outside labour. A concrete example of the middle peasants in an advanced capitalist country is provided by the group of farms of 5 to 10 hectares in Germany, where, according to the census of 1907, the number of farms employing hired labourers is about one-third of the total number of farms in this group.* In France, where the cultivation of special crops is more developed—for example, vine-growing, which requires a particularly large amount of labour —this group probably employs outside hired labour to somewhat larger extent.

The revolutionary proletariat cannot set itself the task—at least not in the immediate future and in the initial period of the dictatorship of the proletariat—of winning over this stratum, but must confine itself to the task of neutralizing it, i.e., making it neutral in the struggle between the proletariat and the bourgeoisie. Vacillations of this stratum be-

---

* Here are the exact figures: the number of farms of 5 to 10 hectares—652,798 (out of a total of 5,736,082); these employed 487,704 hired labourers of various kinds, while the members of the farmers' families (Familienangehörige) working on the farms numbered 2,003,633. In Austria, according to the census of 1902, this group comprised 383,331 farms, of which 126,136 employed hired labour; the hired labourers working on these farms numbered 146,044 and the working members of the farmers' families 1,265,969. The total number of farms in Austria was 2,856,349.

tween these two forces are inevitable, and in the beginning of the new epoch, in developed capitalist countries, its main trend will be towards the bourgeoisie. For among this stratum the outlook and the sentiments of property-owners predominate; it has an immediate interest in profiteering, in "freedom" of trade and in property, and stands in direct antagonism to the wage-workers. The victorious proletariat will directly improve the position of this stratum by abolishing rent and mortgages. In the majority of capitalist countries the proletarian state should not immediately abolish private property completely; at all events, it guarantees both the small and the middle peasantry not only the preservation of their plots of land, but also the enlargement of the latter by the addition of the total area they usually rented (abolition of rent).

The combination of measures of this kind with a ruthless struggle against the bourgeoisie fully guarantees the success of the policy of neutralization. The proletarian state must effect the passage to collective farming with extreme caution and only very gradually, by the force of example, without any coercion of the middle peasant.

5) The big peasants ("Grossbauern") are capitalist entrepreneurs in agriculture who as a rule employ several hired labourers and are connected with the "peasantry" only by their low cultural level, habits of life, and the manual labour they themselves perform on their farms. These constitute the largest of the bourgeois strata which are direct and determined enemies of the revolutionary proletariat. In all their work in the countryside, the Communist Parties must centre their attention mainly on the struggle against this stratum, on liberating the toiling and exploited majority of the rural population from the ideological and political influence of these exploiters, etc.

After the victory of the proletariat in the towns, all sorts of manifestations of resistance and sabotage as well as direct armed actions of a counter-revolutionary character on the part of this stratum are absolutely inevitable. Therefore, the revolutionary proletariat must immediately set to work to prepare, ideologically and organizationally, the forces necessary for completely disarming this stratum, and simultaneously, with the overthrow of the capitalists in industry, dealing it a most determined, ruthless and smashing blow at the very first signs of resistance; for this purpose the rural proletariat must be armed and village Soviets organized in which the exploiters must have no place, and in which the proletarians and semi-proletarians must be ensured predominance.

However, the expropriation even of the big peasants certainly cannot be made an immediate task of the victorious proletariat, for the material, in particular the technical conditions, as well as the social  conditions for the socialization of such farms are still lacking. In individual,  and probably exceptional, cases, those parts of their land which they rent out in small plots, or which are particularly needed by the surrounding small peasant population will be confiscated; the small peasants should also be guaranteed, on certain terms, the free use of part of the agricultural machines belonging to the big peasants, etc. As a general rule, however, the proletarian state must allow the big peasants to retain their land, confiscating it only if they resist the power of the toilers and the exploited. The experience of the Russian proletarian revolution, in which the fight against the big peasantry was complicated and protracted by a number of special conditions, nevertheless showed that, when taught a severe lesson for the slightest attempt at resistance, this stratum is capable of loyally fulfilling the requirements of the proletarian state, and even begins to be imbued, although very slowly, with respect for the government which protects all who work and is ruthless towards the idle rich.

The special conditions which in Russia complicated and retarded the struggle of the proletariat against the big peasants after it had defeated the bourgeoisie, were chiefly the following: the fact that after October 25 (November 7) 1917, the Russian revolution passed through the stage of "general-democratic," that is, basically, bourgeois-democratic, struggle of the peasantry as a whole against the landlords; the cultural and numerical weakness of the urban proletariat; and, lastly, the enormous distances and extremely bad means of communication. Inasmuch as these retarding conditions do not exist in the advanced countries, the revolutionary proletariat of Europe and America should prepare far more energetically, and achieve far more quickly, resolutely, and successfully, complete victory over the resistance of the big peasantry, completely depriving it of the slightest possibility of resisting. This is imperative, because until such a complete and absolute victory is achieved, the masses of the rural proletarians, semi-proletarians, and small peasants cannot be fully brought to accept the proletarian state as a stable one.

6) The revolutionary proletariat must immediately and unreservedly confiscate all the land of the landlords, the big landowners, i.e., those who in capitalist countries, directly or through their tenant farmers, systematically exploit wage-labour and the surrounding small (and, not infrequently, part of the middle) peasantry, perform no manual labour themselves, and are largely the descendants of the feudal lords (the nobles in Russia, Germany, and Hungary, the restored seigneurs in France, the lords in England, the former slave-owners in America), or are rich financial magnates, or a mixture of both these categories of exploiters and parasites.

Under no circumstances is it permissible for the Communist Parties to advocate or practise compensation for the big landowners for the lands expropriated from them, for under present-day conditions in Europe and America this would be tantamount to a betrayal of socialism and the imposition of new tribute upon the masses of toilers and exploited, upon whom the war has imposed most hardship, while multiplying the number of millionaires and enriching them.

As to the method by which the land that the victorious proletariat confiscates from the big landlords is to be cultivated, in Russia, owing to her economic backwardness, the predominating method was the distribution of this land among the peasantry for their use, and only in relatively rare and exceptional cases were there organized what are known as "Soviet farms," which the proletarian state runs on its own account, converting the former wage-labourers into workers of the state and members of the Soviets which administer the state. The Communist International is of the opinion that, in the case of the advanced capitalist countries, it would be correct to keep *most* of the big agricultural enterprises intact and to conduct them on the lines of the "Soviet farms" in Russia.

It would be a great mistake, however, to exaggerate or to stereotype this rule and never to permit the free grant of *part* of the land expropriated from the expropriators to the surrounding small, and sometimes, middle peasantry.

Firstly, the objection usually raised against this, viz., the technical superiority of large-scale farming, very often amounts to citing an indisputable theoretical truth to justify the worst kind of opportunism and betrayal of the revolution. For the sake of the success of this revolution, the proletariat has no right to shrink from a temporary decline in production, any more than the bourgeois enemies of slavery in North America shrank from a temporary decline in cotton production as a consequence of the Civil War of 1863-65. For the bourgeois, production is important for production's sake; for the toiling and exploited population, the most important thing is the overthrow of the exploiters and the creation of conditions that will permit the toilers to work for themselves and not for the capitalists. The primary and fundamental task of the proletariat is to ensure the proletarian victory and its durability. And the durability of the proletarian government cannot be ensured unless the middle peasantry is neutralized and the support of a very considerable section, if not the whole, of the small peasantry is secured.

Secondly, not merely an increase, but even the preservation itself of large-scale production in agriculture presupposes the existence of a fully developed and revolutionary conscious rural proletariat with considerable experience of trade-union and political organization behind them. Where this condition does not yet exist, or where it is not possible to entrust the work expediently to class-conscious and competent industrial workers, hasty attempts at the introduction of large state-conducted farms may only discredit the proletarian government. Under such conditions, the utmost caution must be exercised and the most thorough preparation made before "Soviet farms" are set up.

Thirdly, in all capitalist countries, even the most advanced, there still exist survivals of medieval, semi-feudal exploitation by the big landowners of the surrounding small peasants, as in the case of the Instleute* in Germany, and métayers** in France, the share croppers in the United States (not only Negroes, who, in the Southern States, are mostly exploited in this way, but sometimes whites too). In such cases it is incumbent on the proletarian state to grant the small peasants free use of the lands they formerly rented, for no other economic or technical basis exists, nor can it be created at one stroke.

The implements and stock of the big farms must be confiscated without fail and converted into state property, with the absolute proviso that *after* the requirements of the big state farms have been met, the surrounding small peasants may have the use of these implements gratis, in compliance with conditions drawn up by the proletarian state.

In the period immeditely following the proletarian revolution, it is absolutely necessary, not only to confiscate the estates of the big landlords at once, but also to deport or to intern them all as leaders of counter-revolution and ruthless oppressors of the whole rural population. But as the proletarian power becomes consolidated in the countryside as well as in the cities, systematic efforts must be made to employ (under the special control of highly reliable communist workers) the forces within this class possessing valuable experience, knowledge, and organizing ability for the building up of large-scale socialist agriculture.

7) The victory of socialism over capitalism, and the consolidation of socialism, may be regarded as ensured only when the proletarian state, having completely suppressed all resistance on the part of the exploiters and secured complete stability for itself and complete obedience, reorganized the whole of industry on large-scale collective lines and on a modern technical basis (founded on the electrification of every branch of economy). This alone will enable the towns

* Tenant farmers.—*Ed.*
** Share croppers.—*Ed.*

to render such radical assistance, technical and social, to
the backward and scattered rural population as will create
the material basis for enormously raising the productivity
of agricultural and of farm labour in general, thereby stim-
ulating the small tillers by the force of example and in
their own interests to adopt large-scale, collective, mechanized agriculture. This indisputable theoretical truth, although nominally recognized by all Socialists, is in fact distorted by the opportunism which prevails in the yellow Second International and among the leaders of the German
and British "Independents," the French Longuetites, etc. The
distortion lies in the fact that attention is directed towards
the relatively remote, beautiful, and rosy future; attention is
deflected from the immediate tasks involved in the difficult
practical transition and approach to this future. In practice,
it consists in preaching compromise with the bourgeoisie
and "social peace," that is, complete betrayal of the proletariat, which is now carrying on its fight amidst the unprecedented ruin and impoverishment created everywhere by
the war, amidst the unprecedented enrichment and arrogance of a handful of millionaires resulting precisely from
the war.

It is precisely in the rural districts that the creation of
real opportunities for a successful struggle for socialism demands, firstly, that all Communist Parties should educate
the industrial proletariat to realize that it must make sacrifices, and inculcate a readiness in it to make sacrifices for
the sake of overthrowing the bourgeoisie and of consolidating the proletarian power—for the dictatorship of the proletariat implies both the ability of the proletariat to organize
and lead all the masses of toilers and exploited, and the ability of the vanguard to make the utmost sacrifice and to display the utmost heroism to this end; secondly, success demands that the labouring and most exploited masses in the
countryside obtain as a result of the victory of the workers
an immediate and considerable improvement in their conditions at the expense of the exploiters—for unless this is
so, the industrial proletariat cannot be sure of the support
of the rural districts, and, in particular, will be unable to
ensure the supply of food to the towns.

8) The enormous difficulty of organizing and training for the revolutionary struggle the masses of the agricultural toilers, whom capitalism has reduced to a particular state of wretchedness, disunity, and, often, semi-medieval dependence, makes it necessary for the Communist Parties to devote special attention to the strike struggle in the rural districts, to give increased support to mass strikes among the agricultural proletarians and semi-proletarians and to develop them in every way. The experience of the Russian revolutions of 1905 and of 1917, now confirmed and extended by the experience of Germany and other advanced countries, shows that the developing mass strike struggle (into which, under certain conditions, the small peasants can and should be drawn) is alone capable of rousing the countryside from its lethargy, of awakening the class-consciousness of the exploited masses in the countryside, of making them realize the need for class organization, and of revealing to them in a vivid and practical manner the importance of their alliance with the urban workers.

This Congress of the Communist International brands as traitors those Socialists—to be found, unfortunately, not only in the yellow Second International, but also in the three very important European parties which have withdrawn from that International—who are not only capable of remaining indifferent to the strike struggle in the countryside, but even (like K. Kautsky) of opposing it on the grounds that it threatens to reduce the output of articles of consumption. Neither programmes nor solemn declarations are of any value whatever if it is not proved in practice, by deeds, that the Communists and workers' leaders are able to place the development of the proletarian revolution and its victory above everything else in the world, and to make the greatest sacrifices for it; for there is no other way out, no other salvation from starvation, ruin, and new imperialist wars.

In particular, it should be pointed out that the leaders of the old socialist movement and representatives of the "labour aristocracy," who now often make verbal concessions to communism and even nominally side with it in order to maintain their prestige among the worker masses, now rap-

idly becoming revolutionary, must be tested for their loy-
alty to the cause of the proletariat and their suitability
for responsible positions precisely in those spheres of work
where the development of revolutionary consciousness and
the revolutionary struggle is most marked, the resistance
of the landowners and the bourgeoisie (the big peasants,
kulaks) most fierce, and the difference between the Socialist
compromiser and the Communist revolutionary most striking.

9) The Communist Parties must exert every effort to
begin as speedily as possible the formation of Soviets of
Deputies in the countryside, in the first place, Soviets of
hired labourers and semi-proletarians. Only if they are
connected with the mass strike struggle and with the most
oppressed class can the Soviets perform their functions and
become consolidated enough to influence (and later to in-
corporate) the small peasants. If, however, the strike struggle is not yet developed, and the organizing ability of the
agricultural proletariat still weak, owing both to the severity of the oppression of the landowners and big peasants
and to lack of support from the industrial workers and their
unions, the formation of Soviets of Deputies in the rural
districts will require long preparation by means of the organization of communist nuclei, even if small ones, intensified agitation—in which the demands of communism are
enunciated in the simplest manner and illustrated by the
most glaring examples of exploitation and oppression—
the arrangement of systematic visits of industrial workers
to the rural districts, and so on.

Written at the beginning of
June 1920
Published in July 1920

Vol. XXXI, pp. 129-41

# REPORT ON THE SUBSTITUTION OF A TAX
## IN KIND FOR THE SURPLUS-APPROPRIATION SYSTEM
## DELIVERED AT THE TENTH CONGRESS OF
## THE R.C.P.(B.)

*March 15, 1921*

Comrades, the question of substituting a tax for the surplus-appropriation system is primarily and mainly a political question, for it is essentially a question of the attitude of the working class to the peasantry. We are raising it because we must subject the relations of these two main classes, struggle or agreement between which determines the fate of our revolution as a whole, to a new, or, I would say, perhaps, more careful and correct re-examination and a certain revision. There is no need for me to dwell in detail on the reasons for such a re-examination. You all, of course, know very well the sum total of developments arising mainly from the extreme want caused by the war, ruination, demobilization, and the exceedingly grave crop failure—you know the circumstances which taken together have made the position of the peasantry especially grievous and critical and inevitably increased its vacillation from the proletariat to the bourgeoisie.

A word or two on the theoretical significance or the theoretical approach to this issue. There is no doubt that a socialist revolution can be carried out in a country where the overwhelming majority of the population consists of small agricultural producers only through the implementation of a whole series of special transitional measures which would not be necessary at all in countries with highly developed capitalism, where wage-workers in industry and agriculture make up the vast majority. Coun-

tries with highly developed capitalism have a class of agricultural wage-workers that has taken shape in the course
of scores of years. Only such a class can socially, economically, and politically support direct transition to socialism. Only in countries where this class is sufficiently developed is it possible to pass over directly from capitalism
to socialism without any special country-wide transitional measures. We have stressed in a good many written
works, in all our public utterances, in all our statements
in the press, that this is not the case in Russia, that in
Russia industrial workers constitute the minority and small
tillers of the soil, the vast majority. The socialist revolution can be conclusively successful in such a country only
on two conditions. First, if it is given timely support by a
socialist revolution in one or several advanced countries.
As you know, we have done very much indeed in comparison with the past to bring about this condition, but far
from enough for it to have become reality.

The second condition is agreement between the proletariat which is giving effect to its dictatorship, that is,
holding state power in its hands, and the majority of the
peasant population. Agreement is a very broad concept
which includes a whole series of measures and transitions.
Here it must be said that all our propaganda and agitation must be open and above-board. We must most resolutely condemn people for whom politics is a matter of
pettifoggery, sometimes bordering on deception. Their mistakes have to be corrected. You cannot deceive classes. We
have done very much in the past three years to raise the
political consciousness of the masses. Most of all they
have learned in the course of sharp struggles. In keeping
with our world outlook, the revolutionary experience we
have accumulated in the course of decades, and the lessons of our revolution, we must state the issues point-
blank: the interests of these two classes differ, the small
farmer does not want the same thing as the worker.

We know that so long as there is no revolution in other
countries, only agreement with the peasantry can save the
socialist revolution in Russia. And thus we must put it,
frankly, at all meetings and in the press. Under all cir-

cumstances we must not try to hide anything, but must declare outright that the peasantry is dissatisfied with the form our relations with it have taken, that it does not want this form and will not continue to live as it has hitherto. This is unquestionable. The peasantry has expressed its will in this respect definitely enough. This is the will of the vast masses of the toiling population. We must reckon with this, and we are sober enough politicians to say frankly: let us re-examine our policy in regard to the peasantry. The state of affairs that has prevailed so far cannot be continued any longer.

We must say to the peasants: "If you want to turn back, if you want to restore private property and free trade in their entirety, this will mean falling inevitably under the rule of the landlords and the capitalists. This is proved by a whole series of examples from history, examples of revolutions. The briefest examination of the ABC of communism, the ABC of political economy, will prove that this is inevitable. Let us then look into the matter. Is it in the interest of the peasantry to part ways with the proletariat so as to slip back—and let the country slip back—to rule by the capitalists and landlords, or not? Consider this, and let us consider it together."

We believe that if the matter is given proper consideration, the conclusion will be in our favour, in spite of the admittedly deep gulf between the economic interests of the proletariat and the small farmer.

As difficult as our position is in regard to resources, the needs of the middle peasantry must be satisfied. There are far more middle peasants now than before, antagonisms have been smoothed out, the land has been distributed for use far more equally, the kulak's position has been undermined and he has been in considerable measure expropriated—in Russia more than in the Ukraine, and in Siberia less. On the whole, however, statistics show absolutely definitely that there has been a levelling out, an equalization, in the village, that is, there no longer is the same sharp division into kulaks and cropless peasants. Everything has become more equable, the peasantry in general has acquired the status of the middle peasant.

Can we satisfy this middle peasantry as such, with its economic peculiarities and economic roots? A Communist who thought the economic basis, the economic roots, of small farming could be reshaped in three years was of course a dreamer. We need not hide the fact that there were a good many such dreamers among us. Nor is there anything particularly reprehensible in this. How could one start a socialist revolution in a country like ours without dreamers? Practice has, of course, shown how tremendous a role can be played by all kinds of experiments and undertakings in the sphere of collective agriculture. But it has also afforded instances of these experiments as such playing a negative role when people full of the best of intentions and desires went to the countryside to set up communes, collectives, but did not know how to run them because they had no experience in collective endeavour.

You know perfectly well how many cases there have been of this kind. I repeat that this is not surprising, for it will take generations to remake the small farmer, to remake his entire psychology and habits. The only way to solve this problem of the small farmer, to improve, so to speak, his whole mentality, is through the material basis, technical equipment, the use of tractors and machines on a mass scale in agriculture, electrification on a mass scale. This would remake the small farmer fundamentally and with tremendous speed. If I say this will take generations, it does not mean centuries. But you know perfectly well that to obtain tractors and machines and to electrify our vast country is a matter that at any rate may take decades. This is the objective situation.

We must try to satisfy the demands of the peasants who are not satisfied, who are disgruntled and quite legitimately so, and who cannot be otherwise. We must say to them: "Yes, this cannot go on any longer." How is the peasant to be satisfied and what does satisfying him mean? Where can we find the answer to the question how to satisfy him? Naturally in the very demands of the peasantry. We know these demands. But we must verify them, examine from the standpoint of economic science all that we know of the farmer's economic demands. If we go into this, we shall see at once that the small farmer can be satisfied essentially through two things. Firstly, what is needed is a certain freedom of exchange, freedom for the small private proprietor, and, secondly, commodities and products must be procured. What indeed would free exchange amount to if there is nothing to exchange, and free trade, if there is nothing to trade with! It would all remain on paper, and classes cannot be satisfied by scraps of paper, they want material things. These two conditions must be clearly understood. The second condition—how to get commodities and whether we shall be able to obtain them—we shall discuss later. It is the first condition—free exchange—that we must dwell on now.

What is free exchange? Free exchange is free trade, and free trade means turning back toward capitalism. Free. exchange and free trade mean circulation of commodities among separate petty proprietors. All of us who have studied at least the ABC of Marxism know that this exchange and free trade inevitably lead to a division of commodity producers into owners of capital and possessors of labour power, division into capitalists and wage-workers, i.e., a revival of capitalist wage-slavery, which does not drop down from the skies but springs the world over precisely from agricultural commodity economy. This we know perfectly well in theory, and in Russia nobody who has observed the small farmer's life and the conditions under which he farms can escape noticing this.

How then can the Communist Party recognize free trade and go over to it? Does not the proposition contain irreconcilable contradictions? The answer is that the practical solution of the problem naturally presents exceedingly great difficulties. I can foresee, and I know from the talks I have had with comrades, that the preliminary draft on substituting a tax for surplus appropriation—the draft which has been handed out to you—gives rise to legitimate and inevitable questions mostly as regards permitting exchange of goods within the bounds of local economic turnover. This is set forth at the end of Paragraph 8. What does it mean, what limits are there to this exchange, how is it all to be implemented? Anyone who expects to get the answer at this congress will be disappointed. We shall find the answer in our legislation; it is our task to lay down the principle to be followed, to issue the slogan. Our Party is the Party in government and the decision the Party congress will pass will be obligatory for the entire republic: here we must decide the question in principle. We must decide the question in principle and inform the peasantry of our decision, for the sowing season is almost here. Further we must muster our whole administrative apparatus, all our theoretical forces, all our practical experience, in order to see how it can be done. Can it be done at all, theoretically speaking, can free trade, freedom of capitalist enterprise for the small farmer, be restored to a certain extent without thereby undermining the political power of the proletariat? Can it be done? It can, for the question here is of extent. If we were able to obtain even a small quantity of goods and were to hold them in the hands of the state, in the hands of the proletariat exercising political power, and if we could release these goods into circulation, we, as the state, would add economic power to our political power. Release of these goods into circulation would stimulate small farming, which is in a terrible state of decline owing to the grievous consequences of war and dislocation and the impossibility of developing small farming. The small farmer, so long as he remains small, needs a stimulus, a spur, an incentive corresponding to his economic basis, i.e., the small separate farm. Here you cannot avoid local free exchange. If this turnover gives to the state in exchange for manufactured goods a certain minimum of grain sufficient to cover the requirements of the cities, factories, industry, economic circulation will be revived with the state power remaining in the hands of the proletariat and growing stronger. The peasants want to be shown in practice that the worker who holds the factories, mills, industry in his hands is able to organize exchange with the peasantry. And, on the other hand, the vastness of our agricultural country with its poor transport system, boundless expanses, varying climate, different farming conditions, etc., makes a certain freedom of exchange between local agriculture and local industry on a local scale inevitable. In this respect we are very much to blame for having gone too far; we have pushed nationalization of trade and industry more than necessary, clamping down on local exchange of commodities. Was this a mistake? Undoubtedly it was.

In this respect we have made many outright mistakes, and it would be the greatest crime not to see this and not to realize that we have failed to keep within bounds, that we did not know where to stop. There has, of course, also been the factor of necessity—until now we have been living in conditions of a savage war that laid an unprecedented burden on us and left us no choice but to take wartime measures in the economic sphere as well. It was by a miracle that the ruined country withstood this war, yet the miracle did not come down from the heavens; it grew out of the economic interests of the working class and the peasantry, whose mass uplift created this miracle that rebuffed the landlords and capitalists. But at the same time it is an unquestionable fact that we went further than was theoretically and politically necessary, and this should not be concealed in our agitation and propaganda. We can allow free local exchange to a sizable extent without destroying but strengthening the political power of the proletariat. How this is to be done, practice will show. I only wish to prove to you that theoretically this is conceivable. The proletariat, which wields state power, can, if it possesses any reserves at all, put them into circulation and thereby secure a certain satisfaction of the middle peasant—satisfy him on the basis of local economic exchange.

Now a few words about local economic exchange. First of all I must touch on the question of the co-operatives. The co-operatives, which are now in an extreme state of decline, are of course something we need as an agency of local economic exchange. Our programme stresses that the best distribution agency are the co-operatives left over from capitalism, and that this agency must be preserved. This is what the programme says. Have we lived up to this? To a very slight extent, or not at all, again partly

because we have made mistakes, partly because of wartime necessity. The co-operatives, which brought to the
fore the more business-like, economically more advanced
elements, thereby produced in political life Mensheviks
and Socialist-Revolutionaries. This is a law of chemistry
—you can't do anything about it! (*Laughter.*) The Mensheviks and Socialist-Revolutionaries are people who
either consciously or unconsciously work to restore capitalism or help the Yudeniches. This too is a law. We must fight
them. And to fight means to take action as in war; we had
to defend ourselves, and we did so. But are we bound to
perpetuate the present situation? No, we are not. It would
be a mistake to tie one's hands in this way. Because of this
I submit a resolution on the question of the co-operatives;
it is very brief and I shall read it to you:

"In view of the fact that the resolution of the Ninth
Congress of the R.C.P. on the attitude toward co-operatives was wholly based on recognition of the principle of
surplus-appropriation, which is now replaced with the tax
in kind, the Tenth Congress of the R.C.P. resolves:

"To annul the above-mentioned resolution.

"The congress instructs the Central Committee to draft
and carry out through Party and Soviet channels decisions
that would improve and develop the structure and activity of the co-operatives in conformity with the programme
of the R.C.P. and with a view to the substitution of a
tax in kind for the surplus-appropriation system."

You will say that this is rather vague. Yes, that is so;
it is necessarily vague to a certain extent. Why necessarily? Because to be absolutely definite we must know exactly what to do for a whole year ahead. Who knows that?
Nobody knows and cannot know.

But the resolution of the Ninth Congress ties our hands
by calling for "subordination to the Commissariat of
Food." The Commissariat of Food is a fine institution, but
it would be an obvious political mistake absolutely to subordinate the co-operatives to it and to tie our hands at a
time when we are reviewing our relations with the small
farmers. We must instruct the newly elected Central Committee to work out and implement definite measures and

changes and to check up on every step we take back and forth—to what extent we must do so, how to uphold our political interests, to what extent must there be a relaxation to make things easier, how to check up on the results of our experience. Theoretically speaking, in this respect we are facing a whole series of transitional stages, transitional measures. One thing is clear to us: the resolution of the Ninth Congress presupposed that our movement forward would proceed in a straight line, but it turned out, as has constantly happened throughout the entire history of revolutions, that the movement took a zigzag course. To tie one's hands with such a resolution would be a political mistake. Annulling it, we say that we must be guided by our programme, which stresses the importance of the machinery of the co-operatives.

As we annul the resolution, we say: work with a view to the substitution of a tax for surplus-appropriation. But when shall we do this? Not before the harvest, that is, several months from now. Will it be done in the same way in all localities? Under no circumstances. It would be the height of stupidity to apply the same pattern to Central Russia, the Ukraine, and Siberia. I propose that this fundamental idea of freedom of local exchange be formulated as a decision of this congress. I presume that following this decision the Central Committee will without fail send out a letter within the next few days which will point out, and of course do it better than I can here, that nothing is to be radically changed, that there should be no undue haste, no decisions on the spur of the moment, that things should be done so as to satisfy the middle peasantry to the maximum without damaging the interests of the proletariat. Try one thing and another, study things in practice, through experience, then share your experience with us, and let us know what you have managed to do, and we shall set up a special commission or even several commissions to consider the experience that has been accumulated. This is a highly important question, for money turnover is a splendid test of the state of commodity circulation in the country; when this is unsatisfactory, money turns into worthless scraps of paper. In order to proceed on the basis of experience, we must check up on the measures we have adopted ten times over.

We shall be asked where the goods are to come from. For free trade requires goods, and the peasants are very shrewd people and very good at scoffing. Can we obtain goods now? Now we can, for our economic position on the international arena has greatly improved. We are waging a fight against the international capitalists, who, when they were first confronted by our republic, called us "brigands and crocodiles" (I was told by an English artist that she had heard literally these words from one of the most influential politicians). And crocodiles can only be despised. This was the voice of international capital. This was the voice of the class enemy and from his point of view quite correct. However, the correctness of such conclusions has to be verified in practice. If you are a world power, world capital, and you resort to words like "crocodile" and have all the technical means at your disposal, then try and shoot it! But when world capital tried this, it only hurt itself. It was then that the capitalists, which are forced to reckon with political and economic realities, declared: "We must trade." This is the greatest of victories for us. I can tell you now that we have two offers of a loan to the amount of nearly one hundred million in gold. We have gold, but you can't sell gold, because you can't eat it. Everybody has been reduced to such a state of impoverishment, currency relations between all the capitalist countries are in an incredible state of confusion as a result of the war. Moreover, for communication with Europe a fleet is needed, and we have none. The fleet is in hostile hands. We have concluded no treaty with France, which considers that we are her debtors and, consequently, that every ship we have is hers. They have a navy and we have none. Under these circumstances we have so far been in a position to make use of our gold on a limited, insignificant, ridiculously insignificant scale. Now we have two offers from capitalist bankers to float a loan of one hundred million. Of course they will charge exorbitant interest. Yet until now they have not proposed anything of the kind; so far they have said: "I'll shoot you and take everything for nothing." Now, unable to shoot us, they are ready to trade with us. Trade agreements with America and Britain can now be said to be on the way; the same applies to concessions. Yesterday I received another letter from Mr. Vanderlip who is here and who, besides a whole series of complaints, sets forth a whole series of plans concerning concessions and a loan. He is a representative of finance capital of the shrewdest type connected with the Western States of the U.S.A. which are more hostile to Japan. So we have an economic possibility of obtaining goods. How we shall manage to do it is another question, but a certain possibility does exist.

I repeat, the type of economic relations which at the face of it looks like a bloc with foreign capitalism makes it possible for the proletarian state authority to arrange for free exchange with the peasantry below. I know—and I have had occasion to say this before—that this has evoked some sneers. There is a whole intellectual-bureaucratic stratum in Moscow which is trying to shape "public opinion." "See what communism has come to!" these people sneer. "It's like a man on crutches and face all bandaged up—nothing but a picture puzzle." I have heard enough of this kind of gibes—gibes that are either bureaucratic or just irresponsible. Russia emerged from the war in a condition that can most of all be likened to a man beaten within an inch of his life; for seven years she was beaten and now we can be grateful if she can hobble about on crutches! That is the situation we are in! To think that we can get out of this state without crutches is to understand nothing! So long as there is no revolution in other countries, it would take us decades to come up, and under these circumstances we cannot grudge hundreds of millions' or even thousands of millions' worth of our inestimable wealth, our rich raw material sources, in order to obtain help from the big leading capitalists. Later we shall recover it all and to spare. The rule of the proletariat cannot be maintained in a country ruined as no country ever was—a country where the vast majority are peasants who are equally ruined—without the help of capital, for which, of course, it will extract exorbitant interest. This we must understand. And hence the choice is between this type of economic relations or nothing. He who puts the question otherwise understands absolutely nothing in practical economics and is avoiding the issue by resorting to gibes. We must recognize the fact that the masses are utterly worn out and exhausted. What can you expect after seven years of war in our country, if four years of war are still making themselves felt in the more advanced countries?!

In our backward country, the workers, who have made unprecedented sacrifices, and the mass of the peasants are in a state of utter exhaustion after seven years of war. This exhaustion, this condition borders on complete loss of working capacity. What is needed now is an economic breathing spell. We counted on using our gold reserve to obtain means of production. It would be best of all to make our own machines, but even if we bought them, we would thereby build up our industry. But to do this you must have a worker and a peasant who can work; yet in most cases they are not in a condition to do so, for they are exhausted, worn out. They must be assisted, the gold reserve must be channelled to consumption goods, contrary to our former programme. Our former programme was theoretically correct, but practically unsound. I shall pass on to you some information I have here from Comrade Lezhava. From this data we see that several hundred thousand poods of various items of food have already been bought in Lithuania, Finland, and Latvia and are being shipped in with utmost speed. Today we learned that a deal has been concluded in London for the purchase of 18½ million poods of coal, which we decided to buy in order to revive the industry of Petrograd as well as the textile industry. If we obtain goods for the peasant, it will, of course, be a violation of the programme, an irregularity, but we must have a breathing spell, for the people are exhausted to a point when they are not able to work.

I must say a few words about individual exchange of commodities. When we speak of free exchange, we mean individual exchange of commodities, which in turn means encouraging the kulaks. What is to be done? We must not close our eyes to the fact that replacing surplus-appropriation with a tax will result in the kulaks coming up under this system more than before. They will come up where they could not before. But it is not with prohibitive measures that this must be combated, but by amalgamation under state auspices and measures taken by the state from above. If you can give the peasant machines, you will be helping him to come up, and when you provide machines or electric power, tens or hundreds of thousands of small kulaks will be wiped out. So long as you cannot give all this, you must give a certain quantity of goods. If you hold the goods in your hands, you are in power; to preclude, deny, renounce any such possibility means making any exchange impossible, not satisfying the middle peasantry, and it will not be possible to get along with it. A greater proportion of peasants in Russia have become middle peasants, and there is nothing to fear in exchange being conducted on an individual basis. Everyone can give something in exchange to the state. One can give his grain surplus, another, garden produce, a third, his labour. Basically the situation is this: we must economically satisfy the middle peasantry and go over to free exchange; otherwise it will be impossible, economically impossible, to preserve the rule of the proletariat in Russia in view of the delay in world revolution. We must clearly realize this and not be afraid to talk about it. In the draft decision on the substitution of a tax in kind for the surplus-appropriation system (the text has been handed out to you) you will find many discrepancies, even contradictions, and because of this we added these words at the end: "The congress, approving in substance (this is a rather loose word covering a great deal of ground) the propositions submitted by the Central Committee on the substitution of a tax in kind for the surplus-appropriation system, instructs the Central Committee of the Party to correlate these propositions with the utmost despatch." We know that they have not been correlated, we had no time to do so. We did not go into the details. The forms of carrying out the tax in practice will be worked out in detail and the tax implemented by a law dealing with the matter which the All-Russian Central Executive Committee and the Council of People's Commissars will issue. The procedure outlined is this: if you adopt the draft today, it will be given the force of a decision at the very first session of the All-Russian Central Executive Committee, which too will issue not a law, but modified regulations; the Council of People's Commissars and the Council of Labour and Defence will later make them into a law, and, what it still more important, issue the practical instructions. It is important that people in the localities should understand the significance of this and lend us assistance.

Why must we replace surplus-appropriation with a tax? Surplus-appropriation implied confiscation of all surpluses and establishment of an obligatory state monopoly. We could not do otherwise, for our need was extreme. Theoretically speaking, state monopoly is not necessarily the best system from the viewpoint of the interests of socialism. A system of taxation and free exchange can be employed as a transitional measure in a peasant country possessing an industry—if this industry operates—and if there is a certain quantity of goods available.

This very turnover is a stimulus, an incentive, a spur to the peasant. The proprietor can and will surely make an effort in his own interest when he knows that all his surplus produce will not be taken away from him, that he will only have to pay a tax, which should whenever possible be established in advance. The basic thing is to have a stimulus, an incentive, a spur for the small farmer to till the soil. We must adapt our state economy to the economy of the middle peasant, which we could not remake in three years and shall not be able to remake in another ten.

The state has faced definite responsibilities in the sphere of food. Because of this the appropriation quotas were increased last year. The tax must be less. The exact figures have not been defined, nor can they be defined. Popov's brochure "Grain Production of the Soviet and Federated Republics" cites data issued by our Central Statistical Board giving exact figures and showing why agricultural production has fallen off.

If there is a crop failure, surpluses cannot be collected because there are none. They would have to be taken out of the peasants' mouths. If the crop does not fail, everybody will go moderately hungry and the state will be saved, or, if we are unable to take from people who themselves cannot eat their fill, the state will perish. This is what we must make clear in our propaganda among the peasants. A fair harvest will mean a surplus of up to five hundred million. This will cover consumption and yield a certain reserve. The crux of the matter lies in providing the peasants with a stimulus, an economic incentive. The small proprietor must be told: "It is your job as a proprietor to produce, and the state will take a minimum tax."

My time is nearly up, I must close. I repeat: we cannot issue a law now. Our resolution suffers from the shortcoming that it is not too well phrased according to legislative standards—laws are not written at a Party congress. Hence we propose that the resolution submitted by the C.C. be adopted in essence and that the C.C. be instructed to co-ordinate the various propositions contained in it. We shall print the text of the resolution and local workers in the various localities will try to co-ordinate and correct it. It cannot be co-ordinated from beginning to end; this is an impossible task, for life takes too many forms. To find the transitional measures is a very difficult task. If we are unable to do this quickly and directly, we shall not lose heart, we shall win through in the end. No thinking peasant will fail to understand that we as the government represent the working class and all those toiling people with whom the working peasants (and they make up nine-tenths of the total) can agree, that any turn back will mean return to the old, tsarist government. The experience of Kronstadt proves this. There they do not want either the Whiteguards or our government—and there is no other government—and as a result find themselves in a situation which speaks best of all in our favour and against any new government.

We are now in a position to come to an agreement with the peasants, and this must be done in practice, skillfully, efficiently, and flexibly. We know the machinery of the Commissariat of Food, we know that it is one of the best we have. Comparing it with others, we can see it is the best, and it must be preserved. But administrative machinery must be subordinated to policy. We will have no use for the splendid machinery of the Commissariat of Food if we cannot establish proper relations with the peasants. In such a case this splendid machinery will serve not our class but Denikin and Kolchak. Leaders must be aware when resolute change, flexibility, skilful transition become politically necessary. A strong machinery must be fit for any manoeuvre. But if the strength of a machinery turns into obdurate unwieldiness and interferes with change, then a struggle is inevitable. Hence, every effort must be made to achieve unfailingly the aim that has been set, to subordinate the machinery completely to politics. Politics is the relationship between classes, and this decides the fate of the republic. The stronger the administrative machinery, the better fitted, as an auxiliary instrument, it is for manoeuvring. If it cannot do this, it is completely useless.

I ask you to bear in mind the fundamental fact that it will take several months to work out all the details and elucidations. Right now we must remember that the main thing is to let the whole world know by radio tonight of our decision, to announce that this congress of the government Party in the main substitutes a tax for the surplus-appropriation system, thereby giving the small farmer a whole series of stimuli to expand his economy, to plant more; that the congress by embarking on this course corrects the system of relations between the proletariat and the peasantry and voices its conviction that in this way the relations of the proletariat and the peasantry will be placed on a durable footing. (*Stormy applause.*)

First printed in full in 1921 in
*The Tenth Congress of the Russian Communist Party. Verbatim Report. (March 8-16, 1921),*
Moscow

Vol. XXXII, pp. 191-205

# REPORT ON THE TACTICS OF THE R.C.P.
# DELIVERED AT THE THIRD CONGRESS
# OF THE COMMUNIST INTERNATIONAL

*July 5, 1921*

*(Excerpt)*

As regards the internal political situation within our republic, I must begin with a detailed examination of class
relationships. Here there has been a change in recent
months inasmuch as we have witnessed the formation of
new organizations of the exploiting class directed against
us. The aim of socialism is to abolish classes. In the forefront of the class of exploiters are the big landowners and
industrial capitalists. To do away with them is a rather
simple matter which may be completed in a few months,
and sometimes even in a few weeks or days. We in Russia
expropriated our exploiters, both the big landowners and
the capitalists. During the war they had no organization of
their own, and acted merely as an adjunct of the armed
forces of the international bourgeoisie. Now that we have
repulsed the offensive of international counter-revolution,
a foreign organization of the Russian bourgeoisie and all
Russian counter-revolutionary parties has been formed. The
total number of Russian émigrés who have settled abroad
may be reckoned at one and a half or two million. In practically every country they publish daily papers, and all the
parties, landlord and petty-bourgeois, not excluding the Socialist-Revolutionaries and the Mensheviks, have numerous
ties with foreign bourgeois elements, that is, they receive
enough money to have a press of their own; we find all our
former political parties without exception working together
abroad, and we see how the "free" Russian press published
there, beginning with the Socialist-Revolutionaries and the

Mensheviks and ending with the ultra-reactionary monarchists, supports the big landowners. In a certain measure
this simplifies our task, for it makes it easier for us to ap-
praise the enemy's forces, his organization, and the political trends in his camp. On the other hand, it, of course,
complicates our work, for these Russian counter-revolutionary émigrés use every means to prepare for struggle
against us. This struggle proves once again that on
the whole the class instincts and class consciousness of the ruling classes are still more highly developed than the consciousness of the oppressed classes,
in spite of the fact that the Russian revolution has done
more in this respect than all the previous revolutions.
There is not a single village in Russia where the people, the
oppressed, have not been shaken up. Yet a level-headed
appraisal of the organization and the political clarity of
the Russian counter-revolutionary émigrés living abroad
will show that the bourgeoisie still is more class-conscious
than the exploited and oppressed. These people try everything, they cunningly make use of every opportunity to
attack Soviet Russia in one way or another in order to dis-
member her. It would be highly instructive—and I believe
that our foreign comrades will do this—to follow systematically the most important aims, the most important tactical
moves, and the most important trends of this Russian counter-revolution. Since it operates mainly abroad, our foreign
comrades will not find it particularly hard to watch this
movement. In some respects we must learn from this enemy.
These counter-revolutionary émigrés are very well informed,
they have an excellent organization, they are good strat-
egists, and I think that systematic comparison, systematic
study of their organization and how they make use of one
or another opportunity coming their way may have a strong
propaganda effect on the working class. This is not general
theory, but practical politics, and here we can see how
much the enemy has learned. The Russian bourgeoisie suffered a crushing defeat in recent years. There is an old
saying that defeat teaches an army a great deal. The defeated army of reaction has learned much, and learned it
well. It is learning with the greatest avidity, and it really

has made great progress. At the time when we took power by storm, the Russian bourgeoisie was unorganized, politically underdeveloped. Now, I believe, it stands at the present-day West-European level of development. We must reckon with this, we must improve our own organizations and methods, and to this end we shall exert every effort. We found it comparatively easy to deal with these two exploiting classes, and I believe that other revolutions will find it no harder.

But besides this exploiting class, there exists a class of small producers and small farmers in nearly all capitalist countries—with the exception, perhaps, of Britain. The struggle against the last two classes is now the principal issue in the revolution. To get rid of them, methods other than those used against the big landowners and capitalists are needed. We could simply expropriate and drive out both of these classes, which is what we did. But we cannot do the same with the remaining capitalist classes, the small producers and the petty bourgeoisie, which are to be found in all countries. In most capitalist countries these classes represent a very strong minority, roughly 30 to 45 per cent of the population. If we add to them the petty-bourgeois element of the working class, we get even more than 50 per cent. They cannot be expropriated or driven out—here the fight must be carried on differently. The significance of the period Russia is now entering, from the international standpoint—if we look upon the international revolution as a single process—is essentially that we must solve in practice the question of the attitude of the proletariat toward the last capitalist class in Russia. All Marxists have solved this problem quite easily and well in theory, but theory is one thing and practice another, and solving the question in practice and solving it in theory are two entirely different things. We know definitely that we have made big mistakes. From the international standpoint the fact that we are seeking to determine the attitude of the proletariat which is in power to the last capitalist class, to the very foundation of capitalism, to small property, to the small producer, represents tremendous progress. This question has now confronted us in practice. I think we can solve this task. At any rate the experiment we are making will be of benefit to coming proletarian revolutions, and they will be able to prepare better technically to solve this question.

I have sought to analyze the question of the attitude of the proletariat to the peasantry in my theses. This is the first time in history that there exists a state with only these two classes—the proletariat and the peasantry. The latter constitutes the vast majority of the population. It is of course a very backward class. What practical forms does the attitude of the proletariat in power toward the peasantry assume in the course of the revolution? The first form is alliance, close alliance. This is a very difficult task, but at any rate it is a feasible one economically and politically.

How did we approach this question in practice? We concluded an alliance with the peasantry. We understand this alliance thus: the proletariat emancipates the peasantry from exploitation by the bourgeoisie, from its leadership and influence, and wins it over for joint struggle to defeat the exploiters.

The Mensheviks reason thus: the peasantry constitute the majority, and since we are pure democrats, the decision rests with the majority. But since the peasantry cannot be independent, in practice this means nothing but restoration of capitalism. The slogan is the same: alliance with the peasants. For us, however, this means strengthening and consolidating the proletariat. We have sought to give effect to this alliance between the proletariat and the peasantry, with a military alliance as the first stage. The three-year civil war created enormous difficulties, but in a certain respect it made our task easier. This may sound strange, yet it is so. War was nothing new to the peasants; war against the exploiters, against the big landowners, was something they fully understood. Huge masses of peasants sided with us. In spite of the vast distances, in spite of the fact that most of our peasants can neither read nor write, they readily accepted our propaganda. This proves that the broad masses—just as in the most advanced countries—learn far better through their own practical experience than from books. In our country the accumulation of practical experience by the peasants was facilitated also by the exceptional size of Russia and the fact that different sections of the country could pass through different stages of development at the one and the same time.

The counter-revolution was able to win temporarily in Siberia and the Ukraine because the bourgeoisie there was backed by the peasantry, because the peasants were against us. Peasants often said: "We are Bolsheviks, but not Communists. We are for the Bolsheviks, because they drove out the landlords, but not for the Communists, because they are against individual economy." And so for some time the counter-revolution was victorious in Siberia and the Ukraine, because the bourgeoisie succeeded in gaining influence over the peasants; but a very short period was sufficient to open the peasants' eyes. Within a brief space of time they gained practical experience and soon declared: "Yes, the Bolsheviks are rather unpleasant people; we do not like them, but for all that they are better than the Whiteguards and the Constituent Assembly." For them "Constituent Assembly" is a term of opprobrium. Not only advanced Communists, but the peasants regard it as such. They know by experience that the Constituent Assembly and the Whiteguards mean one and the same thing, and that the first is inevitably followed by the second. The Mensheviks also advocate, for their own ends, a military alliance with the peasantry, but fail to see that such an alliance alone is not enough. A military alliance cannot exist without an economic alliance. For we do not live on air alone; our alliance with the peasants could under no circumstances last long without an economic foundation, which is the basis of our victory in the war against our bourgeoisie, for our bourgeoisie has united with the entire international bourgeoisie.

The basis of this economic alliance between us and the peasants was, of course, very simple, even crude. The peasant received from us all the land and support against the big landowner. We were to get food in exchange. This alliance was something altogether new, and was not founded on the usual relations between commodity-producers and consumers. Our peasants understood this far better than the heroes of the Second and Second-and-a-Half Internationals. "These Bolsheviks are stern leaders," they told themselves, "but for all that they are our own kind." However it was, we laid in this way the foundations of a new economic alliance. The peasants gave their produce to the Red Army, and the Red Army helped them to defend their holdings. This is something that is always forgotten by the heroes of the Second International, who, like Otto Bauer, have no idea whatever of the real situation. We admit that the original form of the alliance was very primitive and that we made very many mistakes. But we had to act with the utmost speed, we had to organize the supply of the army at all costs. During the civil war we were cut off from all of Russia's grain-producing areas. Our position was appalling, and it seems nothing short of a miracle that the Russian people and working class were able to bear so much suffering, want, and privation while possessing nothing but an indomitable will to victory. (*Lively approval and applause.*)

When the civil war ended, a task of a different order confronted us. If the country had not been ruined to the extent it was after seven years of continuous war, a less painful transition might have been possible to a new form of alliance between the proletariat and the peasantry. But the difficult conditions prevailing in the country were aggravated further by crop failure, shortage of fodder, etc. As a result, the privation suffered by the peasants grew unbearable. We had to show the broad masses of the peasantry at once that we were ready, without in the slightest departing from our revolutionary course, to change our policy so that the peasants could say: the Bolsheviks want immediately and without fail to improve our unbearable condition.

So our economic policy changed: the tax in kind took the place of requisitioning. This was not thought out at once. In the Bolshevik press you can find a number of proposals published over a period of months, but no project really promising success was devised. But this is not important. The important thing is that we changed our economic policy exclusively out of practical considerations dictated by the circumstances. Crop failure, shortage of fodder, lack of fuel—all this naturally exercises a decisive effect on economy as a whole, peasant economy included. If the peasantry goes on strike, we shall have no firewood. And if we have no firewood, the factories will have to stop. The economic crisis arising from the disastrous crop failure and shortage of fodder thus assumed gigantic proportions in the spring of 1921. All this was the result of the three years of civil war. The peasantry had to be shown that we can and want to change our policy quickly, in order to alleviate their need immediately. We have always said—this was brought up at the Second Congress too—that the revolution demands sacrifices. There are comrades, however, who resort to the following argument in their propaganda: we are ready to make the revolution, but it should not be too painful. If I am not mistaken, this idea was put forth by Comrade Smeral in his speech at the Czechoslovak Party congress. I read about it in a report published in the Reichenberg *Vorwärts*. They evidently have a slightly Leftist wing there, and hence this source cannot be considered absolutely unbiassed. At any rate I must say that if Smeral made such a statement, he is wrong. Several speakers who addressed the above congress after Smeral declared: "Yes, we shall follow Smeral, for in this way we shall avoid civil war." If all this is true, I must say that agitation of this kind is not communist and not revolutionary. Every revolution naturally entails enormous sacrifices for the class that makes it. What distinguishes a revolution from an ordinary struggle is that the number of people taking part in it is ten times, a hundred times greater, and hence every revolution involves sacrifice not only on the part of individuals, but of a whole class. The dictatorship of the proletariat in Russia entailed such sacrifices, such want, and such privation on the part of the ruling class, the proletariat, as history had never known, and it is highly probable that exactly the same will happen in every other country.

The question arises: how are we to distribute the burden of these hardships? We govern the state. We are to some extent in a position to distribute the burden, to impose it on several classes, and hence relatively to alleviate the condition of certain sections of the population. What principle should we be guided by? The principle of justice or that of the majority? No. We must be practical. We must distribute

the burden so as to preserve the rule of the proletariat. This
is our sole principle. At the beginning of the revolution the
working class had to suffer incredible want. Today I can
note that our food policy has been more and more successful from year to year. And in general the situation has undoubtedly improved. Yet the peasants have certainly gained
more in Russia from the revolution than the working class.
On this score there can be no doubt. When regarded from
the viewpoint of theory, this fact naturally shows that our
revolution has been to a certain degree a bourgeois revolution. When Kautsky advanced this argument against us,
we laughed at him. Obviously, a revolution without expropriation of large land holdings, a revolution that does not
oust the big landowners and divide up the land, is a bourgeois, not a socialist revolution. As it was, however, we
were the only Party that was able to carry the bourgeois
revolution to its consummation and to facilitate the struggle for a socialist revolution. Soviet government and the Soviet system are institutions of the socialist state. We have already established these institutions, but the economic relations between the peasantry and the proletariat are a problem still to be solved. Much still remains to be done, and
the outcome of our efforts will depend on whether we shall
be able to solve this problem or not. And so, distribution of
the burden of hardships is in practice one of the most difficult tasks. Generally speaking, there has been an improvement in the position of the peasantry, while the working
class has had to suffer severely—and suffer precisely because it is giving effect to its dictatorship.

I have already said that the shortage of fodder and the
crop failure caused in the spring of 1921 the most appalling
want among the peasantry, who constitute the majority in
our country. We cannot exist without good relations with
the peasant masses. Hence we set ourselves the task of rendering them immediate assistance. The condition of the
working class is exceedingly grave. It is suffering terribly.
Nevertheless, the politically most advanced elements realize that, in the interests of the dictatorship of the working
class, we must exert every effort to help the peasantry at
whatever cost. The vanguard of the working class has un-

derstood this, but there still are people in this vanguard who cannot grasp it, who are too weary to understand it. They regarded it as a mistake, and began to talk about opportunism. The Bolsheviks, they said, are helping the peasants. The peasant, who exploits us, they said, is getting everything he wants, while the worker goes hungry. But is this opportunism? We help the peasants because without alliance with them the political power of the proletariat would be impossible, it could not be preserved. It was precisely this motive of expediency, and not of fair distribution of the burden, that was decisive for us. We help the peasants because this is absolutely necessary if we are to preserve our political power. The supreme principle of the dictatorship of the proletariat is the maintenance of an alliance between it and the peasantry so that the proletariat should continue to play the leading role and retain state power.

The only means of doing this we could find was to go over to a tax in kind; this transition was an inevitable outcome of the struggle. In the coming year we shall levy this tax for the first time. So far this principle has not been tried out in practice. We must pass over from a military to an economic alliance, and from the standpoint of theory, the only basis for the latter is the introduction of a tax in kind. From the standpoint of theory, this offers the only possibility of arriving at a really solid economic basis for the socialist society. The socialized factory will give the peasant its products, and the peasant will give grain in return. This is the only possible form of existence of the socialist society, the only form of socialist construction in a country where small peasants constitute the majority, or at any rate, a very substantial minority. The peasant will give a part of his product in the form of a tax, and another part in exchange for the products of the socialist factory or through commodity exchange.

First printed in full in *Third World Congress of the Communist International. Verbatim Report,* Petrograd, 1922

Vol. XXXII, pp. 460-66

# POLITICAL REPORT OF THE CENTRAL COMMITTEE OF THE R.C.P. (B.) DELIVERED AT THE ELEVENTH CONGRESS OF THE R.C.P. (B.)

*March 27, 1922*

## (Excerpt)

The main question, of course, is the new economic policy. The predominant question during the year under review has been the new economic policy. If we have any important, serious, and irrevocable gain to record for this year (and I am not so very sure that we have), it is that we have learnt something of the principles of this new economic policy. Indeed, during the past year we have learnt a great deal about the new economic policy. And the test of whether we have really learnt anything, and to what extent, will probably be made by subsequent events of a kind which we ourselves can do little to determine, as, for example, the impending financial crisis. I think that the most important thing that we must keep in mind in connection with the new economic policy, as a basis for all our arguments, as a means of testing our experience during the past year, and of learning practical lessons for the ensuing year, are the following three points.

First, the new economic policy is important for us primarily as a means of testing whether we are really establishing a bond with peasant economy. In the preceding period of development of our revolution, when all our attention and all our efforts were concentrated mainly on, or almost entirely absorbed by the task of repelling invasion, we could not devote the necessary attention to this bond; we had other things to think about. When we were confronted by the absolutely urgent and overshadowing task of warding off the danger of being immediately strangled by the gigantic forces of world imperialism, we could, to a certain extent, afford to, and had to, ignore this bond.

The turn towards the new economic policy was decided on at the last congress with exceptional unanimity, with even greater unanimity than other questions have been decided by our Party (which, it must be admitted, is generally distinguished for its unanimity). This unanimity showed that the need for a new approach to socialist economy had fully matured. People who differed on many questions, and who appraised the situation from different angles, unanimously and very quickly and unhesitatingly agreed that we lacked a real approach to socialist economy, to the task of building its foundation, and that the only means of finding this approach was the new economic policy. Owing to the course taken by the development of military events, by the development of political events, by the development of capitalism in the old, cultured West, and owing to the social and political conditions that developed in the colonies, we were the first to make a breach in the old bourgeois world at a time when our country was economically, if not the most backward country in the world, one of the most backward countries. The vast majority of the peasants in our country are engaged in small, individual husbandry. The items of our communist programme of socialization that we were able to apply immediately were to a certain degree outside the sphere of activity of the broad masses of the peasantry, upon whom we imposed very heavy obligations on the plea that war brooked no hesitation in this matter. Taken as a whole this plea was accepted by the peasantry, notwithstanding the inevitable mistakes that we committed. On the whole, the masses of the peasantry realized and understood that the enormous burdens that were imposed upon them were necessary in order to save the workers' and peasants' rule from the landlords, in order to save ourselves from the noose of capitalist invasion which threatened to rob us of all the gains of the revolution. But there was no bond between peasant economy and the economy that was being built up in the nationalized, socialized factories and state farms.

We saw this clearly at the last Party congress. We saw

it so clearly that there was no hesitation whatever in the
Party on the question as to whether the new economic policy was inevitable or not.

It is amusing to read what is said about our decision
in the unusually extensive press of the various Russian
parties abroad. There are only trifling differences in the
opinions they express. Living in the past, they continue
to reiterate that the Left Communists are still opposed to
the new economic policy. In 1921, they remembered what
had occurred in 1918 and what our Left Communists themselves have forgotten; and they go on repeating this over
and over again, assuring the world that these Bolsheviks
are a very sly and false lot, and that they are concealing
from Europe that there are disagreements in their ranks.
Reading this, one says to oneself: "Let them go on fooling
themselves." If this is what they imagine is going on in
our country, we can judge the degree of intelligence of
these allegedly highly educated old fogies who have fled
abroad. We know that there have been no disagreements in
our ranks—there have been no disagreements because the
practical necessity of a different approach to the task of
building the foundation of socialist economy was clear
to all.

The bond between peasant economy and the new economy we tried to create was lacking. Does it exist now?
Not yet. We are only approaching it. The whole significance of the new economic policy—which our press still
often searches for everywhere except where it should
search—the whole purpose of this policy is to find the bond
with the new economy which we are creating with such
enormous effort. That is what stands to our credit; without
it we would not be Communist revolutionaries.

We began to build the new economy in an entirely new
way, completely ignoring the old. Had we not begun to
build it, we would have been utterly defeated in the very
first months, in the very first years. But the fact that
we began to build this new economy with such audacity
does not mean that we must obstinately continue in the
same way. Why does it follow that we should? It does not
follow at all.

From the very beginning we said that we had undertaken an entirely new task, and that unless we received speedy assistance from our comrades, the workers in the capitalistically more developed countries, we should encounter incredible difficulties and undoubtedly commit a number of mistakes. The main thing is to be able dispassionately to examine where such mistakes have been made and to start again from the beginning. If we begin from the beginning, not twice, but many times, it will show that we are not bound by prejudice, and that we are approaching our task, the greatest task in the world, with a sober outlook.

The main thing in the question of the new economic policy at present is properly to assimilate the experience of the past year. This must be done, and we want to do it. And if we want to achieve this, come what may (and we do want to achieve it, and shall achieve it!), we must know that the aim of the new economic policy, the fundamental, decisive, and overriding aim, is to establish a bond between the new economy that we have begun to build (very dably, very clumsily, but have begun to build nevertheless, on the basis of an entirely new, socialist economy, of a new system of production and distribution), and peasant economy, by which millions and millions of peasants obtain their livelihood.

This bond has been lacking, and it is this bond that we must create before everything else. Everything else must be subordinated to this. We have still to ascertain to what extent the new economic policy has succeeded in creating this bond and not in destroying what we have begun so clumsily to build.

We are building our economy in conjunction with the peasantry. We shall have to alter it many times and build in such a way that it will serve as a bond between our socialist work on large-scale industry and agriculture and the work on which every peasant is engaged as best he can, struggling out of poverty without philosophizing (for how can philosophizing help him to extricate himself from his position and save him from the very real danger of a painful death from starvation?).

We must reveal this bond so that we may see it clearly, so that all the people may see it, so that the whole mass of the peasantry may see that there is a connection be- tween their present severe, incredibly ruined, incredibly im- poverished and painful existence and the work which is being done for the sake of remote socialist ideals. We must bring about a situation when the ordinary rank-and- file toiler realizes that he has obtained some improvement, and that he has obtained it not in the way a few peasants obtained improvements under the rule of landlordism and capitalism, when every improvement (undoubtedly there were improvements and very big ones) was accompanied by insult, derision, and mockery for the muzhik, by vio- lence against the masses, which not a single peasant has forgotten, and which will not be forgotten in Russia for decades. Our aim is to restore the bond, to prove to the peasant by deeds that we are beginning with what is in- telligible, familiar, and immediately accessible to him, in spite of his poverty, and not with something remote and fantastic from the peasant's point of view. We must prove that we can help him and that in this period, when the small peasant is in a state of appalling ruin, impoverish- ment, and starvation, Communists are really helping him. Either we prove that, or he will send us to the devil. That is absolutely inevitable.

This is the significance of the new economic policy; this is the basis of our entire policy; this is the major lesson taught by the whole of the past year's experience in apply- ing the new economic policy, and, so to speak, our main political rule for the coming year. The peasant is allow- ing us credit, and, of course, after what he has lived through, he cannot do otherwise. Taken in the mass, the peasants go on saying: "Well, if you are not able to do it yet, we shall wait; perhaps you will learn." But this cre- dit cannot be inexhaustible.

This we must know; but having obtained credit we must nevertheless hurry. We must know that the time is approaching when this peasant country will no longer give us credit, when it will demand cash, to use a commercial term. "You have postponed payment for so many months, so many years. But by this time, dear rulers, you must have learnt the soundest and most reliable method of helping us to extricate ourselves from poverty, want, starvation, and ruin. You can do it, you have proved it." This is the examination that we shall inevitably have to face; and in the last analysis, this examination will decide everything: the fate of NEP and the fate of communist government in Russia.

Shall we accomplish our immediate task or not? Is this NEP fit for anything or not? If the retreat turns out to be the correct tactics, we must link up with the peasant masses while in retreat, and march forward with them a hundred times more slowly, but firmly and unswervingly, in a way that will always make it apparent to them that we are really marching forward. Then our cause will be absolutely invincible, and no power on earth can vanquish us. We did not accomplish this in the first year. We must say this quite frankly. And I am profoundly convinced (and our new economic policy enables us to draw this conclusion quite definitely and firmly) that if we appreciate the enormous danger that is concealed in NEP and concentrate all our forces on its weak points, we shall solve this problem.

Link up with the peasant masses, with the rank-and-file toiling peasants, and begin to move forward immeasurably, infinitely more slowly than we expected, but in such a way that the entire mass will actually move forward with us. If we do that we shall in time get such an acceleration of progress as we cannot dream of now. This, in my opinion, is the first fundamental political lesson of the new economic policy.

Printed in 1922 in *Eleventh Congress of the Russian Communist Party (Bolsheviks). Verbatim Report*, Moscow, Publishing Department of C.C. R.C.P.

Vol. XXXIII, pp. 238-44

# ON CO-OPERATION

## I

I think that not enough attention is being paid to the co-operative movement in our country. It is hardly likely that everyone understands that now, since the October Revolution, and quite apart from NEP (on the contrary, in this connection we must say, precisely because of NEP), our co-operative movement assumes really exceptional importance. There was much fantasy in the dreams of the old co-operators. Often they were ridiculously fantastic. But why were they fantastic? Because these old co-operators did not understand the fundamental, root significance of the political struggle of the working class for the overthrow of the rule of the exploiters. We have overthrown the rule of the exploiters, and much that was fantastic, even romantic and banal in the dreams of the old co-operators is now becoming the most unvarnished reality.

Indeed, since state power is in the hands of the working class, since this state power owns all the means of production, the only task that really remains for us to perform is to organize the population in co-operative societies. When the population is organized in co-operative societies to the utmost, the socialism which in the past was legitimately treated with ridicule, scorn, and contempt by those who were justly convinced that it was necessary to wage the class struggle, the struggle for political power, etc., automatically achieves its aims. But not all comrades understand how vastly, how infinitely important it is now to organize the population of Russia in co-operative societies. By adopting NEP we made a concession to the peasant as a trader, to the principle of private trade;

it is precisely for this reason (contrary to what some people think) that the co-operative movement assumes such immense importance. As a matter of fact, all that we need under NEP is to organize the population of Russia in co-operative societies thoroughly enough, on a sufficiently wide scale, for now we have found that degree of the combination of private interest, private trading interest, with state supervision and control of this interest, that degree of its subordination to the common interests that was formerly the stumbling-block for very many Socialists. As a matter of fact, the power of state over all large-scale means of production, the power of state in the hands of the proletariat, the alliance of this proletariat with the many millions of small and very small peasants, the assured leadership of the peasantry by the proletariat, etc.—is not this all that is necessary in order to build a complete socialist society from the co-operatives, from, the co-operatives alone, which we formerly treated as huckstering and which from a certain aspect we have the right to treat as such now, under NEP? Is this not all that is necessary for the purpose of building a complete socialist society? This is not yet the building of socialist society, but it is all that is necessary and sufficient for this building.

This is what many of our practical workers underrate. They look down upon our co-operative societies with contempt and fail to appreciate their exceptional importance, first, from the standpoint of principle (the means of production are owned by the state) and, second, from the standpoint of the transition to the new order by means that will be *simplest, easiest, and most intelligible for the peasant.*

But this again is the most important thing. It is one thing to draw up fantastic plans for building socialism by means of all sorts of workers' associations; but it is quite another thing to learn to build socialism practically, in such a way that *every* small peasant may take part in the work of construction. This is the stage we have reached now. And there is no doubt that, having reached it, we take too little advantage of it.

25*

We went too far in introducing NEP not in that we attached too much importance to the principle of free industry and trade; we went too far in introducing NEP in that we lost sight of the co-operatives, in that we now underrate the co-operatives, in that we are already beginning to forget the vast importance of the co-operatives from the two standpoints mentioned above.

I now propose to discuss with the reader what can and should at once be done practically on the basis of this "co-operative" principle. By what means can we and should we start at once to develop this "co-operative" principle so that its socialist meaning may be clear to all?

Politically, we must place the co-operatives in the position of always enjoying not only privileges in general, but privileges of a purely material character (bank rate, etc.). The co-operatives must be granted state loans which should exceed, even if not much, the loans we grant to the private enterprises, even as large as those granted to heavy industry, etc.

Every social system arises only with the financial assistance of a definite class. There is no need to mention the hundreds and hundreds of millions of rubles that the birth of "free" capitalism cost. Now we must realize and apply in our practical work the fact that the social system which we must now assist more than usual is the co-operative system. But it must be assisted in the real sense of the word, i.e., it will not be enough to interpret assistance to mean assistance for any kind of co-operative trade; by assistance we must mean assistance for co-operative trade in which *really large masses of the population really take part.* It is certainly a correct form of assistance to give a bonus to peasants who take part in co-operative trade; but the whole point is to verify the nature of this participation, to verify the conscious motives behind it, to verify its quality. Strictly speaking, when a co-operator goes to a village and opens a co-operative store, the people take no part in this whatever; but at the same time, guided by their own interests, the people will hasten to try to take part in it.

There is another aspect to this question. We have not very much more to do from the point of view of the "civilized" (primarily, literate) European to induce absolutely everyone to take not a passive, but an active part in co-operative operations. Strictly speaking, there is *"only"* one more thing we have to do, and that is, to make our people so "civilized" as to understand all the advantages of everybody taking part in the work of the co-operatives and to organize this participation. *"Only"* this. We now need no other cunning devices to enable us to pass to socialism. But to achieve this "only," a complete revolution is needed; the entire people must go through a whole period of cultural development. Therefore, our rule must be: as little philosophizing and as few acrobatics as possible. In this respect NEP is an advance in that it is suited to the level of the most ordinary peasant, in that it does not demand anything higher of him. But it will take a whole historical epoch to get the entire population to take part in the work of the co-operatives through NEP. At best we can achieve this in one or two decades. Nevertheless, this will be a special historical epoch, and without this historical epoch, without universal literacy, without a proper degree of efficiency, without sufficiently training the population to acquire the habit of reading books, and without the material basis for this, without certain safeguards against, say, bad harvests, famine, etc.—without this we shall fail to achieve our object. The whole thing now is to learn to combine the wide revolutionary range of action, the revolutionary enthusiasm which we have displayed and displayed sufficiently and crowned with complete success— to learn to combine this with (I am almost ready to say) the ability to be an efficient and capable merchant, which is fully sufficient to be a good co-operator. By ability to be a merchant I mean the ability to be a cultured merchant. Let those Russians, or plain peasants, who imagine that since they trade they can be good merchants, get this well into their heads. It does not follow at all. They trade, but this is far from being cultured merchants. They are now trading in an Asiatic manner; but to be a merchant one must be able to trade in a European manner. A whole epoch separates them from that.

In conclusion: a number of economic, financial, and banking privileges must be granted to the co-operatives— this is the way our socialist state must promote the new principle on which the population must be organized. But this is only the general outline of the task; it does not define, depict in detail the entire content of the practical tasks, i.e., we must ascertain what form of "bonus" we should give for organizing the co-operatives (and the terms on which we should give it), the form of bonus by which we shall sufficiently assist the co-operatives, the form of bonus by means of which we shall obtain the civilized co-operator. And a system of civilized co-operators under the social ownership of the means of production, with the class victory of the proletariat over the bourgeoisie, is the system of socialism.

January 4, 1923

## II

Whenever I wrote about the new economic policy I always quoted the article on state capitalism which I wrote in 1918. More than once this has roused doubts in the minds of certain young comrades. But their doubts arose mainly in connection with abstract political questions.

It seemed to them that the term state capitalism cannot be applied to the system under which the means of production are owned by the working class, and in which the working class holds political power. They failed to observe, however, that I used the term "state capitalism," *firstly*, in order to establish the historical connection between our present position and the position I held in my controversy with the so-called Left Communists; and already at that time I argued that state capitalism would be superior to the existing economy. It was important for me to show the continuity between ordinary state capitalism and the unusual, even very unusual, state capitalism to which I referred in introducing the reader to the new economic policy. *Secondly*, I always attached importance to the practical aim. And the practical aim of our new economic policy was to benefit by concessions. Undoubtedly, under the conditions prevailing in our country, concessions would have been a pure type of state capitalism. That is how I conceived the argument about state capitalism.

But there is another aspect of the matter for which we may need state capitalism, or at least, something in juxtaposition with it. This is the question of co-operation.

There is no doubt that under the capitalist state the co-operatives are collective capitalist institutions. Nor is there any doubt that under our present economic conditions, when we combine private capitalist enterprises—but

situated on public land and controlled by the state power
which is in the hands of the working class—with enterprises of a consistently socialist type (the means of production, the land on which the enterprises are situated, and
the enterprises as a whole, belonging to the state) the
question of a third type of enterprise arises, which formerly
was not regarded as an independent type differing in principle from the others, viz., co-operative enterprises. Under
private capitalism, co-operative enterprises differ from capitalist enterprises as collective enterprises differ from private enterprises. Under state capitalism, co-operative enterprises differ from state capitalist enterprises, firstly, in
that they are private enterprises, and, secondly, in that they
are collective enterprises. Under our present system, co-
operative enterprises differ from private capitalist enterprises because they are collective enterprises, but they do
not differ from socialist enterprises if the land on which
they are situated and the means of production belong to
the state, i.e., the working class.

This circumstance is not taken into consideration sufficiently when co-operation is discussed. It is forgotten
that owing to the special features of our state system, our
co-operatives acquire an altogether exceptional significance. If we exclude concessions, which, incidentally, we
have not granted on any considerable scale, co-operation,
under our conditions, very often entirely coincides with
socialism.

I shall explain my idea. Why were the plans of the old
co-operators, from Robert Owen onwards, fantastic? Because they dreamt of peacefully transforming present-day
society into socialism without taking into account fundamental questions like that of the class struggle, of the
working class capturing political power, of overthrowing
the rule of the exploiting class. That is why we are right
in regarding this "co-operative" socialism as being entirely fantastic, something romantic, in seeing something
even banal in the dream of being able to transform the
class enemies into class collaborators and the class struggle into class peace (so-called civil peace) merely by organizing the population in co-operative societies.

Undoubtedly we were right from the point of view of the fundamental task of the present day, for socialism cannot be established without the class struggle for political power in the state.

But see how things have changed now that state power is in the hands of the working class, now that the political power of the exploiters is overthrown, and all the means of production (except those which the workers' state voluntarily loans to the exploiters for a certain time and on definite terms in the form of concessions) are owned by the working class.

Now we have the right to say that for us, the mere growth of co-operation (with the "slight" exception mentioned above) is identical with the growth of socialism, and at the same time we must admit that a radical change has taken place in our whole outlook on socialism. This radical change lies in that formerly we placed, and had to place, the main weight of emphasis on the political struggle, on revolution, on winning power, etc. Now the weight of emphasis is changing, and is being shifted to peaceful, organizational, "cultural" work. I would be prepared to say that the weight of emphasis should be placed on educational work were it not for our international relations, were it not for the fact that we have to fight for our position on a world scale. If we leave that aside, however, and confine ourselves entirely to internal economic relations, the weight of emphasis in our work is certainly shifted to educational work.

We are confronted by two main tasks which constitute the epoch: the first is to reorganize our machinery of state, which is utterly useless, and which we took over in its entirety from the preceding epoch; during the past five years of struggle we did not, and could not, make any serious changes in it. The second is to conduct educational work among the peasants. And the economic object of this educational work among the peasants is to organize them in co-operative societies. If the whole of the peasantry were organized in co-operatives, we would be standing firmly with both feet on the soil of socialism. But the organization of the entire peasantry in co-operative societies presupposes such a standard of culture among the peasants (precisely among the peasants as the overwhelming mass) that this cannot be achieved without a complete cultural revolution.

Our opponents have told us more than once that we are embarking on a rash task in undertaking to implant socialism in an insufficiently cultured country. But they were mistaken, misled by the fact that we did not start from the end that was prescribed by theory (the theory that all sorts of pedants subscribe to), and that in our country the political and social revolution preceded the cultural revolution, the cultural revolution which now confronts us.

This cultural revolution would now be sufficient to transform our country into a completely socialist country; but it bristles with immense difficulties of a purely educational (for we are illiterate) and material character (for to be cultured we must achieve a certain development of the material means of production, we must have some material base).

January 6, 1923

First published in *Pravda*,
Nos. 115 and 116, May 26 and 27,
1923
Signed: N. Lenin

Vol. XXXIII, pp. 427-35

# BETTER FEWER, BUT BETTER

## *(Excerpt)*

The general feature of our present social life is the following: we have destroyed capitalist industry and have done our best to raze to the ground the medieval institutions, landlordism, and thus created a small and very small peasantry, which is following the lead of the proletariat because it believes in the results of its revolutionary work. It is not easy, however, to hold on until the socialist revolution is victorious in the more developed countries merely with the aid of this confidence, because economic necessity, especially under NEP, keeps the productivity of labour of the small and very small peasants at an extremely low level. Moreover, the international situation, too, threw Russia back and, taken as a whole, forced the productivity of the labour of the people considerably below the pre-war level. The West-European capitalist states, sometimes deliberately and sometimes unconsciously, did everything possible to throw us back, to utilize the elements of civil war in Russia in order to spread as much ruin in the country as possible. It was precisely this way out of the imperialist war that seemed to hold out many advantages. These states argued somewhat as follows: "If we fail to overthrow the revolutionary system in Russia, we shall, at all events, hinder her progress towards socialism." And from their point of view they could argue in no other way. In the end, their problem was half-solved. They failed to overthrow the new system that was created by the revolution; but they did prevent it from at once taking the step forward that would have justified the fore-

casts of the Socialists, that would have enabled it to develop the productive forces with enormous speed, to develop all the potentialities which, taken together, would
have produced socialism and thus vividly demonstrated to
all and sundry that socialism contains within itself gigantic forces and that mankind had now entered into a new
stage of development which has extraordinarily brilliant
prospects.

The system of international relationships which has
now taken shape is a system in which one of the states of
Europe, viz., Germany, has been enslaved by the victor
countries. Furthermore, a number of states, namely, the
oldest states in the West, are in a position to utilize their
victory to make a number of insignificant concessions to
their oppressed classes—concessions which, insignificant
though they are, nevertheless retard the revolutionary
movement in those countries and create some semblance
of "social peace."

At the same time, precisely as a result of the last imperialist war, a number of countries—the East, India,
China, etc.—have been completely dislodged from their
groove. Their development has definitely shifted to the general European capitalist lines. The general European fer-
ment has begun to affect them, and it is now clear to the
whole world that they have been drawn into a process of
development that cannot but lead to a crisis in the whole
of world capitalism.

Thus, at the present time we are confronted with the
question: shall we be able to hold on with our small and
very small peasant production, and in our present state
of ruin, while the West-European capitalist countries are
consummating their development towards socialism? But
they are consummating it not as we formerly expected.
They are not consummating it by the gradual "maturing"
of socialism, but by the exploitation of some countries by
others, by the exploitation of the first of the countries to
be vanquished in the imperialist war combined with the exploitation of the whole of the East. On the other hand, precisely as a result of the first imperialist war, the East has

been definitely drawn into the revolutionary movement, has been definitely drawn into the general maelstrom of the world revolutionary movement.

What tactics does this situation prescribe for our country? Obviously the following: we must display extreme caution so as to preserve our workers' government and enable it to retain its leadership and authority over our small and very small peasantry. We have the advantage in that the whole world is now passing into a movement that must give rise to a world socialist revolution. But we are labouring under the disadvantage that the imperialists have succeeded in splitting the world into two camps; and this split is made more complicated by the fact that it is extremely difficult for Germany, which is really a land of advanced, cultured, capitalist development, to rise to her feet. All the capitalist powers of what is called the West are pecking at her and preventing her from rising. On the other hand, the entire East, with its hundreds of millions of exploited toilers reduced to the last degree of human suffering, has been forced into such a position that its physical and material strength cannot possibly be compared with the physical, material, and military strength of any of the much smaller West-European states.

Can we save ourselves from the impending conflict with these imperialist countries? May we hope that the internal antagonisms and conflicts between the thriving imperialist countries of the West and the thriving imperialist countries of the East will give us a second respite, as was the case when the campaign of the West-European counter-revolution in support of the Russian counter-revolution broke down owing to the antagonisms in the camp of the counter-revolutionaries in the West and the East, in the camp of the Eastern and Western exploiters, in the camp of Japan and America?

I think the reply to this question should be that the answer depends upon too many factors, and that the outcome of the struggle as a whole can be foreseen only because we know that in the long run capitalism itself is educating and training the vast majority of the population of the globe for the struggle.

In the last analysis, the outcome of the struggle will
be determined by the fact that Russia, India, China, etc.,
account for the overwhelming majority of the population
of the globe. And it is precisely this majority that, during
the past few years, has been drawn into the struggle for
emancipation with extraordinary rapidity, so that in this
respect there cannot be the slightest shadow of doubt what
the final outcome of the world struggle will be. In this
sense, the complete victory of socialism is fully and absolutely assured.

But what interests us is not the inevitability of this
complete victory of socialism, but the tactics which we,
the Russian Communist Party, we, the Russian Soviet government, should pursue to prevent the West-European
counter-revolutionary states from crushing us. To ensure
our existence until the next military conflict between the
counter-revolutionary imperialist West and the revolutionary and nationalist East, between the most civilized
countries of the world and the orientally backward countries, which, however, account for the majority, this majority must become civilized with all speed. We, too, lack
sufficient civilization to enable us to pass straight on to
socialism, although we have the political requisites for this.
We must adopt the following tactics, or pursue the following policy to save ourselves.

We must strive to build up a state in which the workers
retain their leadership in relation to the peasants, in
which they retain the confidence of the peasants, and, by
exercising the greatest economy, remove every trace of extravagance from our social relations.

We must reduce our state apparatus to the utmost degree of economy. We must remove from it all traces of
extravagance, of which so much has been left over from
tsarist Russia, from its bureaucratic capitalist apparatus.

Will not this be the reign of peasant narrowness?

No. If we see to it that the working class retains its
leadership of the peasantry, we shall be able, by exercising
the greatest possible economy in the economic life of our
state, to use every kopek we save to develop our large-
scale machine industry, to develop electrification, the

hydraulic extraction of peat, to finish the construction of Volkhovstroi, etc.

In this, and this alone, lies our hope. Only when we have done this will we, speaking figuratively, be able to change horses, to change from the peasant, muzhik horse of poverty, from the horse of economy fit for a ruined peasant country, to the horse which the proletariat is seeking and cannot but seek—the horse of large-scale machine industry, of electrification, of Volkhovstroi, etc.

March 2, 1923

*Pravda*, No. 49,
March 4, 1923

Vol. XXXIII, pp. 455-59

# NOTES

[1] On February 19, 1861, the tsarist government carried out a reform which abolished serfdom in Russia. p. 11

[2] The reference here is to the so-called *otrezki*, or cut-off lands, which were taken away from the peasants and given to the land-lords at the time of the abolition of serfdom in Russia in 1861.

The programme of the R.S.D.L.P. adopted at the Second Congress of the Party in 1903 demanded the return of these lands to the peasants. p. 11

[3] One-fourth of the peasant allotment established by law for the given locality. Under the Reform of 1861 part of the former serfs received these pauper allotments from the landlords free of charge, without compensation. Hence these allotments were also called "gift" allotments and the peasants who received them—"gift-land" peasants. p. 11

[4] Temporarily-bound peasants—former serfs who even after the abolition of serfdom were bound to render services (in the shape either of quitrent or of labour) until they began to make payment for their allotments to the landlords.

From the moment the peasants contracted to make these payments they ceased to be "temporarily-bound" and were registered as "peasant proprietors." p. 11

[5] When serfdom was abolished in 1861, the tsarist government appointed from among the hereditary landed nobility the so-called *miroviye posredniki* (from the word "*mirit*," to establish peaceful relations) whose task it was to carry out the reform in the localities—to fix the boundaries between the landlords' and peasants' lands, to approve the charters, etc. p. 12

[6] The charters were deeds drawn up by the landlords on the "emancipation" of the serfs in conformity with the Reform of 1861. In

them were recorded the amount of land occupied by each peasant before the reform and the amount of land and woods, pastures, etc., left to the despoiled peasants after their "emancipation." They also recorded the duties the serfs had formerly performed for the landlords, and served as the basis for calculating the amount of compensation to be paid by the peasants. p. 12

7 All the members of a Russian village community were held collectively responsible for the full and prompt discharge of monetary duties and services to the government and the landlords (taxes, compensation payments, provision of recruits for the army, etc.). This form of peasant bondage remained in force after the abolition of serfdom and was only annulled in 1906. p. 14

8 Under the Statute of February 19, 1861, which abolished serfdom in Russia, the peasants had to pay compensation to the landlords for the land allotments they received after emancipation. The payments greatly exceeded the real value of the land allotted to the peasants and approximated 2,000 million rubles. In reality, the peasants had to pay the landlords not only for the land, which they had long had the use of, but also for their personal emancipation. p. 15

9 *"Emancipation of Labour" group*—the first Russian Marxist group, formed by G. V. Plekhanov in Geneva in 1883, which did much to disseminate Marxism in Russia. p. 17

10. In 1899, with a view to consolidating the power of the landlords over the peasants, the tsarist government established the office of Zemstvo chief. Appointed from among the local landed nobility, the Zemstvo chiefs had wide administrative and even judicial powers, including the right to arrest peasants and to inflict corporal punishment upon them. p. 55

11 *Iskra* (*The Spark*)—the first All-Russian illegal Marxist newspaper; founded by V. I. Lenin in December 1900 abroad, it was secretly transported to Russia. After the Second Congress of the R.S.D.L.P. the Mensheviks (an opportunist wing in the R.S.D.L.P.) seized the newspaper and from November 1903, beginning with issue No. 52, it was turned into a Menshevik mouthpiece. It now came to be known as the "new" *Iskra*.

*Zarya* (*Dawn*)—Russian Social-Democratic theoretical magazine founded by V. I. Lenin. It was published simultaneously with *Iskra* by the editors of the latter. The magazine came out in Stuttgart from April 1901 to August 1902. p. 88

[12] The Third Congress of the R.S.D.L.P. was held in London from April 25 to May 10, 1905. The congress was prepared and convened by the Bolsheviks led by Lenin. It adopted highly important decisions on the tactics of the Party in the bourgeois-democratic revolution that had begun in Russia.                                        p. 92

[13] *Vperyod* (*Forward*)—an illegal Bolshevik weekly directed by V. I. Lenin; published in Geneva from December 22, 1904 (January 4, 1905) to May 5 (18), 1905. Eighteen issues came out.     p. 92

[14] "*Black redistribution*" (*chorny peredel*) was a widespread slogan among the peasants of tsarist Russia which expressed their demand for the abolition of landlord estates and a general redistribution of land.                                                                          p. 94

[15] New *Iskra*-ists—Mensheviks. See Note 11. The Menshevik conference took place in May 1905 in Geneva.                          p. 97

[16] On January 9, 1905, by order of Nicholas II, the tsarist troops shot down a peaceful demonstration of St. Petersburg workers who marched with their wives and children to the Winter Palace to present a petition to the tsar describing their intolerable conditions and utter lack of rights. This massacre of unarmed workers started a wave of mass political strikes and demonstrations all over Russia under the slogan, "Down with the autocracy!" The events of January 9 marked the beginning of the 1905-07 Revolution.                                                                        p. 98

[17] The programme of the R.S.D.L.P. adopted by the Second Congress of the Party in 1903 consisted of two parts: a minimum programme calling for the overthrow of tsarism, a democratic republic, the eight-hour day and other demands attainable under capitalism; and a maximum programme, formulating the ultimate goal of the working class, viz., socialist revolution, dictatorship of the proletariat, the building of a socialist society.                                    p. 100

[18] Economism—an opportunist trend in the Russian Social-Democratic movement in the late 90's and early 1900's. The Economists held that the political struggle against tsarism should be conducted chiefly by the liberal bourgeoisie, while the workers should confine their struggle to such economic demands as better conditions, higher wages, etc. They rejected the principle of the guiding role of the Party and the importance of revolutionary theory, maintaining that the labour movement must develop spontaneously. That the

views of the Economists were utterly untenable and harmful for the working-class movement was shown by V. I. Lenin in his book *What Is To Be Done?* published in 1902.      p. 101

[19] *Zemstvo*-ists—members of the Zemstvos, organs of local self-government in tsarist Russia which had no executive power and consisted mostly of landlords.

*Osvobozhdentsi (Liberationists)*—bourgeois liberals who grouped round the magazine *Osvobozhdeniye (Liberation)* published abroad in 1902-05 under the editorship of Pyotr Struve; in 1904 they formed the Liberation League. The *Osvobozhdentsi* made up the core of the Constitutional-Democratic Party, the principal party of the Russian bourgeoisie.      p. 109

[20] Socialist-Revolutionaries—a party of petty-bourgeois democrats, founded in 1902. They demanded the abolition of the landed estates and advanced the slogan of "equalitarian land tenure." The Socialist-Revolutionaries resorted to individual terror as a method of combating the tsarist regime. After the defeat of the 1905-07 Revolution, a substantial section of the party and its leadership sided with the bourgeois liberals. Following the bourgeois-democratic revolution of February 1917, the Socialist-Revolutionary leaders joined the Provisional Government, sought to suppress the peasant movement and whole-heartedly supported the capitalists and landlords against the working class, which was then preparing the socialist revolution.

After the victory of the October Socialist Revolution the party took an active part in the counter-revolutionary armed struggle waged by the bourgeoisie and the landlords against the Soviet Republic.      p. 109

[21] The reference here is to the Russo-Japanese War of 1904-05 in which tsarist Russia was defeated.      p. 110

[22] *Proletary*—an illegal Bolshevik newspaper, the central organ of the R.S.D.L.P.; issued from May to November, 1905.      p. 112

[23] *Peasants' Union*—a revolutionary-democratic organization founded in 1905. Its chief demand was immediate convocation of a constituent assembly and the granting of political freedoms. Its agrarian programme called for abolition of private landownership and the transfer to the peasants, without compensation, of all state, monastery, and appanage lands. Its policies were half-hearted and vacillating: while insisting on abolition of landlordism, it consent-

ed to partial compensation to the landlords. It was persecuted by the police, and by the end of 1906 ceased to exist.    p. 114

[24] *Black-Hundred* elements—from the monarchist gangs known as the Black Hundreds which the tsarist police organized to fight the revolutionary movement. They assassinated revolutionaries, attacked progressive intellectuals and perpetrated Jewish pogroms.   p. 114

[25] *V.V.* (V. Vorontsov) and *Nikolai—on* (Nikolai Danielson)—Narodniks, authors of a number of works on economics.   p. 128

[26] *Maslov* (pseudonym John)—a Menshevik, author of works on the agrarian question.   p. 135

[27] *Narodnaya Volya* (People's Will)—a secret organization of Russian revolutionary intellectuals founded in 1879. In their fight against tsarism its members resorted to individual terror. They made several attempts on the lives of tsarist officials and on March 1, 1881, assassinated Alexander II. The Narodnaya Volya erroneously held that a handful of revolutionaries would be able to seize power and overthrow the autocracy without the support of a revolutionary mass movement. The Narodnaya Volya ceased to exist in the second half of the eighties.   p. 146

[28] In October-December 1905 the Russian Revolution of 1905-07 reached its highest point.

In October 1905 the workers of Russia, fighting for the overthrow of the autocracy, declared an all-Russian political strike: all the factories and mills of this vast country ceased work, all the railways came to a standstill. On October 17, the tsar was compelled to issue a manifesto which promised to introduce a constitution in Russia and "grant" freedom of speech, assembly, press, etc. The tsar's promises, however, proved a deception and were not fulfilled.

In December 1905 an armed uprising started in Moscow. For nine days the city's factory workers, led by the Bolsheviks, fought heroically on the barricades against the tsarist troops equipped with artillery. The tsarist government was able to crush the uprising only by bringing in troops from St. Petersburg.   p. 146

[29] The Constitutional-Democratic Party, founded in 1905, represented the Russian liberal bourgeoisie and advocated a constitutional monarchy.

During the first Russian Revolution of 1905-07, the Constitutional Democrats called themselves the party of "Popular Freedom," while actually betraying the people and secretly negotiating with the tsarist government on ways and means of suppressing the revolution. They were an "opposition" party in the State Duma, and as such hoped the tsarist regime would allow them to share in the government of the country.

The Constitutional Democrats introduced in the State Duma agrarian reform bills providing for the compulsory alienation of a part of the landlords' lands in favour of the peasants on the basis of what they called a "fair evaluation." Actually, however, the peasants would have had to buy the land at exorbitant prices.

After the February 1917 Revolution, they entered the bourgeois Provisional Government, fought the workers' and peasants' revolutionary movement, defended landlord landownership and tried to force the people to continue the imperialist war. Following the victory of the October Socialist Revolution, the Constitutional Democrats took part in the armed sruggle waged by the counter-revolution against Soviet Russia.                                    p. 147

30  *Zemstvozation*—transfer of the land to the Zemstvos. See Note 19.
                                                                          p. 149

31  See Karl Marx, *Theses on Feuerbach*.                               p. 150

32  *Trepov* was a high tsarist official. In 1905 as Governor-General of St. Petersburg, he took brutal measures against the revolutionary workers.                                                              p. 150

33  *Petrunkevich and Rodichev* were Constitutional Democrats.  p. 150

34  The State Duma was set up as a result of the 1905-07 Revolution. Though formally the legislative assembly of tsarist Russia, it had no effective power and the elections to it were neither direct, nor equal, nor universal. The electoral rights of the working classes and the non-Russian nationalities were greatly curtailed. The vast majority of workers and peasants were denied the right to vote.

When the First Duma (April-July 1906) discussed the agrarian question and the peasant deputies demanded the confiscation of the landlords' land and its transfer to the peasantry, the tsarist government dissolved the Duma. The agrarian question was again put on the agenda in the Second Duma, convened in February 1907, but on June 3, 1907, the tsarist government dissolved the Duma and enacted a new electoral law which curtailed the rights of the workers and peasants still more and ensured a Black-Hundred majority.                                                              p. 151

[35] *Trudovaya* or peasant group, or Trudoviks—a group of petty-bourgeois democrats formed in April 1906 by peasant deputies in the First State Duma.

They demanded the abolition of all estate and national restrictions, democratization of the rural and urban local government bodies, and universal suffrage in elections to the State Duma. Their agrarian programme was based on the Narodnik principle of equalitarian use of land and envisaged the formation of a national land fund to include state, appanage, crown, and monastery lands, as well as private estates exceeding a certain labour norm, with payment of compensation for land taken from private owners. The implementation of the land reform was to be entrusted to local peasant committees.                                                    p. 155

[36] Lenin refers to the granting of "free lands" by the U.S. Government, primarily in the West, in the second half of the nineteenth and early twentieth centuries. The homestead law of 1862 gave every citizen of the U.S.A. the right to acquire free of charge or at a low price up to 160 acres of land. The homestead laws accelerated the development of capitalism in U.S. agriculture.         p. 162

[37] The Popular Socialists were a petty-bourgeois party which split off from the Right wing of the Socialist-Revolutionaries in 1906 and advanced moderate constitutional demands. In the agrarian sphere, they advocated the alienation of landlord lands in favour of the peasants with payment of compensation.                    p. 163

[38] Lenin refers to the voting of the Trudoviks, Popular Socialists and Socialist-Revolutionaries for F. A. Golovin, the Constitutional Democrat candidate for Speaker of the Second State Duma. By "tactics of silence" is meant the attitude of the Trudoviks towards the government's declaration read by Stolypin in the Duma on March 6 (19), 1907. When the Social-Democratic deputies suggested criticizing the government, the Trudoviks announced that they had decided to meet the declaration by "dead silence" and that they had already agreed on this with most of the opposition groups, the Constitutional Democrats included. When the budget was discussed in the Duma, the Trudoviks voted together with the Constitutional Democrats to refer it to the Duma budget commission.
                                                    p. 164

[39] *Stolypin*—Chairman of the Council of Ministers, 1906-11; responsible for the ruthless suppression of the 1905-07 Revolution and for mass shootings of the workers and peasants.

On November 9 (22), 1906, Stolypin issued a new land law enabling the peasants to leave the village communities and to set up separate farms. This law broke down the system of communal land tenure by giving the peasants an opportunity to take possession of their allotments as private property and to withdraw from the communities. They could now sell their land, which they were not allowed to do before. The Stolypin land law, which was advantageous to the kulaks and completely ruined the rural poor, was aimed at making the kulaks a bulwark of the tsarist autocracy in the countryside.                                          p. 167

40 *Razuvayev and Kolupayev*—capitalist sharks described in Saltykov-Shchedrin's works.                                          p. 167

41 For Economists see Note 18.                                          p. 173

42 *Dyelo Naroda* (*People's Cause*)—a Socialist-Revolutionary newspaper.                                          p. 184

43 In April 1917, the Constitutional Democrat Shingaryov, a minister in the bourgeois Provisional Government, sent out a telegram forbidding the peasants to "settle the land question independently" and suggesting "voluntary agreement" between the landlords and the peasants instead. Shingaryov's policy was designed to safeguard the interests of the landlords and to prevent the landlords' land from passing over to the people.                                          p. 184

44 Stolypin agrarian reform—see Note 39.                                          p. 189

45 The reference is chiefly to the Stolypin agrarian law of November 9, 1906. See Note 39.                                          p. 207

46 *Avksentyev and Dan Soviets*—Socialist-Revolutionary and Menshevik Soviets. Avksentyev was one of the leaders of the Socialist-Revolutionaries, and Dan, a Menshevik leader.                                          p. 214

47 *Kornilov* was a tsarist general who tried to engineer a counter-revolutionary coup d'état in September 1917 and organized an armed struggle against the Soviets in the South of Russia in 1917-18.                                          p. 229

48 *The Committees of Poor Peasants* were established by a decree of the All-Russian Central Executive Committee issued on June 11, 1918, "On organizing the village poor and supplying them with

grain, articles of prime necessity and agricultural implements." According to the decree, the functions of the committees included distribution of grain, articles of prime necessity and agricultural implements, and assistance to the local food bodies in taking surplus grain away from the kulaks and the rich. The decree gave various privileges to the poor in the matter of grain and implements distribution.

The Committees of Poor Peasants were a bulwark of the dictatorship of the proletariat in the countryside. They played a tremendous role in the struggle against the kulaks, in the redistribution of the confiscated land, and in supplying the industrial centres and the Red Army with food. The formation of the committees marked a new stage in the development of the socialist revolution in the countryside. They helped to consolidate Soviet power in the villages and were of enormous political significance in winning it the support of the middle peasants.

By decision of the Sixth All-Russian Extraordinary Congress of Soviets (November 1918), the Committees of Poor Peasants, having fulfilled their task, merged with the Soviets of Peasants' and Agricultural Workers' Deputies.                                    p. 235

[49] *The Law on the Socialization of the Land* was enacted on January 18 (31), 1918, at the Third All-Russian Congress of Soviets. It confirmed the abolition of private property in land and transferred it to the Soviet state. A special clause made it incumbent on the Soviet government to promote collective farming with a view of passing over to socialism. To meet the wishes of the peasants, the Bolsheviks agreed to include a clause on equalitarian land tenure though they opposed this slogan of the Socialist-Revolutionaries. "This is not our idea," wrote Lenin, "we do not agree with this slogan, but we consider it our duty to implement it since the overwhelming majority of the peasants demand it. And this kind of idea and demands of the majority of the toilers are something they must *discard of their own accord:* such demands cannot be either *abolished* or *skipped over.* We Bolsheviks will *help* the peasantry to discard petty-bourgeois slogans, to *pass* from them as quickly and as easily as possible to socialist slogans."                                    p. 235

[50] The reference is to the decision of the Council of People's Commissars of August 6, 1918, to treble the fixed prices paid by the state for grain of the 1918 harvest, and the decree, "On supplying agriculture with implements of production and metals," which was signed by Lenin on April 24, 1918, and published on April 27, 1918.                                    p. 235

[51] A counter-revolutionary revolt of the Czechoslovak Corps, organized by the British and French imperialists with the active participation of the Mensheviks and Socialist-Revolutionaries.

The Czechoslovak Corps, which consisted of prisoners of war taken during the First World War, was formed by the Provisional Government in 1917 for action against the German Army. Following the Great October Socialist Revolution, the Russian counter-revolutionaries and British and French imperialists used the counter-revolutionary officers of the corps to engineer an anti-Soviet revolt. It began in Chelyabinsk in May 1918, and with the aid of the Czechoslovak troops the counter-revolutionaries seized the rest of the Urals, the Volga area and, subsequently, Siberia. Making use of the Czechoslovaks, the Mensheviks and Socialist-Revolutionaries set up a government of Whiteguards and Socialist-Revolutionaries in Samara and a Whiteguard government of Siberia in Omsk.

In October 1918, the Red Army liberated the Volga area, and the counter-revolutionary Czechoslovak revolt was finally put down in 1919.                                                                p. 239

[52] A fund of 1,000 million rubles was instituted by decree of the Council of People's Commissars of November 2, 1918, "for the purpose of improving and developing agriculture and its speedy reorganization along socialist lines." Subsidies and loans from this fund were issued to agricultural communes, producers' co-operatives and rural associations or groups of peasants that wished to till the land collectively.                                                          p. 243

[53] Peace of Brest-Litovsk—an onerous peace imposed upon young Soviet Russia in 1918 by imperialist Germany and her allies, Austria-Hungary, Bulgaria and Turkey. It was signed in Brest-Litovsk on March 3, 1918, and annulled by the Soviet Government following the November revolution of 1918 in Germany.          p. 247

[54] *Krasnov*—a tsarist general who, supported by the British, American and French interventionists, organized counter-revolutionary action against Soviet government in the South of Russia in 1918.   p. 254

[55] *Kolchak*—a tsarist admiral. In 1918-19 Kolchak stirred up a counter-revolutionary rebellion in Siberia and instituted a reign of terror against the Siberian workers and peasants. Aided with money, arms and troops by Britain, America, Japan and France, Kolchak launched an offensive against the Soviet country, but in the winter of 1919-20 the Red Army completely smashed his forces and liberated Siberia.                                                        p. 273

[56] The *Statute on Socialist Agrarian Measures and on Measures for Transition to Socialist Agriculture* was adopted by the All-Russian Central Executive Committee in February 1919. Lenin took a direct part in framing and editing it. The statute provided for a series of practical measures to reconstruct agriculture along socialist lines, increase its productivity and extend crop areas. p. 275

[57] The Second International as revived at the conference of social-chauvinist and centrist parties in Berne in February 1919. p. 302

[58] *Kolchak*—See Note 55.
*Denikin*—a tsarist general, led the counter-revolutionary forces in the South of Russia in 1919.
*Yudenich*—a tsarist general, organized a counter-revolutionary offensive in Northwest Russia in 1919. p. 306

## TO THE READER

*The Foreign Languages Publishing House would be glad to have your opinion of the translation and the design of this book.*

*Please send all suggestions to 21, Zubovsky Boulevard, Moscow, U.S.S.R.*